Stemming the Tide

Arms Control in the Johnson Years

Glenn T. Seaborg

with

Benjamin S. Loeb

Lexington Books

D.C. Heath and Company/Lexington, Massachusetts/Toronto

The authors and publisher thank the following for
their kind permission to reprint copyrighted material.

HENRY HOLT AND COMPANY,
for passages from *The Vantage Point,* by Lyndon B. Johnson.
Copyright © 1971 by HEC Public Affairs Foundation.
Reprinted by permission of Henry Holt and Company.

THE EDUCATIONAL FOUNDATION FOR NUCLEAR SCIENCE,
for passages from the *Bulletin of the Atomic Scientists,*
a magazine of science and world affairs.
Copyright © 1986 by the Educational Foundation for Nuclear Science,
Chicago, Illinois, 60637.

THE MACMILLAN PUBLISHING COMPANY,
for passages from *The Diffusion of Power,* by Walt W. Rostow.
Copyright © 1972 by W. W. Rostow.
Reprinted by permission of Macmillan Publishing Company.

WEIDENFELD & NICOLSON LTD.,
for passages from *A Personal Record: The Labour Government 1964–1970*
by Harold Wilson.
Copyright © 1971 by Harold Wilson.
Reprinted by permission of Weidenfeld & Nicolson Ltd.

Library of Congress Cataloging-in-Publication Data

Seaborg, Glenn Theodore, 1912–
Stemming the tide.

Includes index.
1. Nuclear arms control—United States—History.
2. Nuclear arms control—Soviet Union—History.
3. Nuclear nonproliferation—History.   4. Johnson,
Lyndon B. (Lyndon Baines), 1908–1973.   I. Loeb,
Benjamin S., 1914–   .   II. Title.
JX1974.7.S417   1987   327.1'74   86–40444
ISBN 0–669–13105–9 (alk. paper)

Published simultaneously in Canada
Printed in the United States of America
International Standard Book Number: 0–669–13105–9
Library of Congress Catalog Card Number: 86–40444

The paper used in this publication meets the minimum requirements of
American National Standard for Information Sciences—Permanence
of Paper for Printed Library Materials, ANSI Z39.48–1984.

ISBN 0–669–13105–9

87 88 89 90 8 7 6 5 4 3 2 1

In memory of
Alva Myrdal and Olof Palme,
leaders in the quest for a better world.

Contents

Abbreviations and Acronyms

ABM	antiballistic missile
ACDA	Arms Control and Disarmament Agency (U.S.)
AEC	Atomic Energy Commission (U.S.)
ANF	Atlantic Nuclear Force (NATO)
AVLIS	atomic vapor laser isotope separation
ANZUS	Australia, New Zealand, U.S. Treaty
CCD	Conference of the Committee on Disarmament
CSC	Atlantic–Pacific Interoceanic Canal Study Commission
CTB	comprehensive test ban
CTBT	Comprehensive Test Ban Treaty
DOD	Department of Defense (U.S.)
ENDC	Eighteen Nation Disarmament Committee
FOBS	fractional orbital bombardment system
FRG	Federal Republic of Germany
GAC	General Advisory Committee (AEC)
GCD	general and complete disarmament
GCEP	gas centrifuge enrichment plant
HILAC	heavy ion linear accelerator
ICBM	intercontinental ballistic missile
IDO	International Disarmament Organization
IRBM	intermediate-range ballistic missile
JCAE	Joint Committee on Atomic Energy (U.S. Congress)
JCS	Joint Chiefs of Staff
LTBT	Limited Test Ban Treaty
MIRV	multiple independently targeted reentry vehicle
MLF	Multilateral Force (NATO)
MRBM	medium-range ballistic missile
NPT	Nonproliferation Treaty
NSAM	National Security Action Memorandum
NSC	National Security Council
PNE	peaceful nuclear explosive; peaceful nuclear explosion
SLBM	submarine-launched ballistic missile

TTB   threshold test ban
UNAEC   United Nations Atomic Energy Commission
UNDC   United Nations Disarmament Committee

While differing principles and different values may always divide us, they should not, and they must not, deter us from rational acts of common endeavor.

Lyndon B. Johnson
August 26, 1966

Preface

The administration of Lyndon Johnson is not commonly associated with arms control—not nearly so commonly, for example, as with the Vietnam War or the Great Society. Yet, the Johnson presidency was a period of great arms control ferment both within our own government and in international discussion. The period produced, moreover, two very significant results. First of these was the signing in 1968 of the Nonproliferation Treaty, the most widely accepted among Americans of the arms control agreements thus far negotiated with the Soviet Union. Perhaps even more important to the world was the intellectual ground breaking by which President Johnson and his associates—principally Robert McNamara—persuaded the Soviet leadership to embrace the concept of a mutual limitation on strategic weapons, both offensive and defensive. Indeed, but for the Soviet invasion of Czechoslovakia in August 1968, the Strategic Arms Limitation Talks (SALT) would have begun during Johnson's presidency. The Johnson administration deserves much more credit for this accomplishment than it is generally given.

In describing the arms control events of the period it is necessary to consider negotiations on a number of levels. The negotiations among nations involved more active participants than in prior years. It was no longer merely a matter of the United States trying to reach an accommodation with the Soviet Union. The matters under discussion during the Johnson years required that we also work things out with our NATO allies and with nonaligned nations in the Third World and elsewhere. The interests of the former group sometimes, and that of the latter group frequently, diverged from our own. Fully as complex as the negotiations with other nations were those that took place within our own government. Within the Executive Branch there were repeated clashes among constituencies with different points of view.

If the Executive Branch achieved a consensus, there were frequent problems in reaching an accord with influential elements in the Congress. I have tried to trace events in all these arenas.

This book is a study of process as well as of substance. From time to time I find occasion to criticize the Johnson administration in both respects—for the substantive positions it adopted on some issues and, particularly, for some of the processes it employed, which were not always orderly. The hope always is that we may derive maximum instruction from past errors, lest they be repeated.

As in my other venture into arms control history (*Kennedy, Khrushchev and the Test Ban,* University of California Press, 1981), principal sources for this volume included my own diary, maintained religiously every day, plus copies of correspondence and other official papers that crossed my desk in my capacity as chairman of the Atomic Energy Commission during these years. (I should mention in passing that quotations from my diary, though frequently verbatim, are not so in every case. I have taken occasional editorial liberties in the interest of clarity, particularly for the general reader.) Reliance on these primary sources has probably introduced a certain amount of distortion in that I may have given disproportionate emphasis to events in which I personally participated. The positive side of this is that these are the events about which I have the greatest chance of making original contributions to the historical record. I also utilized a variety of secondary sources: government reports, newspapers, periodicals, works of scholarship. I made extensive use of materials in the LBJ Library in Austin, Texas, where David Humphrey and other members of the skilled professional staff offered most expert and generous assistance, not only during research at the library but in following months.

I tried through interviews to scratch the memories and draw on the wisdom of some key players in the arms control events of the period. I am particularly indebted to McGeorge Bundy, George Bunn, Spurgeon Keeny, Walt Rostow, and Dean Rusk for sharing recollections and interpretations of events in which they played such important roles.

Some associates who served with me through the Johnson years provided invaluable help. My fellow AEC commissioner, Dr. Gerald F. Tape, and my disarmament assistant of those years, Allan Labowitz, read the entire manuscript and made important suggestions that helped keep it in balance. Myron Kratzer made especially valuable contributions to the chapters on verification safeguards, his area of great expertise. Gregg Herken also offered helpful comments.

I am pleased to acknowledge my debt to the excellent team at Lexington Books: in particular to Jaime Welch-Donahue, for uniformly helpful contributions as the book's editor; to Marsha Finley, for skillfully guiding the manuscript through the production process; to Kevin Ahern, for an outstanding performance as copy editor; and to Bruce Katz, for his stellar efforts to maximize the book's readership. At the Department of Energy, Roger Anders rendered important archival assistance. Ellen Loeb provided very significant editorial help. Special thanks are due to Jeanne Loeb for research assistance and for heroic efforts in getting the manuscript ready for submission. Finally, I should note that if errors of fact or interpretation have crept in here, I do not share credit for them with anyone.

G. T. S.
Berkeley, California

Part I
Prologue

Let us begin.
John F. Kennedy
January 20, 1961

Let us continue.
Lyndon B. Johnson
November 27, 1963

1
"The Best Way to Begin . . . Is to Begin"

Somehow or other, optimist that I am, I just believe that peace is coming nearer.

—Lyndon B. Johnson
September 16, 1964

"Though the Harp Is Smashed . . ."

In May 1963 I led a delegation of U.S. scientists on a tour of Soviet laboratories. It was a memorable trip, characterized by the greatest cordiality. In November 1963 a Soviet group returned our visit. On Friday morning, November 22, the tour had brought us to the Lawrence Berkeley Laboratory at the University of California, Berkeley, where in prior years I had pursued my academic interest in nuclear chemistry. We were in the laboratory's HILAC building when I was called aside and given the message: President Kennedy had been shot. By a stroke of tragic irony, I was standing in the same spot where, three years earlier, I had received the call from then President-elect Kennedy offering me the chairmanship of the Atomic Energy Commission.

The news threw us all into a turbulence of emotion and confusion. I wrote in my diary:

The personal shock of President Kennedy's death is tremendous. It raises questions in my mind whether I want to stay on as Chairman.

Our Soviet guests seemed as overwhelmed as the rest of us. They placed themselves entirely at our disposal, offering to cancel the remainder of their tour if that was our preference. It was a touchy situation that transcended diplomatic niceties because at first there was speculation that the Soviet Union had somehow been involved in the assassination. After conferring with the State Department, I decided not to call off the tour, but did cancel visits in the San Francisco–Palo Alto area that had been scheduled for the next two days. It was arranged instead for the Soviet group to visit Yosemite National Park until Sunday evening and then to proceed as planned to the National Reactor Testing Station in Idaho. Once there, the visitors asked that a television set be placed in the cafeteria so they could watch the funeral proceedings on Monday. (There were almost no employees about because the day had been declared a national day of mourning.) They told me later how touched they had been to see me among those attending the service at Arlington National Cemetery.

I cannot speak too warmly of the comportment of our visitors at this difficult time. They made the necessary schedule changes and spur-of-the-moment arrangements easier by their unhesitating cooperation. Illustrative of their sensitive behavior was a gesture by one of their number, who, the day after the assassination, rose at dinner to recite the following lines:

> Say not that he has died—he lives;
> Though the chalice be broken,
> The flame still flares;
> Though the rose is plucked,
> It still in color blooms;
> Though the harp is smashed,
> The chord rings on.[1]

On the last day of the scheduled tour, the leader of the delegation, my Soviet counterpart, Andronik H. Petrosyants,* quite unexpectedly announced that he and the rest of the group would like to lay a wreath on President Kennedy's grave. Permission was hurriedly obtained and, without publicity at the time or afterward, it was done.

These were among the indications we received that Kennedy had meant something special to the Russians, that they regarded his passing as their tragedy as well as our own. This feeling seemed to apply,

---

*He was not fully my counterpart. As chairman of the State Committee for the Utilization of Atomic Energy, his jurisdiction was limited to the nonmilitary uses of nuclear energy, whereas mine extended also to the development and testing of weapons. On the other hand, as I told then-President Leonid Brezhnev in an interview during our visit in May 1963, their chairman had more authority to act than our chairman.

indeed, to the entire Eastern bloc. Witness the fact that the government of Poland declared an official national day of mourning for him.

Why They Mourned

The outpouring of grief on Kennedy's death was worldwide and probably unprecedented in modern times. Chester Bowles, then ambassador to India, later furnished this representative account:

> There was a huge turnout in front of the Embassy—thousands and thousands of people. The whole Indian Parliament turned out—everybody—the whole Cabinet. You go into the most remote villages of India and you'll still [1969] find pictures of Kennedy; it's just unbelievable—way, way in the backwoods—pictures of Gandhi and Kennedy.[2]

What explained it? Undoubtedly a large part of Kennedy's appeal had to do with personal attributes. His youth, good looks, wit, and obvious zest for life made him an attractive figure to masses of people in many countries. One had only to travel abroad during the Kennedy years, as I did on many occasions, to appreciate the degree to which he, and also his glamorous family, had captured the popular fancy. The fact that this magnetic young man also bore with dignity and grace his responsibilities as head of a powerful nation in perilous times only added to his appeal.

Important as were these personal factors, I am convinced that the reaction to Kennedy's death would not have been as great had he died fourteen months earlier, before the Cuban missile crisis, before the signing of the Limited Test Ban Treaty. The skill and restraint that Kennedy demonstrated in the missile crisis enhanced his reputation immeasurably. But most of all, I think, it was the Limited Test Ban Treaty, achieved by Kennedy and Khrushchev together in their rapprochement following Cuba, that captured the popular imagination. It was clear that the treaty would not by itself accomplish much beyond cleansing the air of radioactive fallout from atmospheric tests. It was certainly a far cry from the comprehensive test ban that both leaders had sought. Yet the treaty, and the atmosphere of reconciliation in which it was achieved, seemed to bring a resurgence of hope that the overhanging threat of nuclear holocaust might one day be lifted.

On the first anniversary of the treaty, Premier Khrushchev spoke of a certain "fund of confidence" it had engendered, which, if preserved and nurtured, could lead to further benefits for both East and West. I believe that the Soviets and their allies looked forward to four more years in which they could build with Kennedy on this fund. His death may well have filled them with renewed anxiety about the future because they knew how mercurial changes in U.S. policy could be. And so they too mourned, not only for the loss of an admired figure, but from fear of what his death might portend.

"The Chord Rings On"

The circumstances under which Lyndon Johnson assumed the presidency implied a strong obligation to carry forward the policies and programs of his predecessor. In *The Vantage Point,* an autobiographical memoir of his presidency, Johnson described the impact of this obligation on him:

> Rightly or wrongly, I felt from the very first day in office that I had to carry on for President Kennedy. I considered myself the caretaker of both his people and his policies. He knew when he selected me as his running mate that I would be the man required to carry on if anything happened to him. I did what I believed he would have wanted me to do.[3]

Though this statement may be tinged with the hyperbole to which Johnson was addicted, it characterizes reasonably well the spirit that permeated his early days in office.*

In carrying on for Kennedy, Johnson could not but have been aware of the very high priority that his predecessor had assigned to arms control. Kennedy had enlisted himself personally in the quest for a test ban agreement as in virtually no other pursuit. And, though the Limited Test Ban Treaty fell short of the comprehensive test ban he had sought, Kennedy nevertheless derived profound satisfaction

---

*Not that he liked the situation he was in. As he later told Doris Kearns: "I took the oath. I became president. But for millions of Americans I was still illegitimate, a naked man with no presidential covering, a pretender to the throne, an illegal usurper. And then there was Texas, my home, the home of both the murder and the murder of the murderer. And then there were the bigots and the dividers and the Eastern intellectuals, who were waiting to knock me down before I could even begin to stand up. The whole thing was almost unbearable." (Kearns, *Lyndon Johnson and the American Dream,* p. 170).

from its successful negotiation and its ratification by the Senate. The strength of Kennedy's identification with this treaty was such that, when ratification was still in doubt, he confided to associates that he "would glady forfeit his re-election, if necessary, for the sake of the Test Ban Treaty."[4]

But Kennedy never regarded the Limited Test Ban Treaty as an end in itself. In a television address to the nation on July 26, 1963, after the treaty had been initialed in Moscow, he made clear his view that it was but a first step along the path to peace, and one that would have little significance unless additional steps were taken. On October 7, when he signed the instruments of ratification on behalf of the United States, Kennedy again used essentially the same image:

> This small step toward safety can be followed by others longer and less limited, if also harder in the taking. With our courage and understanding enlarged by this achievement, let us press onward in quest of man's essential desire for peace.[5]

This was more than rhetoric. Averell Harriman once told me of a conversation in which Kennedy indicated that if he won a second term its principal thrust would be to seek improved relations with the Soviet Union. The objectives to be sought, moreover, had been quite clearly identified and had been discussed on numerous occasions within the administration. Some had already been the subject of international negotiations.

As vice president, Lyndon Johnson had not delved as deeply into the substance of arms control as had President Kennedy; nevertheless, he was generally familiar with the Kennedy administration's arms control agenda, and indicated early his intention to move forward with it. He identified his main objectives in this field in a January 18, 1964, letter to Chairman Khrushchev:

to prevent the spread of nuclear weapons;

to end the production of fissionable material for weapons;

to transfer large amounts of fissionable materials to peaceful purposes;

to ban all nuclear weapons tests;

to place limitations on nuclear weapons systems;

to reduce the risk of war by accident or design; and

to move toward general disarmament.[6]

The continued pursuit of these objectives, with some variations and additions, provides the subject matter of this book.

Favorable Omens

In carrying forward Kennedy's policies on arms control, Johnson was assisted by a number of institutional factors predisposing toward continuity.

- The Arms Control and Disarmament Agency (ACDA), which had performed research, supplied policy guidance, and conducted negotiations on arms control since its establishment in 1961, continued to be led by William C. Foster, its tenacious first director, and his creative and persuasive deputy, Adrian S. Fisher.
- The Committee of Principals, established by President Eisenhower to coordinate the Executive Branch's review of arms control policy, remained in operation. Greatly expanded during the Kennedy administration, it now consisted of the secretary of state, who acted as chairman; the secretary of defense; the directors of the CIA, the ACDA and the U.S. Information Agency; the chairmen of the AEC and the Joint Chiefs of Staff; the administrator of NASA; and the president's national security and science advisers. None of the individuals occupying these positions changed in the early days of the Johnson presidency.
- Backstopping the Principals was the Committee of Deputies, representing the same agencies with officials one echelon down. It was chaired by ACDA Deputy Director Adrian Fisher. Most of the head knocking needed to resolve agency differences was done in this group, so that by the time issues reached the Principals they were often all but settled.
- The main international negotiating forum for arms control questions, the Eighteen Nation Disarmament Committee (ENDC), also had not changed since 1961. Meeting in Geneva, Switzerland, the ENDC's nominal membership consisted of five NATO countries (the United States, the United Kingdom, Canada, France* and Italy), five

---

*In actuality, France never attended, President de Gaulle haughtily insisting that nuclear disarmament matters should be discussed only by nations that had or soon would have nuclear weapons.

Warsaw Pact countries (the USSR, Bulgaria, Czechoslovakia, Poland, and Romania), and eight nonaligned countries (Brazil, Burma, Ethiopia, India, Mexico, Nigeria, Sweden, and the United Arab Republic).

Another factor conducive to progress in arms control was a momentarily favorable tide in East–West relations. Johnson himself gave the following appraisal of the situation from the American perspective:

> When I took office the atmosphere was somewhat less charged with blind anti-Communist sentiment. Americans felt a renewed confidence. . . . There were many reasons for that change. Sputnik had given the Communists a tremendous psychological boost, but by 1963 most people realized that the U.S. was catching up and soon would pass the Soviets in space exploration. Deepening rivalry between Moscow and Peking helped people to realize that the Communist world was not a tightly disciplined monolith. Facing down the Soviet missile threat in Cuba removed the immediate danger of nuclear blackmail. Our own economy was growing, and it became obvious that Khrushchev's claim that the Soviets would surpass us in economic output by 1970 was an empty boast. Finally, the Soviet leaders had shown, by their participation in the "hot line" and in the Partial Test Ban Treaty,* that they were prepared to consider agreements that involved mutual benefits.[7]

The president conveyed a similar view in a message to the ENDC early in 1964:

> Today your search begins anew in a climate of hope. Last year's genuine gains have given us new momentum. Recent Soviet and American announcements of reduction in military spending, even though modest, have brightened the atmosphere further. Let us pray that the tide has turned—that further and more far-reaching agreements lie ahead.[8]

Johnson meant to see what could be accomplished, and in the same message he set forth the U.S. agenda.

---

*The official name of the treaty is "Treaty Banning Nuclear Weapons Tests in the Atmosphere, in Outer Space and Under Water." Though "Limited Test Ban Treaty" is the short title adopted by the U.S. State Department and preferred generally in American usage, "Partial Test Ban Treaty" is favored throughout most of the rest of the English-speaking world.

First Message to the ENDC

The occasion for the president's message was the reconvening of the
ENDC on January 21, 1964, following one of its periodic recesses.
To help prepare the U.S. position for the new session, a large two-
day meeting had been held on the weekend of December 14 and 15,
1963. It was attended by several top staff representatives from State,
Defense, and ACDA (including in the latter case the agency's director
and deputy director), and by single representatives from AEC (Com-
missioner John Palfrey) and CIA. National Security Adviser Mc-
George Bundy sent in a copy of the detailed agenda to President
Johnson with the following hand-printed note:

> THESE ARE TOP STAFF MEN IN ALL DEPTS, ON ARMS CONTROL, IN 2
> DAY MTG. TO REVIEW U.S. POSITION—AND SEEK IMPROVEMENT
> BEFORE GENEVA MTG. IN JANUARY. THESE ARE ABLE MEN—TOUGH
> PROBLEM—YOU NEED THEM—LONG SLOW PULL—PEACE AS YOUR
> CENTRAL OBJECT.[9]

The fact that Bundy felt the need to send in such a note is an indication of how relatively untutored President Johnson was thought to
be on arms control matters in this early stage of his administration.
(As discussed later in this section, this impression of naïveté, which
Johnson himself fostered, may have been exaggerated.)

Out of this two-day meeting and other governmental processes a
proposed U.S. position emerged, and on January 16, 1964, I attended
a further meeting intended to determine how this position should be
reflected in Johnson's message to the ENDC. The president himself
presided. Also present at this extraordinary Saturday afternoon session were Secretaries Rusk and McNamara, Chairman of the Joint
Chiefs of Staff Maxwell Taylor, CIA Deputy Director Marshall S.
Carter, ACDA Deputy Director Adrian Fisher, and newly appointed
White House assistants Bill Moyers and Jack Valenti. A draft of the
proposed presidential message had been distributed by the ACDA.

The message proposed consideration of five types of potential
agreements. These related to (1) prohibiting the threat or use of force
to settle international disputes; (2) a verified freeze of strategic nuclear offensive and defensive vehicles; (3) halting production of fissionable materials for weapons use; (4) observation posts to reduce
the danger of war by accident, miscalculation, or surprise attack; and
(5) measures to stop the spread of nuclear weapons.

Only one item in the proposed program produced extended discussion at the January 16 meeting. It was in the section on nuclear spread, which, as drafted by the ACDA, read:

> To stop the spread of nuclear weapons to nations not now controlling them, let us agree:
>
> (A) That nuclear weapons not be transferred into the national control of states which do not now control them and that all transfer of nuclear materials for peaceful purposes take place under effective international safeguards;
>
> (B) That the major nuclear powers accept in an increasing number of their peaceful activities the same inspection that they recommend for other states;
>
> (C) On the principles which could lead to the establishment of nuclear-free zones; and
>
> (D) On the banning of all nuclear weapons tests under effective verification and control.

The item that caused controversy was subparagraph C, relating to the establishment of nuclear-free zones. This provoked an objection from General Taylor on behalf of the Joint Chiefs. In view of the already far-advanced negotiations for a treaty establishing a nuclear-free zone in Latin America (see chapter 26), the ACDA had thought that President Johnson could usefully suggest that nuclear-free zones might have merit in other parts of the world as well, for example, in Africa or the Middle East. The Joint Chiefs, on the other hand, felt that U.S. support for nuclear-free zones might play into the hands of the Eastern bloc, which repeatedly since 1956 had been advocating such a zone in central Europe in order to outlaw the emplacement of U.S. missiles in West Germany.

Adrian Fisher later described how this disagreement was resolved:

> The president asked me whether this [the entire list of proposals] was an agreed program. I said: "It's all agreed except point 5C, to which the Joint Chiefs disagree." And Max Taylor said, "Yes, we agree to everything except that." And the president said, "Who wants it in?" I said, "The ACDA would like it in, and we'd like to have you hear us out on it."
>
> He looked at me and he said, "Butch [Fisher's nickname], I will hear you out if you will first answer me this question: Is this point

worth enough to you to have to explain on the Hill that the Joint Chiefs didn't agree to the entire program? Or would you be better off with a program which you can defend as being agreed to across the board? After you've thought that question over, if you still want me to hear you out, I'll do it."

I had to confess he was right. I said, "At this stage in the negotiations we'd probably be better off to be able to say without any ifs, ands or buts that this is an agreed program." He said, "Well, all right, that settles it." And that was the end of that. He was right. I was being a little parochial.[10]

Subsequent events proved that the objections of the Joint Chiefs had been well founded. Within the month Poland circulated a memorandum at the ENDC again proposing a nuclear-free zone in Europe, specifically including West Germany. Had the item about nuclear-free zones been left in the president's message, the United States might have been in an awkward situation in Geneva.

The fascinating thing about this episode is that the president appeared to settle the issue without particular reference to its substance. As a supremely skilled negotiator and persuader, he was acutely sensitive to political realities, to who held the levers of power, and he resolved the matter on that basis.

The episode also serves to indicate the great political power wielded by the Joint Chiefs of Staff. Courageous indeed—or perhaps one should say foolish—is the official who seeks congressional approval of any arms control proposal without the concurrence of the Joint Chiefs. This is a consideration to which we shall return in later pages.

The nuclear freeze proposal included in the president's message is of particular interest because of its revival in more recent times. The proposal was couched in the following terms:

> The United States, the Soviet Union and their respective allies should agree to explore a verified freeze of the number and characteristics of strategic nuclear offensive and defensive vehicles. For our part, we are convinced that the security of all nations can be safeguarded within the scope of such an agreement and that this initial measure preventing the further expansion of the deadly and costly arms race will open the path to reductions in all types of forces from present levels.

This issue was to be thoroughly ventilated at the ENDC (see chapter 29).

The proposal "to reduce the danger of war by accident, miscalculation or surprise attack" announced an intent to frame at a later time specific language on the creation of a system of observation points. In espousing a measure to prevent surprise attack, the message hearkened back to President Eisenhower's 1955 "Open Skies" proposal. As Walt Rostow has recorded, Lyndon Johnson, then Senate majority leader, was one of the first to acclaim Eisenhower's initiative. Still hospitalized by a heart attack he had suffered three weeks earlier, Johnson hailed the proposal as "the daring, imaginative stroke for which a war-weary world has been waiting."[11] The feeling is inescapable that in these early days of his administration Johnson was approaching arms control in just such a spirit—a desire himself to come up with something daring that would cut through the congealed hostility and advance the cause of peace.

The remaining proposal in President Johnson's message, on prohibiting the threat or use of force to settle international disputes, was really part of a propaganda contest that Johnson felt it necessary to wage with Nikita Khrushchev. The latter had sent New Year's messages on December 31, 1963, to chiefs of government around the world. Khrushchev proposed an agreement to settle territorial disputes by peaceful means and denounced "colonizers" and "imperialism" as the major cause of past wars. Johnson was irritated by the one-sidedness of Khrushchev's letter and felt the need to counterbalance it by calling attention to ways in which the Soviet Union and other Communist nations had themselves committed aggression.[12] The president therefore proposed an agreement ". . . prohibiting the threat or use of force, directly or indirectly—whether by aggression, subversion, or the clandestine supply of arms—to change boundaries or demarcation lines; to interfere with access to territory; or to extend control over, or change arrangements for administration of territory."

Johnson concluded his message to the ENDC with an appeal for action: "Each of these proposed steps is important to peace. No one of them is impossible of agreement. The best way to begin disarming is to begin. . . ."

Johnson underscored his own sense of the importance of this message, and amplified its impact, when he took the extraordinary step of requesting television and radio time to tell the American people about it on the same morning it was being received in Geneva. The broadcast address closely followed the text of the formal message until the end, when the president asked for popular support. "Disarmament," he said, "is not merely the government's business. . . . It is everyone's business."

All in all, it was a strong beginning, indicating that at this early stage—before the Vietnam War consumed him—Johnson intended to engage his personal energies and prestige, even as his predecessor had done, in the quest for meaningful progress in arms control. It was important to convey this idea because there was a widespread impression that Johnson lacked experience, knowledge, and skill in foreign affairs. This impression was fostered in the press. For example, Walter Lippmann, the most influential columnist of the day, concluded that "Johnson knows little of the outer world"; and Philip Geyelin, then foreign correspondent for the *Wall Street Journal,* described the president as "king of the river and a stranger to the open sea."[13] The apparent gap in Johnson's background had been a source of concern to European leaders; so much so that, in a trip abroad shortly after the assassination, Dean Rusk had been at pains to point out that the new president had indeed had contact with foreign affairs while vice president and that he was familiar with international issues.[14]

Rusk attributes the impression that Johnson was deficient in foreign affairs to a "sort of snobbishness that a number of people on the Northeastern seaboard had toward LBJ."[15] Rusk points out that for six of Eisenhower's eight years Johnson, as majority leader, had steered foreign policy bills through the Senate, a task that required him to "know everything that could be known about the pending legislation." Later, as vice president, he had been assigned a foreign service officer to see to it that he got a full reading of State Department cable traffic every day.* In addition, Johnson had visited some twenty-five foreign countries while vice president. Before each such visit he received a complete briefing on U.S. relations with the country involved because, as Rusk states, "he wanted to discuss substance with these countries; he didn't want to go on purely protocol visits." Finally, Rusk points out that "during the Kennedy years LBJ sat with us in the National Security Council and in Cabinet meetings. So he had much more experience in foreign affairs than even he himself was willing to confess. LBJ sort of pretended to be an amateur in foreign policy. He was much more than an amateur."

---

*He was also regularly briefed on national security matters by an aide, Air Force Colonel Howard L. Burris (Colonel Burris memos to Vice President, LBJ Library).

Notes

1. Translated from an untitled poem written in 1886 by Nadson Semon, a Russian poet.
2. Transcript, Chester Bowles Oral History Interview, 11/11/69, by Joe B. Frantz, p. 45, LBJ Library.
3. Johnson, *The Vantage Point*, p. 16.
4. Sorensen, *Kennedy*, p. 745.
5. *Documents on Disarmament: 1963*, p. 532.
6. *Documents on Disarmament: 1964*, p. 5.
7. Johnson, *The Vantage Point*, p. 470.
8. *Documents on Disarmament: 1964*, p. 7.
9. National Security File, Aides Files, Bundy Memos to President, Vol. 1, LBJ Library.
10. Transcript, Adrian Fisher Oral History Interview, 10/31/68, by Paige E. Mulhollan, Tape 2, p. 49, LBJ Library. That the ACDA was too parochial was precisely the criticism directed at the agency by others, including—according to Walt Rostow—the president himself (private conversation with Rostow, June 5, 1985).
11. Rostow, *Open Skies*, p. 49f.
12. Johnson, *The Vantage Point*, p. 464f.
13. Geyelin, *Lyndon B. Johnson and the World*, p. 15.
14. *The New York Times*, January 21, 1964.
15. Private conversation, March 13, 1986.

Part II

Production Cutbacks

We must not . . . seek an excess of military
power that could be provocative as well as
wasteful.

Lyndon B. Johnson
January 8, 1964

2
President Johnson's
Bold Start

A Surprising First Meeting

Even before the president sent his message to the ENDC, he had initiated within his administration an approach to one aspect of the American agenda. This related to the production of fissionable materials. The message proposed "a verified agreement to halt *all* production of fissionable materials for weapons use" (emphasis added). What had already been set in motion in Washington—a cutback in the *excess* production of fissionable materials—was much more modest. The tortuous passage of this limited action across the national stage shows much about the obstacles that confront even small attempts to arrest the momentum of the arms race.

The matter came up in my first meeting with the new president, on November 29, 1963, one week after the assassination:

I told the president that the main reason I wanted to see him was to discuss a matter I had taken up with President Kennedy shortly before his death, and upon which no conclusion had been reached. It had to do with the AEC's belief that France might soon reach a thermonuclear weapons capability and with the effect this might have on the world situation. [France had tested its first fission weapon in February 1960.] President Johnson was interested in this but felt that there was nothing we could do other than remain aware of the situation.

We then discussed whether to initiate a cutback in the production of fissionable materials. I pointed out that the economic impact in terms of lost employment and income at the production sites could be severe, and that, consequently, President Kennedy had been inclined to postpone action until after the 1964 election.

> Johnson indicated that his first reaction was *not* to make
> the election a factor in his decision, but he said he wanted to
> study the matter further.

I could not but agree with what the president said about the French matter. France's nuclear weapons program was an irritant in inter-allied relations and an obstacle in arms control negotiations. Experience had taught us, however, that there was not much we could do about it, especially while Charles de Gaulle was president. As to the materials production cutback, I was frankly surprised that Johnson seemed to attach so little importance to the political considerations involved. It was not the last time I would be surprised by this complex and unpredictable man.

Economic Hazards

From the point of view of military or civilian need, there was little doubt that a significant cut in fissionable materials production was warranted. Since the end of World War II, the United States had, at enormous cost, constructed a huge complex of production facilities that were capable of producing far more uranium-235 (U-235) and plutonium than was needed to meet the weapons requirements of the Defense Department. (How this came about is discussed in the next chapter.) Nor could the rapidly expanding civilian nuclear power program utilize more than a fraction of the excess U-235. To keep all the production facilities in operation would therefore achieve no reasonable national goal and be a prodigious waste of money.

But, as I told the president, a cutback in materials production might cause grievous economic hardship at the production sites. Likely to be hardest hit were the communities of Oak Ridge, Tennessee, and Richland, Washington, both of which had been established, literally from the ground up, in the World War II atomic bomb project. These communities were, by design, in isolated areas and had virtually no industry to sustain them beyond that supported in some manner by AEC activity. To make matters worse, homes and commercial facilities in the communities, originally government property, had only recently been sold to private individuals. The communities around the Savannah River Plant, established in 1951 on the border between Georgia and South Carolina, were also highly dependent on continued activity at the complex's plutonium production facilities. Also directly involved were communities around Paducah, Kentucky, and Portsmouth, Ohio, where the newest enriched uranium plants had been built beginning in 1951 and 1952, respectively.

Moreover, though the primary purpose of any cutbacks would be to produce less plutonium in the reactors at the Hanford Works and the Savannah River Plant, and less U-235 in the gaseous diffusion plants at Oak Ridge, Paducah, and Portsmouth, the cumulative effects would spread well beyond those facilities. There would also be reduced activity in plants that processed uranium to prepare it as feed material for the gaseous diffusion plants, or as fuel for the plutonium reactors. The processing plants involved were located in four different states. Uranium concentrates were refined in an AEC-owned plant at Weldon Springs, Missouri. The concentrates were converted into uranium hexafluoride gas (UF_6) at the AEC's Paducah complex and at a Metropolis, Illinois, plant owned by the Allied Chemical Company. Production reactor fuel elements were fabricated at an AEC-owned plant operated by the National Lead Company in Fernald, Ohio.

The ripple effect would go still further. Because the gaseous diffusion plants were prodigious users of electricity—they consumed nearly 10 percent of the nation's total electric power generation in 1956, when the expansion of production facilities reached its peak—it had been necessary to build new power plants especially to supply their needs. These were located at Joppa, Illinois; Madison, Indiana; and Kyger, Ohio. Faced with a curtailment of demand from its sole customer, the fate of each of these power plants and its employees was in doubt. Further, the power plants were all coal-fired, and loss of their business would threaten to shut down coal mines in several states.

Kennedy's Concession to Politics

As I have indicated, this situation had been approached with great wariness by President Kennedy. He had been appalled by the potential economic consequences of the suggested cutbacks. Frightening in a different way was the political hornet's nest that might be stirred up, and this had been fully appreciated by Kennedy. The nine states most likely to be affected had a total of 126 electoral votes. In addition, these states were represented by some of the most formidable members of the Congress, including Senator Richard B. Russell of Georgia, chairman of the Military Affairs Committee; Senator Everett Mc-

Kinley Dirksen of Illinois, minority leader of the Senate; and, perhaps most formidable of all on this issue, Senator Henry M. "Scoop" Jackson of Washington. Jackson had earned a considerable following in the Senate on national security matters through his expert knowledge, acquired by diligent application through the years, and through his skill in expressing himself forcefully and clearly. Years of service on the Joint Committee on Atomic Energy (JCAE) had made him particularly expert in our business. Because a community in his own state might be seriously affected, Jackson had spoken to President Kennedy about the threatened cutbacks on several occasions.

Like President Kennedy, I shrank from the difficulties the cutbacks threatened to arouse, not the least of which would be deciding on which facilities the blows must fall. On June 12, 1963, after presiding over a commission meeting at which we made plans to study the cutbacks' likely effects, I wrote in my diary:

> This is probably the most difficult problem I have faced since I became Chairman.

In the ensuing weeks, while the AEC was pursuing its detailed study of how much to cut and where, President Kennedy evidently had renewed opportunities, with perhaps some help from Senator Jackson and others, to contemplate the economic and political problems involved, to his apparent distaste. I heard of his views from Senator Jackson during a conversation at a private reception. Jackson said the president had asked him to urge me "not to go too far too fast." What this meant was later clarified by McGeorge Bundy. He said that President Kennedy had an understanding with Jackson that no AEC production activity would be slowed down until after the 1964 election. (Jackson was a candidate for reelection in 1964, and Kennedy of course meant to be one.)

Johnson's Decision

Remembering President Kennedy's concerns, I felt ill at ease about President Johnson's apparent indifference to the political implications of a production cutback. I wanted to be sure that he was fully aware of what he might be getting himself into, considering, for example, his own election chances in 1964. During my first meeting with him on November 29, 1963, he had asked me to send him a memorandum pointing out the consequences of starting a cutback as early as July 1964. In my reply a week later I described the status of the study that President Kennedy had asked the AEC to undertake. I noted that there were advantages in waiting until all the results were in, although it was already clear that substantial cuts would be indicated. I then added: "You are probably aware that Senator Jackson has a deep interest and concern about the effects of a cut at Richland, Washington. You might find it profitable to talk to him about the matter." I calculated that a talk with Jackson would tell the president all he needed to know about any political risks.

The die was cast within the week. On December 11:

> I called Senator Jackson to tell him that we had had a budget review session this morning, that, afterward, I had had the opportunity to talk briefly with President Johnson about the production cutback issue, and that he didn't seem to consider employment impact to be nearly as important a factor in making this decision as Kennedy had. The indications were that the president might want to shut down a production reactor or two in order to make some impact on the 1965 budget. Jackson said he had himself been with the president yesterday and had suggested that any cutback be scheduled in a leisurely manner so that loss of employment could be handled on an attrition basis. The president, he said, hadn't seemed very interested in approaching the problem this way.

And that appeared to be that. It seemed quite clear that a cutback in fissionable materials production capacity would soon take place.

3
Flashback: The Buildup

It is my opinion that we must err. . . . on the side of too much rather than too little. . . .

—Secretary of Defense Robert A. Lovett
1951

A Slow Start

How did the overcapacity in the nation's nuclear materials production facilities come about? To answer, one must go back to the period just after World War II.

When David Lilienthal took the oath of office as first chairman of the Atomic Energy Commission in November 1946, the United States had only two atomic bombs in its arsenal. As Lilienthal told an interviewer: "Actually we had one that was probably operable; one that had a good chance of being operable."[1] By June 1947 the arsenal of weapons had increased to thirteen, in various states of readiness.[2] The production rate, still dependent on hand assembly methods in the laboratory, was perhaps two per month.

The rate of fissionable material production did not permit a substantial speedup in weapons manufacture. There were three plutonium production reactors, all at Hanford. Because of technical difficulties (expansion of the large graphite block within the reactor shield), however, one of these had been shut down and the remaining two were operating at reduced capacity. U-235 for direct use in weapons and to fuel the plutonium production reactors was being produced by a single plant at Oak Ridge. After irradiation in the production reactors, much of the U-235 was being lost because the chemical separation process used to separate out the plutonium was unable to recover the uranium. The overall situation was hardly consistent with the nation's foreign policy and military posture, both of which were predicated on the existence of a considerable stockpile of nuclear weapons.

Events in the world soon made the situation even more alarming. In February 1948 a Communist coup seized full control of Czechoslovakia. In June 1948 the Soviets blocked all surface access to West Berlin, leading to the desperate and dangerous Berlin airlift. U.S. civilian authorities and military planners began to consider war with the Soviet Union a distinct possibility. In contemplating this prospect, it was disturbing to realize that the Soviets had great superiority in conventional arms over an America that had essentially demobilized at war's end. The nation's policymakers accordingly turned to a rapid buildup of the U.S. nuclear arsenal as the best way to protect ourselves and the relatively defenseless nations of Western Europe. There was a reluctance to add a conventional buildup, not only because of the cost, but also because of a fear that this might convince the Soviet Union that we would not use nuclear weapons against a Soviet conventional attack.

To support the increase in the weapons stockpile a major buildup in the capacity for producing fissionable materials was clearly essential. Fourth and fifth production reactors were added at Hanford in 1948 and 1949. Thereafter, the buildup occurred in two major spurts, formally approved by President Truman, in 1950 and 1952. How these two efforts were initiated is considered next.

The 1950 Expansion Program: A Stab in the Dark

Although the nation's policymakers were in agreement during the late 1940s that a rapid expansion in fissionable materials production was needed, there was not an adequate information base for determining the proper extent or pace of the expansion. There was, for example, almost no expert knowledge of nuclear technology outside the AEC and its installations. It therefore proved virtually impossible for the armed services to present well-supported statements of nuclear weapon requirements. Indeed, in 1949 the Joint Chiefs of Staff abandoned the attempt altogether and stated their requirements not in terms of weapons required, but rather in terms of the kilograms of nuclear materials and the minimum materials production capacity that should be available. Because the stated requirements involved a substantial increase in capacity with very little supporting data, the AEC asked President Truman to initiate a full-scale review of national security policy.[3]

In the course of this review, Senator Brien McMahon, first chairman of the Joint Committee on Atomic Energy, wrote to Secretary of Defense Louis Johnson urging that the already very high requirements submitted by the Joint Chiefs be "revised upwards."[4] McMahon based his recommendation not on expert knowledge—the joint committee had refused until 1949 to accept any classified information from the AEC—but on the general proposition that atomic weapons were "the keystone of our military policy and a foundation pillar of our foreign policy as well." The first Soviet atomic test, announced by the president on September 23, 1949, provided further support to the arguments for rapid expansion.

Early in October 1949, a special committee composed of the heads of Defense, State, and AEC reported to the president its conclusions that an acceleration of materials production consistent with the requirements submitted by the Joint Chiefs was necessary in the interest of national security. (This report was mainly the work of the Defense Department representatives; AEC's part was limited to commenting on feasibility and estimating the costs of expansion.)[5] A modest expansion, including construction of an additional uranium enrichment plant at Oak Ridge, was already under way by the end of 1949.

Following the Soviet test, an intense debate* also ensued as to whether to undertake development of the hydrogen bomb. Much has been, and continues to be, written about this bitter controversy. It arrayed J. Robert Oppenheimer and most members of the AEC's General Advisory Committee (GAC) that he chaired (who opposed development)† against AEC Commissioner Lewis L. Strauss, Edward Teller, and others (who favored it). Truman settled the issue on January 31, 1950, directing the AEC "to continue its work on all forms of atomic weapons, including the so-called hydrogen or super-bomb."

The momentum toward drastic expansion of uranium and plutonium production capacity received a sharp boost on June 24, 1950,

---

*Although this debate was intense, it was conducted in greatest secrecy and hence had very few participants. Thus, the opportunity to bring to bear the leavening effect of public opinion, so essential in a democracy, was lost, as it has been in other important decisions regarding our fundamental nuclear policies. Looking back, it is hard to see why this particular debate needed to have been carried on in secret.

†When the GAC considered the hydrogen bomb issue during the last week of October 1949, I was on a trip to Sweden. Before the meeting I transmitted my views to Oppenheimer by mail, concluding that "I would have to hear some good arguments before I could take on sufficient courage to recommend not going toward such a commitment." There is some doubt as to whether Oppenheimer told the committee about my letter. My own opinion is that he probably did not. (See Hewlett and Duncan, *Atomic Shield,* p. 384 and note 43, p. 642f.)

when invasion from the north launched the Korean War. In August, Secretary of Defense Johnson and General Omar Bradley, chairman of the Joint Chiefs, testified before the Joint Committee that the rate of production of bomb material should be increased so that it utilized all available uranium in the shortest possible time. Representative Henry M. Jackson wrote to Secretary Johnson that anything short of doubling authorized output would be detrimental to the United States. If we could do more than that, so much the better.[6]

In September 1950, a joint AEC–DOD working group reported that the expansion program being demanded would require essentially all the uranium ore available in the free world.[7] Notwithstanding, the Joint Chiefs formally submitted for presidential approval new and even higher fissionable materials production objectives. These requirements were translated into a major expansion program for materials production facilities. Approved by President Truman on October 9, 1950, the program involved adding:

a sixth plutonium production reactor at Hanford;

five plutonium production reactors plus two chemical separation plants (for separation and purification of reactor-produced plutonium) at the new Savannah River complex near Aiken, South Carolina;

two plants at a new site near Paducah, Kentucky,* that would more than double the nation's capacity for producing enriched uranium;

and two plants—at Savannah River and Dana, Indiana—to produce heavy water for use, instead of graphite, as moderator in the newer Savannah River reactors.

The 1952 Expansion Program: "You Can't Get Enough . . ."

Following the president's approval of the 1950 expansion program, AEC Chairman Gordon E. Dean wrote to Joint Committee Chairman McMahon that the expansion represented "the maximum feasible program without exorbitant or unreasonable expenditure in light of the supplies of ore foreseeable at this time."[8] In effect, Dean seemed

---

*A second enriched uranium site had seemed desirable so as not to offer too concentrated a target and so power demands could be met by more than one utility network.

to be saying: "Enough! Enough!" Nevertheless, a further deterioration in the world political situation soon brought pressures for still another jump in production capacity.

On October 23, 1950, the People's Republic of China entered the Korean War. News from the battlefronts turned so dark that the United States seriously considered the use of atomic weapons. AEC Chairman Gordon Dean recorded in his diary that on April 6, 1951, he was summoned to the White House by President Truman. The president told him

> that the situation in the Far East is extremely serious; that there is a heavy concentration of men just above the Yalu River in the part of Manchuria across from the northwestern corner of Korea; that there is a very heavy concentration of [enemy] air forces on several fields and the planes are tip-to-tip and extremely vulnerable; that there is a concentration of some 70 Russian submarines at Vladivostok and a heavy concentration on southern Sakhalin—all of which indicates that not only are the Reds [Chinese and North Koreans] and the Russians ready to push us out of Korea, but [that they] may attempt to take the Japanese Islands and with their submarines cut our supply lines to Japan and Korea. He told me he had a request from the Joint Chiefs of Staff [portion deleted—classified] that no decision had been made to use these weapons and he hoped very much that there would be no necessity for using them; that before there was any decision to use them the matter would be fully explored by the National Security Council; that in no event would the bomb be used in northern Korea where he appreciated, as I pointed out to him, that they would be fully ineffective and psychological "duds" [because of the ruggedness of] northern Korea terrain.
>
> I told him there were many considerations we would like to bring to the Council table when the question was up as to use. [Portion deleted—classified.] He then said if I saw no objection he would sign the order directing me to release to the custody of General [Hoyt S.] Vandenberg, chief of staff, USAF, nine nuclears [portion deleted—classified].[9]

In subsequent days the "nine nuclears" were indeed transported to the Pacific. The enemy offensive in Korea was thrown back, however, and the feared Communist thrust toward Japan did not materialize.

These events serve to illustrate the superheated atmosphere in which national security decisions were being made at this time. JCAE staff chief William L. Borden expressed the prevailing philosophy in a July 1951 memorandum to Senator McMahon: "If we act to increase our supply of atomic weapons and they turn out to be unnecessary, we may lose a few hundred million dollars. If we fail to produce these weapons and they turn out to be necessary, we may lose our country."[10] McMahon heartily approved of these sentiments and of the recommendations for major further expansion that went with them. He expressed his own conviction that the nation needed "thousands and thousands" of bombs.[11]

In November 1951 the Joint Chiefs proposed a further massive expansion in materials production capacity beyond what had been approved in 1950.[12] As heretofore, the Joint Chiefs did not offer any statement of weapon requirements to justify an effort estimated to cost $5 billion for construction and an additional $1.3 billion per year in operating costs.*

The AEC conveyed its views about the requested expansion in a report to the National Security Council (NSC). The commission indicated that expansion to the extent proposed by the Joint Chiefs was "probably feasible." It went on to comment, however, that the expansion approved in 1950 would place the nation "in a position . . . to reach eventually any military goal." The objective of any additional expansion could therefore only be "to reach any specific military goal at an earlier date."

In the general stampede for increased production capacity, major technical developments that made these very increases less necessary seemed to pass unnoticed. The AEC's report to the NSC called attention to some of these when it asked the council to consider that prospective weapon improvements offered the possibility of "substantial gains in energy release from the same amount of fissionable materials."[13] Also, production technology developed rapidly during the 1940s and 1950s, leading to spectacular increases in the capabilities of the individual materials production plants as compared to their original design ratings.

AEC Commissioner Henry D. Smyth attempted to press home the point about the gains to be expected from weapon improvements in a meeting with the National Security Council staff on December 3 but reported that he made very little impression.[14] He also reported

---

*One would need to multiply these numbers by about four to approximate costs in 1986 dollars. (Producer Price Index data from U.S. Bureau of Labor Statistics.)

that the military representatives present seemed to assume that what the Joint Chiefs wanted, the Joint Chiefs would get. At about the same time Commissioner T. Keith Glennan took issue specifically with the notion that the military should always get all they wanted. He stated that his understanding of the Atomic Energy Act and its legislative history was that "while the rights of the military are to be protected at all times, the notion of a 'blank check' for the military was not developed as a result of the legislative deliberations."[15]

On December 11, Secretary of Defense Robert A. Lovett articulated the military side of this controversy in a statement to the NSC. He said he doubted that it would ever be possible for the Joint Chiefs to indicate a number of weapons that would be sufficient to assure U.S. security. Technological progress in weapon design and new delivery systems, including nuclear artillery, were enlarging opportunities and would continue to do so. Added to this was the uncertainty about Soviet intentions. Accordingly, Lovett said, "[i]t is my opinion that we must err . . . on the side of too much rather than too little, within our economic capabilities and the overall defense effort."[16]

A decision on the new expansion request was reached at a climactic meeting of the NSC convened by President Truman on January 16, 1952. Lovett explained again that rapid developments in weaponry made it difficult to estimate military requirements exactly. Air Force Chief of Staff Vandenberg pointed out that the need to disperse atomic weapons increased the number required. Secretary of State Dean Acheson saw no sign of any easing in international relations that would warrant not going ahead. Gordon Dean stated that, though the AEC believed the program was feasible, it had no opinion on whether it was wise. He dissented from the view that "you simply can't get enough of this material."[17]

In raising his mild objections, Dean could not have hoped to prevail. No hands were raised when the president asked: "Does anyone feel we should not undertake this?" At the end of the meeting he signified his approval and, on February 25, 1952, he signed the directive authorizing the expansion to go forward.[18] The construction effort in this new round of expansion was to be completed in five years. It involved three new Hanford plutonium production reactors; and six new gaseous diffusion buildings for the production of enriched uranium: one at Oak Ridge, two at Paducah, and three at a new site—selected because of the availability of electric power—on the Scioto River north of Portsmouth, Ohio.

What We Built

With the startup of the last units at Portsmouth in November 1955, the expansion approved in 1952 was completed, nearly a year ahead of schedule. The following major facilities were then in place:

twelve gaseous diffusion process buildings for producing enriched uranium;

thirteen reactors for the production of plutonium, some of which could also produce tritium;

seven chemical separation plants for the recovery and purification of plutonium; and

two heavy water production plants.

As we have seen, this huge enterprise proved within a few years to be far in excess of what was needed. It was to leave President Johnson with the difficult problem of cutting back. How he handled this problem is what we will consider next.

Notes

1. Herken, *The Winning Weapon*, p. 197n.
2. Norris, Cochran, and Arkin, "History of the Nuclear Stockpile," p. 107.
3. AEC 1140, "History of Expansion of AEC Production Facilities" (unpublished report), p. 10f. As the citations indicate, this document provides a principal basis for this chapter.
4. Ibid., p. 11.
5. Ibid.
6. Ibid., p. 19.
7. Ibid., p. 20.
8. Ibid., p. 22.
9. Anders, ed., *Forging the Atomic Shield*.
10. Hewlett and Duncan, *Atomic Shield*, p. 523.
11. Ibid., p. 547.
12. Herken, *The Winning Weapon*, p. 563.
13. AEC 1140, p. 39f.
14. Ibid., p. 40f.
15. Ibid., p. 42.
16. Ibid., p. 41f.
17. Ibid., p. 44.
18. Ibid., p. 42ff.

4
First Cuts

Planning under Kennedy

In late 1959, and again in February 1961, the Atomic Energy Commission had put into effect substantial reductions in total electric power demand at its three U-235 production sites. (The electricity consumed by the plants correlated roughly with their output of finished product and, for security reasons, power demand was used as the unit of measure for programming the plants' activity.) These cutbacks marked the first departures from the previous philosophy of striving always for maximum production.

President Kennedy initiated consideration of a further cut in February 1963. In a letter to me he indicated that weapon requirements for U-235 were being reduced and he requested the AEC to adjust production of enriched uranium accordingly. The reductions were occasioned by the president's decision to cancel production (for the British) of the Skybolt missile, to terminate further production of eight-inch artillery shells, and to apply a more stringent weapons retirement policy. These changes reflected the more searching analysis instituted in the Pentagon by Defense Secretary McNamara.

Kennedy's request set in motion a detailed study by the AEC staff, the results of which I reported to the president in May 1963. We recommended a further 24 percent cut in electric power usage at the AEC diffusion plants, from 4,850 megawatts—the level reached after the reductions in 1959 and 1961—to 3,700 megawatts, the reduction to be completed in two years. I told the president that we could not submit any recommendations about plutonium and tritium until he decided on requirements for tactical and antisubmarine weapons.

The information needed to complete the picture was soon available. In August 1963 Secretary McNamara sent the president what was undoubtedly the most precise and detailed statement of nuclear weapon requirements yet to emerge from the Pentagon. It consisted of weapon stockpile objectives extending through June 1972. Significantly, McNamara acknowledged that the Joint Chiefs of Staff were not in full agreement with his estimates. It is doubtful that any prior secretary of defense would have dared to present military requirements without the Joint Chiefs' full concurrence.

Early in October 1963 the AEC staff, having addressed itself to the stockpile objectives recommended by McNamara, came up with a matching ten-year production plan for plutonium and tritium. The plan contemplated the shutdown in fiscal years 1965 and 1966 of six of the nation's fourteen production reactors. Five of the six were to be older reactors located at Hanford. The sixth was to be one of the newer plants at Savannah River. The staff estimated that, despite these shutdowns, weapon stockpile objectives could be met and still leave the nation with a reserve of several thousand kilograms of plutonium in 1972. McNamara's stockpile objectives also permitted a much deeper cut in U-235 output than the AEC had previously recommended, although we did not at once estimate how much deeper.

One-upmanship

As we have seen (chapter 2), President Kennedy was reluctant to implement any of the production cuts he had himself initiated until after the 1964 election. When it appeared that President Johnson was not similarly hesitant, I wrote to him setting forth AEC's recommendations of steps that should be taken. We suggested that a decision be made at once to shut down the six reactors identified in our October 1963 letter to President Kennedy and that we begin a gradual reduction of power demand at the U-235 production sites from 4,850 megawatts to about 2,000 megawatts. This would be a reduction of about 60 percent, not the 25 percent recommended in our letter of May 17, 1963, the difference having been made possible by McNamara's statement of weapon requirements.

A little game of one-upmanship now ensued. The Defense Department wanted to proceed faster than the AEC, recommending that all six reactors be shut down in fiscal year 1965—we had thought this action could be spread over two years. As to enriched uranium, Defense pointed out that virtually all its needs for the next several years would be met by using uranium in weapons withdrawn from the stockpile.* Any incremental requirements that might come along for enriched uranium were therefore likely to be for civilian needs and, as to these, Defense said it would defer to AEC's judgment.

On December 21, McNamara, Budget Director Kermit Gordon, and I met with the president and Bundy to resolve a few small differences among us. We reached the following conclusions:

1. There would be a cut of about 850 megawatts of electric power demand in fiscal year 1965 at the uranium enrichment plants as part of a long-range program to reduce total demand to 2,000 megawatts from the existing level of 4,850 megawatts.
2. Six production reactors would be shut down: one at Savannah River on July 1, 1964; and five at Hanford at three month intervals beginning January 1, 1965.

A Failure of Nerve?

Within the next week it was decided to announce the production cutbacks in the president's State of the Union message on January 8, 1964. On January 7 the proposed text came down. The pertinent sentence read, in part: ". . . we are cutting down our production of enriched uranium by *25 percent*, shutting down *four* plutonium piles and closing many nonessential military installations" (emphasis added).

At a White House meeting convened on January 7 solely to discuss this one sentence:

I pointed out that the sentence might be misleading in that the president had already decided, in the meeting of December 21, to make deeper cuts; namely, he had decided to cut power at the diffusion plants down to 2,000 megawatts, which was a reduction of about 60 percent, not 25 percent; and he had decided to shut down six reactors, not four. To my surprise, [Deputy Budget Director Elmer B.] Staats said he thought the president had left the long-range situation somewhat open. Bundy then said that this could only be resolved by conferring with the president.

---

*The total megatonnage in the stockpile had been reduced by nearly half with the sudden retirement of heavy B36 bombs between August 1961 and January 1962 (Norris, et al., "History of the Nuclear Stockpile," p. 107). Technical discoveries by Edward Teller and Stanislaw M. Ulam in the early 1950s had made it possible to reorient the hydrogen bomb arsenal from the huge and cumbersome early models to lighter, more deliverable bombs requiring far less fissionable material.

The issue was of concern to the AEC mainly because of certain clauses in our contracts with electric utilities. As indicated in chapter 3, it had been necessary to create new sources of power when the enrichment plants were built. Two new companies had been created for this purpose: the Ohio Valley Electric Corporation (OVEC) and Electric Energy Inc. (EEI). Each was essentially a consortium of a number of existing utility companies. OVEC had constructed power plants at Madison, Indiana, and Kyger, Ohio, to furnish power to Portsmouth. EEI had constructed a plant at Joppa, Illinois, to supply part of the power needs of Paducah, the remainder being furnished by the Tennessee Valley Authority (TVA), which had added new capacity to its system solely for this purpose.

As these power plants were being constructed, it became apparent that very favorable rates, approximately four mills (0.4 cents) per kilowatt-hour, could be obtained for the diffusion plants if the AEC was prepared to enter into long-term contracts. In July 1953 the Congress granted AEC the necessary statutory authority, and contracts of twenty to twenty-five years were concluded with OVEC, EEI, and TVA. Along with favorable rates, however, the contracts provided for substantial penalties if the AEC reduced its purchases. The amount of the penalties would vary depending on the supplier involved, the amount of power to be dropped, and the amount of advance notice we could give. The last criterion—advance notice—was the crux of the matter in January 1964. If President Johnson would make a public commitment to the full long-term cut I thought had been agreed to in the December 21 meeting, the AEC could then negotiate relatively lenient penalties with the utilities.

But President Johnson apparently was now becoming concerned about the political implications of announcing very drastic reductions all at once. In a hastily arranged meeting that convened within an hour after the preliminary January 7 meeting adjourned, the president decided that he would stay with the draft text for the State of the Union message. He asked all of those present (Rusk, McNamara, Bundy, Gordon, and myself) not to mention in public any longer-range plan.

Another Try

The decision President Johnson made about the State of the Union message may have spared him a political problem but it did not solve the AEC's financial problem. The power supply contracts, and the potentially stiff cancellation penalties, just would not go away. Therefore, on February 3, 1964, AEC Commissioner James T. Ramey and I gathered at the White House with Bundy, Staats, and others to consider this matter further.

> I pointed out that, if the AEC intended later on to make cuts deeper than the 25 percent announced by the president, it was important that we give the power companies notice of that intention before February 15, which was a formal deadline in our contracts. Otherwise, we would have to pay steep penalties when we actually made the deeper cuts.
>
> After discussion back and forth, the AEC was authorized to negotiate at once with the power suppliers a reduction to about 2,900 megawatts—about forty percent less than the current level. A decision on whether to reduce further to 2,000 megawatts—the level that AEC felt best accorded with military and civilian requirements—was deferred until the end of the year.

But now another factor intervened, calling for a slower pace. This was the president's desire to use the further cutbacks—the ones beyond those he had already announced—as a lure in arms control negotiations with the Soviet Union.

5

The Arms Control Connection

So, let us try.
—Nikita Khrushchev
March 2, 1964

"A Little Private Signaling"

In the first few days of Johnson's presidency, Robert McNamara had suggested to him that the long-pending cutback in fissionable materials production be presented in a challenging and conspicuous fashion so as to evoke some Soviet response in kind. It was this suggestion that led the president to mention the cutbacks in the State of the Union message in the following context:

> [W]e must take new steps—and we shall make new proposals at Geneva—toward the control and the eventual abolition of arms. Even in the absence of agreement we must not stockpile arms beyond our needs or seek an excess of military power that could be provocative as well as wasteful. And it is in this spirit that in this fiscal year we are cutting back our production of enriched uranium by 25 percent. We are shutting down four plutonium piles. We are closing many nonessential military installations. *And it is in this spirit that we today call on our adversaries to do the same* [emphasis added].[1]

The Soviet Union did not at once take the bait and, for over a month, during all of our discussions within the administration about the size and timing of prospective cuts, there was no further mention of an arms control connection. It was suddenly revived at a meeting in Bundy's office on February 12, 1964.

> We discussed making an early public announcement of cuts in power use at the uranium enrichment plants beyond those announced in the president's State of the Union message. There

were no objections to the idea, but Bundy asked [Ambassador-at-Large Llewellyn E.] Thompson whether there would be any value in delaying the announcement in order to use the additional cutback in disarmament negotiations with the Russians. I again warned that any long delay could cost the AEC as much as $16 million in penalty payments under its utility contracts. Thompson doubted that further delay would be worth such a cost in view of the very slight hope that the Soviets would agree to mutual reductions. It was decided, therefore, that I would send the president a letter recommending that the further cuts be approved and announced forthwith.

I did send such a letter the following day, planning to make the announcement two days hence, on February 15, the formal deadline in our contracts. Early on that day, however, Bundy called to say that it had been decided to put the formal announcement "on hold." Notwithstanding Thompson's pessimism, the diplomats would make a try.

What the diplomats had in mind had been described on February 14 by ACDA Deputy Director Adrian Fisher. Referring to AEC's plan to announce energy cuts the next day, Fisher wrote to Bundy that such an announcement would "tend to undercut the president's earlier call on the USSR [in the State of the Union message] to respond to the first cut-back . . . and call into question whether the first announcement was a bona fide offer or merely a halt in unnecessary production." Fisher's memorandum continued:

> Since we intend to make the [new] cut-back regardless of the Soviet attitude, there is very little bargaining leverage available to us. If the announcement were delayed for a short period, we might in the interval persuade the Soviets that it is in their interest to put Chairman Khrushchev's "mutual example" suggestion into practice in this area, or perhaps to respond by making a constructive unilateral move in some other area.* They may possibly decide to do so rather than have the USSR put in a negative position. . . . Nothing will be lost if the Soviets react negatively; much could be gained if we could induce them to respond positively.
>
> Although the AEC's contractors may require legal notice by

---

*Khrushchev's suggestion was that the two superpowers might move forward more rapidly in arms control and disarmament if, instead of trying to negotiate formal agreements, they simply took independent, but reciprocal, actions. (*Documents on Disarmament* 1964, p. 313.)

February 15, I cannot believe that this cannot be handled without public disclosure at this time.

Fisher concluded by saying that he intended to transmit that day a draft of a possible presidential message to Chairman Khrushchev.

(In making this intervention, the ACDA was acting exactly as Hubert Humphrey, then-Senator John Kennedy, and other original sponsors of this "peace agency" within government intended it to act from its inception in 1961. The concept was that the agency would probe ceaselessly for opportunities to take initiatives leading toward disarmament and would act as an advocate of such initiatives within the government. The rationale, which I certainly support, was that disarmament, like defense, labor, commerce, agriculture, or the elderly, is a legitimate interest that deserves representation within government councils. One must note with regret that the ACDA no longer seems to be functioning this way.)

I learned of the pending strategy in a telephone call from Bundy on February 18:

He said that the "disarmament people" had proposed that the United States do a little private signaling to the Soviets before we made our public announcement of the further production cuts. . . . He asked whether I could give him reasonable assurance that there would be no leak for a minimum of two weeks. I said that there were a number of people in the utilities who knew what was coming up, but that they all seemed trustworthy.

Later the same day Bundy called again:

He said the administration was definitely going ahead with the private message we had discussed earlier. He was not optimistic. He said State did not believe there would be any answer to our message, which would be delivered by Thompson to Ambassador Dobrynin.

What Thompson delivered to Dobrynin, on February 18, was a letter from President Johnson to Chairman Khrushchev, reading in part:

With further reference to my announcement on January 8 of the reduction by 25% in the United States output of enriched uranium (U-235) and the closing of some plutonium-producing reactors, I have again reviewed our requirements and have concluded that it will soon be possible to reduce United States production of U-235 by an additional substantial amount.

I am furnishing you this advance notice in the renewed hope that the Soviet Government would find it in its interest to take a parallel step. . . . The reductions need not be by an equal amount. I am sure that another substantial reduction in the United States' output will naturally lead the world to hope that the Soviet Union will follow suit.

Should my suggestion meet your approval, I am prepared to delay my announcement . . . for the time it would require to concert our views on the matter. We could then consider how best to make this public, whether by a joint announcement or other appropriate means. . . .

Noteworthy about this letter was the rather clear implication that what was principally involved was effect on world opinion. The world would be heartened if the Soviet Union went along—both governments would gain by this. On the other hand, if the Soviets did not follow our lead, they would disappoint world hopes. Johnson was putting the squeeze on Khrushchev in an area of great sensitivity to the Soviets—their reputation among the community of nations for being "peace-loving."

Notwithstanding the State Department's pessimism, a reply did come, and relatively soon by Soviet standards. It was read aloud by Dobrynin to Thompson on March 2, and then left behind in written form. The message was vintage Khrushchev: long, rambling, and containing factual errors. It was also replete with the curious ambivalence that had characterized Khrushchev's communication with Western leaders before the 1963 test ban negotiations in Moscow. On the one hand, it was full of complaint and scarcely concealed mistrust. On the other hand, when it came to the main points, it was reasonably forthcoming.

Khrushchev began with a review of Soviet arms control proposals across a broad front, and of arms control agreements already reached, featuring the Limited Test Ban Treaty, by which, like Kennedy, he set great store. He continued: "After thinking it over and consulting our specialists, I came to the conclusion that it may be worthwhile to seek a mutual understanding in this [production cutbacks] area also." But then he let it be known that he was aware of the situation that, as Fisher had noted, made our bargaining position weak:

> I shall confide that our specialists have drawn to my attention . . . that for two decades the United States has accumulated a quantity of fissionable materials which in general exceeds all thinkable and even unthinkable requirements. . . . If this is really true, it means that a kind of crisis of overproduction is about to occur in the United States.

Khrushchev went on to state two more grievances—about a new dual-purpose (power and materials production) reactor being built at Hanford, and a large diffusion plant being built in France. Then, almost as a non sequitur, he added: "So, let us try." He might soon be able to announce the ending of construction on two large production reactors; he would agree to the president's suggestion that the exchange of views be kept confidential for the present. All in all, it was not a bad response.

At the Last Hour: Apparent Agreement

It was administration policy to keep the pressure on the Soviets in this matter. Consequently, on March 3, the day after Khrushchev's response was received, several of us gathered together at the White House to consider what he had said and how President Johnson might best respond. The group included, among others, Bundy (the principal orchestrator of this entire exercise), ACDA Director Foster, Ambassador-at-Large Thompson, Deputy Defense Secretary McNaughton, and CIA Director John A. McCone.

> Thompson said Khrushchev's message seemed to indicate some desire for an agreement. Bundy asked me whether an additional delay was possible in announcing the further cutback in U-235 production without incurring penalties under AEC's utility contracts. I thought another month or two could probably be arranged. The rest of the meeting was taken up with a discussion of what kind of a reply to make to Khrushchev.

Our discussion was pretty well reflected in President Johnson's reply. It contained factual corrections about the capacity of the new

Hanford reactor and the new French diffusion plant, both of which Khrushchev had exaggerated. But, the president wrote, these numbers did not matter. We had previously offered to cut back more than the Soviets did; we were not asking them to match us kilogram for kilogram. Expressing satisfaction that the Soviets might halt construction of the two plutonium production reactors, Johnson noted the absence in Khrushchev's message of any specific reference to enriched uranium, commenting: "I think that this would be particularly appropriate since it is our understanding that you are continuing to expand your already substantial uranium-235 production." The president then cited Khrushchev's questions about the validity of our announced cutbacks as a reason to "reaffirm my previous suggestion on the desirability of some type of verification. . . . I feel that such inspection would add measurably to the confidence of all peoples in the reality of our reductions." Johnson concluded by urging that, "as an initial measure," the two countries try to complete their joint action on materials cutbacks as soon as possible (a concession to AEC's problem with its electricity suppliers), and that they "prepare and exchange independent announcements of [their] intended actions for concurrent release."

It is hard to see how an awkward situation—U.S. production overcapacity—could have been coaxed into serving beneficial ends with greater skill than President Johnson, Bundy, Fisher, Thompson, and others in the administration demonstrated in this instance. We had now to await a further Soviet response.

And wait we did, with the electric utility penalty clauses hanging over AEC's head and setting a limit to our patience. The denouement is best told in President Johnson's own account in his memoirs:

> [B]y April 17 no firm agreement had been reached. I decided that the United States would move on its own. . . . I informed [Khrushchev] that I planned to make the announcement in three days. Unless I heard from him before then, I would not mention the possibility of parallel action.
>
> On April 20 I flew to New York City for the annual Associated Press luncheon, where I planned to discuss the basic principles of our foreign policy. The text of my speech also contained the announcement that we were going to reduce further our production of fissionable material. I was disappointed that I could not say the Russians were taking similar action. Then, just before I was to speak, a courier brought me an urgent message that prompted me to pencil

in a new paragraph. I had barely finished writing before the presiding officer completed his introduction and made room for me at the rostrum.

Halfway through my speech I came to the key section, announcing the additional cutback in our production of enriched uranium. . . . Then I added what I had just written on a sheet of paper: "Simultaneously with my announcement now, Chairman Khrushchev is releasing a statement in Moscow, at two o'clock our time, in which he makes definite commitments to steps toward a more peaceful world. He agrees to discontinue the construction of two big new atomic reactors for the production of plutonium, over the next several years to reduce substantially the production of U-235 for nuclear weapons, and to allocate more fissionable material for peaceful uses."

As I flew back to Washington that afternoon, I felt renewed hope for the future of mankind. The world's two greatest adversaries, history's two greatest powers, had taken a step toward disarmament. It was not a big step, but at least it was movement.[2]

It is to be noted that Khrushchev's announcement went well beyond what he had indicated was possible in his March 2 letter. Then he had mentioned only ceasing construction of two plutonium production reactors, whereas now he was contemplating also a reduction in U-235 output—acceding to the president's suggestion—and a transfer of fissionable material to peaceful uses. Johnson had every reason to feel pleased at the apparent result of his arms control initiative.

Reaction

The AEC issued its own announcement of the additional materials production cuts on April 20, describing them in greater detail than did the president's speech the same day. We stated that the further electric power reductions would take effect gradually, beginning in 1966, with completion in 1968. The cuts would be allocated 500 megawatts to Portsmouth, 445 megawatts to Oak Ridge, none to Paducah. The savings in annual power costs would be $33 million. Employment at the two affected sites would be reduced by about 125 positions out of a total of about four thousand.

The day following, Adrian Fisher appraised the significance of the Johnson and Khrushchev announcements in brief remarks to the

ENDC. He said that they marked "the beginning of what the United States hopes will be a process leading ultimately to a complete and verified cut-off in the production of fissionable materials for weapons purposes and to substantial transfers to peaceful uses."[3] The ENDC itself issued a communiqué stating that the announcements were "received with great satisfaction."

On April 22, Carl Rowan, director of the USIA, reported to the president that the U.S. and Soviet announcements had received "voluminous world acclaim." He said that Latin American and Far East comment was "highly laudatory" and that papers in India gave the United States full credit for the initiative. This was true even of Radio Moscow, which stated: "The idea of reducing the output of fissionable materials came from President Johnson, so that in agreeing to it the Soviet Union met the United States halfway."[4] Rowan noted, however, that mixed in with all the praise were quite a few skeptical editorials pointing out that neither side had actually reduced its military power.

There was a wary reaction also from influential members of Congress. They seemed far from overwhelmed by the symbolic aspects that had so enthused President Johnson. Most of all, they expressed annoyance about not having been consulted in advance. Thus, on the morning of April 20, before the dual announcements that afternoon:

> I appeared before the Joint Committee on Atomic Energy to explain the cutback. [Senator Bourke B.] Hickenlooper and [Representative Craig] Hosmer were very suspicious of the administration's motives and felt it was sprung on them too fast. I tried to explain the long and careful consideration given to the power reduction. Then I met with the House Appropriations Committee to explain the same thing prior to continuation of our budget hearings for fiscal year 1965. [Chairman Clarence] Cannon claimed I hadn't been frank with the committee in a discussion of future cutback plans last week. [I had been under wraps imposed by the White House.]

The following day:

> General Congressional reaction to President Johnson's announcement of the U-235 cutback seemed generally good. There was some Republican criticism, however, to the effect either that the timing of our announcement to coincide with Khrushchev's made this an agreement without inspection, therefore

unacceptable to the Congress; or that it wasn't an agreement at all—merely parallel announcements masquerading as an agreement.

In my regular biweekly report I told the president:

Senator Pastore [chairman of the Joint Committee] gave strong support on the Senate floor on April 21. Senator Jackson, while supporting the cutback, announced that the Joint Committee will hear testimony from General Maxwell Taylor, Chairman of the Joint Chiefs of Staff, to make sure that everything possible has been done to safeguard our nuclear superiority.

Did They or Didn't They?

In the months following the dual announcements of April 20, 1964, the U.S. cutbacks went forward and further reductions were initiated. But no confirmation was received, nor was U.S. intelligence able to ascertain, that the Soviet Union was carrying out the intentions announced by Khrushchev. This subject was thrown into stark relief when word came on October 13, 1964, that he had been removed from office. Would Khrushchev's successors follow through on his commitment? Many suspected they would not.

The matter was raised at a meeting of the Committee of Principals on December 21, 1964:

The consensus view was that the Soviets had not initiated the promised cutback. Bundy suggested creation of an interdepartmental group to look into the matter. I mentioned that AEC and Defense were studying a still further reduction in U-235 production and suggested that, if such a cutback were decided on, it could possibly provide a means for prying some information from the Russians.

The Bureau of the Budget added its voice in subsequent days with a recommendation for a drastic further cut in power demand at the uranium enrichment plants—from the 2,970 megawatt level announced on April 20 all the way down to 1,500 megawatts. The matter came to a head at a White House meeting I attended on January 26, 1965. Bundy, Budget Director Gordon, and others from Budget, the White House, and AEC were present. It was decided to

accept the AEC's more moderate recommendation of a gradual reduction to 2,000 megawatts, to be initiated in 1966 and completed
in 1969.

This time I was careful to brief the Joint Committee in advance.
Having obtained the committee's assent to the planned reduction, I
was preparing to write to the president to request his formal approval
when I learned that someone had leaked the news to John Finney of
The New York Times. This gave us some nervous moments because
we knew that President Johnson was particularly phobic about press
leaks; on more than one occasion he changed a planned action so as
to discredit a press report. On the evening of February 2, 1965, I
contacted the president by telephone to tell him of the letter I was
sending him and also of the leak to Finney. Johnson expressed disgust
about the leak.

Although the president told me on the telephone that he would
approve the recommended action, he delayed in doing so. Meanwhile,
another February 15 deadline for escaping a cancellation penalty was
approaching—$5 million was at stake this time. Accordingly, I made
urgent contact with the White House, and the president finally signed
on February 13. I don't doubt that his delay related to the press leak.

AEC duly announced the new cutback on February 15, and two
days later Llewellyn Thompson gave a copy of our release to Ambassador Dobrynin. As discussed at the December 21 Principals meeting, the hope was that this might smoke out some information from
the Soviets about whether they had carried out Khrushchev's commitments. Months passed, however, and we in the AEC heard nothing. Meanwhile we were receiving many inquiries about what the
Soviet Union might have done. Several members of Congress, including Senator Jackson, expressed skepticism that the Soviets had made
any cutbacks at all; some implied that President Johnson had been
duped into a disadvantageous deal. The heat on this matter finally
grew to the point where the AEC felt it necessary to issue a statement
of "clarification," which we did on November 25, 1965.

The statement began by summarizing the status of U.S. cutbacks.
It next quoted Khrushchev's announcement of Soviet decisions to take
parallel action. We then commented: "There is no evidence to confirm that the Soviets have indeed done what they stated they would
do." Finally, to disarm those who felt we might have fallen victim to
Soviet trickery, we said:

The original United States decision to cut back its fissionable material production was based on defense requirements. The U.S. action was not contingent upon any agreement with the Soviets nor contingent upon the Soviets adhering to their public statements.

Then, and only then (that is, after the AEC had issued its press release) did we learn that the attempt to pry some information from the Soviets with our February 15, 1965, announcement had indeed borne fruit. On March 17, 1965, Ambassador Dobrynin had handed the following statement to Llewellyn Thompson:

> In conformance with the April 20, 1964, statement of the Chairman of the Council of Ministers of the USSR, the construction was halted in the Soviet Union of two new large atomic reactors for the production of plutonium. There also is being undertaken a curtailment, projected for the next several years, of the production of Uranium-235 for nuclear weapons. Correspondingly more fissionable materials are being designated for use for peaceful purposes.
>
> The communication transmitted by the American side concerning further U.S. plans for the curtailment of the production of Uranium-235 in 1966–1969 is being taken under consideration by the Soviet side.

Although this Soviet statement was not necessarily to be taken at face value, there was a good chance that it was an honest representation of fact. There had been no public pressure on the Soviet Union to make any statement at all, and the risk in bilateral relations of being discovered in duplicity hardly seemed worth taking. Whatever one may conclude about the Soviet statement's veracity, however, it was clear that State had committed a gaffe of considerable magnitude in failing for more than eight months to make the AEC aware of the statement's existence.

Further Actions

The cumulative effect of the curtailments initiated in 1964 spread through the entire chain of plants that supplied feed materials to the diffusion plants and fuel to the production reactors. On January 11, 1964, the AEC announced that the uranium concentrate plants at Weldon Springs, Missouri, and Fernald, Ohio, would remain open, but at reduced levels; that the feed material plant at Paducah would

be placed in standby; and that the Metropolis, Illinois, plant of Allied
Chemical Company would not be kept under contract after June 30,
1964. In April 1966, it was decided to shut down Weldon Springs
and consolidate all uranium concentrate operations at Fernald.

When the first reactor shutdowns at Hanford were announced, it
was explained that this would eventually lead to the closing of one
of the two Hanford plants for the chemical reprocessing of reactor-
produced plutonium. Such a closing did in fact take place at the end
of 1966.

An additional Hanford reactor was shut down in July 1967. Then
in January 1968 it was decided to place in standby one reactor at
Hanford and one at Savannah River. An additional reactor was then
shut down in each of the years 1969, 1970, and 1971. Following
these actions, only four of the fourteen production reactors that had
been operating in mid-1964 remained in operation.

In the Reagan administration the Department of Energy has undertaken various initiatives to increase the supply of plutonium and
tritium in keeping with the president's decision to "revitalize the
stockpile." These steps include converting the three currently operating Savannah River reactors to the production of a higher grade of
plutonium, blending stocks of fuel-grade plutonium that was being
stored for the cancelled breeder reactor program in order to raise it
to weapons grade; increasing production at Savannah River by changing the reactor cores and operating the reactors at higher power;
converting the dual-purpose (power and plutonium) N Reactor at
Hanford from the production of fuel-grade plutonium to the production of weapons-grade plutonium; and, finally, upgrading and restart-
ing one of the deactivated reactors at Savannah River.[5] One additional
reactor there remains in standby condition, permitting it to be reac-
tivated over a period of some eighteen months should some unfore-
seen development so require. The other eight shutdown reactors still
stand, mute testimonials to some great wartime and postwar accomplishments and to some fairly large errors in judgment.

Notes

1. *Documents on Disarmament: 1964*, p. 4.
2. Johnson, *The Vantage Point*, p. 466f.
3. *Documents on Disarmament: 1964*, p. 169.
4. National Security File, NSC Meetings, Box 1, Vol. 1, LBJ Library.
5. Arkin, Cochran, and Hoenig, "Fueling the Arms Race," p. 7.

6
The Economics Connection

We must not operate a WPA nuclear project, just to provide employment,
when our needs have been met.

—Lyndon B. Johnson
April 20, 1964

Protests and Consequences

As expected, the shutdown of nuclear material production facilities
produced a wave of concern and protest from the political and economic constituencies involved. It was in fear of this reaction that
President Kennedy had shied away from taking action in an election
year and that President Johnson had retreated somewhat from his
early bold approach.

AEC's estimate of personnel impact from the cuts we initially
recommended (a reduction to 2,000 megawatts at the uranium enrichment plants and the shutting down of six reactors), as I communicated it to President Johnson in a letter of December 19, 1963, had
included some fairly frightening numbers:

Site	Reduction in Personnel	Total Employment before Reduction	Period for Reduction
Hanford	3,000	8,300	1964–67
Savannah River	550	6,500	1964
Oak Ridge	1,130	14,482	1964–68
Paducah	320	1,197	1964–68
Portsmouth	270	1,367	1964–68
Coal and utility industries	5,075	—	1964–68

The overall numbers were not made public. However, as each
cutback was actually made, its estimated personnel impact was an-

nounced. The announcements caused a sense of shock in the affected communities. There was evident surprise at the unexpected reversal in what had previously been a steadily rising trend in defense-related employment. Nuclear weapons production had been one of the major boom industries in the United States since the end of World War II, and there may have been an expectation that this would continue indefinitely.

I received many distressed communications. A fair number of them urged the AEC to find some peaceful atomic energy activities that could be placed in the communities to ease the loss in employment. One such request came from the governors and combined congressional delegations of South Carolina and Georgia. They proposed that a site within the Savannah River Plant be used for construction of a power reactor prototype in AEC's growing program for development of civilian nuclear power technology. I informed the delegations that the AEC could not go along with this suggestion because we had neither the funds nor the technological need for such a prototype.

Twelve Southeastern electric utilities proposed a study to determine the feasibility of converting part of the Savannah River facility to the production of electricity. I had to inform the utilities that the facility had been designed for a specialized purpose; to change that purpose would be too costly.*

Senator Carl Hayden of Arizona suggested using Hanford reactors as a source of energy for pumping to relieve water shortages in the Pacific Southwest. We indicated that nuclear power might well be used for such a purpose but that we did not favor conversion of existing Hanford reactors because of their age and relatively outmoded technology.

Representative Kenneth J. Gray wrote in considerable agitation about the prospective loss of three hundred jobs at the Allied Chemical Company's uranium feed processing plant and the Joppa electric power plant in southern Illinois. Referring to the economic distress coal mine closures had already caused in the area, he termed our proposed action "almost inhuman," and difficult to square with President Johnson's war on poverty. We could do no more than express regret.

---

*The utilities conducted their own study. After a year they reached the conclusion that the cost of electricity from a converted production reactor would exceed that from a new nuclear power plant.

The cutbacks aroused apprehension even in communities not directly affected. Representative Thomas G. Morris of New Mexico inquired "whether any consideration was being given to the future of the Los Alamos community should a more general weapons cutback occur." I wrote Morris that we did not foresee a decrease in weapons research and development work at Los Alamos.

I had telephone conversations with several senators from affected states, including some of the Senate's most powerful members. Generally speaking, they were temperate and understanding in their questions and comments. Washington State Senators Henry Jackson and Warren G. Magnuson both wanted to know how many people would be affected at Hanford. After I gave them the numbers, Jackson went on to make the reasonable suggestion that in any diversification we undertook at Hanford we make "overall contribution to employment in the area" a principal criterion. Senator Richard Russell of Georgia wanted to know how the cutback would be carried out as between Savannah River and Hanford. He reported that President Johnson had called him at his apartment before Christmas 1963—about two weeks before the first cutback announcement—to tell him that only three to four hundred people would be affected at Savannah River. I had to tell Russell that he had been fed the more optimistic of the numbers I had given the president. (I had said it would be four to five hundred. In our December 1963 memo we had estimated it would be 550.)

Representative Catherine May, whose Washington district included Hanford, noted that it had been announced that three reactors were to be closed down at Hanford, but that the AEC had not yet revealed which specific ones were to close. She took this as an indication that the whole process by which Hanford was being made to bear a larger share of the burden than Savannah River was an arbitrary one. I informed Mrs. May that the performance of the five oldest reactors at Hanford was so nearly identical that it had not been thought important to make an early choice among them. We were quite clear, however, that to shut down more at Savannah River and less at Hanford would result in greater expense to the government and the taxpayer.

Senator Dirksen inquired whether a delay in the power cuts at Joppa might be possible. I told him that we were stockpiling a little more than we needed of the enriched uranium produced at Paducah with Joppa power, looking toward the 1970s when we might need some of it for civilian nuclear power plants. The big question, therefore, was whether we should be cutting faster, not slower. He mentioned that the reduction in power demand varied between utilities. I said we had tried to equalize the impact as much as possible but that there was also the matter of what our contracts with different utilities would let us do. Joppa might have suffered a little more because its contract was relatively lenient.

The AEC tried to cooperate with local interests in joint efforts to "diversify the economic base" of the affected communities. Consideration of such possibilities had begun as early as 1962 when it became apparent that future shutdowns were inevitable. Other federal agencies as well as private companies were made aware of the capabilities of the sites for various activities. Strengthening this effort became a major concern as the shutdown periods approached. On May 6, 1964, I announced the establishment within AEC of an Office of Economic Impact and Conversion, whose job it was to coordinate our efforts to find new sources of employment. We had a fair measure of success. For example, some private laboratories moved into the communities to take advantage of the available pool of trained personnel.

Wider Implications

In the end, the production cutbacks passed into history without nearly the degree of economic and political trauma that I and others involved, including the two presidents, had feared. By making the shutdown announcements well in advance, and by carefully controlling hiring rates throughout the AEC establishment, we were able to help many employees find jobs elsewhere. Some others took advantage of early retirement opportunities. The communities of Oak Ridge and Richland (near Hanford) continued to expand in total population, and the quality of municipal services they were able to offer remained at a high level.

This relatively mild experience nevertheless brought us into contact with a phenomenon that has wider implications. What we experienced, on a relatively small scale, was an instance of what has come to be considered routine in American life, the attempt by local economic interests, abetted by their political representatives, to better themselves through participation in military preparedness programs.

These pressures can be even more significant when linked to those applied by affected laboratory and military interests.

The attitudes and pressures we encountered in such mild form, when brought to bear on behalf of major weapons systems, can introduce serious distortions into the making of public policy. When the decision to be made is whether or not to produce a new weapon, our national leaders can be induced to accede by the massed influence of technical, military, industrial, and congressional advocates, even though the security need for the weapon may be questionable. Once a weapon has entered production, moreover, resistance to ceasing or diminishing its production can be equally overwhelming.

Interventions by pressure groups on behalf of weapons production have been so frequent, vigorous, and effective as to lead some observers to conclude that such activity has been largely responsible for the failure to make greater progress toward disarmament.* That economic or professional self-interest should be so prominent a factor in decisions potentially affecting the survival of the human species seems to me utterly unacceptable. How as a practical matter to reduce the influence of these extraneous considerations on public policy is a difficult question. It is one our society needs to address on a more urgent basis.

---

*Daugherty, *Arms Control and Disarmament*, p. 6. One should note here a comment by Arthur H. Dean, President Kennedy's principal disarmament negotiator. Dean writes that when the administration was attempting to put together a U.S. plan for general and complete disarmament in 1961, "protests came from politically powerful representatives of states with defense industries, especially California and Texas, who feared any disarmament measure which might have a deleterious effect on the economies of their states" (*Test Ban and Disarmament*, p. 26).

Part III

Proliferation: The Mounting Problem

I ask you to stop and think what it would mean to have nuclear weapons in so many hands, in the hands of countries large and small, stable and unstable, responsible and irresponsible, scattered throughout the world. There would be no rest for anyone then, no stability, no real security, and no chance for effective disarmament.

John F. Kennedy
1963

7
Proliferation Begins

What nature tells one group of men, she will tell in time to any group
interested and patient enough in asking questions.
—Albert Einstein
1946

Although U.S.–Soviet cooperation on cutbacks in fissionable materials production attracted President Johnson's attention and aroused his enthusiasm at the outset of his presidency, this issue soon paled into relative insignificance before the dominant arms control issue of the Johnson years, which was how to prevent the spread of nuclear weapons to additional nations. As that issue arrived on President Johnson's desk, it was already freighted with history. There is no escape from that history; we must consider it briefly.

The Franck Report

Before the atomic bomb was used—indeed, before it was ever tested—the likelihood of proliferation was very much on the minds of scientists in the wartime atomic bomb project. We were only too aware that the principles involved in atomic fission, as revealed in the work of scientific teams in Germany, France, Italy, England, and Denmark, and as published in the open literature, were well known throughout the world. Indeed knowledge that work on a bomb was under way in Nazi Germany had been one of the spurs to our own work.*

Nor did we share the view, so widespread in this country, that the industrial steps needed to proceed from the known scientific principles to an actual bomb were beyond the skills and resources of other countries. On the contrary, we felt that our use of the bomb could

---

*Bombing raids were conducted during the war to destroy the Norwegian heavy water factories that were of basic importance to the German program.

lead directly and immediately to a nuclear arms race, with incalculable consequences. There was only one important secret about the bomb and that was whether it would work. Our use of it would settle that question.

At the code-named Metallurgical Laboratory (commonly abbreviated "Met Lab") at the University of Chicago, where I headed a section of the chemistry division,* meetings were held and reports circulated in which postwar policy was anxiously discussed. The issues involved were often of a type that most of us, by training, and perhaps also by temperament, were not particularly qualified to consider. Aware though we were of our limitations, there seemed no choice but to address the issues. By an accident of history, we were among a very few who were aware of a new, world-threatening peril, and we felt obligated to express our views to those in authority.

In June 1945 six committees were established at the Met Lab to make recommendations to the government regarding postwar policy. One was a Committee on Social and Political Implications. It was headed by German-born James Franck, a venerated Nobel laureate (1925) in physics.† I was a member of this group. Other members, all chosen by Franck, were Donald Hughes, James Nickson, Eugene Rabinowitch, Joyce Stearns, and Leo Szilard. The committee's report, shaped mainly by Szilard, with some drafting help from Rabinowitch, was completed on June 11, 1945, and signed by every member of the group. It made, basically, three points. The first was that the United States could not avoid a nuclear arms race through a policy of secrecy. The second was that the best hope for national and world safety from the consequences of the bomb lay in international control of atomic energy. The third was that the military use of the bomb against Japan was "inadvisable" because it would "sacrifice public support throughout the world, precipitate the race for armaments and prejudice the possibility of reaching an international agreement on the future control of weapons." We suggested, instead, that the power of the bomb first be demonstrated in an uninhabited "desert or barren island."

---

*The task of my section was to conceive and develop chemical processes for the separation and purification of plutonium.

†Franck had made it a condition of his participation in the bomb project that he "could present his views on using the weapon to the nation's leaders before they reached a decision to use it" (Kurzman, *Day of the Bomb*, p. 313f).

The Franck Committee's recommendation of a demonstration rather than direct military use received very little consideration in Washington. In fact, the decision to use the bomb on two Japanese cities, without warning, appears to have been made before the Franck Report was delivered.

The Chicago Conference

Six weeks after Hiroshima, a number of the other Met Lab scientists and I were invited to attend an Atomic Energy Control Conference sponsored by the University of Chicago. There were some fifty participants, including Secretary of Commerce and former Vice President Henry Wallace; prominent theologian Reinhold Niebuhr; Beardsley Ruml, chairman of the Federal Reserve Bank of New York; David Lilienthal, then chairman of the Tennessee Valley Authority and soon to be the first chairman of the Atomic Energy Commission; Charles A. Lindbergh; and many distinguished academicians from various disciplines.

During the conference ideas flew so thick and fast and in such unstructured variety that it was difficult to jot them all down. I did my best to register in my diary at least the flavor of what was said.

September 19, 1945

University of Chicago President Robert M. Hutchins made opening remarks; these included a message from General Groves on security.

Leo Szilard described the Hiroshima and Nagasaki bombs. The latter, despite the fewer casualties (a matter of terrain and poor aiming), was the stronger. In ten years it would be possible to make bombs whose radius of destruction would be ten miles, not one mile. Russia could produce a bomb in two and a half years [actually it took them four] They could have enough bombs in six years to destroy all our cities. In that time we could have enough to destroy all major cities of the world. Szilard suggested a ten-year plan under which 60 million Americans would be relocated at a cost of $15 billion per year. To decrease their vulnerability, the new cities should be elongated rectangles one mile wide and fifty miles long, and contain from 100,000 to 500,000 people each. Someone warned that such dispersion could be a *causus belli* because it might seem to indicate we were preparing for military action.

Szilard said it was necessary to have international control to prevent cheating. This meant inspection of all pertinent mining and manufacturing activities. We should use our current bargaining power as the only nation with the bomb to force Russia to accept inspection. Otherwise there could be war within three years. Inspection could provide the rest of the world a warning time of one-half to one year if any nation set out to make bombs. Permanent peace could be attained only with world government, which could be achieved, if possible at all, only through a step-by-step process requiring 15 to 20 years. (At another point he said 20 to 30 years.) He thought there was only a ten percent chance to get world government without war. If there were a war, the victor would impose world government and it would be a tyranny not worth having.

Niebuhr felt that achieving world government was not a realistic possibility in our era. This was tragic, since without it there was a threat of complete annihilation. He felt that the task before us was a more modest one—to develop a bomb policy that mitigated rather than increased the dissension between the United States and Russia. What was needed was some sort of psychological pacification of the two countries that would keep the peace between them for the next 20-30-40 years.

Szilard's estimate of Russian capability was challenged on the basis that they lacked industrial capacity. But Irving Langmuir (General Electric Research Laboratory) expressed the opinion, based on a recent visit to the Soviet Union, that they had tremendous potential, having the largest government support for science and technology of any country. He predicted they would catch us in five years and be way ahead of us in ten.

A letter was read from Percy W. Bridgman (professor of mathematics and natural philosophy, Harvard University).* He said it would take the Russians 10 years to make a bomb. There was a chorus of disagreement, in which I joined. Someone asked if spreading radioactive poisons might not be worse than bombs. Hutchins asked Franck and me what we thought. We both felt that bombs were worse because radioactive poisons could not cover so large an area, nor could they be stockpiled.

September 20, 1945

This day's session began with a discussion of the secrecy issue. Oswald Veblen (professor of mathematics, Institute for

---

*Bridgman was to win the Nobel Prize in physics for 1946.

Advanced Study, Princeton, N.J.) said the need for secrecy stopped when the bomb was used. It was time to let the public and the Russians know everything that we knew.

A letter from Albert Einstein was read, saying that the only questions left were political, not scientific. Niebuhr agreed that all information should be released, and without bargaining. Several other speakers chimed in to the effect that trying to preserve secrecy would be futile, resulting only in adding to the existing ill will and tension.

Philip M. Hauser (director of the census, U.S. Department of Commerce) said that the thinking in Washington on the secrecy issue was highly confused. There were nine bills before Congress prescribing penalties for revealing "the secret of the bomb." It was not safe to assume that President Truman was getting other than military advice on this question.

Jacob Viner (professor of economics, University of Chicago) stated that nuclear weapons were the cheapest method of killing and that as many as twenty countries could afford them. Uranium was also widely available on the earth's surface, as were facilities for the quick training of personnel. He felt that the spread of atomic weapons might enable small countries to come out from under the shadow of giants and again become truly independent as they had been before the Napoleonic wars and again just before World War I. He thought the worst case would be if only two nations had the bomb because of the danger if they had a dispute. It would be better to universalize the weapon. He felt that the atomic bomb could make wars less frequent, since even the victor would have to pay too high a price.

Jacob Marschak (also a professor of economics, University of Chicago) took issue with his colleague. He said that although the bomb might slightly reduce the frequency of wars—say one war per 1.2 generations instead of one per generation—the loss in war would be increased by a factor of 25.

William T. R. Fox (Yale Institute of International Study) said no country would have moral inhibitions about using the bomb against the United States, since we used it first. Complete abolition of bomb manufacture was the only type of control that should be considered. The control system should be attached to the UN and be policed by inspectors whose loyalty would be to the UN, not to any nation state. Inspection should be far-reaching, extending into mine-heads, factories, laboratories and testing grounds, and including also budgets and the whereabouts and activities of scientists, engineers and students. The United States should stop bomb production while the international control system was being discussed, provided no other nations constructed production facilities. The United States should make complete disclosure as soon as the control system was in operation.

Edward Shils (assistant professor of sociology, University of Chicago) continued along the same lines. The UN control organization should not maintain a stockpile of bombs—he agreed there should be none in the world—but it should maintain a skeleton installation for producing bombs in some international enclave outside national boundaries. This installation could be energized for the protection of all should there be a violation, e.g., if any nation abrogated the inspection agreement. That agreement should guarantee UN inspectors free access to and within every national territory. With everything out in the open, there could be no laws against atomic espionage; only laws requiring atomic publicity.

September 21, 1945

Kurt Riezler (professor of philosophy, New York University) thought that the international control ideas voiced yesterday by Shils and Fox had gone beyond what was reasonable or practical. The type of intrusive inspection they suggested would require the Russians to change their system; this could not be expected. Franck doubted that U.S. industrial firms would consent either. He thought inspection of mines, only, might be accepted.

Szilard said we should not prejudge the Russian response. Why not ask Stalin? Russia had a good record of doing things that were in her interest, and a world without atomic weapons certainly seemed to be in her interest. Riezler warned that negotiation itself was dangerous because it could breed distrust if each side rejected the other's proposals. An arms negotiation with this result was one of the causes of World War I.

Further on the subject of inspection, Thorfin R. Hogness (professor of chemistry, University of Chicago) doubted that even inspection of mining was practical, since uranium deposits were so numerous and so widely scattered. Franck doubted there were enough scientists in the world to accomplish all the inspections that would be needed for an international control system such as had been proposed. He felt also that scientists who spent their time inspecting would become poor scientists.

Harold D. Lasswell (director of war communications research, Library of Congress) discussed the technical possibilities of achieving a world state, beginning with a federation of the United States and the United Kingdom. Rabinowitch asked whether such a federation might not be a step *away* from world union if the Russians perceived it as a threat. Eugene Staley (Institute of Pacific Relations, San Francisco) said there was no conflict between taking some immediate steps through the UN Security Council and working long-term toward a world state.

As the conference neared its end there was discussion of whether what was being said should be made public. Franck's opinion was that "making a lot of noise" might weaken the bargaining position of the government in upcoming negotiations. Riezler, also, doubted that this conference should embark on a publicity campaign without consulting the government. Ruml and Niebuhr took issue. Ruml felt we should use all the techniques of Madison Avenue to make our positions known. Niebuhr contended we were under no obligation to consult the government—this conference had a different perspective. Viner felt also that it was not for us to ask the U.S. government what to do but rather for the government to provide us with information in defense of its position. The government got its direction from the public, not the other way round. But Karl K. Darrow (Bell Telephone Laboratories, New York) asked how we could dare risk embarrassing our government at a time when negotiations with the Russians were impending.

On this inconclusive note, the conference ended.

The Chicago conference revealed how the radically new situation that had burst on the world appeared to well-informed, serious-minded individuals. All were trying to discern some way in which mankind could escape from what was agreed to be a dire predicament. Unencumbered by the details of national bargaining positions (which had not yet emerged), or of the nuclear arms race (which had not yet begun), the participants were able to raise very broad questions that would prove increasingly difficult to consider as the years passed and the political and military landscape became more cluttered. Yet, no clear picture emerged of how one could achieve the objective nearly all of those present had in mind—a world without nuclear weapons. It was as though the seeds of a nuclear arms race were imbedded in the nature of man and his political institutions.

The Baruch Plan

If there was one predominant theme sounded at the Chicago conference it was that some form of supranational control was necessary to
cope with the bomb. This idea was soon to have an airing in the
practical world of international politics.

In January 1946 the UN General Assembly voted to establish a
UN Atomic Energy Commission, consisting of the eleven members
of the Security Council, plus Canada. The UNAEC was instructed to
study methods for controlling atomic weapons. Secretary of State
James F. Byrnes then directed Under Secretary Dean Acheson to head
a committee to formulate a U.S. proposal to the UNAEC. (Other
members were Dr. Vannevar Bush, Dr. James B. Conant, Leslie R.
Groves, and John J. McCloy.) To help with its work, the committee
named a panel of consultants that included David E. Lilienthal and
Robert Oppenheimer. Out of the work of this committee and panel
came the so-called Acheson–Lilienthal Report, which was mainly the
work of Oppenheimer.* The report proposed that all "dangerous
activities"—basically, all activities in the chain leading to a nuclear
weapon—be turned over to an international authority. This authority
would have the exclusive right to perform nuclear research, would
develop peaceful uses for the benefit of all nations, and would police
the plan's prohibitions through a corps of international inspectors.
The plan was meant to reach fruition in stages. The first stage was
to include a world survey of uranium resources. Only in the final
stage would the United States be required to turn over its weapon
laboratories and its stock of weapons.

To present the U.S. proposal to the UNAEC, Secretary of State
Byrnes selected a fellow South Carolinian, seventy-five-year-old Bernard Baruch, a successful financier who had been head of the War
Industries Board in World War I. Baruch and his advisers succeeded,
after a spirited controversy within the government, in gaining approval for a new proposal that differed from the Acheson–Lilienthal
Report in several ways. The most important of these had to do with
enforcement. The report had provided what was primarily a warning
system. The inspectors would detect and report any violation; the
nations would then determine their individual or collective response.
Baruch was not satisfied with this and succeeded in gaining President

---

*For an authoritative, fascinating, and more detailed account of this history, the reader is urged
to consult Hewlett and Anderson, *The New World.*

Truman's approval for a system whereby the control organization, through the Security Council, would actually mete out punishment to offending nations. In the council's exercise of enforcement, moreover, there could be no exercise of the veto power.

The Baruch Plan, presented to the UN on June 19, 1946, has been canonized as an act of supreme generosity by the United States—an offer to surrender our nuclear monopoly. As recent scholarship has emphasized, however, the plan did not require us to turn over our weapons until some indeterminate time when the international control scheme would be in effective operation.[1] Even then, we would have retained the knowledge, personnel, skills and much of the industrial infrastructure needed to resume production speedily. In the intervening stages the Soviets would have been required to open their borders to international inspectors and could have been subject to a devastating attack in the name of the UN for any suspected violation. (The Baruch Plan did not rule out the use of atomic bombs against a violator.) Without the protection of the veto power, which had been a precondition for Soviet acceptance of the UN in the first instance, the USSR would have been at the mercy of the huge UN voting majority then enjoyed by the United States. No Soviet government could have accepted such a surrender of control over the nation's future destiny.

One is left with the conviction that, in offering a proposal that was virtually certain to be rejected, U.S. policymakers had made the fateful decision to rely on our prowess in nuclear arms to keep us safe, rather than on international agreements. Meanwhile, we would be satisfied with the propaganda victory made possible by the apparent generosity of the Baruch Plan.

If the U.S. proposal could thus be considered self-serving, the one the Soviets submitted in response was equally and more transparently so. Five days after Baruch's presentation, the young Andrey A. Gromyko called for a multilateral treaty prohibiting atomic weapons "in any circumstance whatever" and providing for the destruction of all existing stocks of weapons. Only after this was done could some form of international control and inspection be introduced under the jurisdiction of the Security Council, with veto power intact. Moreover, international control was not to extend to punishments. It would be up to each nation to punish its own violators.

Details aside, one should note the fundamental difference in approach between the U.S. and Soviet proposals. We were for controls first, disarmament later. They were for disarmament first, controls later. Why did we want controls first? Essentially because we thought the Soviets would cheat, using agreements as a shield behind which they could covertly eat away at our lead in nuclear arms. Why did the Soviets want disarmament first? Essentially because they felt vulnerable to American attack while they were inferior in nuclear arms and feared we would use controls to ascertain how weak they were and to pinpoint the location of military and industrial targets for bombing attacks. This dichotomy was to persist and keep the two sides apart on issue after issue in the years ahead.

Two New Club Members

Some on the American side may have believed that the Soviets would accept the Baruch Plan because they had no reasonable alternative. But indeed they had one. Their own nuclear weapons program, following about the same path we had traversed before them, was in reality quite far advanced. Their first nuclear reactor went critical on Christmas Eve, 1946. In August 1949, much sooner than generally expected—General Groves thought it would take them twenty years[2]— the Soviets exploded their first nuclear device. When confronted with evidence of the test, President Truman at first refused to believe that "those Asiatics" had been capable of such a feat. The Soviet achievement tilted the balance finally toward a U.S. decision to develop the hydrogen bomb, as announced by Truman in January 1950. Our first thermonuclear device was detonated in November 1952; the Soviets followed suit less than a year later, surprising us again with the speed of their accomplishment and with the sophistication of their device. The nuclear arms race had entered a new and more deadly phase.

After the Russians, the British: Before Pearl Harbor the British were probably ahead of us in atomic research, such that President Roosevelt suggested at one point that development of the bomb be a joint endeavor. During the war, British scientists and technicians, transplanted to the United States, made important contributions in development of the bomb. Bertrand Goldschmidt, a founder of the French Atomic Energy Commission and a participant in the British wartime effort, has written that without the British work "it is very unlikely that . . . the first atomic bombs would ever have been ready in time to end the war."[3]

Under an agreement reached by Roosevelt and Churchill at Quebec in August 1943, the United States was required to get British assent to the use of the bomb against Japan. A further accord reached at a Hyde Park summit in September 1944 promised "full collaboration . . . in developing atomic energy for military and commercial purposes" after the war. Second thoughts soon prevailed in Washington, however. Under pressures from General Groves and others, Truman was induced to renege on these commitments at a Washington meeting with Clement Attlee in November 1945. The president promised future collaboration in "scientific" but not in "industrial"—that is, weapons—matters. This experience undoubtedly strengthened British determination to forge ahead with their own program. It could only have been strengthened further by the passage in July 1946 of the U.S. Atomic Energy Act, with its implicit reliance on continued secrecy to preserve our monopoly.

Early in 1947 Prime Minister Attlee, recognizing that nuclear collaboration with the United States was no longer available to Britain, and that an international control agreement would not be achieved, made the decision to proceed toward a British nuclear weapon. On October 3, 1952, the British exploded their first atomic bomb off the west coast of Australia. They would follow with a thermonuclear test in May 1957.

Notes

1. See for example, Herkin, *The Winning Weapon.*
2. Hewlett and Anderson, *The New World,* p. 354.
3. Goldschmidt, *The Atomic Complex,* p. 57.

8
Toward an International Approach

A curse fell on the whole future of mankind when the atomic bomb fell.
                                                                —Alva Myrdal

"Atoms for Peace"

The Soviet hydrogen bomb test in August 1953 produced a profound shock in U.S. government circles. One of the first casualties was what confidence had remained that denying nuclear materials, equipment, and information to other nations could head off proliferation. Some had clung to the belief that the rapid Soviet achievement of a fission bomb had only been possible because of disclosures by Klaus Fuchs and other atom spies. The Russians' thermonuclear achievement offered a convincing demonstration that they had capabilities of their own. (Scientists familiar with the situation never doubted this, but there were other opinions.)

There had already been dissatisfaction with the policy of denial because it inhibited progress toward the peaceful use of nuclear energy. After the Soviet test there no longer seemed sufficient reason for keeping a lid on technologies that offered rich opportunities for commercial endeavors and human betterment. Accordingly, President Eisenhower embarked on a new, less restrictive course. Addressing the UN General Assembly on December 8, 1953, he proposed that governments with stocks of nuclear materials progressively turn over increasing amounts to a new international agency. That agency, to be established under UN auspices, would assure that the materials were used for peaceful purposes only.

As a further part of this Atoms for Peace Program, President Eisenhower submitted recommendations for liberalizing the Atomic Energy Act of 1946. As finally signed into law on August 30, 1954, the new Atomic Energy Act enabled the AEC to transmit peaceful atomic energy information, research tools, and nuclear materials to other nations under agreements pledging the recipient not to use what was received for any military purpose. The first Agreement for Cooperation, with Turkey, was signed in June 1955. In time, such agreements would be concluded with more than thirty nations. A remarkable feature of the agreements was a safeguards provision that permitted U.S. personnel to enter the territories of the recipient nations and carry out audits and inspections to assure that there had been no diversion to military use. The willingness of nations to compromise their own sovereignty in this way testified to their eagerness to embrace the new technology. As an adjunct to the bilateral agreements, the United States began accepting a large number of young scientists and engineers from other countries for training at AEC and private laboratories.

The worldwide enthusiasm engendered by the American initiatives led to the convening in 1955, under UN auspices, of a massive international conference on the peaceful uses of atomic energy. This conference, held in Geneva, Switzerland, was probably the largest scientific meeting held up to that time. Over twenty-seven hundred participants from thirty-eight nations attended. More than a thousand papers were submitted. By mutual agreement among the more advanced nations, the veil of secrecy was drawn aside at this conference from many aspects of nuclear technology never before discussed in public. Optimism abounded, particularly about the prospects for generating electric power in nuclear plants. (Similar UN Geneva Atoms for Peace conferences followed in 1958, 1964, and 1971.)

In due course negotiations at the United Nations led to establishment of the International Atomic Energy Agency proposed in President Eisenhower's speech. It commenced operations in Vienna, Austria in October 1957. The main purpose that Eisenhower had proposed for the new agency—to receive nuclear materials from the principal powers for disbursal to others—was not achieved, however. The Soviets refused to take part in this plan, ostensibly because there was no prior agreement to do away with atomic weapons. Their real reason may have been that they were striving with might and main to catch up with us in nuclear weapons and needed all their fissionable materials for that purpose.

Although the Eisenhower initiative did not achieve what was billed as its main objective, it did have a revolutionary effect on the worldwide approach to the control of proliferation. It had been one of the premises of the Baruch Plan, and of the Acheson–Lilienthal Report from which it sprang, that an international authority was needed because to leave atomic energy development in national hands was too dangerous. The Atoms for Peace Program stood this idea on its head by implying that nation states could, after all, be trusted with nuclear materials and technology provided they renounced military use under proper verification. What the United States had essentially done, according to one apt description, was to reverse the policy of denial and inaugurate one of "constructive engagement."[1]

Some criticized the Atoms for Peace approach on the grounds that it allowed many nations to approach the threshold of a nuclear weapons capability. But, as I noted in a 1966 speech (to the British Nuclear Energy Society, London):

> Most of us knew that it was only a matter of time before other countries could achieve a nuclear weapons capability independently of the U.S., the USSR, and the U.K. . . . Many countries had their own supplies of natural uranium and, perhaps more importantly, their own scientists. We also considered that, if we failed to cooperate in sharing peaceful nuclear technology and nuclear materials, other countries might be willing to do so, without, however, insisting as we did on a firm assurance as to peaceful end use. Aside from this, we could not overlook the positive aspects of nuclear energy and its possible contributions to human betterment.

The last consideration was probably the dominant one in many minds. It was an article of faith with nuclear scientists, perhaps particularly with those of us who had contributed to the development of weapons, that the development of this great new source of energy, with its multitude of beneficial applications, could provide a significant turning point in human history. There have been disappointments along the path to fulfillment of this vision. There have also been accomplishments that indicate our hopes may yet be validated.

The last chance for having a world without nuclear weapons probably disappeared in 1946 with the rejection of both the Baruch Plan and the Soviet counterproposal. It may well have disappeared before that, with the decision to use the weapon against Japan, or even before that, with the decision to develop it. To use an expression of which John F. Kennedy was fond, the genie was long out of the bottle by 1953. I am persuaded that Eisenhower's choice in establishing the Atoms for Peace Program—to extract what benefit was possible from the new force, while trying to create conditions and controls that would discourage proliferation—was the best one available.

After the British, the French

No one could accuse the Atoms for Peace Program of having contributed to Britain's first bomb, which preceded it. Nor did the program play any part in developing the weapon of the next nation to join the nuclear club.

Before World War II, important progress toward a nuclear chain reaction had been made in Paris by a team under Frédéric Joliot-Curie. While Joliot-Curie elected to remain in France after the German invasion, five of France's leading nuclear scientists fled to England and later to Canada. There they played an active part in Anglo-Canadian-American reactor research.* Following the war, three of the five returned home to help provide the foundation for a French atomic energy establishment.

Directly after the end of the war, France embarked on a modest atomic energy effort emphasizing scientific research and peaceful uses. In 1948, uranium ore deposits were found in France and a small research reactor went into operation. In the early 1950s, French political leaders became increasingly alarmed over the gap in influence developing between nuclear-armed nations and all others. As Pierre Messmer, French defense minister, observed: "One is nuclear or one is negligible."[2] France's historical position as a major power in Europe seemed threatened. In 1952 the French atomic program was expanded. Construction began on two large reactors for the production of plutonium. No public mention was made of nuclear weapons at this time, but the option was being created. Feasibility studies and preparations for building nuclear weapons were initiated in 1954. In 1955 a unit of the Commissariat à l'Energie Atomique (CEA) was secretly authorized to design a bomb. In November 1956 a secret four-year program to produce a prototype bomb was begun. All this

---

*One of these, Bertrand Goldschmidt, spent three months in 1942 working in my section at the Met Lab because the British wanted him to become familiar with the chemistry of plutonium. This was the beginning of an enduring friendship between us that on various occasions helped to smooth over some strained relationships between our two governments in the nuclear field.

was done informally, outside democratic channels—that is without a formal cabinet decision and without parliamentary concurrence or, apparently, even awareness.[3] Then, in 1958, the French publicly announced their intention to become a nuclear weapon power. Their first nuclear test, of a plutonium device, took place in the Sahara on February 13, 1960. As Prime Minister Pompidou later told Secretary of State Rusk, "France had taken the choice between being a secondary power and playing a first class role."[4]

Athough power and prestige factors were undoubtedly dominant in the French decision, they were also influenced by three events on the world scene. One was the apparent lack of progress toward general disarmament, which French negotiators repeatedly insisted was a precondition for French abstinence. A second factor was the Suez debacle of November 1956. When President Eisenhower pressured Britain and France to cease military operations in Suez, serious questions were raised about the dependability of the American ally. (The British also took sober note of this incident and undoubtedly grew more determined as a consequence to persist in their independent weapons effort.) The third event was Sputnik, in October 1957. This space achievement appeared to substantiate Soviet claims that they had an intercontinental ballistic missile capability. General de Gaulle and other French spokesmen repeatedly emphasized from that time forward that the United States, faced now with a threat to its own territory, could no longer be relied on to intervene vigorously on the continent in defense of Europe.

Sputnik's Impact on U.S. Policy

Sputnik had major repercussions on this side of the Atlantic as well. It called into question the presumed scientific superiority of the United States, leading to a great emphasis on scientific education for the next several years. Specifically, it seemed to indicate that the Soviets were ahead of us in the development of long-range missiles. This feeling was compounded by the Gaither Report of October 1957, which made alarming estimates about the strategic balance.

A near panic ensued in official Washington. One of the reactions was to seek an additional whittling down of the constraints of secrecy. The feeling grew that the Soviets were so far ahead in important aspects of the arms race that an interallied effort was needed to catch up with them. As President Eisenhower expressed it in his State of the Union message of January 8, 1958:

> It is wasteful in the extreme for friendly allies to consume talent and money in solving problems that their friends have already solved— all because of artificial barriers to sharing. We cannot afford to cut ourselves off from the brilliant talents and minds of scientists in friendly countries. The task will be hard enough without handcuffs of our own making.

Accordingly, the administration sought a further amendment to the Atomic Energy Act to permit under certain conditions the transfer to allies of sensitive information, fissionable materials, and nonnuclear components useful in nuclear weapons. When the legislation finally emerged, however, it was limited in scope to nations that had "already made substantial progress in the development of atomic weapons." As these words were interpreted by the Joint Committee on Atomic Energy, only Great Britain qualified. The net effect, apparently intended from the first, was to discriminate in favor of the British and against the French. Our action served to validate and strengthen Britain's independent deterrent. (In time there would be second thoughts about whether this was a wise step.) We also succeeded in adding greatly to the disenchantment of the French, leading, over the years, to their increasing alienation and disengagement from the Atlantic Alliance.

Mounting Concerns

The United States was careful to limit the nuclear assistance it rendered under the Atoms for Peace Program's bilateral agreements to activities with a peaceful purpose. The safeguards provisions appeared to be effective in preventing any immediate diversion of nuclear materials to military ends. Nevertheless, one had to face the fact that all nuclear technology emanated from a relatively few basic principles, and the more the knowledge of these principles was spread throughout the world, the greater the long-run danger of nuclear weapons proliferation.

The inevitability of proliferation was recognized, as we have seen, in the Chicago conference of 1945. By the mid-1950s the danger was understood by politicians as well as scientists, and dire predictions began to be made. As concern grew, antagonistic neighbors in various regions of the world began to eye each other's "peaceful" nuclear activities with nervousness and suspicion. Each feared being at its rival's mercy if the latter were to possess even one nuclear weapon. Prestige was also heavily involved. It was already becoming apparent that the possession of nuclear weapons might enable a country to win preeminence in its region, and even "to sit at the big table" as a major power. The temptation was great.

The United States faced a special difficulty. As Walt Rostow expressed it:

> The emergence of additional nuclear weapons states could weaken the structure of collective security in the non-communist world at critical points. . . . If any state to which the United States was committed produced nuclear weapons and asserted an independent right to fire them, the U.S. would confront a grave dilemma: to avoid the possibility of another nation—by its own initiative—drawing the U.S. into nuclear war, the U.S. would have to dilute or withdraw its security commitments in parts of the world judged vital to U.S. interest.[5]

The Soviet Union may well have felt itself in a similar dilemma, causing it, for example, to withdraw nuclear assistance from its Chinese ally in 1959, with grave consequences to the relationship between the two countries.

It was recognized that there was no technical fix for the proliferation problem. Nor did there seem to be any exercise of power by which the superpowers could *require* the rest of the world to abjure nuclear weapons. The task was more nearly, as McNamara expressed it in his testimony supporting the Limited Test Ban Treaty, "to create a climate in which nuclear weapons [were] not a good bargain," so that voluntary national self-abnegation would follow. To achieve such a climate, action on a multilateral basis seemed to be required.

In one respect, the mounting international focus on nonproliferation came at an awkward time for the United States. In the aftermath of Suez, the Sputniks, and the emplacement of Soviet medium-range missiles targeted on Western Europe, NATO had suffered a quite severe loss of confidence. The Eisenhower administration's response, for both military and psychological reasons, was to move toward greater nuclear sharing with the allies. Jupiter missiles were emplaced in Turkey and Italy. Nuclear weapons were deployed to Western Europe and agreements were negotiated for their use by NATO commanders in time of war. As previously mentioned, the Atomic Energy Act was amended to permit greater nuclear cooperation with the British. It was not easy to reconcile this type of activity with the objective of nonproliferation. Yet it was the task of U.S. policymakers to attempt just such a reconciliation.

A crude early effort came as part of an omnibus Western disarmament proposal submitted to the UN Disarmament Committee in 1957. The package included a provision forbidding transfer of nuclear weapons, "except for self-defense." The Soviets were quick to point out the ample opportunities for evasion offered by this formula. They countered with a proposal designed primarily to embarrass the United States, namely, that nuclear weapon states agree not to install any nuclear weapons beyond their national frontiers.

With each superpower unable, or unwilling, to come forward with ideas that had a chance of being accepted by the other, initiative at the UN passed to the government of Ireland, whose foreign minister, Frank Aiken, had adopted nonproliferation as a sort of personal specialty. Ireland submitted draft resolutions on nonproliferation in each of the years 1958, 1959, 1960, and 1961. The 1958 draft, brought before the UN as a side issue to the discussion of a ban on nuclear testing, suggested merely that the UN conduct a study on how to prevent the further spread of nuclear weapons. The resolution was withdrawn when the United States indicated it could not give its support. (The Eisenhower administration, deeply absorbed in its efforts to shore up NATO's confidence and nuclear strength, appeared to feel that supporting the resolution would convey mixed signals to the allies.)

The 1959 resolution took a new approach. It called on nations producing nuclear weapons "to refrain from handing over control of such weapons to nations not possessing them." Introduction of the concept of "control," interpreted by the United States to mean the unilateral right to fire, was sufficient to overcome our objections. When it came time to vote, however, the Soviet bloc abstained.

The 1960 resolution expanded on the obligations of the nuclear powers. It called on them to refrain not only from relinquishing control of nuclear weapons but also from transmitting "information needed for their manufacture." This time it was the Soviet bloc that voted in favor and the United States, joined by some, but not all, of its allies, that abstained. This U.S. vote, cast in December 1960, has been interpreted as a reluctance on the part of the lame-duck Eisenhower administration to prejudice the positions of its successor.[6] The administration was showing similar restraint at this same time in the test ban negotiations in Geneva.

Though the Irish resolution of 1961 hardly deviated from that of 1960 in its requirements of the nuclear powers, the Kennedy administration found it unobjectionable, and the resolution passed the General Assembly unanimously on December 4, 1961. The resolution's salient paragraph—actually only a single sentence, though undoubtedly one of the longest in diplomatic history—called upon:

> all States, and in particular upon the States at present possessing nuclear weapons, to use their best endeavors to secure the conclusion of an international agreement containing provisions under which the nuclear States would undertake to refrain from relinquishing control of nuclear weapons and from transmitting information necessary for their manufacture to States not possessing such weapons, and provisions under which States not possessing nuclear weapons would undertake not to manufacture or otherwise acquire control of such weapons.

This resolution was to provide a point of departure for future nonproliferation proposals and negotiations.

Nonproliferation and General Disarmament

The attention being given to nonproliferation at the UN merged for a time with that being given to proposals for general and complete disarmament (GCD). GCD had been a staple of discussion at the UN since the early 1950s. The Soviets took the lead in these exercises, doubtless because it suited their diplomatic and military positions. Being far behind in nuclear arms, they had nothing to lose by advocating the rapid abolition of such weapons. On the contrary, by forcing the United States to reject the proposals, they were able to win some costless propaganda victories. The United States felt during the 1950s that it had to take part in this diplomatic charade by submitting proposals of its own. As Morton Halperin has written:

> No one in the U.S. government took the possibility of GCD seriously. The Soviets had proposed it and it was decided, for diplo-

matic reasons and to compete with the Soviets in the Third World, that we had to feign interest and engage in negotiations and so we did.[7]

GCD prospects changed suddenly—from hopeless to barely possible—following a remarkable two-man negotiation between John J. McCloy, President Kennedy's special adviser on disarmament, and Soviet UN Ambassador Valerian A. Zorin. Between March and September 1961 the two succeeded in hammering out a Joint Statement of Agreed Principles for Disarmament Negotiations, which the U.S. and USSR submitted jointly to the General Assembly on September 20, 1961. Among other provisions the agreement stipulated that:

Disarmament was to take place by stages within specified time limits.

Steps were to include, among others, disbanding armed forces, eliminating stockpiles of weapons of mass destruction and their means of delivery, and the end of military expenditures.

Disarmament was to be supervised by an International Disarmament Organization (IDO) within the UN. IDO inspectors were to be "assured unrestricted access without veto to all places as necessary for the purpose of effective verification."*

At the end of the process nations were to have only those nonnuclear armed forces needed to maintain internal order.

A UN peace force was to be established with sufficient strength to suppress any aggression.

Agreement on disarmament was to be sought at the earliest possible date.

After this wholly unexpected diplomatic achievement, both sides hastened to complete GCD plans conforming to the agreed principles. The Soviet package was submitted on March 15, 1962; ours a month later. Both plans envisaged disarmament to the level required for internal security and that this level would be reached in three stages.

---

*An unresolved issue was what could be inspected. The Soviets insisted that inspection be limited to those munitions brought to terminals for destruction. The United States maintained that articles that remained should also be inspected. McCloy dispatched a letter to all UN delegations disclosing this difference.

There were wide differences, however, on the pace of the reductions and the application of control procedures. The U.S. approach, speaking generally, was that only if control procedures were found to work well with small doses of disarmament should the process be made complete. The Soviets' more rapid pace was guided by the view that if all weapons were abolished inspection and control would prove to be subsidiary and manageable problems.[8]

Significantly, both plans would have assigned to the first stage a nonproliferation agreement following the main outline of the 1961 Irish resolution. The proposed agreements were alike in that both would have bound nuclear weapon powers not to transfer control of nuclear weapons and nonweapon powers not to manufacture them. They differed in that the Soviets would also have bound the nonweapon states to "refuse to admit the nuclear weapons of any other State into their territories."

It was clear from the GCD exercise as well as from other indications that the major difference between the two sides on a nonproliferation treaty—seemingly the only difference that prevented an agreement—continued to be about U.S. nuclear sharing with its NATO partners. By 1961, however, the discord no longer revolved around the general idea of such cooperation, as it may have done throughout most of the 1950s. It now focused on a specific plan that was under intense scrutiny on both sides of the Atlantic. This was to establish a NATO naval force, jointly financed, manned by crews of mixed nationality, and armed with U.S.-controlled Polaris missiles. This so-called Multilateral Force (MLF) was to occupy center stage in the nonproliferation controversy for several years, extending well into the Johnson administration.

Notes

1. National Academy of Sciences, *Nuclear Arms Control,* p. 233.
2. Quoted in Kolkowicz, et al., *The Soviet Union and Arms Control,* p. 107.
3. Dunn, *Controlling the Bomb,* p. 9.
4. Rusk cable from Paris to Department of State, 12/14/64, National Security File, MLF Cables, Vol. 3, Box 24, LBJ Library.
5. Rostow, *The Diffusion of Power,* p. 379f.
6. Bader, *The United States and the Spread of Nuclear Weapons,* p. 13.
7. Halperin, "Arms Control: A Twenty-Five-Year Perspective," p. 4.
8. Bloomfield, *Disarmament and Arms Control,* p. 51.

9

The MLF before Johnson

It is the nature of big government that a good measure of mystique, a rich variety of motives, and evangelical zeal are almost essential to propel anything controversial or revolutionary through the bureaucratic bogs and on up to the bureaucratic peaks.

—Philip Geyelin[1]

Origins

The Multilateral Force, "the flotilla that never put to sea," was an attempt to deal with a web of interlocking aspirations and problems affecting the Atlantic Alliance at the beginning of the 1960s.* These included:

1. The perceived military threat from the Soviet deployment of medium-range missiles targeted on Western Europe.

2. The need to preserve allied cohesion in the face of the Soviet threat and the diminished credibility of U.S. protection after Sputnik.

3. The belief that major Western European countries with revived economic and political strength—most notably Germany—aspired to a greater role in the planned use of nuclear weapons for their defense.

4. The desire of the United States to prevent the emergence of additional independent nuclear powers who might target medium-range missiles on the Soviet Union, and also to pre-

---

*Much has been written about the MLF. Outstanding accounts of its early history are provided in Buchan, "The Multilateral Force," and Henry A. Kissinger, *The Troubled Partnership*. Philip Geyelin has an informative chapter on President Johnson's handling of this matter in *Lyndon B. Johnson and the World*.

vent others, again particularly Germany, from nuclear weapons cooperation with France.

5. The desire of the United States to encourage the movement
   toward a united Europe.

6. The desire of the United States to create an alternative that
   might in time tempt the United Kingdom and France to give
   up their independent nuclear deterrents.

7. The desire of the United States to have its allies bear a larger
   share of the financial and military burdens of mutual defense.

Relative emphasis among these motives varied from time to time
and, at any given time, from proponent to proponent.

Dean Rusk traces the first stirrings of the MLF back to the summer of 1960, when General Lauris Norstad, NATO military commander, and Paul-Henri Spaak, NATO secretary-general, jointly
approached the U.S. NATO delegation and stated that the European
members of the alliance wanted greater participation in its nuclear
affairs.[2] Thereupon, a plan for having a nuclear-armed flotilla that
would be jointly financed and have mixed crews from several NATO
nations was nurtured in the State Department's Policy Planning Staff
under the direction of Robert R. Bowie. The plan received its first
public airing in December 1960, when Secretary of State Christian
Herter presented it to a NATO ministerial meeting. The proposal at
that time was to give NATO five submarines armed with eighty Polaris missiles, if a system of multilateral control could be devised.[3]

As the Kennedy administration began, only West Germany and
Italy seemed interested in the proposal. President Kennedy's own initial reaction was cool. He wanted the allies to meet their NATO-
assigned goals in conventional forces before giving serious thought to
an MLF. This was in keeping with a new strategic doctrine fostered
by Secretary of Defense McNamara, which supplanted John Foster
Dulles's policy of automatic nuclear response to a Soviet attack in
Europe with a policy of "flexible response," that is, meeting each
level of attack with a comparable level of retaliation. Kennedy's early
view, moreover, as he expressed it repeatedly in public and in private,
was that the MLF should be established only if our NATO allies
clearly indicated that they wanted it.

President Kennedy's lack of enthusiasm left the MLF moribund
through most of 1961. A State Department group that included Under

Secretary George Ball and Walt Rostow, director of the policy planning staff, continued to press for it, however, and Kennedy gradually was induced to give it more support. In the spring of 1962 he formally approved, as Executive Branch policy, a U.S. offer to join our allies, *if they wished,* in developing an MLF having about two hundred missiles, a scale-down from a previous concept calling for three hundred missiles.

Nassau and Its Aftermath

In late 1962 and early 1963 there occurred a series of diplomatic confrontations among the leading NATO allies that, for a while, seemed to enhance prospects for the MLF. In November 1962, Secretary McNamara informed a stunned British government that our production for them of Skybolt air-to-surface missiles would have to be cancelled because of escalating costs and repeated technical failures. Britain had planned to use Skybolt for arming its V-bomber force with nuclear missiles that could be released at great distances from their targets. (Direct over-the-target bombing was thought no longer feasible because of the improvement in antiaircraft defenses.)

In an ensuing summit meeting at Nassau, President Kennedy succumbed to Prime Minister Macmillan's pleas and agreed to sell the British, as a substitute for Skybolt, Polaris missiles—without warheads—for use in British submarines. Britain, in return, agreed to subscribe the Polaris-armed submarines to NATO, but as an all-British national contingent, not as part of a mixed-manned force.

To assuage the feelings of the French, President Kennedy offered them the same deal on Polaris missiles as he had offered the British. The equality of treatment was more apparent than real, however, because, as Bertrand Goldschmidt has pointed out: "France would not possess for several years either the nuclear submarines to carry the rockets or the thermonuclear warheads to arm them—unlike the British, who alone were receiving American help with these items."[4] The French had long been suspicious of the U.S.–U.K. relationship and Nassau apparently confirmed their beliefs that Britain's tie was to the United States, not Europe, and that partiality to Britain was primary in U.S. nuclear policy. President de Gaulle's response to the Nassau developments came at a press conference on January 14, 1963. He rejected Kennedy's Polaris offer, reaffirmed France's determination to maintain an independent deterrent, and dealt the cause of European integration a major blow by stating that France would vote against British entry into the European Common Market. A week later the French signed a Treaty of Friendship with West Germany, increasing U.S. fears of Franco–German nuclear collaboration.

These events persuaded the Kennedy administration that the MLF should be more vigorously promoted by the United States, if for no other reason than to offer the Germans an alternative to collaboration with France. As McGeorge Bundy would later express it in a memo to Kennedy: "It was necessary after Nassau to take a direct initiative in favor of the MLF and to find out by making it a U.S. proposal whether in fact there was any real support for it."[5]

Within a few days of de Gaulle's news conference, President Kennedy authorized a mission headed by Ambassador Livingston T. Merchant to open official talks with NATO governments on behalf of the MLF.

A Side Issue: What Type of Ship?

The first rudimentary plan for an MLF, the one proposed by Herter in 1960, contemplated the use of submarines. This concept remained unchallenged through 1962. Enter now Admiral Hyman Rickover, who headed naval reactor units in both the Navy Department and the AEC. Rickover, the acknowledged father of the nuclear navy, commanded enormous respect in Congress, particularly in the Joint Committee on Atomic Energy.

On January 18, 1963:

I attended a White House meeting at which President Kennedy attempted to persuade JCAE members of the merits of the MLF. [More about that meeting anon.] I stayed behind after the meeting to talk briefly with the president and Bundy. I indicated to them that it would be important for the president to meet with Admiral Rickover at the proper time to enlist his support, if possible, for the concept of using submarines in the MLF.

On February 11, 1963:

Admiral Rickover called to give me a report on his meeting with the president today. He said that it lasted 45 minutes, with no one else present. He said he pointed out to the president the "vast difficulties" that would be involved in multi-national manning of a nuclear submarine. I asked how the president reacted, and Rickover said he didn't know. However, the president did indicate he might make up his mind in a hurry.

In his oral history interview for the Kennedy Library Rickover indicated that he told the president it was "inadvisable to try out the multinational idea on so complex a ship as an atomic submarine, which can be safely entrusted only to highly intelligent and specially trained officers and men, working in close harmony with one another." He thought that "differences in training and language were bound to cause many difficulties and to lower the effectiveness and safety of these ships." Yet, he told the president, "if we absolutely had to make it work we could make it work." What he could not see a way around, however, was the problem of security: "We would be giving away information about our nuclear submarines which inevitably would leak to the Russians, long before they could develop [the knowledge] themselves." He added that "since our Polaris system was probably the best deterrent we had, and would continue so into the 1980's, it was foolhardy to jeopardize it."

Rickover's points apparently persuaded the president. A report of a National Security Council meeting held the same day included the following:

> The president said Admiral Rickover had convinced him that the multinational manning of Polaris [missiles] should be on surface ships and not on submarines because of simplicity, the time element, security issues, and possible difficulty of obtaining Congressional approval.

When the decision to reject submarines was cabled to Ambassador Merchant and Thomas K. Finletter, permanent U.S. representative to NATO, they were admonished that the new dispensation was to be communicated to the allies with delicacy:

> While we have clear preference for surface ship option, our tactic will be to attempt persuade others this point of view . . . without seeming to foreclose submarines. To convey impression we are seeking to force this choice might well increase desire on part of others for subs and prejudice prospects for MLF on grounds it a "second-class force."

Anticipation of difficulty in selling the surface ship concept was well founded. In my diary for March 9, 1963:

> It appears that the AEC should have pressed harder to acquaint the president with the difficulties of his Nassau agreement with Macmillan regarding a NATO submarine force. It seems clear that Merchant is running into trouble selling the use of surface ships to the allies. They prefer the original concept—the use of submarines.

The reason for this preference was understandable. Predominant sentiment among the allies was that submarines, being harder to find, would be less subject to attack. The president attempted to come to grips with this argument in his press conference on March 6, saying:

> It's not easy to find merchant ships at sea. It took us more than two days to find that recent Venezuelan ship in the Caribbean. They are not easy to find. It took us longer to find the Portguese ship some months ago. The ocean is a large ocean.

The wishes of the United States in this matter prevailed, as of course they had to. From the spring of 1963 on, discussion of the MLF was in terms of a flotilla of about twenty-five surface vessels, camouflaged as merchant ships. But this scheme did not advance easily. Despite the arguments of the president and others, the substitution of surface ships for submarines undoubtedly degraded the MLF in European eyes and may have contributed in some measure to its eventual demise.

The Congressional Hurdle

President Kennedy made it unmistakably clear that he intended to submit any MLF agreement negotiated with the allies to the Senate for its advice and consent. The legal requirement to do so did not appear to be ironclad. Former President Eisenhower, for example, expressed the view—according to the minutes of a briefing on the MLF conducted for him in January 1964—"that the administration might well seek Congressional authorization to make *executive agreements* . . . under which an MLF arrangement might be consummated" (emphasis added). Such an agreement would presumably have entered into force on signature. In advancing this suggestion Eisenhower undoubtedly had in mind that any MLF treaty submitted to the Senate for advice and consent would have to be referred in the first instance to the Joint Committee on Atomic Energy. As president he had had eight years of experience with the JCAE and was familiar with its negative attitude toward any sharing of nuclear weapons or military information. Altogether, he had not found working with the JCAE either enjoyable or beneficial, to put it mildly. As the minutes of the 1964 briefing record: "General Eisenhower at several points expressed concern about the preemption by the Joint Committee on Atomic Energy of international nuclear weapons policy." Later, in his memoirs, Eisenhower would recommend that the Joint Committee be abolished as "worse than silly."[6]

Kennedy was as familiar as Eisenhower with the views of the JCAE and yet had no intention of trying to evade its scrutiny. I believe Kennedy's attitude reflected his own continued ambivalence toward the MLF and a desire to husband all the senatorial goodwill possible for what he considered more important measures, such as a test ban. Perhaps more fundamental was the fact that the MLF would not have been permissible in any case without amendment of the Atomic Energy Act (to permit transfer of warheads from U.S. to MLF custody), and any such amendment would have had to originate in the Joint Committee.

Knowing the key role the JCAE might play in determining the fate of the MLF, various members of the administration made repeated efforts to sell the committee on the plan's merits. The president's own efforts were not very strong. I attended a White House meeting on January 18, 1963, at which Kennedy spoke to the entire JCAE membership.

The president went over the history of relations with de Gaulle and the basis for the latter's antagonism to the United States, Great Britain, and NATO. [This was but four days after de Gaulle's negative press conference.] He also described the possible ambitions of the West Germans to obtain some sort of nuclear capability. They had pledged in 1954 that they would not make the weapon themselves.* Nevertheless, the president noted, they might acquire it through alliance with France or through purchase. He said that the United States did not support the

*The Germans made this commitment to fellow-members of the Western European Union as the price for admission to that organization.

MLF because of any dissatisfaction with the existing arrangement within NATO. On the contrary, we were satisfied with the status quo, but other countries were not; therefore, a change had to be sought. The concept of a multilateral force had the virtue that it would preclude development of a number of independent national nuclear forces, or of a joint Franco–German force.

Kennedy's presentation to the JCAE certainly did not convert that body. On February 20, 1963:

I attended an executive session of the JCAE where Ambassador Livingston Merchant and the other two members of his MLF mission—Gerard Smith and Admiral John M. Lee—explained the purpose of their forthcoming sales trip to Paris, Rome, and Brussels. They met with almost unanimous opposition from committee members, mainly on security grounds.

There were hopes that the JCAE might eventually soften its opposition, and plans for the MLF went forward more or less on that assumption. The committee did not relent, however, and, as we shall see, Lyndon Johnson ultimately felt compelled to confront this reality more seriously.

Hard Realities

In spite of misgivings about the attitude of Congress, a specific treaty proposal was drafted and a mission headed by Ambassador Merchant was dispatched to European capitals in March 1963 to negotiate on its behalf. Our demand for a prior buildup of conventional forces was dropped. Optimism—fostered largely by reports from Merchant and his fellow missionaries—reached such a level that, at the end of March 1963, President Kennedy suggested that heads of government might sign a preliminary agreement during his visit to Europe, scheduled for June. This timetable contemplated submission of a treaty to the Senate in September. As the date for Kennedy's trip neared, however, it became apparent that the schedule was far too optimistic. In a June 15, 1963 memo to the president, Bundy sketched out the hard realities as he saw them. In general, he found that support for the MLF in Europe was slight and "grudging." One of the problems was cost. "It is striking," Bundy wrote, "that such support as the MLF has is almost always in Foreign Offices and very seldom in Treasuries or Ministries of Defense, where the resources must be found."* Portraying the situation in individual countries, Bundy found problems everywhere. In France, the MLF was considered "an attack on the French nuclear effort, which [had] support . . . far beyond de Gaulle." In Great Britain, "almost no one with any political standing [was] personally favorable to the MLF. . . ." A decision favoring it "would be regarded as . . . subservience to U.S. pressure." In Italy, there was "no enthusiasm for the MLF as such: at best there [was] a willingness . . . to walk with American leadership and keep up with the Germans." Even in Germany Bundy found "no strong affirmative sentiment for the MLF as something the Germans themselves wanted." And Bundy introduced, "as a new factor of real importance," the attitude of the Soviet Union. If the MLF moved into action, he wrote, we would be vulnerable to a Soviet accusation that we were "the nuclear rearmers of Germany," a charge that would add to the disenchantment of many in Western Europe. Bundy added that Soviet antagonism to the MLF was so great that, if we pressed it, we might lose some agreements otherwise possible. (This was to become a key issue as negotiations for a nonproliferation treaty went forward.)

Bundy attributed the current advancement of the MLF to "the people with direct responsibility" in State, who, he said, had "pressed the case more sharply and against a tighter timetable, at every stage, than either you or the Secretary [Rusk] would have chosen."† He blamed himself for not having watched them as closely as he should have. He recommended that our policy be to "switch from pressure to inquiry." Without backing away too sharply, which he thought would damage American prestige, Bundy recommended that we "take away any sense of a deadline . . . and try to widen the discussion to include other elements in the nuclear problem, instead of pressing in a somewhat nervous and narrow way for a single specific solution."

Bundy later reported to President Johnson that Kennedy responded to this memo "very strongly and affirmatively."[7] One indication of this occurred at a White House meeting I attended on June 21, 1963. The meeting was called to prepare for Averell Harriman's

---

*As of early 1964, it was generally believed that the fleet would cost somewhere between $3 and $5 billion over an eight- to ten-year period.

†Rusk confirms that the strong advocates of MLF in State grew "very impatient" with him because he was unwilling to put full U.S. "diplomatic muscle" behind the proposal. (Private conversation, March 13, 1986.)

forthcoming mission to Moscow to negotiate the Limited Test Ban Treaty, and for the president's own European trip. During the discussion:

> Fisher raised the question about a possible agreement to curb proliferation of nuclear weapons. President Kennedy suggested that to obtain such an agreement *the United States might offer to give up the MLF concept.* . . . Bundy felt that it was too early to do this—the MLF should be kept alive as a bargaining chip. Rusk pointed out that the MLF involved the Allies so deeply that giving it up should not be considered a possible position for the present.

At a meeting of his staff advisers in December 1964, President Johnson asked Bundy why Kennedy had been so tentative and careful about the MLF. Bundy's reply, submitted in writing the next day, was that "there were different reasons at different times, but in the last half of 1963 the reasons were, I think, dominated by his feeling that if we could only get the MLF by major and intense U.S. pressure, it was not worth it."[8]

There was another factor. On December 6, 1963, Bundy reported to Johnson that "President Kennedy's instruction to me was to watch [MLF] negotiations closely and make sure we did not present him with a debatable treaty in 1964."[9] The reason for this instruction was undoubtedly the upcoming presidential election. As we have observed in connection with the cutback in nuclear materials production, Kennedy appeared to be "running scared," and seemed reluctant to take bold actions that might antagonize any significant political constituency.

When the president made his European trip in late June 1963, he found that only the West Germans seemed willing to proceed with the MLF. The British, whom State Department zealots still hoped to convert, were unwilling to contemplate any action until after their own election, scheduled for October 1964. There seemed no choice, therefore, but to hold the MLF in abeyance. Work nevertheless continued on its development through the remainder of Kennedy's presidency. In October 1963, a NATO working group of seven nations that included the United Kingdom met in Paris to consider legal and political aspects. Another group met in Washington to discuss military matters. At the time Lyndon Johnson became president, the force was not in a very vigorous state of health, but it was still alive.

Notes

1. Geyelin, *Lyndon B. Johnson and the World,* p. 159.
2. Dean Rusk, private conversation, March 13, 1986.
3. Schlesinger, *A Thousand Days,* p. 851.
4. Goldschmidt, *The Atomic Adventure,* p. 190.
5. Bundy to President, 6/15/63, National Security File, Memos to President—McGeorge Bundy, Vol. 1, LBJ Library.
6. Quoted in Rostow, *The Diffusion of Power,* p. 629n.
7. Bundy to President, 12/6/64, National Security File, Memos to President—McGeorge Bundy, Vol. 7, LBJ Library.
8. Ibid.
9. Bundy to President, 12/6/63, National Security File, Memos to President—McGeorge Bundy, Vol. 1, LBJ Library.

10
The MLF, 1964:
A Sea of Troubles

This is a most complex issue of tactics and timing.
—McGeorge Bundy
in a memo to President Johnson

How Hard to Push?

On November 8, 1963, two weeks before President Kennedy's assassination, Vice President Lyndon B. Johnson made a strong endorsement of the multilateral force in a speech in Brussels. Perhaps of greatest significance was his statement that "[e]volution of this missile fleet toward European control, as Europe marches toward unity, is by no means excluded."[1] The concept was that if, in time, the British and/or the French chose to turn over their independent deterrent(s) to a European force, American control—even American participation—might not be necessary. (This idea became known as "the European option," and was to figure prominently in future negotiations.) In making this speech, Johnson was probably not voicing independent views, but rather expressing U.S. policy as formulated by others. As president he would have to grapple personally with this most difficult of problems.

On December 6, 1963, when President Johnson had been in office but two weeks, he met with Rusk, McNamara, Ball, Bundy, Merchant, and Walt Rostow about the MLF. In a briefing note sent in beforehand, Bundy described the meeting's purpose:

This is a most complex issue of tactics and timing on which no big decision is needed. Today you will be asked only for two authorizations on which there is general agreement: (a)to let administration advocates of MLF brief selected Congressional leaders on current

state of Paris negotiations with seven other interested nations;* and
(b)to let the same people brief General Eisenhower in the hope of
holding his support for this force.²

The fact that permission to brief Congress was being sought is an
indication of how diffident President Kennedy had been toward the
project. He had made clear that he would submit any MLF agreement
to Congress, but he had refused to engage his own prestige to the
extent of permitting normal congressional consultation on the
negotiations.

In this same note to President Johnson, Bundy summarized his
impression of where matters stood with the MLF:

> Behind these simple [requests] is a tension which existed for many
> months between MLF advocates in State Department and President
> Kennedy. President Kennedy wanted to avoid getting pinned to a
> very complex and difficult treaty commitment that might not be easy
> to get through the Senate. Thus he felt the main initiative and pres-
> sure should come from Europeans rather than from U.S. State De-
> partment advocates (not so much Dean Rusk) have felt that U.S.
> must get MLF into being by active leadership and diplomatic pres-
> sure on every front. This view has now been adopted by Dean
> Acheson.†
>
> I should add that Bob McNamara has always been cool to this
> force although willing to have it staffed out and proposed. Navy is
> for it as another element of Naval nuclear power. The Europeans
> are divided every which way, with only the German Government
> clearly and solidly in favor.

As though to bear out Bundy's comment about the diversity of
views on the MLF issue, President Johnson received a second written
briefing before the meeting. This one, eight pages long, was not signed,
but clearly represented the work of the MLF's State Department advocates, and it presented an overview quite different from Bundy's.³
It led off with an upbeat summary of the current status of the working
group discussions in Paris and Washington. Next came a section de-

---

*The Paris working group included the U.S., U.K., West Germany, Italy, Belgium, the Neth-
erlands, Greece, and Turkey. Their task was to work out an MLF treaty that was technically
feasible, but without committing their respective governments to its adoption.

†The former secretary of state, although no longer in the government, was consulted frequently
on important issues.

voted to argumentation for the MLF. A ten-point rationale for the force was presented, following generally the points listed at the beginning of the last chapter. Next, under the heading "Present Acceptance in Europe," came an optimistic country-by-country summary. At the conclusion of this section was the following note, variants of which appeared several times in State Department documents during this period:

> It should always be borne in mind that whatever the apparent defects of the MLF—and no solution to the nuclear problem is perfect—*no other serious alternative* to solve the major problems has been offered (emphasis in original).

The minutes of the December 6 meeting, written by Rostow,[4] record the following decisions:

> The President affirmed that we were to proceed with the briefing of General Eisenhower and the Congressional leaders; and that we would return to the MLF issue when we knew the results of these briefings; where the Washington and Paris MLF discussions fetched up; the shape of the Italian political discussions, etc.

Reports on the briefings were received by the president on April 8 in the form of a memorandum signed by Dean Rusk.[5] The memo reported that General Eisenhower had "indicated his enthusiastic support and his willingness to make that support known." Congressional leaders had shown "interest and receptivity, and no strong opposition." The memo acknowledged, however, that the briefings had not included the Joint Committee on Atomic Energy, which had reacted so negatively in February.

The memo continued with another country-by-country status report, optimistic in tone. Discussions with the allies were progressing "favorably, but slowly." West Germany, Greece, and Turkey were "anxious to act as soon as possible." The British attitude continued to depend on October election results: a Conservative government would probably join; a Labour government might do so, but not quickly. Belgian and Dutch participation probably depended on what the British did.

The memo concluded that there was a "substantial possibility" of reaching informal agreement on an MLF charter in the spring or summer of 1964, that a formal signing conference could be held in

November or December, and that the necessary amendments to the Atomic Energy Act could be presented to Congress early in 1965. The president was asked to approve not only expanded congressional briefings but also increased public discussion.

With this memorandum as background, the president met on April 10, 1964, with the MLF's principal sponsors: George Ball (acting secretary of state in Rusk's absence), Ambassador Finletter, Gerard Smith,* and Walt Rostow. Also present were ACDA Director Foster, McGeorge Bundy, and William R. Tyler (assistant secretary of state for European affairs). According to the unsigned minutes of the meeting,[6] Ball led off with a briefing that paralleled Rusk's memo of two days before, probably indicating a common authorship. Finletter reported that the Paris working group had reached the end of its "educational phase" and that, if the president would give the go-ahead sign, drafting of an MLF charter could begin. The president then asked Bundy for a summary of views on the MLF within the government. The minutes report Bundy's answer that

> there was a consensus supporting it, but that McNamara, the Joint Chiefs of Staff and Foster [ACDA] had serious reservations. The MLF, he said, could provide an Atlantic solution to the problem of the nuclear defense of the West and weaken French and British determination to hold on to their national nuclear establishments provided it were not forced upon the Europeans.

Finletter favored a much more aggressive approach to the Europeans than Bundy's summary implied. According to the minutes:

> It was his [Finletter's] view that the U.S. had to stop being diffident about the MLF. [Labour candidate] Harold Wilson had told him bluntly the British had the impression that President Johnson, as President Kennedy, was not really interested in the project. [Italian foreign minister Giuseppe] Saragat had also expressed concern about the situation. He said the American attitude had complicated the problem for the Italians, since Harold Wilson kept insisting that the U.S. really did not want the MLF. Therefore, Saragat wanted President Johnson to give specific endorsement to the project so there would be no misunderstanding the American position. Moreover, it

---

*Smith, who held the title of special adviser to the secretary of state, headed an MLF task force in the State Department. During the Nixon administration he was to be director of ACDA and the chief American negotiator of the SALT I agreements.

was Finletter's view that even a Wilson government in Britain would join the MLF. He was sure that in the long run Wilson would do what the U.S. wanted. [How wrong he was! See chapter 12.]

Finletter's recommendation of a less diffident stand reflected his own practice as chief MLF salesman abroad. In spite of instructions not to do so, it was Finletter's tendency to lean rather hard on the allies. For example, on one occasion he is reported to have told the French representative to NATO (Seydoux) that it was difficult for the United States to believe that none of its allies other than Germany would respond to policy advocated by the United States at the highest level. On another occasion he went so far as to say: "As goes this fleet, so may go the defense of the West and our efforts to prevent war."[7]

For what happened next at the April 10 meeting, we cite a recollection by Gerard Smith:

> [A]fter all the arguments had been made and the president had pretty clearly made up his mind to go ahead with the MLF, Bill Foster spoke up. I remember his exact words. He said, "Mr. President, I feel like a skunk in a garden party, but if you go ahead with this MLF you must recognize it's going to make my chances of negotiating a nonproliferation treaty harder."[8]

Foster specifically took issue with a conclusion in the State Department memo of April 8 that the MLF was not preventing disarmament agreements. He said that estimate "did not coincide with his impressions from his talks with the Soviets at Geneva."

Foster did not prevail. At the conclusion of the meeting, according to the minutes, the president directed (1) that congressional briefings be broadened; (2) that the Europeans be told, without trying to "shove the project down their throats," that in his judgment the MLF was the best way to proceed; and (3) that agreement on the MLF be sought by the end of the year.

This meeting seemed to have been a significant triumph for the proponents of the MLF. They had apparently obtained from Johnson a commitment more decisive than any ever given by Kennedy. (Bundy recalls being surprised at the firmness of the president's endorsement.)[9] Again, Gerard Smith:

I wouldn't represent that [the president] really understood all the details of the MLF, but he seemed to feel, "Well, this is the best arrow that we've got in the quiver. Let's go ahead with it." In effect, he said to Finletter, "You go ahead and get this thing done, and I'll be ready to move the day after election." I remember going back with Finletter to talk to the press about it, and Finletter of course was elated, because he had a firm commitment from the president to go ahead and get the thing negotiated.[10]

Just as with Kennedy the year before, there was later some dispute about whether the president had committed himself to the extent the MLF proponents thought he had; Johnson argued that he had not meant to do so.[11] In that case, he only confused matters further when he publicly affirmed his support of the MLF during the April 20 speech at the Associated Press luncheon in New York—the occasion when he announced American and Soviet cutbacks in materials production facilities. "We realize," the president said, "that sharing the burden of leadership requires us to share the responsibilities of power. As a step in this direction we support the establishment of a multi-lateral nuclear force composed of those nations which desire to participate."[12]

Immediately following the April 10 meeting, marching orders were sent out from State Department headquarters in the form of a cable from George Ball, still acting secretary, to all U.S. missions in NATO countries. It conveyed President Johnson's directives at the meeting, as noted above.[13] In an answering cable, Finletter expressed unhappiness about the last part of the following instruction:

> Europeans would be advised in U.S. judgment MLF best answer now available. However, in discussion with Europeans no REPEAT no attempt will be made force solution upon them. . . .[14]

He reported that this instruction had "already raised doubts among those who have seen message in this mission."* These doubts included a question "in minds of our allies as to whether we will ever be serious about MLF." All had been "waiting for U.S. decision to move." After such a decision had apparently been made at the White House on April 10, it was disheartening to have the old policy of

---

*This gives the impression that Finletter was showing his instructions to representatives of other governments, surely an odd way to proceed.

diffidence reasserted. Finletter cited as an example a conversation in which Wilhelm Grewe, German permanent representative to NATO, had said that "Bonn needs to be left in no doubt as to the seriousness of American intentions." Finletter felt that there was a middle ground between the old diffidence and "shoving down the throat." This was "to believe in policy, to urge courteously and without pressures that it be accepted by our allies for common good, to explain policy as best we can, and to use reasonable persuasion to ask our allies to work in common with us." Anything less than this, Finletter wrote, would "be misunderstood by allies who cannot understand that most powerful member of alliance is as diffident as all that."

Finletter's suggestion found a sympathetic audience in Ball, who promptly sent out new instructions. Acknowledging that the previous ones might have given "too negative an impression," he issued, as "a fuller formulation of our position," an almost verbatim statement of Finletter's "middle ground."*

To support the new policy USIA Director Carl Rowan sent a circular to U.S. Information Service officers in all NATO countries instructing them that in the next six months an effort was to be made "to persuade public opinion leaders that the MLF [was] an effective, efficient, and desirable response to the threat of Communist arms. . . ." The officers were to be prepared "intelligently to discuss the MLF" and were to treat it "as a matter of high priority."[15]

The project seemed at last to be moving strongly forward. But now it began to encounter new problems on a number of fronts.

Problems with the British

A key factor in determining the attitude of several NATO countries, notably Belgium and the Netherlands, was what position the United Kingdom might adopt. Much seemed to depend on the outcome of Britain's October 1964 election, with the Conservatives considered

---

*Ball telegram, 4/15/64, National Security File, Subject File, MLF Cables, Vol. 2, LBJ Library. As to the relationship of Ball and Rusk on this issue, Bundy has the following to say: "I think that Ball was more closely in touch with and on top of this particular question than the secretary was. At the same time I'm sure that Dean Rusk kept informed and therefore felt that these were his people doing this. It wasn't like some other cases where you might feel the assistant secretary or some other subordinate was carrying his own ball. George was in that sense a careful political bureaucrat and he would have had the secretary with him. But it was 'the secretary with him,' not he doing what the secretary independently had put his own energy behind" (private conversation, January 22, 1986).

more likely than Labour to favor an allied force. Both British parties found difficulty in the rapid German–American schedule that contemplated a treaty signing by the end of 1964. Both were in agreement also in preferring some alternative form of NATO force that would not involve mixed-manning at sea—they didn't think that was any way to run a navy—and that would be less costly than the MLF seemed likely to be. (Implementation of the 1962 Nassau agreement, involving the purchase of Polaris missiles, had already saddled the British with enormous costs.) Accordingly, the Macmillan government began late in the spring of 1964 to submit alternative proposals that included mixed-manned operation of land-based missiles, both on the continent and in the United States, and to suggest that the scheduled MLF decision date be delayed. There was a question in many minds whether the British were serious about their proposals or whether their true intent was to defeat or delay the MLF.

Assuming that the British might be employing delaying tactics, U.S. and West German spokesmen began in June 1964 to suggest that, much as all parties would regret it, their two countries might launch the project without initial British participation, so long as at least one other country went along. The expectation was that, under this kind of pressure, the British would cave in. As an internal Navy Department assessment said, "neither [British political] party could afford to be outside of an arrangement that gave Germany any degree of control over nuclear weapons."[16]

Despite the British problem, Finletter was able to report a large measure of agreement among the nations participating in the Paris working group. On July 13 he cabled that seven members of the group (all except Britain) had "expressed desire to complete [their] work by the end of the year to permit governments that wish to proceed at that time to do so." He also reported a "heavy presumption" in favor of the U.S. concept—a mixed-manned force of surface vessels armed with Polaris missiles.[17]

A new element was added to the British position in August. This was to insist that in any MLF there be a British as well as a U.S. veto over any use of nuclear weapons. This requirement seemed to be based on a deep-seated and widespread fear in the British public of any arrangement that could lead to a German finger on the nuclear trigger. The initial terms of the proposed MLF did not seem to lead to such an eventuality; yet the British were reportedly disturbed by stories that some day the United States might give up its veto.[18]

Problems with the French

Although it had never been expected that Charles de Gaulle's France would join the MLF, the French attitude toward the project was at first relatively mild and detached: no, the MLF was not something France was interested in joining but yes, they could understand and would not actively oppose participation by West Germany and other countries. When de Gaulle visited Chancellor Ludwig Erhard on July 23, 1964, however, he took a much harder line. As reported by U.S. Ambassador George C. McGhee, he presented a series of issues, including the MLF and Southeast Asia, "in terms of the necessity of choice between French and American policies."[19]

When U.S. Ambassador to France Charles E. Bohlen sought clarification from Foreign Minister Maurice Couve de Murville in October, he received the impression that the French were indeed moving toward greater and more open opposition to the MLF. Bohlen reported Couve as stating France's belief that "including Germany [in an MLF] was merely to whet their appetite for nuclear matters"— the French shared the Soviet view on that. Couve also mentioned that France's doubts had recently been reinforced by the possibility that the MLF would be only a U.S.–German force.[20]

The idea that Germany and the United States might actually go it alone in the initial stages of an MLF was publicly suggested by Erhard at a press conference on October 6, 1964.* De Gaulle responded with fury, saying that in such an event France would have to reexamine its relationship with the Federal Republic. Other members of NATO were also dismayed and two days later Rusk denied there were any plans to consider Erhard's suggestion.

There is no doubt that France's change in attitude, from scornful indifference to vigorous opposition, diminished German ardor for the MLF; it was a cardinal principle of German policy to avoid, if at all possible, having to choose between the U.S. guarantee and French friendship.[21] In a cable at the end of October, Bohlen warned his superiors that de Gaulle's threats should be taken seriously. He thought the chief French objection to the MLF was that it would bind Germany, "a key member of the European community," to the United States, and thus foreclose the possibility of a "French-style European

---

*Erhard had made this suggestion in a letter to President Johnson at the end of September. He made his injudicious press conference comment before the president had had an opportunity to reply (Barnes, "The Nuclear Non-Proliferation Treaty," p. 232f).

unity centered around the Franco–German relationship." He predicted that France would oppose "any REPEAT any" MLF with increasing vigor and that such opposition might include "countervailing action," even including withdrawal from NATO. He had no specific recommendations to make; he merely wanted to sound this alarm about an approaching confrontation.[22] In November de Gaulle lent credence to Bohlen's predictions by issuing a strong denunciation of the MLF, coupled with some vague threats to retaliate against NATO.

Problems with the Germans

Germany and the United States had reciprocal interests in the MLF. For the United States it offered a way of binding Germany to NATO. As President Johnson is reported to have said at the April 10, 1964 White House meeting, "The Germans have gone off the reservation twice in our lifetime, and we've got to be sure that this doesn't happen again, that they don't go berserk."[23] (At all times Johnson appeared to have had greater sympathy for German concerns that did Kennedy. He seemed wholly persuaded that it was in the best interests of the United States and the Western alliance to restore Germany to a position of respect and influence commensurate with its economic strength.) For the Germans the MLF represented a way of binding the United States more firmly to the defense of Europe; most of all to the defense of Germany. Unable to have nuclear weapons of their own, the Germans felt themselves to be naked in the heart of Europe and sorely in need of a nuclear protector. As Chancellor Erhard expressed it, "Soviet medium range rockets on the boundaries of this country are a reality. We have never demanded control over nuclear weapons, but we desire to be defended with the same weapons as threaten us."[24]

While Kennedy and Chancellor Konrad Adenauer were in office, there had been widespread skepticism about the MLF within the German leadership, particularly in the military. By June 1964, however, much of this skepticism had been dispelled, largely by U.S. persuasion efforts, and the German position had shifted "from one of intelligent interest to something more closely resembling a demand."[25]

The German attitude was also affected by the warming atmosphere between Washington and Moscow at the end of Kennedy's term, which Johnson seemed interested in continuing.[26] The Germans were alarmed by the manner in which the Limited Test Ban Treaty had been negotiated without consulting or even informing NATO allies, and by the apparent U.S. willingness to discuss bilaterally with the Soviets various other arms control proposals that affected Germany's future. These trends raised in Bonn the nightmarish specter of some future Soviet–American deal that would sacrifice Germany's vital interests. Chancellor Erhard was also said to fear the possibility of a U.S.–French rapprochement that might isolate Germany.[27] The MLF seemed to offer a means of preventing these eventualities by fixing the American connection to Germany more permanently. This, at least, was the view of Erhard and leading members of his government. A further reported German motive in wanting a nuclear role was to have a bargaining card in negotiations with the Russians for German reunification.[28]

Germany's situation impelled its leaders to urge speed in bringing the MLF into being. The time-table the Germans had in mind was conditioned by their own political calendar. German national elections were scheduled for September 1965. Intensive campaigning, during which thorough consideration of the MLF would scarcely be possible, was expected to begin about June 1. About four months would be required for parliamentary consideration of the treaty, once submitted. This worked back to about February 1. It therefore appeared that, if German consideration was not to be delayed by many months, a treaty had to be submitted by January 1965.[29]

When Chancellor Erhard came to Washington in June 1964, he is reported to have told the president that if an MLF treaty was not signed by December, German assent could not be assured.[30] The joint communiqué issued after this meeting affirmed that "efforts should be continued to ready an agreement for signature by the end of the year." Walt Rostow has characterized this dual statement of resolve as "perhaps the high point of MLF diplomacy in the post-Nassau period."[31] It certainly seemed to indicate a degree of personal commitment by President Johnson that contradicted later denials.

Problems with the Russians

Soviet statements of hostility toward the MLF were frequent and uncompromising throughout 1964. They found their most troubling expression in the context of negotiations for a nonproliferation treaty. The superpowers had both endorsed the Irish resolution of 1961, which seemed to provide the main outlines for such a treaty, that is, nations having nuclear weapons would not transfer control of such weapons or information needed for their manufacture; nations without nuclear weapons would not seek to acquire or manufacture them. This formula, emphasizing "control," would have permitted the MLF to go forward. The problem was that the Soviet Union wanted to add a provision forbidding any nation to *physically transfer* nuclear weapons outside its own territory. In essence, what the Soviets seemed to be insisting on was that the United States abandon not only the MLF but all other nuclear sharing with its NATO allies as well.

The Soviet Union's opposition to the MLF focused, of course, on West Germany. The Soviets were well aware of U.S. arguments that under the contemplated MLF security arrangements there would be no German fingers on the Polaris trigger. They were said to feel, however, that through participation in an MLF the Germans might over time acquire essential technical information about warheads and missile systems. A future West German government might then be in a position to undertake speedy development of a national nuclear force.[32] There was no fear more deeply rooted in the Russian psyche at this time than that of a revanchist Germany with nuclear weapons.

The bitter Soviet hostility toward the MLF presented a serious obstacle to progress on a nonproliferation treaty, which had been a staple of discussion at the ENDC since the UN adopted the Irish resolution in December 1961. On February 6, 1964, ACDA Director Foster told his colleagues at the ENDC that he and his Soviet counterpart, Semyon K. Tsarapkin, had agreed to hold private talks in an attempt to break the NPT impasse. "As an immediate step, and to facilitate progress in these discussions," he said, "the United States, for its part, does not intend to take any actions inconsistent with the terms of the Irish resolution." Foster went on to assert the U.S. view that "the creation of multilateral defense forces within the framework of existing collective security arrangements would not result in additional States obtaining national control of nuclear weapons." "Therefore," Foster maintained, "the creation of such forces would be fully consistent with the Irish resolution and would, in fact, reinforce common policies to prevent wider dissemination of national nuclear weapon capabilities."[33]

The Soviet Union was not buying any of this, and Foster and Tsarapkin were unable to make progress in their private talks. Foster could say nothing to make the Soviet Union accept the MLF; Tsarapkin could say nothing to make the United States abandon it. In the following month the barrage of Soviet statements against the MLF persisted. In June, Khrushchev told Harold Wilson—not yet prime minister—that the MLF was a bar to a nonproliferation treaty. On July 2, Deputy Foreign Minister Valerian Zorin condemned the MLF as aimed at "quenching the nuclear thirst of German revenge seekers," and warned that there could be no disarmament accord unless the West scrapped plans for the project.[34] On July 11, the Soviet government addressed a formal note to the United States saying that further pursuit of the MLF was irreconcilable with the "adoption of collective measures to prevent the dissemination of nuclear weapons," measures that the Soviet government would otherwise favor.[35] On July 27, Tsarapkin told newsmen in Geneva that unless the MLF was dropped the USSR could not "subscribe to any agreement to prevent the spread of nuclear weapons."

There was much support for the Soviet position in the West, even in the United States. The Russians had been attacked by the Germans twice in a generation and, having lost twenty million lives in World War II, seemed to have moral grounds for wanting to assure that they would not be attacked again. Some on our side thought at first that Soviet objections to the MLF could be argued or bargained away. For example, in his April 8, 1964, memorandum to the president, Rusk depicted the Soviet reaction to the MLF proposal as

> critical, but lacking the fire and brimstone that usually connote genuine Soviet concern. . . . There is no evidence MLF is preventing disarmament agreements that the Soviets might otherwise favor and that would be in our interest.

In time it became clear, from the force and frequency with which the Soviets expressed themselves, that this was too optimistic an assessment.

The Voyage of the *Claude V. Ricketts*

The problems that the MLF was having through mid-1964 were almost entirely political in nature. Aware of this, the strategy of the plan's managers in the State Department was to play down politics and to concentrate instead on building the necessary technical and legal foundations. Virtually all NATO countries found it possible to participate in discussions to this end, although several made it clear they were not thereby committing themselves.

The working groups in Paris (legal) and Washington (military) made excellent progress, and by the end of the summer of 1964 a treaty proposal was in readiness. It contemplated a force of twenty-five surface ships, disguised as freighters, which would ply the European coastal waters of the Mediterranean and the Atlantic. Each would carry eight Polaris missiles and be manned by crews of at least three nations. The United States and West Germany would bear the largest financial burdens, each contributing about 40 percent of the total cost.

Planning began at this time for a demonstration project involving the actual operation of a mixed-manned ship. The United States made available a guided missile destroyer, the USS *Claude V. Ricketts*. Six nations—West Germany, Greece, Italy, the Netherlands, Turkey, and, somewhat surprisingly, Britain—agreed to provide about 50 percent of the ship's eighteen officers and 316 enlisted men. The plan was for the personnel from the other countries gradually to replace part of the U.S. complement during the duration of the exercise. The State Department was at pains to point out that the purpose of the project was "to provide training and gain experience rather than to test the feasibility of mixed-manning," of which, the department said, it was "already thoroughly convinced."[36]

After months of training, the project was officially launched in a ceremony held aboard the *Ricketts* at the Washington Navy Yard on October 20, 1964. Secretary Rusk made some affirmative remarks about the MLF. Many other high U.S. officials were present, as were the ambassadors of all the participating countries. The *Ricketts* then headed for the open sea to join the U.S. Atlantic Fleet.

The demonstration continued for more than a year, until December 1, 1965. Mixed-manning seemed to work reasonably well on the voyage, although not so well as to encourage anyone to believe it would have been effective in so complicated a craft as a nuclear submarine. While the experiment was in progress, however, events were occurring in the international arena that greatly diminished its significance.

Notes

1. National Security File, Subject File, MLF Cables, Vol. 1, LBJ Library.
2. Bundy to President, 12/6/63, National Security File, Memos to President—McGeorge Bundy, Vol. 1, LBJ Library.

3. Briefing for the President, 12/6/63, National Security File, Subject File, MLF General, Vol. 1, LBJ Library.

4. Memorandum for the Record, 12/6/63, National Security File, Subject File, MLF General, Vol. 1, LBJ Library.

5. Rusk to President, 4/8/64, National Security File, Subject File, MLF General, Vol. 1, LBJ Library.

6. Memorandum of Discussion, 4/11/64, National Security File, Subject File, MLF General, Vol. 1, LBJ Library. One can surmise that these minutes, as those of the December 6, 1963 meeting, were written by Rostow.

7. Kissinger, *The Troubled Partnership*, p. 104.

8. Transcript, Gerard Smith Oral History Interview, 4/29/69, by Paige E. Mulhollan, Tape 1, p. 12f., LBJ Library.

9. Private conversation, January 22, 1986.

10. Gerard Smith Oral History Interview, p. 6.

11. Geyelin, *Lyndon B. Johnson and the World*, p. 160.

12. *Documents on Disarmament: 1964*, p. 183.

13. Ball cable to European missions, 4/12/64, National Security File, Subject File, MLF Cables, Vol. 2, LBJ Library.

14. Finletter to Department, 4/14/64, National Security File, Subject File, MLF Cables, Vol. 2, LBJ Library.

15. USIA Circular from Rowan, 6/1/64, National Security File, Subject File, MLF Cables, Vol. 2, LBJ Library.

16. J. J. Lynch to Secretary of Navy, 6/18/64, National Security File, Subject File, MLF General, Vol. 1., LBJ Library.

17. Finletter (Paris) to SecState, 7/13/64, National Security File, Subject File, MLF Cables, Vol. 2, LBJ Library.

18. Cable, O'Shaugnessy (London) to DOS, 8/7/64, National Security File, Subject File, MLF Cables, Vol. 3, LBJ Library.

19. McGhee (Bonn) to DOS, 7/23/64, National Security File, Subject File, MLF Cables, Vol. 3, LBJ Library.

20. Bohlen (Paris) to DOS, 10/23/64, National Security File, Subject File, MLF Cables, Vol. 3, LBJ Library.

21. Kelleher, *Germany and the Politics of Nuclear Weapons*, p. 232; Geyelin, *Lyndon B. Johnson and the World*, p. 61.

22. Bohlen (Paris) to DOS, 10/28/64, National Security File, Subject File, MLF Cables, Vol. 3, LBJ Library.

23. Transcript, Gerard Smith Oral History interview, 4/29/69, by Paige E. Mulhollan, Tape 1, p. 6, LBJ Library.

24. From a speech made in Berlin 1/12/65. Quoted in cable 1/15/65 from McGhee (Bonn) to DOS, National Security File, Subject File, Vol. 4, LBJ Library.

25. Buchan, "The Multilateral Force," p. 9.

26. Kelleher, *Germany and the Politics of Nuclear Weapons*, p. 241ff.

27. McGhee cable to DOS, 1/14/65, National Security File, Subject File, MLF Cables, Vol. 4, LBJ Library.

28. Memo, Walt Rostow to Secretary, 10/19/65, National Security File, Subject File, MLF, LBJ Library. In the margin of a copy of this memo, Bundy wrote: "Something to be given away?"

29. Finletter (Paris) to DOS, 2/28/64, National Security File, Subject File, MLF Cables, Vol. 1, LBJ Library.
30. Kelleher, *Germany and the Politics of Nuclear Weapons,* p. 245.
31. Rostow, *The Diffusion of Power,* p. 192.
32. Buchan, "The Multilateral Force," p. 14.
33. *Documents on Disarmament: 1964,* p. 34f.
34. Ibid., p. 241ff.
35. Ibid., p. 276ff.
36. Cable to American Embassies in NATO countries, 2/16/64, National Security File, Subject File, MLF Cables, Vol. 1, LBJ Library.

11

And Then There Were Five

If and when the time comes to do something about China, the Soviet Union would expect the United States to help.

—A Soviet official
1967

News from All Over

Satellite observations and other intelligence reports indicated in September 1964 that the Chinese were preparing for their first nuclear test. It had long been recognized that it was only a matter of time before such an event would take place. The prospect was regarded by many in the United States with the greatest alarm. When Averell Harriman went to Moscow in 1963 to negotiate the Limited Test Ban Treaty, he was instructed by President Kennedy: "to elicit [Khrushchev's] view of means of limiting or preventing Chinese nuclear development and his willingness either to take Soviet action or to accept U.S. action aimed in this direction."[1] Khrushchev did not appear to be interested. According to Harriman's account, he belittled the prospect that China would be a formidable nuclear threat in the near future.[2]

On September 15, 1964, with a Chinese test imminent, the question of joint action with the Soviets came up again. Bundy summarized the circumstances in a Memorandum for the Record:

We discussed the question of Chinese nuclear weapons today, first in a lunch at the State Department given by Secretary Rusk for McNamara, McCone, and myself, and later at a meeting with the president in which Rusk, McNamara and I were with him in the Cabinet Room (McCone having left at a time when we thought the president would not be able to join us).

At the luncheon we developed the following position:

(1) We are not in favor of unprovoked unilateral U.S. military action against Chinese nuclear installations at this time. We would

prefer to have a Chinese test take place than to initiate such action now. If for other reasons we should find ourselves in military hostilities at any level with the Chinese Communists, we would expect to give very close attention to the possibility of an appropriate military action against Chinese nuclear facilities.

(2) We believe that there are many possibilities for joint action with the Soviet Government if that Government is interested. Such possibilities include a warning to the Chinese against tests, a possible undertaking to give up underground testing and to hold the Chinese accountable if they test in any way, and even a possible agreement to cooperate in preventive military action. We therefore agreed that it would be most desirable for the Secretary of State to explore this matter very privately with Ambassador Dobrynin as soon as possible.

[Portion deleted from copy publicly available.]

These preliminary decisions were reported to the president in the Cabinet Room, and he indicated his approval. The Secretary of State now intends to consult promptly with the Soviet ambassador.[3]

Dean Rusk recalls that there was some discussion, "particularly in the staff," about taking some action against China but that the idea "never got anywhere when it reached the top levels of policy. We simply knew that we were not going to deliver any preemptive strikes against China, with or without the Soviet Union." Rusk does not recall any specific talk with Dobrynin on the subject.[*]

In short order the expected came to pass. On October 16, 1964:

The big news today is that at 3 A.M. Washington time the Red Chinese exploded an atomic bomb in the atmosphere. Our electromagnetic and acoustic detection devices picked it up and the Chinese announced it. President Johnson announced it after the Chinese announced it.

The president's announcement was designed to still any alarm, particularly on the part of nations that might feel threatened by China,

---

[*]Private conversation, March 13, 1986. But an Intelligence Information Cable of July 3, 1967, quotes a "Soviet official" as saying that if after Mao's death there did not come "an improvement in the situation insofar as the Soviet Union is concerned, the USSR should take direct action against China to put down the threat. Times have changed," the official continued, "and if and when the time comes to do something about China, the Soviet Union would expect the United States to help" (Intelligence Information Cable, 7/3/67, National Security File, Country File, USSR, Vol. 15, LBJ Library).

for example, India, Japan, and Australia. He was at pains to point out that it was "a crude device" (we would soon learn that this was not entirely true) and that China was still a long way from having a stockpile of reliable weapons with effective systems for delivering them.

The week of the Chinese test was remarkable for other developments as well. The day before the test, word came from Moscow that Nikita Khrushchev had been relieved of his duties and that Leonid Brezhnev, as head of the Communist party, and Aleksey N. Kosygin, as chairman of the Council of Ministers, were to share power.* Earlier in the week there had also been a change of leadership in the United Kingdom. British voters had turned out the Conservatives and given power to the Labour party led by Harold Wilson.

These three events, occurring within the same week in distant places, produced a wave of uncertainty and, indeed, some anxiety here at home. The news media began at once to probe for explanations and evaluations. The president had some questions of his own. Some of these were addressed at an emergency White House meeting I attended on October 17. (The meeting was remarkable for the number of its assessments and predictions that later turned out to be erroneous.)

> The first topic was the Chinese test of the day before. McCone reviewed China's nuclear facilities as they were known to us: a 10 megawatt research reactor; a gaseous diffusion enriched uranium plant under construction, which apparently would not be operable for two or three years; and two possible plutonium production reactors. The uncertainty in McCone's estimate of their facilities came from the fact that it had not been possible to cover one area of China with photographic reconnaissance. He said that what they had exploded was probably a plutonium device. [This was incorrect; see below.]
>
> McCone went on to discuss the Soviet situation, saying that Khrushchev had been removed due to general discontent with his conduct of office, not any one trouble. He had made a strong

---

*I received a number of phone calls from news media asking my impressions of Brezhnev, who was relatively unknown to Americans. While in the Soviet Union in 1963 I had had an extended conversation with him. He occupied then the largely ceremonial position of President of the USSR. I was informed at the time that I was only the second American Brezhnev had ever met, the other having been Gus Hall, head of the American Communist party. This startling information reenforced the view that one of our most difficult problems in relations with the Soviet Union has been the insularity of its leaders. Khrushchev, who travelled a great deal, was a notable exception. Gorbachev may yet prove to be another exception.

demand in September for greater emphasis on consumer goods rather than heavy military products, and this may have contributed to his downfall. [Another factor, not mentioned by McCone, may have been the USSR's humiliating setback in the Cuban missile crisis, for which Khrushchev was undoubtedly blamed.]

McCone said that the relationship of Kosygin and Brezhnev was not yet clear. Either one, or a third person, might move in a little later and take over the leadership. In his opinion neither of the new leaders was imaginative or likely to play a world role comparable to Khrushchev's. The president asked McCone whether the CIA had had any forewarning of the change. McCone said there had been evidence of dissension but no indication of an immediate change.

[Ambassador-at-Large Llewellyn] Thompson predicted there would be few changes in Soviet policy. He noted that in the last seven years Khrushchev had spent $2\frac{1}{4}$ years away from Moscow, so that others had been running the country much of the time, with Kosygin very important. Thompson thought the first changes we might notice would be within the satellite nations rather than in the Soviet Union itself, and then there might be some changes in Soviet relationships with the outside. Rusk agreed with Thompson that there would be little immediate change in Soviet policy. He saw indications, however, that Gromyko might be replaced. [We would have to wait more than twenty years for fulfillment of that prophecy!]

Rusk warned against downgrading Chinese capabilities too much, perhaps having in mind the president's belittling announcement of the day before. Rusk believed the nuclear test would add to China's prestige in the long run. I agreed with Rusk: we should be very careful not to underestimate what China could do or might intend to do.

The president asked [USIA Director Carl] Rowan what people around the world were saying. Rowan replied that they were saying a lot. The Japanese and Yugoslavs had let loose a blast against the Chinese, but much of the reaction elsewhere was favorable to China. Scandinavian countries were saying China should now be admitted to the UN.* Rowan felt that the United States would have to use every persuasive effort in its power to counter these effects.

---

*Dean Rusk was asked during this period whether it mightn't tame the Chinese to bring them into the UN. Rusk replied, aptly, that the UN was "not a reform school."

The discussion then turned to the British election. Rusk reported that Labour had only a four-seat margin of victory. The president thought this meant it wouldn't be much of a government and that it wouldn't last long. Rusk said our Embassy in London gave Wilson ten months to a year. [The Wilson government survived until June 1970, a period of five years and eight months!]

President Johnson said it was important to avoid a panic reaction and to make it clear to the American people that we were alert to the situation. He then asked McCone whether there was anything else coming up of an alarming nature. McCone thought not.

Also discussed at this meeting was the recent arrest of presidential assistant Walter Jenkins on a morals charge. The president admonished us all on the importance of thorough security checks of all our employees. He said that the FBI and the Secret Service had had information about a prior Jenkins arrest (in 1959) but that he, the president, had not been informed of it until this latest episode broke. The president spoke bitterly about the McCarthyite tactics of those who were seeking to exploit the Jenkins case. He said that one of the country's largest corporations had been paying large sums to investigators seeking derogatory information about himself and Mrs. Johnson. The president then arose, in some agitation, and left the room.

The president addressed the nation on TV the following night, October 18. What he said departed in some respects from the briefing he had received at the White House meeting. He characterized Kosygin and Brezhnev as "experienced, but younger men, . . . perhaps less rooted in the past . . . said to be realistic." He added: "We must never forget that the men in the Kremlin remain dedicated, dangerous Communists." He predicted that there would be turmoil in the Communist world. The president said that the Chinese test had not surprised us, that it was a long road from a single test to an effective weapons system, and that our own strength was overwhelming and would be kept that way. He drew the lesson that nuclear proliferation was dangerous to all mankind and that "we must continue to work against it." He asked the Soviet Union to consult its self-interest and join in this endeavor.

The president then addressed an issue that was to become central in coming nonproliferation treaty negotiations, that of security guarantees. He said: "*[T]he nations that do not seek nuclear weapons can be sure that if they need our strong support against some threat of nuclear blackmail, then they will have it."* (Emphasis added.) Although this pledge sounded very strong, its meaning was far from clear. Was the president promising, for example, to guarantee India against China to the same extent that we guaranteed our NATO partners against the Soviet Union? These and other questions were asked, but answers were not forthcoming. Despite its lack of precision, this statement by the president hung in the air and remained part of the political atmosphere for more than three years, until it was replaced by an almost equally vague UN resolution (see chapter 28).

Views on the Chinese Test

On October 19 I gave a short press conference following an address at a Metals/Materials Congress in Philadelphia. When queried about the Chinese test, I ventured the opinion, as McCone had done at the White House meeting, that it was a plutonium bomb. This was the consensus view of the intelligence community, of which the AEC was a part. I repeated this statement later the same day at a meeting the president conducted with congressional leaders. The very next day, however, I had to reverse myself. During the period since the test the AEC had been conducting analyses of the radioactive cloud as it drifted eastward over Japan (October 17), the Aleutians (October 18), the northern Pacific (October 19), and Canada and the western United States (October 20). The analyses convinced us, to our surprise, that the Chinese had detonated a device employing U-235. (The other four nuclear weapon powers had used plutonium devices for their first tests.) Further, we were persuaded that the Chinese bomb had been more sophisticated in design than our own Hiroshima U-235 weapon, employing an advanced form of implosion trigger to detonate the fission materials. I reported these conclusions to a Cabinet meeting on October 20, advising everyone to be very cautious about estimating Chinese capabilities until more was learned.

On October 21 the AEC issued an announcement of its findings. We at once began to receive inquiries about the source of the U-235. All we could say was that we did not know where it came from and that we were studying the matter. Two months later I was able to report at a meeting of the Committee of Principals that the debris seemed to show, though not conclusively, that the U-235 did not come from material that Khrushchev said he had given the Chinese before the Sino–Russian rift; nor from U-235 supplied by the United States to its European partners. On the contrary, the indications were that the bomb material had been produced by the Chinese themselves. This implied a more advanced and more sustainable nuclear weapons effort than had been thought within China's capability.*

The AEC's findings had ominous implications for the possibilities of further proliferation. The fact that the Chinese device had been developed indigenously was further confirmation that the existing nuclear weapon states could not prevent proliferation through policies of denial toward nonweapon states. The event also greatly expanded the stage on which the proliferation drama would be played out. The problem would no longer be confined to the advanced countries of Europe nor to the superpowers and their allies. Consideration would now have to be given to many more nations, and to virtually all regions of the world. An immediate question was raised, for example, as to the intentions of India.

The View from India

On November 3, 1964, the Indian ambassador to the United States, B. K. Nehru, called on ACDA Director Foster. Foster made a detailed record of the conversation and circulated it within the government.

Nehru began by recalling that India had made a formal decision prior to the Chinese explosion not to develop nuclear weapons. The government had reviewed and confirmed this decision after the explosion. He added, however, that "there were strong pressures in India to have the government explode a nuclear device so as to offset the genuine psychological advantages which the Chinese had obtained in Southeast Asia by virtue of their explosion." Nehru stated that this act by the Chinese, "instead of being condemned by most nonaligned nations, was actually being commended to some extent on the basis of showing that the white world was not better than they and that the United States, at least in the Far East and Africa, was not the superpower it used to be."

---

*The intelligence report cited in this chapter quoted the "Soviet official" as saying that Chinese nuclear progress was not surprising in view of the fact that the Soviets had "trained a very large number of Chinese scientists, who are extremely good, and given them about 45 complete factories" (Intelligence Information Cable, 7/3/67, National Security File, Country File, USSR Cables, Vol. 15, LBJ Library).

Nehru cited estimates that India could develop a reasonable nuclear capability for only $20 million.* He added that, unless India did so, China could within a year or so develop a makeshift capability to drop a bomb on New Delhi without fear of retaliation. He warned, moreover, that the Chinese bomb had the potential for seriously degrading India's position in the Far East and therefore "political pressures within India might indeed build up so that it would be politically impossible to resist proposals for an Indian bomb." When Foster called attention to President Johnson's statement on October 18 that the United States would support nations subject to nuclear blackmail, Nehru expressed skepticism, saying, "But the United States would not come to our aid by attacking China if at the same time the Soviet Union said it would assist China under such an attack."

If anyone needed a primer on why nations were tempted to develop nuclear weapons, Nehru's conversation with Foster provided it. Nehru made it clear that India was tempted in order: (1) to protect her security against a nuclear-armed neighbor, and (2) to maintain or add to her regional and worldwide prestige and influence.†

Notes

1. State Department telegram "For Governor Harriman from the President," 7/15/63, released in response to Freedom of Information Act request.
2. Seaborg, *Kennedy, Khrushchev and the Test Ban,* p. 239.
3. Bundy to President, 9/15/64, National Security File, Memos to the President—McGeorge Bundy, Vol. 6, LBJ Library.

---

*This was a surprisingly small amount considering that the wartime Manhattan Project had cost the United States over $2 billion. Much of the difference was based on the fact that we had to do pioneering research and development work that India would not have to repeat, and also that our effort aimed at producing a larger nuclear arsenal than India had in mind.

†For more about India's approach to undertaking a nuclear weapons program, see chapter 21.

Part IV

Nonproliferation: Toward an International Agreement

If effective arms control is not achieved, we may see the day when these frightful, fearful weapons are in the hands of many nations. Their concern and capacity for control may be more limited than our own.

Lyndon B. Johnson
September 16, 1964

12

Backing Away from
the MLF

Wavering

By emphasizing the dangers of proliferation, the Chinese test made a nonproliferation treaty seem more urgent. This, in turn, weakened the case for the MLF, which, because of Soviet objections, seemed to stand in the way of an NPT.

In the gathering state of doubt that the MLF proposal could be kept on track, some of the officials principally concerned with the issue convened for a two-hour discussion on October 31, 1964. Those present included Bundy, Ball, Assistant Secretary of State (European affairs) William Tyler, Deputy Defense Secretary McNaughton, and Columbia University Professor Richard E. Neustadt, who had been brought aboard as an adviser to the president. The minutes of the meeting reported a general agreement that the MLF proposal would have to be modified.[1] The question was how much could be, or should be, salvaged. Bundy seemed willing to accept drastic modification. He suggested that any scheme that "met German emotional needs for first class membership in the immediate future" should be considered satisfactory. At another point in the meeting he said he would be willing to settle "for anything we could get that would include U.K., German, Italian and U.S. participation and would provide something we could build on." Ball, revealing perhaps the true focus of his interest, stated that he viewed the MLF as just "a step in an evolutionary process toward greater European integration."*

Those present all seemed to agree that French opposition and British indecision made it virtually impossible to achieve the rapid

---

*Ball, whose specialty was economic affairs, had been an attorney for Jean Monnet, the French economist who was the acknowledged leader of the movement for a united Europe. Monnet was said to feel that the MLF was the most important forward step being contemplated toward that objective.

MLF consummation the Germans appeared to want. The question was then raised whether it would be feasible to let the whole question slide for two to three years. Bundy thought this should be considered, but Ball argued that our number-one asset in Europe was "confidence in U.S. judgment and initiatives" and that such confidence would be lost if there was much further delay in resolving the issue. This point seemed to prevail, but Bundy expressed the hope that the pace of advance would not be dominated by the need to meet German desires. Finally, there was discussion of whether the force might be made "plausibly open to the French." It was concluded that there was no such possibility because the MLF was in direct conflict with the French objective of an "independent Europe," namely, one not dominated by the United States.

After his decisive election victory on November 3, 1964, President Johnson began to show more interest in the MLF question. The political calendar indicated that important decisions related to this issue might have to be made in the coming months. These concerned not only the MLF negotiations in Paris but also the interests and concerns of the new British government and the intentions of France regarding NATO. (Johnson, an inveterate conciliator, never accepted the view that France was a lost cause.) Most immediate was an impending visit from Prime Minister Wilson, scheduled for December 7 and 8, 1964.

While campaigning for office Harold Wilson had given the impression that he would be willing to transfer Britain's nuclear deterrent to NATO, although not as part of a mixed-manned force. After his election with a bare four-seat majority, he and his Cabinet colleagues determined that their best course would be to continue opposing the MLF, while making clear the reasons for their opposition, and at the same time to develop a more acceptable alternative.[2]

In advance of Wilson's trip to Washington, extensive preparations were made by both sides. Part of the U.S. preparation was to try to find out what the British had in mind. In his memoirs, Wilson speculates that a prime reason for U.S. curiosity was a desire not to repeat the "calamity" of the Nassau meeting of 1962 when "lack of preparation and continual misunderstanding led to an unsatisfactory result." He recounts that President Kennedy had asked Richard Neustadt to carry out an inquiry as to what went wrong at Nassau and that Kennedy had intended to dig into Neustadt's report, "the length of a full-sized novel," upon return from the fateful November 1963 trip to Texas.[3]

Neustadt was now, in 1964, again sent to London. Wilson was also visited by Ambassador David K. Bruce and George Ball. According to Wilson, all three indicated "that the success of the talks would depend on the acceptance of MLF." Ball was reported to be the most blunt of all. "He made it clear that there could be no question of going back on the MLF, that the American Government could expect us to support it, and that unless I was going to be in a position to say so, it would be better if I cancelled my visit."* Wilson wondered whether the line taken by Ball had been authorized by President Johnson.[4]

The U.S. reconnaissance in London made it clear that Wilson intended to propose an alternative to the MLF along the same lines the previous British government had been advocating. The proposal was that there be an "Atlantic Nuclear Force" (ANF) comprising three or four Polaris submarines and some eight V-bomber squadrons (sixty-four aircraft) committed by the United Kingdom; a matching number of Polaris submarines made available by the United States; and a small mixed-manned, jointly owned element—to include land-based missiles—in which nonnuclear NATO countries could participate. The British plan could be expected to have little appeal to West Germany because it essentially provided for a federation of national nuclear forces that the Germans, not having such a force, could participate in to only a minor degree.

Immediately preceding Wilson's arrival, President Johnson began five days of intensive meetings with his principal advisers in search of a policy position of his own. The discussion appeared to have been stormy at times. It was reported that at one meeting, when Johnson had verbally abused several of his advisers one after the other, Dean Acheson broke in to say: "Mr. President, you don't pay these men enough to talk to them that way."[5]

---

*In a letter of August 20, 1986, Ball states that he has no recollection of this specific incident but that "I am certain I did not express myself to Harold Wilson as forcefully as he recalls for I never felt that the issue was as important as he suggests." Ball acknowledges that he supported the MLF "even though it was a military monstrosity because I was greatly concerned, for political reasons, to have the Germans involved at least tangentially in the management of nuclear weapons; otherwise, I feared they might become as disenchanted as they had been after the first World War. In retrospect, it seems clear that I overestimated the danger since I find little enthusiasm in Germany today for having a role of any kind in the nuclear deterrent." As regards Wilson, Ball states: "We knew one another for many years—long before he became prime minister—but we rarely agreed."

A factor that President Johnson introduced into the equation based on his own knowledge was the likely reaction of Congress. On this matter several of his advisers were, in the president's view, too optimistic. From soundings he had apparently taken himself, or that the new vice president, Hubert Humphrey, had taken for him, the president was convinced that the Senate would never ratify a treaty that surrendered custody of any U.S. nuclear weapon to an allied force. The strongest opposition, based largely on security concerns, centered, as we have seen, in the Joint Committee on Atomic Energy. On October 3, 1964, Representative Chet Holifield, vice chairman and chairman-to-be of the Joint Committee,* had written to Johnson requesting that there be no commitment to the MLF before the new Congress convened in January. This was a pointed request in view of the president's previously announced intention to reach an agreement by the end of 1964. Holifield's language was blunt indeed. He wrote:

> If this plan is the first step toward relinquishing U.S. control of nuclear weapons, we should consider the important concept very thoroughly before we become wedded to signing an agreement. On the other hand, if it is a fuzzy attempt to deceive our Allies by offering the possibility of removing the U.S. veto sometime in the future when our intentions are clearly to do otherwise, then our motives will be transparent and our political objectives for creating the MLF will be defeated.

Holifield added that he was joined in his doubts by "Senator Jackson and several other members of the JCAE." He attached a highly critical analysis prepared by the staff.[6]

Objections with a different basis had been voiced by Senate liberals. On September 7, 1964, eight senators—Joseph Clark, Lee Metcalf, Eugene McCarthy, Philip Hart, Maurine Neuberger, George McGovern, Gaylord Nelson, and Gale McGee—had written to the president to communicate their "concern about any hasty implementation of the MLF proposal before it had been subjected to Senate examination." They feared that the MLF "would further imperil the prospects of arms control and divide the NATO alliance, all without adding to the defensive security of the United States." What these senators meant by "Senate examination" was quite clearly a review

---

*By statute, the chairmanship of the committee alternated from session to session between a Senate member and a House member.

by the Foreign Relations Committee, and their letter implied that this committee could become a further congressional focus of opposition to the MLF to add to that already supplied by the Joint Committee.

In the staff discussion on December 5, President Johnson asked Bundy what President Kennedy's position had been on the MLF. (That Johnson did not know was another indication of how isolated he had previously been from the issue.) Bundy responded in writing the next day. We have previously (at the end of chapter 9) quoted that part of Bundy's memo that referred to Kennedy's attitude. Bundy went on to expound at some length on widespread current opposition to the MLF. We quote extensively (from a sanitized version in the public record), because this memo seems to have figured prominently in the president's final decision. Emphasis is as in the original.[7]

1. You asked yesterday why President Kennedy was tentative and careful about the MLF. It was rightly pointed out that there were different reasons at different times, but in the last half of 1963 the reasons were, I think, dominated by his feeling that if he could only get the MLF by major and intense U.S. pressure, it was not worth it. . . .

2. The new force [Bundy presumably had in mind a compromise that would contain some of the elements the British were suggesting], even though wider and better than the old MLF, will have many opponents, and their voices will be heard, whatever specific leaders of governments may say. The most important of them are as follows:

General de Gaulle's hostility is fixed and strongly supported by all French Gaullists. Tactically, the violence of French feeling can probably be somewhat moderated if you visit Paris and reason with him, but the underlying hostility of France will remain. . . .

Most professional military men are cool at best, and many are openly opposed. [Lyman L.] Lemnitzer [supreme NATO commander in Europe, who under the U.S. concept would have been in command of the MLF] is warning against this enterprise as divisive within the alliance. Norstad [former supreme NATO commander] is publicly against it. The JCS will be loyal but probably not enthusiastic. General Eisenhower may not be any better than neutral and could be opposed. [Rusk had given a different report about Eisenhower. See chapter 10.]

American commentators like [Walter] Lippmann and George Kennan are violently opposed. Lippmann believes that there is no

serious support for this force anywhere except among a few faddists
in the State Department. . . .

  The Joint Committee and the Armed Services Committee are
very wary of any treaty which seems to affect U.S. nuclear power
and still more wary of any amendment of the McMahon [Atomic
Energy] Act. . . .

  Hubert Humphrey summarizes *Senatorial sentiment* as strongly
opposed and on many grounds. . . .

On December 5, two days before the summit, President Johnson
is said to have read Bundy's memo aloud to his assembled advisers,
to the reported consternation of Ball.[8] The memo apparently helped
to convince the president that there was not enough merit in or support for the MLF to risk having to battle Congress over it.[9] Consequently, by the time Wilson and his entourage landed in Washington,
the president's inclination was to back away from active U.S. advocacy of the MLF as a near-term "hardware solution" to NATO's
nuclear problem. What transpired during the two-day summit meeting seemed only to strengthen this resolve.

Wilson's Visit

The fullest report I could find of the Johnson–Wilson summit December 7–8, 1964 is that provided in Wilson's own memoirs. According
to this account, the two leaders first had a get-acquainted private chat
at which, after pleasantries, there was some discussion of economic
matters. Then, after lunch, there was a larger meeting where each was
"flanked by . . . senior colleagues, advisers, and note takers." It was
at this meeting that the MLF was first discussed. Wilson recalls that
he first rehearsed British military objections to the MLF. From another source, one can deduce that this part of the presentation made
the point that the MLF would create an entirely new nuclear force
which was both expensive and strategically unnecessary.[10]

  To these military objections Wilson added some political ones,
including "opposition in Europe, not least in Britain, to any suggestion, however indirect, of a German finger even influencing the nuclear trigger." He recounted the vehemence of Soviet feeling on this
score, personally encountered by him on two visits to Moscow. He
summed up British feeling about a NATO force by saying that "collective planning and a collectivised deterrent answerable to NATO

were needed, but the deterrent should be one which made military (and naval) as well as political sense." The British thought their alternative ANF proposal made such sense and Wilson asked Johnson to consider it overnight, which the president promised to do.[11]

The next day's meeting, according to Wilson's account, was delayed for two hours because the president was closeted with his advisers in a meeting that British Defense Secretary Denis Healey predicted would be "Ball's last stand." Referring to Healey's comment, Wilson writes:

> So it proved. When the President met us he said that he was very prepared to consider our ideas of the Atlantic Nuclear Force. . . . The President then made clear that he was not accepting it there and then, nor committing the US Administration to it, but he was instructing his delegation at NATO to enter into full discussions with us and other colleagues and to prepare a full study of what was involved. Clearly we had won the day.[12]

There is no doubt that the situation was more comfortable for the British after the summit than before it—they were no longer being pressed by the United States to agree to the MLF. It is questionable that their presentation alone had "won the day," however, because it seems clear that President Johnson had decided before Wilson's arrival to remove the United States from its position as active sponsor of the MLF.[13]

The U.S. side was at pains to give the impression that our position had really not changed at all. One such effort was a December 9 letter from McGeorge Bundy to British Ambassador Sir William David Ormsby Gore, who apparently had not been present at the Washington discussions. According to Bundy, the president had told the prime minister that he knew what a close election was like and thought it would be unfair to force a decision on Wilson, with his four-seat majority, and also with a grave economic crisis on his hands. Instead, the president encouraged the British to try to work out an agreement directly with the Germans. Meanwhile, Bundy continued, the president was gravely concerned that the prime minister might give others the impression that the United States had in any way backed off from its previous position. "The fact that the president himself did not press the argument was merely an indication of his desire not to force the judgment on the prime minister now."[14]

After Wilson departed, the president attempted to make clear to the bureaucracy just what he had decided and how he wanted his decisions implemented. He did this by issuing a National Security Action Memorandum and then by taking the extraordinary step of leaking the entire document to James Reston of *The New York Times*.

The NSAM was addressed to Secretaries Rusk and McNamara, with instructions that its contents be communicated to their associates in Washington and in allied capitals. Reston paraphrased the memorandum in an article printed on December 21, 1964. According to Reston's article (paraphrasing his paraphrase), the main points of U.S. policy toward nuclear sharing were to be as follows:

The United States continued to believe that the defense of the West was "indivisible," but it wanted the fullest possible discussion within the alliance on views about how the nuclear defense of the West was to be organized.

The president would approve no defense plan that was not acceptable to both Britain and West Germany and would not agree to any plan that was not discussed in advance and in detail with France.

It was the policy of the United States to encourage the maximum unity of Europe and nothing proposed in Washington for the development of the Atlantic alliance was to be interpreted by any U.S. official as opposing this movement toward the economic and political integration of Europe.

No "pressure tactics" were to be used on the allies. The United States was not interested in establishing "special arrangements" with any single ally or in confronting anyone with "deadlines" for acceptance of U.S. proposals.

The president would approve no plan that did not leave the door open for any ally to join in the defense of the Atlantic alliance at any time in the future. This applied particularly to France.

Thus, President Johnson appeared to have adopted in 1964 the advice Bundy had given to President Kennedy in 1963—to "switch from pressure to inquiry." In essence he had determined that the United States, though not opposing the MLF, would no longer actively try to bring it about. Still, while willing to see the MLF die, the president was at pains not to seem to be its murderer. There were important political reasons for adopting this stance. Moderate German politicians had committed themselves to the plan at our urging, and an abrupt repudiation by us would have soured U.S.–German relations severely, possibly driving the Germans into the arms of the French. As Bundy wrote to the president on December 16: "The Germans are watching us like hawks to see whether we are letting them down on this."[15] American prestige also would have suffered had it appeared that we were succumbing to French or Soviet pressure.

Although the new policy thus did not overtly abandon the interallied force concept, it was greeted with bitter disappointment by some MLF enthusiasts. Within a few weeks, Finletter resigned as ambassador to NATO, feeling that he had been deceived into going out on a limb, which was then sawed off.[16] Gerard Smith also resigned, and his special MLF unit in the State Department was dismantled.

In fact, the MLF concept, as a near-term "hardware" solution to NATO's nuclear problem, did not recover from the damage sustained in December 1964, and a general historical consensus fixes its demise at that time. Yet the project was not officially abandoned then. While some, like Finletter and Smith, lost heart, there was still a strong element in the State Department that wished, as Bundy phrased it, "to return to the charge."[17] Thus, shortly after the president announced his new position, the State Department instructed our embassies in Europe that, although the MLF had been referred to the NATO allies for decision, it was not to be considered a dead issue.[18] For nearly two years thereafter, until President Johnson took a more active interest in the nonproliferation treaty negotiations, our diplomats continued to insist on keeping open the possibility of a NATO nuclear force in the text of any proposed nonproliferation treaty. This clinging to what most observers regarded as a bankrupt idea proved a continuing impediment to final Soviet–American agreement on a treaty.

Notes

1. Summary of Discussion, 10/31/64, National Security File, Subject File, MLF General, Box 25, LBJ Library.
2. Wilson, *A Personal Record*, p. 44.
3. Ibid., p. 49f.
4. Ibid., p. 46.

5. Geyelin, *Lyndon B. Johnson and the World*, p. 162.
6. Information on Holifield's letter is from an unpublished chronology prepared 10/23/86 by George Bunn.
7. Bundy to President, 12/6/64, National Security File, Memos to the President—McGeorge Bundy, Vol. 7, LBJ Library.
8. Geyelin, *Lyndon B. Johnson and the World*, p. 172. Bundy does not specifically recall that this was done, or that it was not done (private conversation, January 22, 1986).
9. Transcript, Harlan Cleveland Oral History Interview, 8/13/69, by Paige E. Mulhollan, Tape 1, p. 37f., LBJ Library.
10. John Silard, "The Multilateral Force: The Case Against," p. 18.
11. Wilson, *A Personal Record*, p. 49.
12. Ibid., p. 50.
13. Barnes, "The Nuclear Non-Proliferation Treaty," p. 243; Rostow, *Diffusion of Power*, p. 393.
14. Memorandum, Bundy to Ambassador Bruce, 12/9/64, National Security File, MLF General, Vol. 3, LBJ Library.
15. Bundy to President, 12/16/64, National Security File, Memos to the President—McGeorge Bundy, Vol. 7, LBJ Library.
16. Transcript, Harlan Cleveland Oral History Interview, 8/13/69, by Paige E. Mulhollan, Tape 1, p. 38, LBJ Library.
17. Bundy to Vance, 2/2/65, National Security File, Agency File, Department of Defense, Vol. 2, LBJ Library.
18. Barnes, "The Nuclear Non-Proliferation Treaty," p. 251.

13
A Tale of Two Committees

[E]ven major efforts on our part may not succeed in halting or greatly retarding the spread of nuclear weapons. But we are unanimous in our agreement that such efforts should be made.

—The Gilpatric Committee Report
January 1965

An ACDA Initiative

While leaders of Western governments were debating the merits of alternative proposals for a NATO nuclear force, a parallel discussion was continuing on the closely related matter of a nonproliferation treaty. Well before the Chinese nuclear test of October 1964 focused world attention on the proliferation problem, the ACDA had been strongly advocating such a treaty within the government.

On June 15, 1964, Adrian Fisher wrote a comprehensive memorandum to Secretary of State Rusk conveying ACDA's recommendations on what should be done to advance the cause of nonproliferation, giving particular attention to the relation of that issue to the MLF negotiations. He noted that nonproliferation was "a basic tenet of American foreign policy," and that the decision to move forward with the MLF was not at variance with that policy. Rather "it was intended to support our nonproliferation policy in the light of the growing nuclear ambitions of the Federal Republic." Nevertheless, the two undertakings were in conflict because of Soviet objections to the MLF. This had caused some to advocate relaxation of the nonproliferation efforts pending the conclusion and early implementation of an MLF treaty. Fisher felt this would be a mistake that "might well result in our foreclosing our last chances to close the floodgates to national proliferation and in the process create conditions which would render the MLF ineffective or even dangerous as an instrument of U.S. foreign policy."

Fisher pointed out that what we did or seemed likely to do regarding the MLF would have a significant bearing on the course of other potential nuclear powers, particularly "states now poised at the point of decision." (He named Israel, Sweden, and India.) If any of those states moved toward a nuclear weapon in the next few years, Fisher continued, it seemed inescapable "that the Germans would not remain content with MLF participation . . . for under such circumstances there would be strong forces to argue that Germany would remain a second class nation so long as she had less nuclear capability than Israel or Sweden or India, however small that capability might be." Therefore, Fisher concluded that it might be necessary "to balance some discomfort to the implementation of the MLF" in order not to delay too long the efforts to get a general nonproliferation agreement.

Fisher's memorandum concluded with four recommendations: (1) that at the time an MLF came into being, its nonnuclear participants commit themselves not to acquire a weapons capability; (2) that U.S. officials be instructed to emphasize our firm opposition to proliferation; (3) that we inform the Soviet Union that we were willing to go forward with a nonproliferation agreement without the participation of China; and (4) that "as soon as MLF negotiations [were] assured, the U.S. should, as a matter of highest priority, initiate an intensified effort to obtain a world-wide nonproliferation agreement."

Fisher's memo was discussed briefly at the end of a Committee of Principals meeting on June 16, 1964. Somewhat surprisingly the discussion indicated that nonproliferation was still not an agreed-upon object of U.S. policy. (The following account is based both on my diary and a sanitized version of the minutes of the meeting, obtained from the Department of Energy's archives.)

Rusk questioned whether we would be prepared to have a general nonproliferation agreement without the participation of China. He recalled that at one time the West Germans had conditioned their participation on China's and felt that previous expressions of interest by the Soviets might have been designed to bring pressure on the Chinese. Also, Rusk said, going ahead without China might cause problems with Congress. Fisher thought that China could be handled much as in the case of the Limited Test Ban Treaty, that we could continue to bring international pressure on the Chinese to adopt a sane nuclear policy even after they tested a nuclear weapon.

Rusk then said *he wasn't sure we might not want to give India and Japan nuclear weapons after China attained them.* He suggested that instead of trying to negotiate a general treaty right away we ask individual nations to sign a "letter of intent" about such a treaty, but without formal commitment. This would provide each country with a clue to the intentions of others and would provide us with an indication of how many nations would join us and who would be missing. Several attendees indicated concurrence with this approach. (In spite of this agreement, there did not appear to be any later follow-up of this idea.) Rusk felt that nonproliferation was an area in which there might be sufficient community of interest with the Soviet Union to obtain an agreement.

Rusk and others objected to Fisher's recommendation that MLF members be asked to make nonacquisition declarations that would not at that time be required of others. It was agreed that Fisher would redraft the statement of the U.S. government position on nonproliferation based on the discussion at this meeting.

The Thompson Committee

The inability to reach a definite U.S. policy on nonproliferation presented a very unsatisfactory situation because the subject was clearly heating up on the international scene. The heads of state of the Organization of African Unity (OAU), at their summit conference held in Cairo July 17–24, 1964, declared their "readiness to undertake, through an agreement to be concluded under United Nations auspices, not to manufacture or control nuclear weapons" and called for an international conference to conclude such an agreement. This proposal was in part unacceptable to the United States because we feared such a large conference could get out of control. We preferred the ENDC as a forum for discussion of the nonproliferation problem. In addition, intelligence reports through the summer indicated that China's first nuclear test was imminent. This brought urgently into focus the question of India's nuclear intentions.

In addition, both the OAU conference and India had indicated an intent to introduce nonproliferation resolutions at the UN General Assembly scheduled to start on December 7, 1964. These resolutions contained clauses that were inconsistent not only with the MLF but also with existing NATO defense arrangements. For example, some of the proposals would have forbidden the transit of nuclear weapons across national boundaries. It was further expected that the Soviet

Union would use the General Assembly as a platform from which to launch strong attacks on the MLF.

Beset with all these problems and uncertainties, Secretary Rusk decided in late August to establish an intragovernmental committee to consider how the United States ought to proceed in the nonproliferation arena, with special attention to the problem of India. The panel's membership was basically that of the Committee of Deputies. However, Llewellyn Thompson was designated chairman in place of Adrian Fisher, the Deputies' usual head, and the group thereupon became known as the Thompson Committee. Two officials were added, moreover: Henry Owen, the chairman of the State Department's policy planning staff, a stronghold of pro-MLF sentiment; and Phillips Talbot, the assistant secretary of state for Middle East and South Asian affairs, to speak to the particular concern about India.

While the Thompson Committee was deliberating, the nonproliferation problem faced by the United States was compounded. A summit conference of heads of nonaligned states adopted a resolution similar to that previously endorsed by the OAU and, additionally, recommended establishment of denuclearized zones in Europe and "the oceans of the world." Then, on October 16, the long-awaited Chinese test took place.

On November 12, 1964, Foster transmitted a report by Thompson's group to the Committee of Principals. The problem addressed by Foster's memo and the committee's report was how to devise tactics that would effectively support the movement toward a nonproliferation agreement, show the United States in a favorable light in relation to that movement, and at the same time ward off UN resolutions that attacked, or were inconsistent with, the MLF. (The Thompson Committee's report was written before President Johnson backed away from aggressive advocacy of the MLF at the time of the Wilson visit in December 1964.)

To meet this situation, the Thompson Committee recommended that the United States undertake a series of tactical maneuvers, namely:

1. Induce an appropriate UN member, "probably Ireland," to introduce a nonproliferation resolution the United States could accept.

2. Induce another appropriate UN member, "preferably a nonaligned state," to introduce a procedural resolution remanding to the ENDC all resolutions unacceptable to the United States.

3. Strongly oppose any resolutions or amendments hostile to the MLF.

The committee's report included sample resolutions of the type it was hoped the "appropriate UN members" might be induced to sponsor.

The committee wanted the resolutions we favored to be introduced by others because they "would gain wider acceptance among the neutral countries if the United States were not openly associated" with them. The reason for wanting uncongenial resolutions referred to the ENDC was that it was thought we could gain a more favorable vote in that body than in the General Assembly or in the UN Disarmament Commission, where Third World countries unsympathetic to some of our positions had commanding numbers.

The recommendations of the Thompson Committee provide an illustration of how the United States at times, to use Alva Myrdal's words, plays "the game of disarmament."[1] It is something we continually, and with justice, accuse the adversary of doing. But in truth we both do it.

In transmitting the Thompson Committee's report to the Principals, Foster remarked that it was "based on the assumption that it remains U.S. policy to prevent or curtail proliferation of national nuclear capabilities." When the Principals considered the report on November 23, however, Dean Rusk again questioned this assumption.

> Rusk said he thought a basic question was whether we really should have a nonproliferation policy prescribing that no countries beyond the present five might acquire nuclear weapons. Were we clear that this should be a major objective of U.S. policy? For example, might we not want to be in a position where India or Japan would be able to respond with nuclear weapons to a Chinese threat? Rusk mentioned the possibility of having an Asian group of nuclear weapon countries, pointing out that the real issue was among Asian countries and not between northern countries and the Asians.
>
> McNamara thought it would take decades for India or Japan to have any appreciable deterrent strength. Nevertheless, he thought the question Rusk had raised should be studied. He pointed out that adoption of a nonproliferation policy by the United States might require us to guarantee the security of nations that renounced nuclear weapons.

I expressed doubt that a policy condoning further proliferation should be considered, saying that, once a process of
making exceptions was started, we would lose control and that
this would inevitably lead to serious trouble.

Foster somewhat impatiently pointed out that while valid
points were being made in this discussion, the United States
would be faced with a number of resolutions when the General
Assembly convened in less than two weeks and we had to be
ready with some course of action. Rusk then suggested that we
continue the discussion on the assumption that U.S. policy favored nonproliferation. He thought the basic policy issue of
whether this should indeed be our policy ought to be settled
by about January.

Bundy warned about the need to keep very quiet the fact
that we were discussing the basic question of whether U.S. policy should be nonproliferation, because everyone assumed that
this was our policy. [It had already been so stated by the president
on several occasions, the most recent having been a TV speech less
than a week before.] Any intimation to the contrary would be
very disturbing throughout the world. McNamara added that
we had to stop the leaks that came out of meetings like this.
He agreed with Bundy that the fact that the U.S. commitment
to nonproliferation was being questioned simply must not be
allowed to leak.

When Bundy and McNamara cautioned against leaks about the
U.S. policy debate on nonproliferation, and when Rusk suggested that
the issue might be settled by January, they had more in mind than
the discussion of the Thompson Committee's recommendations. Occurring at this same time was a much more thoroughgoing examination of these same issues by a much more prestigious group.

The Gilpatric Committee

Initiation

In the immediate aftermath of the Chinese nuclear test, amid the
resulting alarm about the further spread of nuclear weapons, President Johnson decided to appoint a special panel of distinguished citizens to advise him on how the United States should approach the
proliferation problem. The November 1, 1964, announcement of the
panel's appointment stated that the president had asked the group
"to explore the widest range of measures that the United States might

undertake in conjunction with other governments or by itself" to limit the spread of nuclear weapons.

Appointed as chairman was Roswell L. Gilpatric, who had been deputy secretary of defense from the beginning of the Kennedy administration until January 1964, and the panel thereafter became familiarly known as the Gilpatric Committee.* The president was reported to have told Gilpatric that "humanity cannot tolerate a step-by-step spread of nuclear weapons," and that while the problem was difficult in 1964, it would be more so in 1974.[2]

Also appointed to the committee were:

Former Defense Secretary Robert A. Lovett;

Former Secretary of State Dean Acheson;

Former White House National Security Adviser John J. McCloy;

Former disarmament negotiator Arthur H. Dean;

Former White House Science Adviser George B. Kistiakowsky;

James A. Perkins, president of Cornell University;

Former Director of Defense Research and Engineering Herbert F. York;

Former CIA Director Allen W. Dulles;

IBM Chairman Arthur K. Watson;

William Webster, president of the New England Electric System,† and

General Alfred B. Gruenther, former military commander of NATO.

It was as distinguished a group as one could reasonably have expected to assemble at that time. Although none of its members was currently a government employee, the committee was supported by a staff of highly placed and very talented individuals from within the

---

*Its formal name was the President's Task Force on Preventing the Spread of Nuclear Weapons.

†I personally recruited Webster and persuaded Bundy to have him added to the committee. Knowing that nuclear power might take some hits as a potential contributor to proliferation, the AEC wanted someone on the committee who could speak accurately on that subject.

government under the direction of Spurgeon Keeny, Jr, who held at that time the lengthy title of National Security Council staff representative for arms control and military technology.* AEC Commissioner John Palfrey was a member of this staff.

Because the panel was announced just two days before the presidential election, some dismissed it as an election-year gimmick.† The committee obviously did not share this view of itself, setting to work in a most searching and vigorous manner.

Plenary Meetings

The Gilpatric Committee held three plenary meetings: the first on December 1, 1964; the second on December 13 and 14, 1964; and the third on January 7 and 8, 1965. Before the first meeting, and in the interim between meetings, Gilpatric and the staff kept busy conferring with key individuals about some of the principal issues. On November 27, for example, Commissioner Palfrey and I had lunch with Gilpatric to discuss whether the U.S. dissemination of nuclear materials, equipment, and information under the Atoms for Peace Program constituted a dangerous stimulus to weapons proliferation. My diary records that we offered the standard AEC defense of Atoms for Peace:

> We described the program and the irrationality of trying to stop or curtail it in view of U.S. commitments and the efforts of other nations to sell reactors without safeguards as stringent as those imposed by us.

In his opening comments at the December 1 plenary meeting, Gilpatric established the group's tasks.[3] They would, he said, "be concerned with studying several conflicting strands of policy" and seeking to harmonize them, or at least to understand their likely consequences. Such a review was necessary, he said, "in view of the absence of any regular and effective mechanism in Government, aside from the Committee of Principals, for reflective discussion of conflicts between various agency interests and programs affecting prolifera-

---

*Keeny is now (1986) president and executive director of the Arms Control Association.

†There may have been something to this accusation in the sense that Gilpatric was given only a few days after his appointment to pull together a core group of members in time for a presidential announcement on November 1. It was some time after the election before the committee was fully constituted.

tion." He then stated a key question: "whether nuclear proliferation may not be inevitable and in some cases even desirable." A U.S. policy on this had to be determined. The committee needed also to take a position on some closely related issues: on the MLF, on a comprehensive test ban, on peaceful uses of atomic energy, on export controls, and on the dispersal and control of U.S. weapons. Thus, the committee's mandate, as its chairman saw it, was broad indeed.

At the end of the first plenary meeting the committee met with President Johnson in the Cabinet Room of the White House. The minutes state that the president "emphasized his personal concern with . . . proliferation, reaffirmed his desire to work toward an international agreement . . . , and indicated his desire to benefit from the judgment of the committee."

At the third plenary meeting the committee members were given an opportunity to state their individual conclusions on a single basic question: Should the United States strive for a world in which there would be no additional nuclear weapon countries—referred to in the discussion as "Model A"—or should the United States countenance a world in which there would be a limited amount of further proliferation—referred to as "Model B." The issue had been propounded in this form by McNamara. The circumstances were explained in a memorandum from McCloy to Gilpatric:[4]

> [I]t has been generally assumed that a world in which there was non-proliferation of nuclear weapons was more desirable, at least from the point of view of the United States, than a world in which there was a proliferation of such weapons. Mr. McNamara has suggested that perhaps the assumption should be examined and that the general acceptance of the desirability of non-proliferation may be more instinctive than analytical. He has further suggested that it might be the duty of this Committee to look deeper into the question than the Government has thus far done, if only to give consideration to the price we might be willing to pay for non-proliferation if we find it to be desirable. The significance of proliferated guarantees which might be an incident of a series of non-proliferation agreements is one of the elements which has to be weighed in trying to arrive at a conclusion.

In raising this question, McNamara may have been playing devil's advocate, responding to the sort of doubts that, as we have noted, had been expressed by Rusk on more than one occasion. McNamara's own clear preference, as he expressed it to the committee, was for Model A.

When the committee met to consider the issue, Gilpatric also stated his preference for Model A, "finding it implausible that additional proliferation could be compartmentalized, quarantined, or regionalized." Webster favored taking all steps necessary to slow proliferation on a case-by-case basis. Thus, he felt he was nearer to Model A than to Model B. McCloy, on the other hand, thought a guarantee of others' security might be too high a price for the United States to pay for a Model A world. Dulles thought we should begin with efforts to hold proliferation where it was and then seek targets of opportunity to roll it back; this was Model A and then some. Watson thought Model A was the preferred solution, but he was puzzled how we could achieve it without the cooperation of France. Kistiakowsky said that thoughts about his grandchildren committed him strongly to support Model A. Dean and General Gruenther both indicated that they had changed their original views to become supporters of Model A. York also came out strongly for Model A. He said guarantees were possible but that the United States must also be able to withdraw from them, if necessary. Staff director Keeny believed that the net security advantage for the United States rested with Model A.

Thus, three weeks before its report to the president was due, a majority of the committee clearly favored a policy of preventing any further proliferation, but with different degrees of enthusiasm, and not without misgivings.

The Written Report

The Gilpatric Committee Report, drafted mainly by Keeny, was delivered to President Johnson at a White House meeting on January 21, 1965.* What was probably its most basic finding was announced at the very start of the document:

> We have noted a significant diversity of views within the Government about the feasibility of preventing nuclear proliferation, and consequently about appropriate policies for the United States. Among ourselves there was also a diversity of opinions at the outset of our study. As a result of our study, however, the Committee is now

---

*Large portions of the report are still considered classified. References herein are to a sanitized version obtained pursuant to a request under the Freedom of Information Act.

unanimous in its view that preventing the further spread of nuclear weapons is clearly in the national interest despite the difficult decisions that will be required. We have concluded, therefore, that the United States must, as a matter of great urgency, substantially increase the scope and intensity of our efforts if we are to have any hope of success. Necessarily, these efforts must be of three kinds: (a) negotiation of formal multilateral agreements; (b) the application of influence on individual nations considering nuclear weapons acquisition, by ourselves and in conjunction with others; and (c) example of our own policies and actions.

The report followed with an analysis of how further proliferation would threaten U.S. security. It would "add complexity and instability to the deterrent balance" between the superpowers, aggravate regional suspicions and hostility, diminish U.S. influence, and cause strong pressures within the country "to retreat to isolation to avoid the risk of involvement in nuclear war." But isolation would be no protection, because there "would be additional nuclear powers—perhaps some in this hemisphere—individually possessing the capability of destroying millions of American lives. Major defensive efforts [a reference to the budding ABM controversy] might . . . diminish such limited threats, but millions of American lives would always be at risk."

The idea of countenancing Indian or Japanese acquisition of nuclear weapons, which Rusk had flirted with, was specifically rejected; the spread could not be stopped there; a chain reaction spreading into Europe could follow.

The report noted that the proliferation problem affected a broad range of U.S. interests and policies, including peaceful atomic energy programs, and argued that "those areas of interest, as well as the agencies of Government which deal with them, . . . must give nonproliferation policies far greater weight and support than . . . in the past." (I had no doubt that this sentence looked in the AEC's direction.)

An issue that was to loom large in the future was next identified: "[I]t is unlikely that others can be induced to abstain indefinitely from acquiring nuclear weapons if the Soviet Union and the United States continue in a nuclear arms race." To meet this problem, the report recommended lessened superpower emphasis on nuclear weapons, and agreements with the Soviet Union on broader arms control measures.

The committee sensed that the time was ripe for this reorientation of policy and that a major effort by the United States might succeed.

The report observed that there was broad support among nations for a multilateral agreement, that the Soviet Union probably shared a strong interest in the problem, and that the USSR's recent change in leadership provided an opportunity. The committee acknowledged that

> even major efforts on our part may not be successful. . . . But we are unanimous in our agreement that such efforts should be made. The rewards of long-term success would be enormous; and even partial success would be worth the costs we can expect to incur.

The report concluded with an enumeration of specific recommendations, most of which were implicit in the preceding discussion. First and foremost was "to seek the early conclusion of the widest and most effective possible international agreement on non-dissemination and non-acquisition of nuclear weapons." Significantly, the committee added: "Our initiatives in this area should not wait, or be dependent upon, the resolution of any issues relating to an Atlantic nuclear force, however helpful such resolution might be."

Largely based on a report in *The New York Times* of July 1, 1965, there was a public impression that the commission had confronted head-on the matter of choosing between an NPT and the MLF, and had recommended that the latter be abandoned. It probably did not go quite that far, but it may have come close. The sanitized version now available to researchers contains the following passage:

> [A]ny conflict between our non-proliferation and [NATO Nuclear Force] objectives may not become critical until the future of the MLF/ANF is known; but if it arises before then, the priorities of the two proposals with respect to our overall national security should be carefully reviewed.

Other specific recommendations in the report included a litany of the measures being espoused by arms control enthusiasts at home and abroad, namely, a comprehensive test ban; Latin American and African nuclear-free zones; a cutoff of nuclear materials production; a freeze on strategic vehicles; a reexamination of our policies shutting China out of the society of nations; strong safeguards for all peaceful atomic energy programs; efforts to strengthen the International Atomic Energy Agency; and revision of NATO strategy to give greater relative emphasis to nonnuclear weapons.

Appended to the written report was a draft of a National Security Action Memorandum that the committee recommended the president send to all the principal officers of the government involved with arms control policy, basically the membership of the Committee of Principals. The draft began with this statement: "It is the policy of the United States to prevent the proliferation of nuclear weapons to the control of other nations." Referring to the new, more urgent situation created by the Chinese test, it stated: "[W]e must take immediate steps on a broad front to intensify and expand our efforts to implement our non-proliferation policy." Then followed these key sentences, a veiled reference to the MLF:

> There will be instances where the objective of preventing proliferation may conflict with other United States objectives. In the resolution of such conflicts, I desire that our non-proliferation policy receive substantially more weight than has been the case in the past.

The remainder of the NSAM was taken up with an enumeration of the steps that the committee wanted the president to order, beginning with a nonproliferation agreement, and continuing with the other actions the committee had recommended in the body of its report.

Of particular interest to the AEC was this statement: "Every effort shall be made to assure that peaceful atomic energy programs do not unreasonably contribute to potential proliferation of nuclear weapon capabilities." This was another signal to us that the arms control community looked at the peaceful atom with a dubious eye.

Before the report was presented to the president, Gilpatric asked each member of the committee to affix his signature to it. This procedure, unusual in government report practice, was a way of emphasizing to the president that the members had all participated in the work of the committee and that each and every one stood behind the report.

Presentation to the President

The January 21, 1965, meeting at which the report was presented to President Johnson was attended by Vice President Humphrey, Secretaries Rusk and McNamara, Joint Chiefs Chairman Earle G. Wheeler, CIA Director McCone, ACDA Director Foster, Science Adviser Donald Hornig, Under Secretary of State George Ball, myself, and all the members of the Gilpatric Committee.

Gilpatric led off by saying it was appropriate that this discussion should take place as one of the first items following the previous day's Inauguration. He told the president that the Committee was now placing the report before him and that it was a unanimous one. He then summarized the report's findings on the importance of a nonproliferation policy for the United States.

Various members of the committee next took the floor to present other conclusions in the report that were of particular importance to them. Dean spoke urgently about the necessity of negotiating a comprehensive test ban. Kistiakowsky spoke on what our policy should be toward non-nuclear weapons states—we should not contribute to their ability to make nuclear weapons. McCloy cautioned against downplaying the problems of the Atlantic Alliance.*

Perkins urged that we encourage the U.K. and France to turn over their nuclear weapons to a NATO force, and that China be brought into the UN within ten years. General Gruenther recommended that the United States strike a better balance between the nuclear and non-nuclear components of its forces.

At this point the president commented sardonically that it seemed like implementation of the committee's report would be "a very pleasant undertaking." [This comment may have indicated that the president had already become somewhat disenchanted with the sweeping nature of the committee's recommendations.]

Gilpatric then said that this was all of the report's recommendations that would be presented orally. Other matters included in it he would leave to a reading of the report itself.

The rest of the meeting was taken up with a discussion of implementation. Gilpatric thought it very important that follow-up be by the president himself and that it not be delegated. The president responded that this subject matter would consume a great deal of his personal attention. He asked Rusk to have a government group make a report on the recommendations. [I am not aware that anything of this sort was ever done.] He commended Gilpatric for this additional evidence of his patriotism and said he would confer with him as the governmental evaluation went forward. [I don't think this was done either.] Johnson continued that, despite the landslide victory in Novem-

---

*Keeny recalls that other members of the committee were somewhat irritated by McCloy's presentation. He took more than his allotted share of the available time and addressed a subject that was somewhat off the committee's main topic. (Private conversation, November 24, 1986.)

ber and the pleasant sunshine on the previous day's Inauguration, not everything on the horizon was pleasant.*

The president asked Rusk, McNamara and Bundy to comment. Rusk said that *the report was as explosive as a nuclear weapon* and that its premature disclosure could start the ball rolling in an undesirable manner. The president emphasized the need to prevent any leaks to newspapers. Rusk said that such items as nonproliferation and arms limitation consumed more discussion time with the Russians than all other topics combined. He observed that we could have an agreement on nonproliferation by 6 P.M.—it was then about 2 P.M.—if we would abandon the MLF, and that this was an area in which we might have to make a choice.

Bundy said that the report should be handled on a personal basis by the Principals only and not be shown to anyone else in their organizations. The president again reiterated the need to guard against newspaper leaks. He mentioned that he had FBI reports of government people talking to columnists under what appeared to be unauthorized circumstances. He said there would be a short release for the press but *there must be no mention of the existence of a written report*. The press then came in and took a number of pictures of the group.

I received my copy of the committee's report the following day. It came with a specific directive from the president that I was not to show it to anyone, not even my fellow commissioners. This was awkward and embarrassing for me because it was not the way we did business at the AEC. I was but one commissioner of several, a chief among equals, not an executive head.†

It is not easy to cast oneself back in time to reconstruct the reasons for the extraordinary secrecy, or the reasons why the report was considered, in Dean Rusk's words, "as explosive as a nuclear weapon." Very likely a principal factor was what the report had to say about

---

*George Ball, who saw the president from time to time during this period, reported that he seemed a very troubled man. Within less than three weeks the United States would begin its major escalation in Vietnam, bombing targets in the North and reinforcing U.S. forces in the South.

†There was much sentiment during this period and throughout the remainder of the AEC's life for converting it from a commission form to an agency with a single head, but such a move was consistently, and effectively, opposed by the Joint Committee. When the AEC was split up in 1974, the commissioners went with the regulatory arm (Nuclear Regulatory Commission); the remaining functions, grouped in the Energy Research and Development Administration, precursor of the present Department of Energy, were placed under a single administrator.

the NPT/MLF controversy, strongly suggesting that the United States throw its weight behind the movement for a worldwide nonproliferation treaty and give only secondary priority to alliance nuclear arrangements. Thus, on the day the report was submitted, Bundy wrote to the president that Dean Rusk was "very much opposed" to its principal conclusion.[5]

Notwithstanding the secrecy, existence of the report soon became common knowledge and pressures appeared for its release. This pressure was increased by Robert Kennedy's maiden speech to the Senate on June 23, 1965. The speech had been long awaited and was greeted by maximum publicity—*The New York Times* printed its entire text. Some of Kennedy's recommendations were like those in the Gilpatric Committee Report in both substance and wording, and he specifically urged that the work of the committee "be carried forward by all agencies of the Government at once." Without criticizing President Johnson directly, Kennedy alleged that "we have not ourselves done all we can" to obtain a nonproliferation treaty.

> The day following Kennedy's speech I travelled with the president to San Francisco, where he spoke at ceremonies commemorating the establishment of the United Nations twenty years before. One of the subjects I discussed with the president en route was the Gilpatric Report. I said that as a result of Presidential Press Secretary George Reedy's announcement at a press conference that there was a written report and that it was in the hands of various agencies—Reedy had mentioned the AEC—the Joint Committee had requested a copy from us. The president's first suggestion was that we not give them a copy but say it was an oral report and that the only written material was a compilation of notes. [On June 28, I relayed this to Bundy who said it was no longer possible to describe the Gilpatric Report as an oral report and that he would discuss this with the president. Bundy also agreed, however, that we should not give a copy to the JCAE but merely say that the disposition of this report to the president was up to the president.]
>
> The president then showed me a copy of the speech he was to give in San Francisco. I was surprised and disappointed that AEC-written passages on scientists providing a common ground between nations and extolling the IAEA, which were present in earlier drafts, had been omitted. White House assistant Horace Busby then told me in confidence that the material had been deleted at the last moment, along with some words about

halting nuclear spread, because the president had been annoyed by Kennedy's speech, which contained some of the same
language as had been in the president's speech draft. Busby
thought this material and the Gilpatric Report must have been
leaked to Kennedy by the State Department and Bill Foster.
Later in the flight the president asked me how I liked his speech
and I was somewhat noncommittal, saying that I liked a section
where he referred to the prospects of a better future through
science. He then asked, somewhat annoyed, "Is that the only
part you liked?" The audience at the San Francisco Opera House
also seemed disappointed by the president's speech and this
seemed to annoy the president further.

Although President Johnson was irate about Robert Kennedy's
address to the Senate, it did appear to sting him into taking action of
a sort. On June 28, five days after Kennedy's speech, the White House
issued National Security Action Memorandum 335, directing the
ACDA to come up with a new arms control program that would
include means to prevent the spread of nuclear weapons.[6] This seems
to have been the president's belated way of responding to Kennedy's
criticism that he had failed to implement the Gilpatric Report, which,
as we have noted, urged an NSAM, albeit a more pointed and specific
one. NSAM 335 did not seem to have any marked effect on the
government's business. The ACDA already had the duty that the president urged it to exercise, and I observed no special measures of implementation following the president's directive. As for the president
himself, it would be more than a year before he became actively and
decisively involved in the pursuit of a nonproliferation treaty.

The issuance of NSAM 335 was not publicly revealed, so it did
nothing to ease the public pressures on the president about the Gilpatric Committee Report. The situation was exacerbated further on
July 1, when *The New York Times* carried a long article, which began
with the following lead sentence:

A top-secret report to President Johnson is understood to have recommended that a treaty to halt the spread of nuclear weapons be
given priority over the establishment of an Atlantic nuclear force.

The *Times* article continued with references to the secrecy surrounding the report and with a discussion of the MLF controversy
and its relation to NPT negotiations. It was then stated that Robert

Kennedy's call for giving nonproliferation greater emphasis in U.S. policy "closely parallelled the Gilpatric panel's findings."

The publicity resulting from Kennedy's speech and the *Times* article brought fresh pressure on President Johnson to release the report. On July 2:

> I received a telephone call from Charles Johnson, White House. He said that Bundy and Gilpatric had looked again at the report, at the president's request, to see whether any part of it could be released. They concluded, and the president concurred, that nothing could be said publicly about the report, nor could it be used in any way. He, Charles Johnson, reported further that Senator Clinton Anderson, a leading member of the Joint Committee, was very unhappy about not having been brought into this, and that Bundy would so advise the president, who might invite Anderson to the White House. I told Johnson we might have a similar problem with other members of the Joint Committee as well. I asked him the official position about acknowledging the existence of the report because Bundy, in an earlier conversation, had hesitated to suggest denying its existence. Johnson said that I should say "no comment" if queried, since that was what both McNamara and Foster planned to do.

Impact

The extraordinary secrecy had predictable consequences. In the months that followed its issuance, I would not hear the Gilpatric Committee Report cited within the administration as an argument for or against any particular course of action. The work of the government in the committee's subject area seemed to go forward as though the report had never been written. The time and conscientious effort of distinguished private citizens and a superbly qualified government staff were thus to a large extent wasted.*

---

*I hasten to add that there is another view on the Gilpatric Report's impact. Spurgeon Keeny contends that although President Johnson wasn't kindled to immediate action by the report, it was nevertheless very significant in sowing the intellectual soil for future actions. It was indeed the most thorough exposure to nonproliferation issues that the president had yet received, and perhaps the first time he had focused on the subject in depth for any length of time. Keeny also observes that Johnson could not but have been impressed by the unanimity of view of these "big name establishment people" on the importance of taking purposeful action on nonproliferation. The report therefore marked, in Keeny's view, a point of departure, the time when Johnson "lost his innocence" about nonproliferation, and a significant preparation for the critical moment, more than a year later (chapter 15), when he had to decide whether to push ahead with nonproliferation despite opposition from our allies. (Private conversation with Spurgeon Keeny, November 24, 1986.)

I have recently had occasion to examine again a sanitized version of the report, obtained through the Freedom of Information Act. (Under our dubious classification policies, some parts of this twenty-two-year-old document are still considered unsuitable for public viewing.) It is a tightly reasoned, well-crafted presentation of the arms control point of view. Much of what the committee recommended would, within three years, become national policy. McNamara called it "as good a report done on a short time scale as any I've seen since coming to Washington."

A fitting epitaph for the committee might be found in a handwritten letter that General Gruenther sent to Bundy from his Washington apartment following the meeting on January 21, 1965:

> During the past eight years I have served on a number of Governmental Commissions. I don't believe there has been a better Chairman than Ros Gilpatric. He has everything. Then there was the size of the Committee, ten. That is about ideal. Most have been too large. . . . Next, the Committee was a wise one. . . . I have never served with a more knowledgeable group. Finally, the staff, headed by Spurgeon [Keeny] was tops. . . . It should follow that the Committee eased the job of the President. I fear that was not the case. . . .[7]

The Tuesday Lunch

On July 3, 1965, Bundy included the following in a note to the president:

> In the light of the fact that the Gilpatric Panel has not worked out to your satisfaction, I want to be quite sure that our next efforts in this critically important field are along lines you approve.[8]

As Bundy now recalls it,[9] Johnson's dissatisfaction with the committee was not based on anything deeply substantive, but rather on the fact that the press leaks and the public discussion by Bobby Kennedy and others tended to deprive the president of control over "what happened next." Nor was the standing of the report with the president helped by the fact that Gilpatric himself was thought to have assisted Kennedy in preparation of his June 23 speech, at least to the extent of reviewing it before it was delivered. (Whether because of this circumstance or for other reasons, Johnson came to have what Bundy describes as "a very dim view" of Gilpatric.)

To allow a highly publicized group like the Gilpatric Committee to have a perceptible influence on policy was simply contrary to President Johnson's style. For reasons bound up with his complex psychological makeup, Johnson needed to be, or at least to appear to be, in control of events. He also seemed disinclined to admit large numbers of people into the policymaking process, especially if they were people he did not know. In this he was quite unlike President Kennedy. Kennedy had seemed to be stimulated by the give and take in large discussion groups. Someone characterized his approach as "government by seminar." Johnson seemed to prefer dealing with a very limited number of trusted advisers.[10]

Johnson's preference gave rise to a new institution for considering important foreign policy and national security matters: the Tuesday lunch. At the outset attendance at the lunches was limited to the president, the secretaries of state and defense, and the national security adviser. Later on, the chairman of the Joint Chiefs, the CIA director, and the White House press secretary were added, with the latter's deputy present as note-taker.[11] The lunches began in February 1964. During Johnson's first three years in office there were periods when they were held regularly; then they would be suspended for a while, as during the heat of the 1964 electoral campaign. Beginning in January 1967, however, the meetings were convened an average of four out of every five weeks. They were generally well-organized affairs, with an agenda and briefing papers prepared in advance, although the discussion might ramble depending on the president's mood. Although Vietnam inevitably became the most frequent topic, the subject matter discussed at the lunches extended over the whole range of U.S. foreign and national security policy.

David Humphrey, who has studied the Tuesday lunches carefully, states that they soon came to surpass National Security Council meetings in significance. The latter became less and less frequent and tended to become "a forum for briefing members but not for actually consulting them."[12] As William Bundy expressed it: "[A] number of the NSC meetings were . . . simply recitals. . . . You knew nothing was going to be decided. . . . The Secretary of State would recite, and the Secretary of Defense would recite. . . . [I]t really wasn't the nitty-gritty."[13]

One reason why the president valued the Tuesday lunch was because he could be assured that it would not produce that, for him, abomination of abominations, the leak. By contrast, he felt that NSC meetings were "like sieves." Another reason was that Johnson had a strong preference for dealing with persons whose points of view were compatible with his own and of whose loyalty he felt assured. As Richard Helms points out, attendance at NSC meetings was established by custom. The statute establishing the NSC dictated the presence of certain individuals. Through the years others had been invited and had become accustomed to attending.[14] The Tuesday lunch apparatus gave Johnson the opportunity to invite to lunch those members of the NSC with whom he wanted to deliberate, and to exclude the others.

Participants have praised the Tuesday lunches for the opportunity it gave them to speak candidly. Bromley Smith noted that "even Dean Rusk" would speak frankly in these meetings.[15] Others, however, have criticized the institution on various accounts. William Bundy thought it was "an abomination . . . in all bluntness, because it was so unstructured, so without any opportunity to know what might be discussed. There was no preparation. And there was almost no readout."[16] As *The Washington Post* expressed it, there was "an inadequate upflow of ideas and an inadequate downflow of results."[17] But Bromley Smith counters:

> Such meetings make the staff miserable because they're not participants—the middle level bureaucrats will attack any system which does not give them a full readout or get something in the record that is meaningful to them. I understand their point of view but, being terribly biased toward the presidency, [I feel] this is a price they ought to be willing to pay. . . . The criticism of the Tuesday lunch comes not from those who participated in them. . . . It was useful to them. And, frankly, in the modern world, I am not too unhappy that the middle-range bureaucrats are unhappy, except insofar as they talk to the press and that may jeopardize the president's image.[18]

There was another danger, however. By speaking only to men who agreed with him, and only on topics of his choice, the president may have unwittingly shielded himself from difficult decisions, unpleasant news, and some of the larger considerations that should enter into the making of policy. As people who were disquieted about his policies left the government (Ball, McNamara, Moyers, Bundy), generally with the president's tacit encouragement, the Johnson administration began more and more to take on some characteristics of a court—a dominant figure surrounded by loyal and quiescent subjects. Although the president's own psychological needs may have brought this about, it was probably not, on balance, helpful to him. The Tuesday lunch abetted this process.[19]

Notes

1. Myrdal entitled her major book on disarmament policy: *The Game of Disarmament: How the United States and Russia Run the Arms Race* (New York: Pantheon Books, 1976).
2. *The New York Times,* November 2, 1964, p. 1.
3. Minutes of Discussion, 12/1/64, National Security File, Committee File, Committee on Nuclear Proliferation, Box 1, LBJ Library.
4. Memorandum for the Chairman, 1/8/65, National Security File, Committee File, Committee on Nuclear Proliferation, Box 1, LBJ Library.
5. Bundy to President, 1/21/65, National Security File, Memos to the President—McGeorge Bundy, Vol. 8, LBJ Library.
6. Information from George Bunn, private conversation, November 24, 1986.
7. Gruenther to Bundy, 1/21/65, National Security File, Committee on Nuclear Proliferation, Box 378, FG 643, LBJ Library.
8. Bundy to President, 7/3/65, National Security File, Memos to the President—McGeorge Bundy, Vol. 12, LBJ Library.
9. Private conversation, January 22, 1986.
10. Transcript, Richard Helms Oral History Interview, 4/4/69, by Paige E. Mulhollan, Tape 1, p. 24, LBJ Library.
11. For a careful and detailed study based on complete documentation, see Humphrey, "Tuesday Lunch at the Johnson White House."
12. Humphrey, "Tuesday Lunch," p. 85.
13. Transcript, William Bundy Oral History Interview, 6/2/69, by Paige E. Mulhollan, p. 42, LBJ Library.
14. Transcript, Richard Helms Oral History Interview, 4/4/69, by Paige E. Mulhollan, Tape 1, p. 23, LBJ Library.
15. Transcript, Bromley Smith Oral History Interview, 7/29/69, by Paige E. Mulhollan, Tape 1, p. 26, LBJ Library.
16. Transcript, William Bundy Oral History Interview, 6/2/69, by Paige E. Mulhollan, Tape 5, p. 12, LBJ Library.
17. Quoted in Humphrey, "Tuesday Lunch," p. 92.
18. Transcript, Bromley Smith Oral History Interview, 7/29/69, by Paige E. Mulhollan, Tape 1, p. 24f., LBJ Library.
19. For a strong presentation of this point of view, see Kearns, *Lyndon Johnson and the American Dream,* pp. 317–24.

14
NPT: First Draft Treaties

My nation is ready. If others are equally prepared, then we can move, with growing confidence, toward the light.
—President Johnson to the ENDC
July 1965

Rusk in Paris: "Facing a World Fact"

It seemed axiomatic that efforts to prevent proliferation could be abetted if all five nuclear powers would simply agree not to disseminate nuclear weapons or weapons technology. Based on past performance, the nations that seemed least likely to join the others in a common effort were France and China. Aside from recently initiated ambassadorial conversations in Warsaw, the United States had no diplomatic contact with China. It was possible to sound out the French, however, and in mid-December 1964 Rusk journeyed to Paris for that purpose. On December 15, he spoke to Prime Minister Pompidou; the following day to President de Gaulle. The secretary was blunt in his questioning of both men; they seemed equally candid in their answers, occasionally expressing bitterness about U.S. postwar nuclear policies, which the French felt had discriminated against them in favor of the British. The following summary of the conversations is derived from the reports cabled from the U.S. Embassy in Paris.[1]

Rusk asked Pompidou what French policy was on the question of nonproliferation. "Did France feel that other countries should be discouraged from acquiring nuclear weapons or not?" The prime minister answered that France's policy was that there should be no proliferation beyond France but the question was how could this be accomplished? "It had not been possible to prevent China acquiring nuclear weapons. It was not possible to go to war to prevent proliferation. France would not help anyone to make a nuclear bomb but that was about all she could do." Rusk suggested that "perhaps the five [nuclear powers] might agree among themselves not to pass on technical information and this was why he wanted the opinion of the French government." Pompidou answered that Rusk's suggestion might be considered "in the future." He assured the secretary that France intended to give no one any information on atomic weapons. France had tried to establish a complete blackout in this field but still did not know whether she had been as successful as the United States had been with regard to France. Rusk said that the United States had the impression that France was a little reticent about saying to others that they should not make weapons. We ourselves were not reticent. Pompidou said that the United States was the headmaster in the art and that "France was only a pupil trying hard."

The discussion with Pompidou concluded with a few words about Franco–American relations in general. Rusk said the United States was "anxious to clear up any misunderstandings." Pompidou responded "cordially." He said that "in spite of any divergencies, France remained deeply attached to the alliance with the United States." Rusk concluded by saying that we wanted to "exchange views more precisely and in more detail than hitherto. . . . It was hard to shake hands in a dark room and there was need to clarify the situation."

A sidelight of the Pompidou–Rusk conversation was a brief colloquy about Israel. The secretary said that the United States was not "one thousand percent sure" that Israel had abandoned the idea of making a bomb. Pompidou answered that France was not entirely sure about Israel either, nor about Egypt.

The talk with de Gaulle followed similar lines, but de Gaulle was more pessimistic. Rusk began by asking whether the five powers with nuclear weapons might in some way act together to limit their further spread. He was thinking, he said, of some sort of public commitment not to proliferate. Perhaps India could be induced to give up the idea of making weapons in return for suitable guarantees. Rusk suggested as a preliminary that the United States, the United Kingdom, and France get together "to see whether our three policies were aligned on the subject of nondissemination." He had not suggested this to London; he wanted first to know de Gaulle's views.

De Gaulle asked what the secretary thought could be achieved by this. Rusk thought there might emerge "a common line of policy, stricter control of use of fissionable materials, and discouraging certain governments from making bombs by exerting appropriate diplomatic influence." De Gaulle answered that the French were not about to give the bomb to anyone, nor was the United States, nor for that matter were the Chinese or the Soviet Union. However, as several other powers would probably have the means of making them in the next twenty years he did not see how we could prevent dissemination. The only way he thought we could prevent the spread of nuclear bombs was to destroy them. This could not be done. He was afraid that we were "facing a world fact." He thought nothing could be done "until the next war." Trying to prevent the nuclear bomb was like the attempts to ban the crossbow in the middle ages.

From these conversations it appeared that the nonproliferation movement would not get much help from the French.

Debate at the UNDC

Rusk may have thought it sufficient to address the proliferation problem through concerted action by the nuclear weapon powers, but those who were being asked to abjure nuclear weapons also wanted to be heard. In response to this sentiment, and prior to the recess of the UN General Assembly in February 1965, the United States proposed that the ENDC be reconvened by mid-March or early April to consider a nonproliferation treaty. After a seven-week interval, Ambassador Dobrynin notified Foster on March 30 that his government had decided instead to request a meeting of the UN Disarmament Committee (UNDC),* a body in which all 114 member states were represented. The State Department regarded the Soviet initiative mainly as a propaganda exercise, an opportunity, for example, to bludgeon the United States about the MLF. As noted in an internal White House memorandum: "historically, when the Soviets want to talk seriously about disarmament, they use the ENDC."[2] Though not enthusiastic about a UNDC session, the United States went along. UN Ambassador Stevenson said we would have preferred "a negotiating committee to a debating committee," but if other nations wanted a UNDC meeting we would "participate constructively."[3]

When the UNDC convened on April 26, 1965, the various strands of opinion regarding a possible nonproliferation treaty were well delineated for all to see. The U.S. position was to advocate an agreement

---

*The UNDC was established in 1952 by the General Assembly to combine the work previously performed by the UN Atomic Energy Commission and the UN Committee for Conventional Armaments. It reported to both the General Assembly and the Security Council. It seldom met because most UN members thought the Eighteen Nation Disarmament Committee was more likely to obtain results in this difficult field.

along the lines of the Irish resolution of 1961, whose artful use of the word "control" provided for the possibility of some form of nuclear sharing within NATO. The Soviets uncompromisingly opposed any agreement that would allow West German access to nuclear weapons "in any form whatsoever." The non-nuclear-weapon states contended that their renunciation of nuclear weapons under an NPT could have meaning only if accompanied by certain related measures indicating that the major powers intended to make "tangible progress towards disarmament." Prominently mentioned among such related measures were a comprehensive test ban, a strategic weapons freeze as suggested by President Johnson in January 1964, and a complete cutoff in the production of fissionable materials.

On June 15, 1965, after all points of view had been fully aired and debated, the UNDC passed a U.S.-sponsored resolution that called on the ENDC to reconvene, to take up the nonproliferation question as a matter of priority, and to give close attention "to the various suggestions that agreement could be facilitated by adopting a programme of certain related measures." The resolution asked that the ENDC be ready to report on its progress to the General Assembly when that body met in September. The vote was 83 to 1 (Albania), with 18 abstentions. The Soviet Union and its allies were among those who abstained, objecting that the resolution did not contain language that would bar West German "access" to nuclear weapons. The Soviet Union also registered its opposition to making nonproliferation "dependent on the solution of a whole series of other complex problems."

The Soviet abstention caused concern because it seemed to prevent the reconvening of the ENDC, of which the USSR and U.S. representatives were cochairmen. Following the June 15 vote, therefore, Foster met in New York with his Soviet counterpart, Tsarapkin, to urge that this aspect of the matter be reconsidered. On July 12, the USSR notified the United States that it was agreeable to resumption of ENDC negotiations on the previously scheduled date, July 27. This was considered sufficiently important to be announced by President Johnson. He termed it "an encouraging development."*

---

*The Soviet assent was widely interpreted as a slap at Communist China, which was advocating a militant line against the United States and opposed all negotiations (*The New York Times*, July 14, 1965).

The day following the Soviet acceptance Bundy sent the president a draft message to the ENDC, adding the following comments:

> As I said on the phone, I think it is very important for us to keep in front on the subject of disarmament. I doubt if the Geneva meeting will produce any new agreements, but it is a meeting on our terms and it is one which the Soviets have resisted. Moreover, we are all confident that we can have a sensible and cool-headed set of proposals for this meeting.
>
> We can also fend off Soviet propaganda against the MLF as long as we are smart about it.
>
> It is true that it would be good to have more time, but this kind of last-minute Soviet acceptance is a standard Russian ploy, and it would surely not be smart now for us to back away from our proposal [that the ENDC meet]. And if we are to be in a disarmament meeting at all, surely it should be under your banner and with your leadership.
>
> Right from the beginning of 1964 you have been in a strong position on this subject, and my belief is that you will want to keep the lead. And one really never knows when the Soviets may be about to make a real concession—in April of 1963 no one would have predicted a test ban treaty [agreed to three months later].[4]

Bundy's memo may have been aimed at rekindling President Johnson's interest in disarmament initiatives; this seemed to have dwindled somewhat following the president's initial burst of energy in 1964. It may also have been an early recognition by Bundy of what became only too apparent later on, that there could be little forward movement on this front without active presidential involvement.

Instructing Foster

As though to serve warning on the United States not to proceed too precipitously toward a nonproliferation agreement with the Soviets, West Germany issued an announcement on July 12 stating that, though it was not seeking to acquire nuclear weapons, it could not bind itself never to do so until its interests were secured.[5] This demarche helped set the stage for a Committee of Principals meeting convened on July 22, 1965, for the purpose of instructing Foster as to the positions he should take at the upcoming ENDC session. Remarkable at this meeting was the extent to which the MLF continued to be a sticking point in the formulation of a U.S. negotiating stance more than six months after the Johnson–Wilson summit.

> Rusk pointed out that the ENDC's opening date, July 27, 1965, would be a "hell of a day" to be making a statement on arms control because on that very day President Johnson might be announcing a significant escalation of our effort in Vietnam. [He announced it July 28.] Rusk asked Foster what he proposed to say in his opening statement. Foster suggested that, after stating why we were in Vietnam, he would refer to the Khrushchev and Johnson letters of January 1964 with their lists of arms control proposals. He would describe the nuclear threat facing the world, especially the proliferation problem. Then he would go to Tsarapkin to talk privately, emphasizing that, in spite of Vietnam, the nuclear race needed to be controlled; that 114 nations participating in the UNDC meeting had urged that this be done.
>
> Rusk thought Foster should deal with Vietnam more directly, pointing out that we were willing to cooperate but that our peace overtures—which he thought Foster should recapitulate—had not borne any fruit. Foster protested that too much detail on Vietnam might create a wrong impression of our objectives in Geneva. He noted that the Soviets would be the first to speak and would certainly bring up Vietnam, so that his comments would be in the nature of a rebuttal. Bundy and Vice President Humphrey agreed that on Vietnam Foster's tactic should be to be ready to respond to the Soviet opening statement with "rebuttal and counterattack."

The next item discussed was an argument the British were having with our State Department and with West Germany. In June 1965 Britain had presented to the North Atlantic Council a draft nonproliferation treaty providing for existing nuclear states to have veto power over the use of nuclear weapons by any future collective nuclear force.[6] In presenting this concept, the British had run head-on into the Germans, who were not yet prepared to give up on the MLF, in which there was to have been a measure of multilateral control. The United States then had made an alternative suggestion that tended to support the Germans more than the British, and the latter had not taken kindly to that.

> Rusk commented that NATO had never before been confronted with so sharp a disagreement between the U.S. and the

U.K. He read from a message he proposed sending to the British that would be sharply critical of their response to our suggested alternative to their draft treaty. Bundy suggested some milder language that he hoped might appease the Germans and still be acceptable to the U.K. Rusk asked Bundy if his language would permit the MLF and Bundy responded that it would. Rusk thought Germany still was not ready to give up on the MLF.

Bundy suggested that perhaps the Soviets would go back to a position they had seemed to adopt in 1963: they would consent to an NPT more or less on our terms and then withdraw from it if an MLF actually came into existence. Rusk thought it entirely possible that by the time an NPT became effective the Soviets might be willing to agree that the MLF was not a step toward proliferation.

Foster indicated he would like to go beyond the NPT and put before the ENDC U.S. proposals for: 1. a comprehensive test ban treaty; 2. destruction of nuclear warheads, with the contained fissionable material to be transferred to peaceful uses; and 3. a cutoff in the production of fissionable material. Rusk doubted that Foster should say anything about the destruction of warheads in view of the president's forthcoming statement on Vietnam. Vice President Humphrey agreed: if the president, as expected, told the nation next week that we were "in a hell of a mess and had a hell of a job in Vietnam," then we shouldn't at the same time say we were cutting back on warheads. Humphrey thought Foster should limit his statement to the NPT and the test ban, or at least give these the emphasis. He suggested that Foster proceed like a boxer, feeling out the other countries before committing himself. Humphrey said that the things to worry about most in Geneva were the Russians on Vietnam and the attitude of some of the nonaligned countries on the NPT. Foster thought we need not worry about the nonaligned; the vice president hoped Foster was right. [He was not: see "The Nonaligned Speak Up," below.]

Opening Salvos in Geneva

President Johnson's brief message of greeting to the ENDC on July 27 was eloquent indeed. It deserves to be remembered:

I send my greetings to the members of the disarmament committee as they renew the most important task on earth.

The bible describes death as the fourth horseman of the Apocalypse, saying: "And hell followed after him." Our genius has changed this from a parable to a possibility. For the wasting power of our weapons is beyond the reach of imagination and language alike. Hell alone can describe the consequences that await their full use.

Therefore, if we love man, nothing is more important than the effort to diminish danger—halt the spread of nuclear power—and bring the weapons of war under increasing control.

Many proposals to this end now sit on your conference table. My delegation, and others, will make new proposals as the conference continues.

I have instructed the American delegation to pursue the following objectives with all the determination and wisdom they can command:

First, to seek agreements that will limit the perilous spread of nuclear weapons, and make it possible for all countries to refrain without fear from entering the nuclear arms race.

Second, to work toward the effective limitation of nuclear weapons and nuclear delivery systems, so that we can diminish present danger as well as prevent expanding peril.

Third, to work for a truly comprehensive test-ban treaty.

Many nations will, and should, share in these discussions.

No difference among any of us, on any other issue, can be allowed to bar agreement in this critical area. This is not in any single nation's interest, nor is it in the interest of the multitude of nations whose future is so tied to the good sense of those at this conference table.

My nation is ready. If others are equally prepared, then we can move, with growing confidence, toward the light.[7]

For the moment, the president's support of arms control seemed limited to such rhetorical bursts. His strong personal commitment to some of the specific objectives mentioned in this message would not come until later.

The opening session at the ENDC meeting followed closely the script laid out in the Principals' discussion.[8] Tsarapkin, as chairman, opened with an attack on U.S. foreign policy, concentrating on our presence in Vietnam. Foster replied with a brief Vietnam defense and then proceeded to elaborate on the points in the president's message.

He proposed an NPT "consistent with the Irish resolution"; consideration of security guarantees; acceptance of IAEA safeguards by "all governments . . . in all their peaceful nuclear activities"; a cutoff of all fissionable materials production; a freeze on strategic nuclear bombers and missiles; and a comprehensive test ban. The Italian foreign minister (Amintore Fanfani) then made the unexpected suggestion that, in advance of a nonproliferation treaty, the nonnuclear countries renounce equipping themselves with nuclear weapons for a specific length of time, "it being understood that if their . . . demands [for example, commitment by the nuclear powers to a program of nuclear disarmament] were not complied with during that time-limit, they would resume their freedom of action."

The day after the opening day's debate in Geneva, President Johnson announced the anticipated escalation in Vietnam. He ordered an increase in U.S. military forces there from 75,000 to 125,000; in monthly draft calls from 17,000 to 35,000. In an emotional TV speech, Johnson portrayed the need for the United States to protect the non-Communist states of Asia. "We did not choose to be the guardians at the gate," he said, "but there is no one else." He offered once again to seek a negotiated settlement. Failing that, he pledged to send even more arms and men if they were needed to fulfill commitments to South Vietnam made by three U.S. presidents. "We will stand in Vietnam," he declared. It was recognized that the decision to escalate, which was taken with dissent only from George Ball* among the president's senior advisers, would be a diplomatic liability for the United States, and an obstacle to success in arms control negotiations.

The Nonaligned Speak Up

After the representatives of East and West had spoken at the ENDC, it was the turn of "The Eight" nonaligned countries. In presentations by the representatives of India (V. C. Trivedi), the United Arab Republic (Abdel Fattah Hassan), and Sweden (Alva Myrdal), they launched a vigorous attack on the one-sidedness of the NPT ideas offered by the nuclear weapon states. Mrs. Myrdal made clear that her delegation preferred a comprehensive test ban to a nonproliferation treaty. A CTB would be at least as effective as an NPT in pre-

---

*After his arguments against widening the war were repeatedly rejected, Ball left the government in September 1966.

venting further additions to the nuclear club and had the virtue of imposing obligations on the nuclears as well as the nonnuclears. It would deprive the nuclears "of some prospects of further perfecting their nuclear weapons—that is, make more static a situation which is now dangerously dynamic and which would continue to be dynamic even under a non-proliferation treaty."[9]

Trivedi associated proposals that would dictate only to nonnuclear countries with an Indian emperor who lived at the beginning of the seventeenth century. "He himself was a drunkard, but he prohibited drinking in the empire." Trivedi proposed a treaty in two stages. In the first stage the nuclear powers would agree not to transfer weapons or weapons technology to others and also to cease all production, and reduce their stocks, of nuclear weapons and delivery vehicles. Only then would nonnuclear countries agree not to acquire or manufacture nuclear weapons.[10]

Subsequently, the Eight joined in a formal statement expressing their conviction that "measures to prohibit the spread of nuclear weapons should be coupled with or followed by tangible steps to halt the nuclear arms race and to limit, reduce, and eliminate the stocks of nuclear weapons and their means of delivery." Only thus, they warned, could a draft NPT receive the support of "the entire international community." Some, but not all, of the Eight also raised the question of security guarantees against nuclear attack. The Nigerian representative (Lucius C. N. Obi) stated the matter bluntly: "As long as states feel threatened . . . it will be impossible to prevent the spread of nuclear weapons. . . ."

So much for Foster's prediction (at the Principals meeting on July 22) that there need not be any concern about the nonaligned countries at the ENDC!

Foster's Article

Another means used to convey the U.S. position on a nonproliferation treaty was an article published by Foster in the July 1965 issue of *Foreign Affairs* under the title "New Directions in Arms Control." Several delegates spoke most respectfully of this article in their presentations at the ENDC—it obviously was widely read. Foster's target audience appeared to be the new Soviet leadership; his article, reportedly written mainly by George Rathjens, his special assistant,[11] was a strong appeal to Soviet self-interest.

Foster began by painting a generally optimistic picture of the trend in Soviet–American relations since the Cuban missile crisis. He contrasted this with the trend in proliferation, which had been "decidedly unfavorable." He noted that there was

> a difference in the time scale for action in the two areas. For a decade and a half the Soviet Union has had nuclear weapons; hence, the prospect of a delay of, say, a year or two in reducing the capabilities of the Soviet Union and the United States to damage each other may not seem terribly critical in itself. But a delay of a year or so, or perhaps even of months, in the implementation of measures bearing on the nuclear-proliferation problem could well mean the difference between failure and success.

He dismissed the case for allowing limited proliferation—the Model B world discussed by the Gilpatric Committee—on the grounds that the superpowers could not control proliferation selectively nor avoid involvement in nuclear conflicts, even those in remote regions. He described the increased potential for proliferation: nuclear weapons were becoming moderate in cost and peaceful atomic technology had disseminated the know-how. He pointed out that nuclear weapons in the hands of more nations would be a "great equalizer"—it would erode "the margin of power" that the superpowers enjoyed relative to the rest of the world. Thus, a nonproliferation treaty seemed "overwhelmingly" in the interest of both superpowers.

Foster then identified the issue that prevented agreement: Soviet refusal to go along with an MLF/ANF. He conceded that the Soviet position, linking the MLF/ANF with German acquisition of a nuclear capability, might reflect genuine concern "to a certain extent." It was also clear, however, that the Soviets were using the issue "for propaganda value and for whatever divisive effect it [might] have in NATO." Whether we would be able to overcome this impasse depended in large measure "on the Soviet assessment of the relative advantages of actually getting a proliferation agreement or of continuing to use the MLF/ANF issue for its political effect."

Perhaps most significant was Foster's prediction that U.S.–Soviet cooperation on a nonproliferation program would lead to a certain "erosion of alliances" and his intimation that the United States might be willing to accept this consequence. "As regards NATO," he wrote, "the best we might hope and strive for would be movement toward a substantial measure of East–West détente—hopefully sufficient to enable us to hold the line on nuclear proliferation—with perhaps progress on European union offsetting at least in part the fact that the cement holding NATO together will weaken with any further erosion of the fear of attack." Here were contained broad hints of a future settlement—an NPT in which the United States would give up on the MLF/ANF in return for Soviet countenancing of the European option.

Although Foster's article was cleared before publication with Rusk, McNamara, and Bundy, it represented the ACDA point of view more than a consensus view of the entire administration, and it was reported to have caused some consternation in other places.[12] Such discord on administration policy pronouncements was another manifestation of the lack of strong presidential leadership during this period.

The U.S. Draft Treaty

Foster unfurled a U.S. draft of a nonproliferation treaty at the ENDC on August 17, 1965. It was based mainly on the draft the British had submitted to the North Atlantic Council in June, with just enough changes to reflect U.S. insistence on holding the door open for some form of European collective force along lines acceptable to West Germany. (ACDA was far from having won its point within the administration to the extent of being able to offer a sacrifice of the MLF/ANF, as hinted at in Foster's article.) Presentation of the treaty became possible when, after some five weeks of negotiation, it was concurred in by the United Kingdom, Canada, and Italy, the other Western members of the ENDC, and by West Germany. British support was grudging, however. Lord Chalfont, the British disarmament minister, commented that the draft left open one possibility the United Kingdom "would prefer to see closed," namely, the establishment of a collective force that could use nuclear weapons based on majority vote.[13]

As the British intimated, the draft treaty was carefully phrased to keep open the possibility both of the MLF/ANF and of an eventual European force. Its first two articles closely followed the Irish resolution of 1961, emphasizing the concept of "control." Article I pledged the nuclear powers "not to transfer nuclear weapons into the national control of any non-nuclear weapons state or . . . any association" of such states and "not to take any action that would cause an increase in the total number of states having control of nuclear weapons." Article II pledged the nonweapon states not to receive nuclear weapons into their national control. There was also an Article III under which all parties were to "facilitate" the application of IAEA "or equivalent" safeguards to their peaceful nuclear activities. (This was soon to provide a new source of controversy—the subject of chapters 22 and 23.) In addition, as a concession to the nonweapon states, the draft provided for a review of progress under the treaty after a period of time. Presumably, if the nonweapon states were not satisfied with the steps the major powers were taking toward disarmament, they could then reconsider their adherence to the treaty. The elapsed time before this review would take place was not specified.

Coincident with the presentation of the U.S. draft treaty, President Johnson issued a statement hailing it as an "important step forward" in the search for disarmament. He called proliferation "the gravest of all unresolved human issues." Waxing eloquent once again, he said: "There is no sane description of a nuclear war. There is only the blinding light of man's failure to reason with his fellow man, and then silence. The time is now. The hour is late. The fate of generations yet unborn is in our hands."

Predictably, the Soviet Union promptly rejected the U.S. draft because it left the door open for a collective European force with West German participation. In reply, Foster stated that the United States did not want to foreclose forever the possibility of European unification. This comment seemed to hint again at future compromise: giving up the MLF/ANF in the short run if the possibility of a European option could be kept open for the long run.

Foster's suggestion of flexibility was not sufficient to mollify the Soviets. At a meeting of the Committee of Principals on August 25, he reported that prospects for a nonproliferation agreement were "very dim." Commenting editorially on the deadlock, *The New York Times* said on August 18:

> The melancholy conviction grows that neither in Moscow or Washington is there available the high statesmanship or the sense of history required to meet what may well be the greatest crisis humanity has faced.

A Soviet Draft

After the ENDC recessed on September 16, 1965, discussion of the nonproliferation issue was transferred to the UN General Assembly. Here a new U.S. ambassador, Arthur J. Goldberg—Adlai Stevenson had collapsed and died on a London street on July 14—urged that an NPT be given first priority. He advocated General Assembly action to provide assurances to nonnuclear countries threatened by nuclear blackmail, but he was not specific as to what form such assurances should take.

Soviet Foreign Minister Gromyko, agreeing on the importance of an NPT, responded on September 24, 1965, by introducing a Soviet draft treaty. It is significant that the Soviets unfurled their draft, not in the ENDC, but in the General Assembly, which provided a better forum for propaganda attacks on West Germany and the MLF/ANF. (It was the same consideration that had prompted the Soviets earlier in the year to suggest convening of the UNDC rather than the ENDC.) The Soviet draft featured an effort to close every conceivable avenue to nuclear sharing in Europe, or anywhere else. Taking dead aim at MLF/ANF proposals, the Soviet draft enjoined nuclear weapons powers not to transfer nuclear weapons "in any form—directly or indirectly, through third States or groups of States—to the ownership or control of States or groups of States not possessing nuclear weapons and not to accord to such States or groups of States the right to participate in the ownership, control, or use of nuclear weapons." A further prohibition seemed to outlaw even existing NATO arrangements. It forbade transferring "nuclear weapons, or control over them or over their emplacement and use, to units of the armed forces or military personnel of States not possessing nuclear weapons, even if such units or personnel are under the command of a military alliance." The severity of the Soviet draft seemed to dash all hope for a near-term agreement.

Gromyko also used the General Assembly debate to respond to the views of the nonaligned nations regarding the alleged discriminatory nature of a nonproliferation agreement. He contended that such a treaty would by itself be a major step toward nuclear disarmament. He denied that it was "simply a method of . . . formalizing the nuclear monopoly of the present five great Powers." Unpersuaded, the nonaligned continued their criticism. In general, they questioned that anything would be gained by their renunciation of nuclear weapons if the superpowers persisted in amassing larger and more deadly arsenals. As the General Assembly session neared its end, the non-aligned nations introduced a compromise resolution. It called on the ENDC to reconvene as early as possible to negotiate a nonproliferation treaty based on five main principles. These principles, particularly the first two, soon became a sort of litmus test by which the non-nuclear-weapon states were to judge future NPT proposals. They read as follows:

(a) The treaty should be void of any loop-holes which might permit nuclear or non-nuclear Powers to proliferate, directly or indirectly, nuclear weapons in any form;

(b) The treaty should embody an acceptable balance of mutual responsibilities and obligations of the nuclear and non-nuclear Powers;

(c) The treaty should be a step towards the achievement of general and complete disarmament and, more particularly, nuclear disarmament;

(d) There should be acceptable and workable provisions to ensure the effectiveness of the treaty;

(e) Nothing in the treaty should adversely affect the right of any group of States to conclude regional treaties in order to ensure the total absence of nuclear weapons in their respective territories.[14]

Supported by the superpowers and their allies, General Assembly Resolution 2028 was adopted on November 19, 1965, by a vote of 93 to 0, with five abstentions.

Soon after completion of the disarmament debate in the General Assembly and its First Committee, the Soviet and U.S. cochairmen of the ENDC, Tsarapkin and Foster, agreed to reconvene that body. The new session was scheduled to begin on January 27, 1966. The fact that both sides were willing to continue the dialogue, despite their wide differences, offered some grounds for optimism.

Notes

1. Rusk to DOS, 12/14/64 and 12/15/64, National Security File, MLF Cables, Vol. 3, LBJ Library.
2. Gordon Chase to Bundy, 4/2/65, National Security File, Country File, UN, Box 290, LBJ Library.
3. *Documents on Disarmament: 1965*, p. 31.

4. Bundy to President, 7/13/65, National Security File, Memos to the President—McGeorge Bundy, Vol. 12, LBJ Library.
5. Barnes, "The Nuclear Non-Proliferation Treaty," p. 273.
6. Ibid., p. 279.
7. *Documents on Disarmament: 1965,* p. 281.
8. Ibid., pp. 281–89.
9. Ibid., p. 316.
10. Ibid., p. 326ff.
11. Barnes, "The Nuclear Non-Proliferation Treaty," p. 254.
12. Ibid., p. 258.
13. U.S. ACDA, *International Negotiations on the Treaty on the Nonproliferation of Nuclear Weapons,* p. 18.
14. *Documents on Disarmament: 1965,* p. 533f.

15
Drawing Closer to an NPT

It was in the U.S. interest in 1964 to attempt to hold the number of nuclear powers to four and it is now in 1966 in our interest to attempt to hold the number of nuclear powers to five.

—Robert S. McNamara

Multilateral Confusion

After President Johnson backed away from active U.S. sponsorship of an interallied force in December 1964, it may seem odd that the prospect of such a force should have proven such an obstacle to NPT negotiations through most of 1965. In fact, however, it is only in retrospect that one can conclude that the MLF/ANF was essentially killed in December 1964. At the time it was by no means clear that this was the case. Largely because of his concern about German sensibilities, the president had been very careful, as we have seen, not to convey the impression that U.S. policy had changed drastically. In the absence of any firm presidential pronouncement, State Department elements at home and U.S. diplomats abroad hung on to the interallied force as a future possibility. The NATO allies were understandably confused. It is time, therefore, that we double back a bit to see how the position regarding the MLF/ANF gradually became clarified, thereby opening a path to the NPT.

After the Johnson-Wilson summit, Britons who had participated spread the word that we had accepted their ANF proposal completely.[1] This of course corresponded to Wilson's diary entry quoted earlier that Britain had "won the day." One is led to conjecture that the impression the president gave at his meeting with Wilson and the one he tried to convey afterward were not the same. Whatever the source of the confusion, a perception took root in Bonn that the United States had abandoned the MLF. This caused great unrest there and Ambassador McGhee entreated Washington for a reassuring statement.

Such a statement was forthcoming in the form of a letter from Rusk to his counterpart, Foreign Minister Gerhard Schroeder. No, wrote the secretary, our views had not changed, despite what people were saying. We had not lost interest in the "problems the MLF was designed to deal with." But we wanted what emerged to truly represent the views of the major participants and not be the result of U.S. pressure on unwilling allies. Congressional support could not be had otherwise. We were prepared to move ahead without France, but not on a strictly bilateral basis. It was vital to find the means that met the needs of the largest members of the alliance. The British approach might through negotiation accommodate the MLF "substantially as it was initially conceived [that is, utilizing submarines instead of surface ships]." Also, it created the possibility of the British divesting themselves of their independent deterrent, "the first step which will ever have been taken *away* from . . . proliferation." We hoped for "constructive forward movement."[2]

McGhee reported that Schroeder was in a grim mood when he received Rusk's letter, but brightened somewhat as he read it. He was relieved to know that the United States had not lost interest. But he added: "It is difficult for smaller countries to proceed in an undertaking if the big power that starts it attempts to leave it to them alone." The Germans had been particularly concerned by the appearance that the United States had changed its attitude to appease France. The chancellor had to have the feeling that U.S. policy was firm if he was to stand up to de Gaulle at their scheduled meeting a week hence. Moreover, the impression that we had lost interest in MLF was so widespread that it could only be dispelled by an authoritative *public* statement.

McGhee added his own comments. The secretary's letter "could not have been better." He underscored, however, Schroeder's request that the policy reassurances in the letter be stated publicly. He, McGhee, was to meet with Erhard the next day. He hoped very much he could assure the chancellor that Germany would not be "bypassed by a U.S.–French rapprochment."[3]

The same day there was a very similar cable from Ambassador Reinhardt in Rome reporting on a conversation with a Foreign Ministry official (Cattani). Italy was still for the MLF and wanted to know where the United States really stood. Cattani was familiar with all recent U.S. statements, yet the impression persisted that U.S. intentions had changed. He understood why we might prefer to have

Europeans settle their differences without U.S. intervention, "but in his view this was unrealistic. . . . It was simply not possible for European powers to resolve matters of this kind in absence of a strong and clear U.S. position."[4]

When McGhee saw Erhard the following day, the chancellor told him that there seemed insufficient time to resolve the MLF matter before the West German elections in October. He did not want the issue to become an "apple of discord" during the campaign but hoped finalization of the MLF would not be delayed unduly. He stated that "Germany cannot, will not, and must not renounce the nuclear protection of the U.S."[5]

The need for a public statement of reassurance was met on January 16 by President Johnson himself. In a news conference at his Texas ranch the president again expressed continued U.S. interest in "nuclear arrangements within the alliance that will allow the non-nuclear members to participate in their own nuclear defense while avoiding the spread of national nuclear systems." Referring to upcoming talks between Wilson and Erhard, the president expressed hope that there would be progress that would "allow us to move on to fruitful multilateral discussions."

Following the rather hectic diplomacy of December 1964 and January 1965, a lull now ensued on the MLF/ANF matter. The subject appeared scarcely to have been mentioned in the Erhard–de Gaulle meeting. Then when Wilson and Erhard held their long-heralded meeting on March 9 and 10, 1965,* Erhard was reported to have told Wilson that Germany did not intend to discuss MLF/ANF issues seriously during the remainder of 1965.[6] Wilson told a news conference afterward that he did not expect interallied negotiations on the matter to "go forward at breakneck speed."[7]

McNamara Floats an Alternative

Late in February 1965 Dean Rusk sought to give the nuclear sharing issue a broader European perspective when he suggested to the president that letters be sent to the leaders of the United Kingdom, West Germany, Italy, and the Netherlands for the purpose of setting up renewed multilateral discussions on the MLF/ANF. Rusk received his

---

*Originally scheduled for January 24, 1965, the meeting had been postponed because of the death on that date of Winston Churchill.

answer in the form of a March 4 memorandum from McGeorge Bundy.[8] Bundy began by saying he had discussed Rusk's suggestion with the president:

> The president believes that neither Wilson nor Erhard is in any doubt as to his own basic position, and he thinks it is also very clear that unless the situation changes sharply as a result of [their] meeting in Bonn, it is very unlikely that there will be any prospect of agreement before the German elections. In this situation he thinks it is better to wait and hear what happens between Wilson and Erhard. [As noted above, that meeting produced nothing of consequence.]

Bundy then returned to his familiar role as the raiser of hard questions. There was nothing wrong with holding multilateral discussions but

> my own growing conviction is that the MLF as such is never going to be the right next step for the necessary number of nations all at the same time—at least not until we have made progress in some other way first. *I therefore wonder if we should be giving close thought to other possibilities for nuclear coordination within the Alliance which may be more modest but which are also more likely to happen* [emphasis added]. I have mentioned this personal view to the President, and he has suggested that I raise it with you and Bob McNamara and George Ball for discussion.

Consistent with Bundy's challenge, McNamara came forward with just such "another possibility for nuclear coordination" at a May 31, 1965, meeting of NATO defense ministers in Paris. With the agreement of Rusk,[9] he proposed the establishment of a "Select Committee of four or five Ministers of Defense" to provide "a greater degree of nuclear participation for . . ." Alliance members. . . . (A similar idea had been mentioned in the communiqué following the 1962 meeting of the North Atlantic Council in Athens.) Specifically, the committee proposed by McNamara was to address two major aspects of the nuclear sharing problem:

> first, possible ways of improving and extending allied participation in planning for the use of nuclear forces . . . and, second, possible ways . . . of insuring that agreed consultation concerning the decision to use nuclear forces can take place as expeditiously as advanced technology will permit.

McNamara's specification that the committee should have "four or five" members was a way of making clear that it would not be confined to the three nuclear-armed members of the alliance—West Germany, and perhaps Italy as well, would have a part.[10] He dutifully pointed out that the committee would be "additional to whatever action may be taken on the MLF/ANF," but international speculation began at once that his suggestion was intended as a substitute for the force.

McNamara's proposal did not at first fare well within the alliance. The fact that it was to be limited to five members connoted to the smaller allies that they would not be allowed to participate. Even the Italians were not sure they would qualify. Both the Germans and Italians let it be known that, though they thought the committee was a good idea, they did not want it to be used as a substitute for some form of allied nuclear force. The British felt that continuation of their "special relationship" with the United States on nuclear matters was preferable to any committee arrangement. How this impasse was resolved is described by Harlan Cleveland in his book, *NATO: The Transatlantic Bargain:*

> There followed a complex and private negotiation among the [NATO] Permanent Representatives in Paris. [Cleveland had himself become the U.S. permanent representative when Finletter resigned in December 1964.] The circle was squared by establishing a Special Committee of all the Defense Ministers who wanted to join, which turned out to be ten. This became the holding company for three smaller groups, on crisis management, on communications, and on nuclear planning. A further negotiation narrowed participation in the "nuclear planning working group," which everybody knew was destined to be the center ring of this little circus, to five. The United States and Britain would be members because they had nuclear weapons; France opted out of the whole enterprise; Germany and Italy would be members because they are big countries; and one member [Turkey, drawn by lot] would represent the small countries.[11]

This settlement was reached in November 1965. In the same month Joint Committee Chairman Holifield publicly endorsed what the newspapers had begun to call "the McNamara Committee" in a speech in which he also restated his opposition to the MLF/ANF.[12]

McNamara approached the new committee, particularly the Nuclear Planning Group, with utmost seriousness, quickly disspelling the
idea that it was meant merely as an escape valve for emotions generated by disappointment over this country's retreat on the MLF.
Through four intense sessions during 1966, he immersed his European opposite numbers in the complexity of nuclear issues as he himself confronted them, revealing all the uncertainties, dangers,
limitations, and compromises that had to be dealt with in establishing
nuclear strategy, and disclosing a lot of hitherto secret information in
the process. As word spread about the benefits of taking part in the
group, other nations aspired to participate. In consequence, the Nuclear Planning Group was expanded to seven members, a permanent
group of four (the United States, the United Kingdom, West Germany,
Italy) and a rotating group of three drawn from the rest of NATO,
except France, Norway and Portugal, all of whom elected not to
participate.

The MLF/ANF Runs Aground

While the Special Committee was gaining support as a sufficient answer to NATO's nuclear-sharing needs, the MLF/ANF concept continued to lose ground. Among the most convincing indications of its
near demise was a single sentence in a September 12 memo from
Bundy to the president. Reporting on a meeting among himself,
McNamara, Rusk, Ball, and CIA Director William F. Raborn,* Bundy
wrote, undoubtedly with satisfaction, "at long last George [Ball] himself has concluded that the MLF is not the solution to the nuclear
defense problem."[13]

Another nail in the MLF/ANF's coffin was the continuing opposition of Britain. The British attitude was made unmistakably clear
on November 9, 1965, by Disarmament Minister Chalfont when he
paid a call on Foster during the General Assembly proceedings in New
York. Chalfont was quoted as saying: "I think we will look with a
fairly beady eye at nuclear sharing proposals and if they don't contribute to a nonproliferation agreement we will probably not give
them much weight." He added that he personally was "ready to sink
several MLF fleets" to gain a nonproliferation treaty.[14] There had
been speculation all along that in proposing the ANF the British pur-

---

*Raborn had succeeded John McCone on the latter's resignation, April 28, 1965. He was
himself succeeded by Richard Helms on June 30, 1966.

pose had been to kill the MLF, that they were not really serious about the alternative.

When all indications pointed to an early and peaceful burial for the notion that there was a hardware solution to NATO's nuclear problem, Erhard came to Washington on December 21 and 22, 1965, with one more proposal, one which tilted far over toward the previous British plan. (Erhard had won a decisive election victory in September, the Social Democrats having failed to make expected gains.) President Johnson reported the proposal in a letter to Prime Minister Wilson:

> The nuclear force [Erhard] describes would appear to fall within the broad framework of your ANF proposal. Unlike the MLF, it would not contemplate the creation of a new weapons system. From our discussion, it would appear that the Chancellor and his Ministers have been generally thinking in terms of an assignment by the United Kingdom of its Polaris submarines and a matching contribution of Polaris submarines by the United States. These submarines would form the basic elements of the force, which might be added to later. It is our impression that the questions of mixed-manning, veto rights, and a "European clause" can be worked out in a manner consistent both with your requirements and ours.[15]

Sympathetic as always to the German point of view, the president urged a forthcoming attitude on Wilson.

> The proposals presented by the Chancellor will give me some problems with Congress, and I am sure they will not be easy for you. But what is essential is a stable and healthy Germany that can play a constructive role on the side of the West. On balance it seems to me that you and I should make a serious effort to respond to the German proposals. . . .

Press reports attributed much significance to the fact that neither the MLF nor any other specific plan was mentioned in the communiqué or in the postconference remarks of either leader. Instead, the communiqué emphasized the discussions that NATO defense ministers were conducting to improve alliance nuclear arrangements—the McNamara Committee. There was also an endorsement of the principle of nonproliferation together with a statement that "Alliance nuclear arrangements would not constitute proliferation."[16]

In fact, there never appeared to be any public discussion of Erhard's proposal, and in appearing to take the plan seriously President Johnson may have been trying to let the chancellor down easily. The key to the fate of the hardware proposals may perhaps be found in the earlier comments made by the West German and Italian diplomats. To repeat, Schroeder had said: "It is difficult for smaller countries to proceed in an undertaking if the big power that starts it attempts to leave it to them alone." And Cattani had said: "It is simply not possible for European powers to resolve matters of this kind in absence of a strong and clear U.S. position." Thus, we can come back to the conclusion that the MLF was indeed sunk in December 1964 when President Johnson pulled the plug on active U.S. sponsorship of the idea.

The focus of administration attention in nuclear diplomacy began now, at the end of 1965, to shift strongly toward attempts to negotiate a nonproliferation treaty.

The Superpowers Edge Closer Together

On January 27, 1966, President Johnson sent a strongly worded message to the reconvening ENDC. On the subject of nonproliferation the president said:

> Let us seek a nonproliferation treaty which, in the words of the United Nations General Assembly, is "void of any loopholes which might permit nuclear or non-nuclear Powers to proliferate, directly or indirectly, nuclear weapons in any form." We are prepared to sign such a treaty, making it applicable to nuclear and non-nuclear countries alike. We are prepared to work with other countries to assure that no non-nuclear country acquires its own nuclear weapons, gains national control over nuclear weapons, achieves the power itself to fire nuclear weapons or receives assistance in manufacturing or testing nuclear weapons. We are prepared to agree that these things should not be done directly or indirectly through third countries or groups of countries, or through units of the armed forces or military personnel under any military alliance.[17]

The president's choice of words was designed to conciliate other elements in the NPT debate. The quotation in the first sentence above was from one of the five principles enunciated in General Assembly Resolution 2028 of November 1965. The words quoted seemed obviously intended to rule out the MLF. Further, in his references to "groups of countries" and a "military alliance," the president adopted the semantics of the Soviet draft nonproliferation treaty. On this point he actually yielded no substantive ground, however. He still spoke only of preventing additional nations from acquiring "control" of nuclear weapons. At Geneva, Soviet Ambassador Tsarapkin was quick to offer the usual Soviet objection that this formula, as embodied also in the U.S. draft treaty, would permit West Germany to gain "access" to nuclear weapons within the framework of a NATO collective force such as the MLF.

On February 1, Premier Kosygin answered President Johnson's message to the ENDC with a strong one of his own, saying that "[t]he Soviet Government insists on the necessity of concluding without delay a treaty on the nonproliferation of nuclear weapons."[18] Tsarapkin followed up by suggesting that there be an article-by-article discussion in Geneva of both the U.S. and Soviet draft treaties. This procedure seemed early in March to be drawing the two sides closer together. In an apparent clarification of the Soviet position, Tsarapkin said that the Soviet Union was not satisfied with the U.S. provision forbidding any nonnuclear nation to acquire *national control* of nuclear weapons. What they insisted on, in addition, was a provision that "would equally prohibit the *transfer* of nuclear weapons to multilateral control within the framework of military alliances, for instance, NATO." If such a provision were added, he said, his country could readily agree to an NPT along the lines of the U.S. draft.[19] This was quite an advance from the Soviet draft treaty which, in denying nonnuclear states "the right to participate in the *ownership, control or use*" of nuclear weapons, seemed to outlaw not only a collective force but also existing NATO bilateral two-key security arrangements for use of nuclear weapons as well as the newly established Special Committee of NATO defense ministers.

Responsive to the Soviet objection, the United States submitted amendments to its draft treaty on March 22, 1966. Most significant of these was the addition of a definition of the key word "control." It was defined as "the right or ability to fire nuclear weapons without the concurrent decision of an existing nuclear-weapon State." Foster sought to persuade the Soviets that this definition guaranteed that there would be an American veto over every contemplated use of a U.S. nuclear weapon by a NATO collective force.[20] (Although no such nuclear force was being actively considered, our diplomats still insisted on keeping the possibility alive.)

The new Soviet delegate, Alexey A. Roshchin—Tsarapkin had been appointed ambassador to Bonn—was not persuaded. He maintained that "control," even with the new definition, was still too narrow a concept, and asked why the United States was not willing to go a step further and forbid *transfer of* and *access to* nuclear weapons. Roshchin argued that the reliability of the U.S. veto was open to question. What would happen if one or more NATO countries, having *access* to nuclear weapons, rejected the veto? Nor did locks protect against thieves. The Soviet Union, he said, recognized the "reality and existence" of NATO. It did not, however, recognize the right of additional NATO members to have nuclear weapons.[21]

It is significant that in its annual report for 1966 the ACDA presented the Soviet arguments at considerable length and in almost sympathetic terms. The report noted that "the Soviet views were presented in a manner relatively free of polemic. . . ." It characterized the discussion as a whole as "an illuminating clarification and exposition of the position of the two sides rarely matched in the conference's open debate."[22] It was as though the ACDA were lobbying for the Soviet position against remaining MLF/ANF advocates in the State Department.

Prospects for accord on an NPT now seemed improved, but there was another cloud on the horizon. It emanated from some new mischief by Charles de Gaulle.

De Gaulle Drops the Other Shoe

On March 23, 1965, word came from the U.S. Embassy in Paris about a remark de Gaulle made to the French ambassador to Washington (Hervé Alphand). As overheard by a British Embassy officer, de Gaulle said:

> The MLF is dead. It is I who killed it. Yet I almost regret having done so since [if alive] it would have permitted me to do sooner that which I intend to do.[23]

Our embassy's conjecture was that the action envisaged was French withdrawal from NATO. On March 7, 1966, de Gaulle validated this

prophecy. He wrote President Johnson that France intended to withdraw its armed forces from NATO and asked that the organization's
headquarters be removed from French soil.

To some in the administration, de Gaulle's action seemed to un-
derscore the need to retain at least the possibility of a NATO collective nuclear force in order to keep Germany from following France
out of NATO. To minimize that likelihood, President Johnson wrote
to Erhard immediately on receipt of de Gaulle's letter, saying in
part:

> General de Gaulle's decisions will have the most serious and far-
> reaching consequences for all the members of NATO. In view of the
> geographical position of the Federal Republic they are particularly
> significant and important to your Government. I want you to know
> that I am prepared to stand shoulder to shoulder with you in face
> of the serious problems which they pose. We are in this together
> and I know that our partners will look to us as nations which are
> carrying heavy burdens in the common defense to see to it that
> the Alliance is strengthened rather than weakened in the weeks
> ahead.[24]

On March 22, the president sent de Gaulle a preachy but for-
bearing reply[25] in which he set forth what he termed "the fundamentals" about NATO. He took issue with de Gaulle's contention that
the presence of allied military forces on French soil impaired the sovereignty of France. He noted, with respect, de Gaulle's pledge that
France would "fight beside her allies if any member of NATO should
suffer unprovoked aggression." But he contended that "reliance in
crisis on independent action by separate forces" was not the way to
proceed. Members of the alliance should be prepared to act in any
emergency "through their mutual organization and in accordance with
mutual plans." Retaining his confidence that the prodigal would ultimately return, the president concluded on a hopeful note:

> [W]e find it difficult to believe that France . . . will long remain
> withdrawn from the common affairs and responsibilities of the At-

lantic. As our old friend and ally her place will await France whenever she decides to resume her leading role.*

De Gaulle's action seemed to require a demonstration of allied cohesion, particularly as regards solidarity with West Germany. One form that this took was an increase in rhetorical support of the MLF/ANF. This in turn caused hopes for an agreement between the superpowers at Geneva to fade once again. In the meantime, however, pressure for an NPT had begun to build from another source.

Involving the President

The Pastore Resolution

On January 18, 1966, Senator John O. Pastore of Rhode Island, vice chairman of the Joint Committee on Atomic Energy, and fifty-five cosponsors, introduced in the Senate a resolution containing the following operative paragraph:

> *Resolved,* That the Senate commends the President's serious and urgent efforts to negotiate international agreements limiting the spread of nuclear weapons and supports the principle of additional efforts by the President which are appropriate and necessary in the interest of peace and for the solution of nuclear proliferation problems.

---

*John Leddy, who was assistant secretary of state for European affairs, reports that a group of top advisers, including Rusk, Rostow, Ball, Bohlen, and Dean Acheson, had gotten together and presented the president with a very different letter to send to de Gaulle. Their idea was "to do battle with the General in the public domain—to argue with him and . . . have a big public debate about it." Leddy continues: "This was in the Oval Room over there. We were sitting around there and the President was in his rocking chair. . . . [E]veryone spoke up and said, 'We ought to challenge the general's basic theories,' and so forth. The President listened to all of this and said, 'It looks like all you fellows voted on this, haven't you?' And he said, 'I want to think about it a little bit more.' As a result of his thinking about it a little bit more, the tone of that letter was very considerably changed. It [became] a polite letter. . . .

"What the President did [by making these changes] was to set the policy tone of the administration in dealing with de Gaulle, which was don't get into big arguments with him. Always be polite. . . . There's no point in arguing with him because he's not going to change his mind. He's asked us to get out of France. We'll get out of France.

"This was a very personal decision, and in effect he disagreed with all of the advice he got around the table. I remember George Ball, I guess a few weeks after that, made some public speech in which he took the general on. And sure enough we had a memo from the White House shortly after that saying, 'Stop it. We're just not going to have that kind of stuff' " (transcript, John Leddy Oral History Interview, 3/12/69, by Paige E. Mulhollan, Tape 1, p. 11, LBJ Library).

The key words in this resolution were "additional efforts by the President." We have already observed that although Johnson had made a number of public pronouncements indicating that he favored a non-proliferation treaty, he had not shown a strong personal interest in the subject. Pastore's initiative seemed to be a subtle and adroit way of holding the president's feet to the fire.

Well-publicized hearings on the Pastore Resolution were held by the Joint Committee on February 23, March 1, and March 7, 1966. Secretary Rusk was the sole witness on February 23. He began by describing the dangers of further proliferation and by indicating that it was an objective of U.S. foreign policy to try to stem the tide. He was at pains to point out, however, that proposed NATO nuclear arrangements did not constitute proliferation because they did not increase the number of "independent nuclear weapon entities." Rusk went on to warn that the Soviets might be seeking to weaken NATO under the guise of seeming to oppose proliferation. Nor did he believe that adoption of an NPT was a matter of desperate urgency. "I think we have a little time," he said.[26]

The witnesses on March 1 were Foster and myself. My testimony was devoted exclusively to the issue of safeguards and is best considered in a subsequent chapter (see chapter 22). Foster's testimony provided a summary of the efforts at Geneva. He expressed encouragement about what seemed greater seriousness by the Soviet Union, as evidenced by their having submitted a draft treaty. The questioning of Foster by members of the committee bore down hard on the issue that still seemed to be preventing agreement:

> Senator PASTORE. Mr. Foster, I think you are familiar with the fact that the overwhelming majority of this Joint Committee is reluctant to accept the concept of the multilateral force, not because anyone here believes that it is proliferation. It is just in opposition to the concept. You are familiar with that?
> Mr. FOSTER. Yes, sir.[27]

Pastore's way of putting it was particularly cogent because it seemed to cut the ground out from under Rusk's argument in defense of an interallied nuclear force, namely, that it did not constitute proliferation.

Secretary McNamara, the concluding witness, was heard on March 7. Unlike Rusk, he presented the security implications of proliferation in stark and urgent terms:

It was in the U.S. interest in 1964 to attempt to hold the number of nuclear powers to four and it is now in 1966 in our interest to attempt to hold the number of nuclear powers to five. . . . All of the other nuclear powers share this interest with us—any increase in the number of nuclear powers is an increase in the danger of nuclear war.[28]

Although he echoed Rusk's assurance that a NATO collective nuclear force would not involve proliferation, McNamara also felt that our allies' need for greater participation in the nuclear affairs of NATO could be met by the consultative committee of NATO defense ministers he had fathered. He noted that the Soviets had not specifically objected to this committee. In answer to a question, McNamara made a veiled criticism of the administration's cautious approach to NPT negotiations:

I do think that as a nation we sometimes fail to accept small penalties in order to achieve large gains. I think if one were to look back over the past two decades one could find many illustrations of that. . . . [T]here are certain problems associated with the nonproliferation treaty. I have no doubt of that. But there are many more serious problems associated with a world in which we don't have a nonproliferation treaty.[29]

This was about as close as McNamara would ever get to disagreeing with Dean Rusk in public.

On May 17, 1966, the Senate approved the Pastore Resolution by a vote of 84 to 0. On June 13, the president sent a letter of congratulations to the senator, saying in part:

Now your resolution has been approved by the Senate without one dissenting vote. This overwhelming expression of sentiment is more than an indication of the support of the American people for our unremitting efforts to stop further proliferation of nuclear weapons. It is clear and unequivocal evidence of the depth of our commitment. As such, it is there for the whole world to see. I know it will reinforce Mr. Foster's position at Geneva, where on my instructions he will shortly renew our urgent pursuit of a treaty.

It is curious that the president waited nearly a month after the Senate's action to send this letter. I think that in general Johnson did not take kindly to being told what he should do—he wanted very much to feel that he was in control of his own agenda. That he broke his silence about the Pastore Resolution was probably related to certain contacts—to be considered next—that strengthened his resolve on the subject of nonproliferation.

Efforts within the Administration

The insight that underlay the Pastore Resolution was that President Johnson would have to become more personally involved if NPT negotiations were to be moved off dead center. One attempt to get the president involved was made by UN Ambassador Arthur Goldberg. On March 19, 1966, he phoned presidential assistant Jack Valenti seeking an appointment with the president in order to present an idea for a bold initiative.[30] His idea, as Valenti wrote it down in a memo to Johnson, was for the president to "fly to Geneva and personally . . . push for a non-proliferation treaty." Goldberg argued that this was "the one field that would preempt Vietnam as a news issue and send the president's stock soaring throughout the world." "I asked him," Valenti wrote, "how would we be able to get an NPT without serious reactions in Germany. . . . His answer was: It can be done. But, he said, the key point is for the president to rise above Vietnam. . . ." Johnson's penned instructions to Valenti at the bottom of the memo were: "Read this to Bill [Moyers], Rusk, Clifford* & give me their reactions." The fact that Johnson wanted the views of three such trusted advisers indicates that Goldberg's idea may have had some appeal for him. But nothing came of it.

A more influential intervention began later in the spring. The key figure was Bill Moyers, who had given up his duties as White House press secretary in order to become an adviser to the president, concentrating on foreign affairs. Various government officials sought Moyers's help in getting the president to focus on the nonproliferation issue. Walt Rostow, who had succeeded McGeorge Bundy as national security adviser at the end of March,† would have been a more obvious channel for such an effort in terms of the White House's formal organization, but his known bias in favor of the MLF was an obstacle.

---

*Clark Clifford, who was to succeed McNamara as secretary of defense in 1968, was at this time in private law practice. President Johnson frequently consulted with him and/or Supreme Court Justice Abe Fortas before making important decisions.

†Bundy had accepted a position as president of the Ford Foundation. There was speculation that he was finding it increasingly difficult to give full support to the president's Vietnam War policies.

One of those who contacted Moyers was Spurgeon Keeny, who had been staff director for the Gilpatric Committee. Keeny recalls having several conversations with Moyers on the NPT issue, sometimes alone and sometimes in the company of one or more of Adrian Fisher, Hayes Redmon (an assistant to Moyers), and John T. McNaughton (assistant secretary of defense for international security affairs and a close associate of Secretary McNamara).[31]

There can be little doubt that McNaughton, besides representing his own views, was acting as McNamara's emissary in this matter. McNamara underscored his own views on May 18 in a widely heralded speech to the American Society of Newspaper Editors, in which he said:

> In the calculus of risk, to proliferate independent national nuclear forces is not a mere arithmetical *addition* of danger. We would not be merely adding up risks. We would be insanely *multiplying* them (emphasis in original text).[32]

Moyers also consulted during this period with ACDA Director William Foster and was so impressed with the latter's presentation on behalf of a nonproliferation treaty that he arranged for him to brief the president directly.[33] Such contact between the president and the ACDA head was fairly frequent under Kennedy—by law the agency reported directly to the president. But Johnson tended to deal with arms control matters through the triumvirate that attended the regular Tuesday lunches: the secretary of state, the secretary of defense, and the national security adviser. As Adrian Fisher observed:

> [W]e tended to work more directly with Mac Bundy and very often with the President himself, under President Kennedy, than we did with President Johnson. . . . We send something up there, he wants to know what the Secretary of State thinks about it.[34]

This was in accord with Johnson's general mode of administration, but in ACDA's case there was an additional reason. President Johnson later communicated to me in a private conversation that he was quite skeptical about the value of the ACDA and its place in the government. (See chapter 17.) Walt Rostow explains Johnson's attitude toward the ACDA as "disappointment with their parochialism."[35]

In this instance, what Foster told President Johnson about the need for a nonproliferation treaty gained credibility because it reinforced messages that were funneling in from a number of other sources. In due time the president responded. On June 13, he sent his congratulatory message to Senator Pastore. Then on July 5, answering a question at a news conference, the president seemed to intimate that the United States was prepared to modify the language of its draft treaty in order to reach a compromise solution with the Soviets:

> We are doing everything we can to reach an agreement on such a [nonproliferation] treaty. We are very anxious to do it. We hope the Soviet Union will meet us and find an acceptable compromise in language which we can both live with. . . . We are going to do everything within the power of our most imaginative people to find language which will bring the nuclear powers together in a treaty which will provide nonproliferation. We think it is the most important decision of our time and we are going to do everything to bring people together on it.[36]

Following the president's news conference, Moyers conducted a background briefing that, judging from the press accounts that followed, gave the impression that Johnson had ordered State and Defense to find a solution to NATO's nuclear sharing problem that might be acceptable to the Soviet Union. It was implied that the president had the McNamara Committee in mind.[37]

George Bunn recalls that the president's press conference statement had an electric effort on the arms control bureaucracy.* It conveyed the sense that Johnson had made a basic decision and that movement would now be possible.[38] Thus energized, U.S. arms control negotiators were ready to proceed to the next step, which was to engage the Soviet Union in some hard and detailed negotiation.

Notes

1. Cable, McGhee (Bonn) to SecState, 1/11/65, National Security File, Subject File, Vol. 4, LBJ Library.
2. Letter, Rusk to Schroeder, 1/13/65, National Security File, Subject File, MLF Cables, Vol. 4, LBJ Library.

---

*Bunn was ACDA general counsel from 1961 to 1968. He also acted regularly as deputy to ACDA Director Foster on U.S. negotiating teams at the ENDC in Geneva and at the UN in New York. He has contributed most generously to the writing of this book by sharing his firsthand recollections and impressions of those years, particularly as regards the negotiation of the Nonproliferation Treaty.

3. Cable, McGhee (Bonn) to SecState, 1/14/65, National Security File, Subject File, Vol. 4, LBJ Library.
4. Cable, Reinhardt (Rome) to SecState, 1/14/65, National Security File, Subject File, MLF Cables, Vol. 4, LBJ Library.
5. Cable, McGhee (Bonn) to SecState, 1/15/65, National Security File, Subject File, MLF Cables, Vol. 4, LBJ Library.
6. Reinhardt cable from Rome, 3/12/65, National Security File, Subject File, MLF Cables, Vol. 4, LBJ Library.
7. *The New York Times,* March 10, 1965.
8. Bundy to Rusk, 3/4/65, National Security File, Subject File, MLF General Box 23, LBJ Library.
9. Cleveland, *NATO: The Transatlantic Bargain,* p. 53.
10. McNamara address at Defense Ministers meeting, Paris, 5/31/65, National Security File, Agency File, Department of Defense Vol. 3, LBJ Library.
11. Cleveland, *NATO: The Transatlantic Bargain,* p. 53f.
12. Barnes, "The Nuclear Non-Proliferation Treaty," p. 314.
13. Bundy to President, 9/12/65, National Security File, Memos to the President—McGeorge Bundy, Vol. 14, LBJ Library.
14. Telegram, USUN New York to DOS, 11/10/65, National Security File, Country File, UN Disarmament, Vol. 1, LBJ Library.
15. Letter, President to Prime Minister, 12/23/65, White House Confidential File, ISI–NATO, LBJ Library.
16. *Documents on Disarmament: 1965,* p. 633f.
17. *Documents on Disarmament: 1966,* p. 6.
18. Ibid., p. 10.
19. Ibid., p. 89. (Emphasis added.)
20. Ibid., p. 162ff.
21. Ibid., p. 180ff.
22. Quoted in *Documents on Disarmament: 1966,* p. 826.
23. Bovey (Paris) to DOS, 3/23/65, National Security File, Subject Files, MLF Cables, Vol. 4, LBJ Library.
24. LBJ to Erhard, 3/7/66, National Security File, Head of State Correspondence, Germany, Box 3, LBJ Library.
25. LBJ to De Gaulle, 3/22/66, White House Confidential File, ISI-IT 47-9, Box 58, IT 34 NATO, LBJ Library.
26. JCAE, *Nonproliferation of Nuclear Weapons, Hearings,* February–March 1966, p. 28.
27. Ibid., p.43.
28. Ibid., p. 74.
29. Ibid., p. 98.
30. Valenti to President, 3/19/66, National Security File, Aides Files, Valenti Memos, LBJ Library.
31. Private communication, October 21, 1985.
32. *Documents on Disarmament: 1966,* p. 323.
33. Anderson, *The President's Men,* p. 344.
34. Transcript, Adrian Fisher Oral History Interview, 10/31/68, by Paige E. Mulhollan, Tape 1, p. 32.

35. Private conversation, May 31, 1985.
36. *Documents on Disarmament: 1966*, p. 405.
37. Barnes, "The Nuclear Non-Proliferation Treaty," p. 338.
38. Private conversation with George Bunn, November 21, 1986.

16
Agreement on Articles I and II

It has become clear in Geneva that the impasse reached in our discussions with the Soviets will continue so long as each side attempts to include in its draft treaty explicit language protecting a position known to be unacceptable to the other.

—Adrian Fisher
July 1966[1]

"Personal Discussions"

In the late spring of 1966, very likely in response to President Johnson's increasing interest after Bill Moyers's intervention (chapter 15), and possibly in response to a specific directive from the president, Dean Rusk became more actively involved in the pursuit of a nonproliferation treaty. Rusk's intervention was of key importance to the achievement of a treaty. The active leadership of the secretary of state was essential because, as had already been demonstrated, this was a multilateral matter that various people in this and other countries could complicate for all kinds of reasons. In addition, Rusk personally had tremendous credibility with our allies as someone who had supported their interests in the past and could be relied on to do so in the future. Thus, from mid-1966 on, Rusk, in the eyes of NPT adherents, "ceased being part of the problem and started being part of the solution."[2]

On June 23, 1966, the secretary wrote to the Committee of Principals urging that simplified draft language be found for a new U.S. draft treaty. Adrian Fisher responded for the ACDA on July 8. Agreeing that a new draft was desirable, Fisher proposed revised language that he thought "would afford the basis for initiating serious negotiations." His suggested text adopted the word for which the Soviets had been contending, forbidding nuclear powers to *transfer* nuclear weapons "to any nation or group of nations." Fisher argued that forbidding transfer was in accord with a similar prohibition in the

Atomic Energy Act, which Congress had indicated it would not change. He contended further that his suggested language would not affect bilateral NATO two-key security arrangements, because these did not involve transfer. Nor did the language, in his view, prejudice "realistic options" for future European nuclear forces—a clear reference to the European option. What Fisher was offering was essentially the compromise hinted at by Foster in his 1965 *Foreign Affairs* article.

Within the next three weeks Foster and Fisher did one of their periodic flip-flops, Fisher going to Geneva and Foster returning to Washington. A new tactic was now devised. This was for Fisher, without the knowledge of the rest of the U.S. delegation, to approach Soviet Ambassador Roshchin and seek his "personal views" on a treaty idea that Fisher would submit, also "on a personal basis." Foster's further cabled instructions to Fisher read, in part:

> You should tell him you have been impressed with emphasis he seems put on barring "transfer" of nuclear weapons. You should add that you have been thinking about recommendations to send Washington . . . and would appreciate exchange views on a personal basis so that you can submit your recommendation before end week. You understand neither he nor his government is in any way bound by such views just as neither you nor your government are by your suggestion.[3]

The text Fisher was to suggest was the simplest yet: "Each of the nuclear-weapon states party to this treaty undertakes not to transfer nuclear weapons to any non-nuclear-weapon state, and not to assist, encourage, or induce any non-nuclear-weapon state to manufacture or otherwise acquire nuclear weapons." A significant omission in this draft was any prohibition against transfer to a "group" or "association" of states, such as had been included in the revised U.S. draft presented to the ENDC in March and in Fisher's suggested text of July 8. The Soviets were not expected to overlook this omission, and Fisher was instructed further:

> If Roshchin asks about absence reference to groups of states . . . you should say purpose of your suggestion is to see if simple formula can be found to avoid some of difficulties that have created impasse. You should not volunteer further explanation but seek his reaction. . . .

The Soviets reacted to the U.S. proposal more or less as expected. As Foster reported to Rusk, they found the search for a new formulation a hopeful sign, a step in the direction of the Soviet position. Without a provision regarding groups or associations of states, however, they said it could not serve as the basis for successful negotiation.[4]

Discussion at Higher Levels

Following his private discussions Fisher cabled to Washington a revised treaty text he thought might be negotiable.[5] Its Article I retained the language he had suggested to Roshchin but added a separate article specifying that none of the prohibited actions could be taken through third states, groups of states, or units of armed forces, even if in a military alliance. Fisher also suggested a major new clause decreeing that the treaty would remain in force for only five or ten years, with a review conference to be held six months before the treaty's expiration to determine whether its life should be extended. He explained this as "designed to lessen impact on potential nuclear states by avoiding the impression that a decision to forswear nuclear weapons was being taken forever, and to make it more palatable to FRG [Federal Republic of Germany] on the basis that future NATO developments would not be forever blocked."

President Johnson stepped up the pressure in behalf of the NPT in a speech at the National Reactor Testing Station in Idaho on August 26, 1966. Speaking of the NPT negotiations, the president said, "I believe that we can find acceptable language on which reasonable men can agree. We just must move ahead—for we all have a great stake in building peace in this world in which we live."[6]

Foster summed up the prospects in Geneva in an August 30 memo to Rusk.[7] Based on Fisher's "personal" discussions, he foresaw the possibility of a treaty that did not ban consultative arrangements like the McNamara Committee or embarrass U.S. bilateral arrangements with NATO partners. It would not, however, be possible to negotiate a treaty that did not deal at all with the question of transfer to groups of states. "I think, however," Foster continued, "we might be able to negotiate a treaty which does not foreclose any option *we could realistically expect to exercise*" (emphasis added). Foster next concerned himself with procedure. He recommended that the president write to Erhard that a NATO force involving mixed ownership of weapons supplied by the United States was no longer feasible and that a European nuclear force seemed likely to come into being only in the context of a true political federation to which either Britain or France would assign its nuclear weapons. Foster thought we could then seek final agreement with the Soviet Union either by presidential correspondence or Rusk–Gromyko discussions.

I could find no evidence that Johnson wrote the suggested letter to Erhard. The chancellor did visit the White House on September 26 and 27, however. It is significant that this visit's communiqué, unlike those that followed Erhard's previous visits to the president, made no mention of any hardware solution to NATO's nuclear problem. Moreover, Rusk and Gromyko did indeed meet. In New York to attend the opening of the General Assembly, they held private meetings on September 22 and 24. These discussions more or less confirmed the boundaries of agreement that had been established at Geneva.[8] As a follow-up to the Rusk–Gromyko sessions, a bilateral working group headed by Foster and Roshchin began deliberations in New York on specific language. Reports to Washington indicated that in this group the Soviets accepted a series of retreats from the severity of their draft treaty. The working group draft did not, for example, retain the Soviet draft's denial of "the right to *participate* in the control or use of nuclear weapons." Thus, the way seemed to be cleared for McNamara's consultative committees. Nor did the working group retain the Soviet draft's prohibition on transmitting "*information* . . . which can be employed for the . . . use of nuclear weapons." This could have interfered with NATO training exercises. Most significantly, the Soviets agreed to give up their previous insistence on banning *access* to nuclear weapons by non-nuclear-weapon states. As advice from our delegation noted: "Given the nature of some of our existing deployment arrangements, this word ["access"] could have given us real difficulties."[9]

On September 28, the working group reached tentative agreement and submitted a draft of Articles I and II of a nonproliferation treaty to their respective governments. The key provision of Article I required nuclear weapon states not to transfer nuclear weapons to any other country "directly or indirectly, either individually or collectively with any other member of a military alliance or group of states."[10]

What happened next is described by Lyndon Johnson in his memoirs:

After reading reports of the Rusk–Gromyko talks and discussing the problem with the Secretary of State and others, I invited several senior advisers to Camp David on October 1. . . . . After dinner, we reviewed the progress of discussions on the nonproliferation treaty. . . . The next morning, October 2, we continued our talks. Much of the time we wandered over the paths and through the autumn-colored woods at Camp David. I sounded out my advisers on their opinions and recommendations. They gave me not only their own views but those held by others in government who had been working on non-proliferation for a long time. Some of them believed that we had reached a point where agreement with the Soviets was within easy grasp, and that we should move ahead quickly. But others, especially Rusk, believed that we would be taking serious risks if we moved too fast and without thorough consultations with our major allies. I shared this view completely and asked Rusk to inform all concerned of my decision. We could not undertake a treaty obligation, I said, if it committed us to act as if there were no Atlantic Alliance. We could not tell our allies that these matters were none of their business. We should continue to push for a nonproliferation treaty, I told the Secretary, but not at the risk of tearing NATO apart.[11]

Another recollection of the discussion at Camp David has been offered by Eugene Rostow:

[T]here was a two-hour discussion of NPT with McNamara and Rusk and me and Walt [Rostow] and Arthur Goldberg. Finally, the President summed it up; he said, "I'm not going to get into the details of drafting, but there are two principles here. One, there can't be any transfer of nuclear weapons. The statute [Atomic Energy Act] forbids it. American public opinion forbids it. It's just impossible even to contemplate. The second is, I'm not going to eliminate the possibility of an . . . Alliance solution. I don't want one now, and we may not want one in the future, but that possibility has to be preserved because it may be necessary to keep the Germans locked in and for many other reasons.[12]

Beyond all these statements of principle, the essence of what happened at Camp David seems to have been to approve the concept that "transfer" of nuclear weapons should be forbidden but to disapprove the specific language agreed to in New York. Its explicit reference to "a military alliance or group of states" may have seemed too pointed for allied consumption, and also perhaps subject to interpretations that might, down the road, conflict with a European option type of solution. In addition, George Bunn, a member of Foster's team for the New York negotiations, speculates that it may have seemed injudicious to reach an agreement with the Soviets clearly outlawing the MLF so soon after the September 26 and 27 visit of Chancellor Erhard. The upshot was that ACDA negotiators were sent back to New York for another try.[13]

Agreement

As the General Assembly session continued, good progress appears to have been made in the New York discussions between the Foster and Roshchin teams. Then, on October 10, Gromyko met first at the White House with President Johnson and then with Secretary Rusk at the State Department. Gromyko said afterward that "it looks like both countries are striving to reach agreement and facilitate conclusion of an international agreement." By October 20, the USSR representative in the UN Political Committee was able to say that there were no major obstacles in the way of a nonproliferation treaty.

The auguries of superpower accord now stirred anxiety in the Germans, for whom the possibility of a Soviet–American deal at German expense was an abiding nightmare. On October 26, Ambassador Heinrich Knappstein called on Acting Secretary of State Nicholas Katzenbach to inquire about the status of NPT negotiations, regarding which he had heard "contradictory information." He wanted to know what concessions the United States had made. He said that the FRG would not produce or acquire nuclear weapons, but could not consider participation in an NPT until the nuclear problems of the alliance had found a satisfactory solution. He maintained that the defense of Europe should take precedence over accommodation of the USSR. Katzenbach told Knappstein that there ought to be things we could agree on with the Soviets that would be acceptable to the FRG. But, in any case, we would not do anything to damage NATO and there would be no agreement with the Soviets without prior consultation with our allies.[14]

In New York the United States and the Soviet Union continued to exchange drafts as the General Assembly session proceeded. Both Rusk and Gromyko stayed actively involved. At length, the long and difficult process bore fruit. On December 5, 1966, the two negotiating teams reached tentative agreement on a Soviet draft of Articles I and II of a nonproliferation treaty. The key element that made this draft acceptable to the United States (whereas the draft considered at Camp David was not) was that, instead of trying to spell out all those to whom transfer of nuclear weapons was forbidden, it merely forebade transfer *"to any recipient whatsoever."* The effect of this simpler version does not seem to have been substantially different from that of the version rejected at Camp David. Yet it was believed that, by omitting specific reference to alliance solutions that would no longer be permitted, it would be more palatable to the allies. It may have outlawed the MLF but it did not rub the Germans' noses in it.

The full text of Articles I and II, as recommended by the New York negotiators, was as follows:

ARTICLE I

Each nuclear-weapon State Party to this Treaty undertakes not to transfer to any recipient whatsoever nuclear weapons or other nuclear explosive devices or control over such weapons or explosive devices directly, or indirectly; and not in any way to assist, encourage, or induce any non-nuclear-weapon State to manufacture or otherwise acquire nuclear weapons or other nuclear explosive devices, or control over such weapons or explosive devices.

ARTICLE II

Each non-nuclear-weapon State Party to this Treaty undertakes not to receive the transfer from any transferor whatsoever of nuclear weapons or other nuclear explosive devices or of control over such weapons or explosive devices directly, or indirectly; not to manufacture or otherwise acquire nuclear weapons or other nuclear explosive devices; and not to seek or receive any assistance in the manufacture of nuclear weapons or other nuclear explosive devices.

It will be seen that Article II, prescribing the obligations of non-nuclear-weapon states, was a mirror image of Article I. It had been the subject of very little negotiation, the thought being that it would follow along in step with Article I.

True to its word, the United States now entered into a long series of consultations with its allies during which many questions were raised about the effect of the draft articles on NATO defense arrangements.* Following these consultations the United States issued

---

*There was some complaint from the allies about the fact that we were presenting to them for review a text already worked out in secret with the Soviets. John Leddy comments: "The NATO countries didn't like that. But . . . on all of the rest of the negotiations, on all the other clauses, we consulted NATO like mad, as well as bilaterally with the Germans. So they have no complaint for almost all of the negotiating period of 1967" (Oral History Interview, 3/12/69, by Paige E. Mulhollan, Tape 1, p. 15, LBJ Library).

a series of interpretations of what Articles I and II would and would not cover. We considered that they would apply to nuclear weapons and other nuclear explosive devices—meaning, peaceful nuclear explosives. They would bar transfer (including ownership or control) to any recipient, including a multilateral entity. On the other hand, the articles would not apply to delivery systems, nor prohibit NATO consultations on nuclear defense (for example, the McNamara Committees), nor prevent the deployment of U.S.-owned and controlled nuclear weapons on the territory of other NATO nations. Most important, we considered that they would not prevent a federated European state, if one ever developed, from legally succeeding Britain or France, or both, as a nuclear power—the European option.

These interpretations played a pivotal role in the final U.S.–Soviet accord on the NPT—a role that is not generally understood. As Dean Rusk explains, the interpretations were of vital importance to the Western alliance, particularly those concerning consultations on nuclear defense and the European option. The Soviets, on the other hand, insisted that they could not publicly endorse any language that implied a possible West German participation in nuclear weapons matters. Rusk thereupon worked out an all-important arrangement with Gromyko. Knowing full well how the Soviets felt on the German matter, but knowing also what was needed to get the assent of our allies, he told Gromyko that we intended at the time of the signing of the treaty to issue the interpretations. We did not insist that the Soviets publicly accept the statement we would issue. If, on the other hand, they publicly *objected* to it, then we would not ourselves ratify the NPT and it would be "back to the drawing board."

In the actual event, the interpretations were issued in question-and-answer form under the title of "Questions on the Draft Non-Proliferation Treaty Asked by U.S. Allies Together With Answers Given by the United States." They were attached by Secretary Rusk to his Letter of Submittal formally presenting the treaty to President Johnson on July 2, 1968, the day after it was opened for signature. The president, in turn, transmitted Rusk's letter, with this and other attachments, to the Senate when he sent forward the treaty for ratification.[15] The Soviet Union made no public objection, and the U.S. interpretations thereupon became an essential part of the transaction between the United States and its allies, on the one hand, and the Soviet Union, on the other.

Articles I and II, in the tentative formulation agreed to on December 5, 1966, survived as part of the treaty's ultimate language. It was a significant achievement, one of the high-water marks of post-World War II diplomacy. I am convinced that it could not have happened had President Johnson not become personally involved. After a long period in which he had confined his participation to giving rhetorical support, he let it be known to U.S. diplomats, to our allies, and to the Soviet Union that he was committed to obtaining an agreement on reasonable terms. His decision at Camp David—to shut the door on the near-term establishment of a NATO collective force—made agreement possible. As for the Soviet Union, Walt Rostow has an interesting observation:

> Moscow had to sit side by side with the United States and stare, with a common understanding, at the problems confronted by EURATOM and NATO, and India, Japan, and many other nations, if the NPT was going to be accepted. . . . One could glimpse during the NPT negotiations a little of what the world might be like if Moscow decided that its maximum attainable objective was a reasonably orderly and safe environment for the Soviet Union, achieved by close collaboration with the United States.[16]

One must also note with appreciation that the Soviets did not apply the doctrine of linkage in this situation. There had been statements on several occasions by Premier Kosygin and other Soviet officials to the effect that U.S. activity in Vietnam made it impossible to have normal relations with us. What the Soviets finally recognized—and what we need to recognize—is that neither of us engages in arms control as a favor to the other. It is something we each do in our own best interest.

Finally, one must ask how it was that the Soviet Union tacitly consented to a treaty interpretation that allowed for the possibility of a united Western European force, something the Soviets certainly would not welcome. They did so, in all likelihood, because they regarded such a united force as being a possibility so remote that, to gain the nonproliferation treaty, it was a chance worth taking. Thus interpreted, the Soviet action represents an object lesson in political pragmatism.

Although articles I and II were undoubtedly the core of the Nonproliferation Treaty, they were by no means the whole of it. Realizing that unless there was agreement on I and II, there could be no treaty, the United States and USSR had paid little attention to determining whether their views were in concert on other aspects. There was, for example, the matter of enforcement safeguards, which the United States had addressed in its drafts but which the Soviet Union had thus far ignored. Moreover, although both superpowers regarded this as something of an irritant, the non-nuclear-weapon states would seek certain assurances and compensation before agreeing to remain in their second-class status. As we shall consider in later chapters, there was much difficult negotiation ahead, involving a number of subjects and many participants. It would be another year and a half from the date of agreement on Articles I and II until a complete NPT could be readied for signature. It would be more than two years before it would enter into force, during the presidency of Richard Nixon.

Notes

1. Fisher to Rusk, 7/8/66, National Security File, Security Council History, Non-Proliferation Treaty, Vol. 2, LBJ Library.
2. This description is attributed to Spurgeon Keeny.
3. Foster to Fisher, 7/27/66, National Security File, National Security Council History, Non-Proliferation Treaty, Vol. 2, LBJ Library.
4. Foster to SecState, 9/15/66, National Security File, National Security Council History, Non-Proliferation Treaty, Vol. 2, LBJ Library.
5. Fisher to Foster, 8/25/66, National Security File, National Security Council History, Non-Proliferation Treaty, Vol. 2, LBJ Library.
6. *Documents on Disarmament: 1966*, p. 620.
7. Foster to SecState, 8/30/66, National Security File, National Security Council History, Non-Proliferation Treaty, Vol. 2, LBJ Library.
8. Barnes, "The Nuclear Non-Proliferation Treaty," p. 351.
9. National Security File, Security Council History, Non-Proliferation Treaty, Document 79a, LBJ Library.
10. George Bunn, private conversation, November 21, 1986.
11. Johnson, *The Vantage Point*, p. 478.
12. Transcript, Eugene Rostow Oral History Interview, 12/2/68, by Paige E. Mulhollan, Tape 1, p. 15, LBJ Library.
13. George Bunn, private conversation, November 21, 1986.
14. Telegram Bonn to DOS, 10/26/66, National Security File, National Security Council History, Non-Proliferation Treaty, Vol. 2, LBJ Library.
15 The attachment is reprinted in *Hearings on the Nonproliferation Treaty*, Senate Committee on Foreign Relations, July 1968, p. 262f.
16. Rostow, *The Diffusion of Power*, p. 383.

Part V

Testing after the Test Ban

A comprehensive test ban can go forward only
when it is decided by politically responsible
persons that the possible arms control benefits
. . . (calculated in terms of non-proliferation and
arms race avoidance) outweigh the probable
security risks . . . (calculated in terms of Soviet
evasion and a freeze on modernizing weapons).

Ploughshares Fund Press Packet
May 1986

17
1964: Dim Prospects
for a CTB

The Limited Test Ban Treaty was the most positive event I have ever been associated with.

—McGeorge Bundy
October 1983

Background: The LTB

To obtain a nonproliferation treaty was the number-one arms control priority during the first three years of the Johnson administration. Nonproliferation had also been a dominant concern of President Kennedy, but he had a different solution in mind. Kennedy believed that the most effective way to prevent proliferation was to bring an end to all nuclear testing. That he succeeded only in achieving the Limited Test Ban Treaty—which forbids tests in the atmosphere, in space, and under water, but permits them to continue underground—was for Kennedy a major setback. He regarded it as only temporary, however—he thought of the Limited Test Ban Treaty a being "a first step."

I have written in detail elsewhere of the history that culminated in the Limited Test Ban Treaty.[1] In this place I will provide only a brief summary to orient the reader to the situation as the Johnson administration found it.

The United States, United Kingdom, and USSR began serious negotiations on a test ban treaty late in 1958. Impelled to the bargaining table in part by a worldwide concern over radioactive fallout from atmospheric tests, each of the three leaders—Eisenhower, Macmillan, and Khrushchev—recognized the appalling potential consequences of a runaway arms race propelled by nuclear testing. Each would have been glad to arrest the competition on terms that did not disadvantage his nation's security. Soon after the tripartite negotiations began in Geneva, Switzerland, however, they became bogged down in disagreements about the details of a control system. Underlying the disagreements were basic elements of mistrust that had divided the superpowers since the nuclear age began. As at the very beginning, the United States insisted on extensive controls because of a suspicion that the Soviets might attempt to conduct clandestine tests in violation of a treaty; the Soviet Union resisted controls, especially those on its own soil, because of a suspicion that the United States intended to use the controls for purposes of espionage, as in the selection of bombing targets.

After many months of arguments about what controls were needed and how effective they would be, a compromise agreement was almost reached in the spring of 1960 on a treaty that would have banned all tests considered to be verifiable; namely, all except underground tests producing signals of less than 4.75 on the Richter earthquake magnitude scale. Along with the treaty, a moratorium would have been declared on those smaller underground tests, during which time a seismic research program would have been undertaken to improve verification techniques. It was widely expected that final agreement on this treaty might be reached at a May 1960 Big Four summit meeting in Paris. Shortly before the summit, however, Francis Gary Powers and his U-2 high-altitude reconnaissance plane were shot down over Sverdlovsk. This incident and the way it was handled diplomatically so poisoned the atmosphere that, though the test ban talks continued in Geneva, there could be no hope of agreement during the remaining months of the Eisenhower administration.

Early in his administration, President Kennedy ordered a thorough review to determine what concessions could be offered to meet Soviet objections to the U.S. test ban position while not impairing U.S. security. The concessions were embodied in a draft treaty introduced by the United States and United Kingdom in April 1961. The draft would have banned all but smaller underground tests; offered a longer moratorium on such tests; and allowed the Soviets to inspect nuclear devices we proposed to use in seismic research or for the AEC's Plowshare (peaceful nuclear explosions) program. We also agreed to a Soviet suggestion that the number of on-site inspections on the soil of each party be limited to an annual quota.

The most serious Soviet objection to the Western draft concerned the number of inspections in this annual quota: we proposed there be twenty; they offered to accept three. Over the ensuing two years the United States several times modified its quota demand until in February 1963 it reached seven as an official offer, with our chief negotiator authorized to produce the number six as a final fall-back position. The Soviets never went higher than three. Some have commented that the difference between three and six inspections was so insignificant that some compromise ought to have been possible. I believe, however, that this difference in numbers masked a more serious problem. This concerned our proposed procedures for the conduct of each inspection. The Soviets were never willing to discuss these, whether at the Geneva conference or in private. Considering that the procedures were quite rigorous and intrusive—involving, for example, low-flying helicopter flights over up to five hundred square kilometers in each inspection—I share Averell Harriman's view that the Soviets probably would not have agreed to them even if we had yielded on the number of inspections.[2]

Test ban negotiations during the Kennedy years were punctuated by tests. In August 1961 the Soviet Union took us completely by surprise—a signal failure of American intelligence—when they suddenly broke an informal test moratorium begun three years earlier and launched a massive series of atmospheric tests.* Analysis of the tests showed that the Soviets had made great progress. This brought strong pressures on President Kennedy to respond in kind. Kennedy, always skeptical about testing, limited the U.S. response at first to a relatively puny underground series. When the full implications, technical and political, of the Russian tests became clear, however, he resisted British attempts to stay his hand and authorized U.S. atmospheric tests. They took place in the Pacific between April and November 1962 and, despite some embarrassing mishaps, proved instructive, particularly regarding the possibilities of missile defense.

Then in October 1962 came the Cuban missile crisis. A paradoxical effect of this brush with catastrophe was that it seemed to draw President Kennedy and Chairman Khrushchev closer together. A by-product of their enhanced rapport was a shared desire to make progress in arms control. Each was limited in what he could agree to, however, by hard-line elements in his own country. Moreover, ne-

---

*Memory of this incident has clouded arms control negotiations from that time forward. Although the Soviet tests were not in violation of any formal agreement, their sudden onset after long and secret preparations was regarded as a breach of faith. Those who oppose particular arms control proposals, or arms control in general, frequently cite this experience as proof that "we can't trust the Russians" and therefore should not make further agreements with them.

gotiations in Geneva, conducted now for the United States by a new
agency, the Arms Control and Disarmament Agency, and before a
new forum, the Eighteen Nation Disarmament Committee, continued
to be frustrated by disagreements over on-site inspection.

The tide began to turn early in 1963. The Soviets agreed in April
to discuss U.S. proposals for a Hot Line agreement; this was signed
in June. In the generally improved atmosphere, the president's private
correspondence with Khrushchev quickened and warmed considerably. Yet, the diplomats in Geneva were mired in continuing deadlock. Kennedy and Macmillan thereupon took a bold initiative. They
proposed to Khrushchev that he receive high-level emissaries to discuss a test ban in private. Khrushchev's favorable reply arrived just
before the president's conciliatory American University speech of June
10, which had a dramatic effect in establishing a friendly atmosphere
for the talks. Khrushchev made it clear, however, before the emissaries arrived on July 15, that he was prepared to accept only a limited
test ban. In twelve days of intensive negotiation, Foreign Minister
Gromyko and Averell Harriman, leader of the small U.S. delegation,
reached agreement on a treaty. (A British delegation led by Lord Hail-
sham played a minor part in the negotiations.) The treaty was initialed on July 25 and signed in an atmosphere of celebration on August
5, 1963, almost exactly eighteen years after Hiroshima.

President Kennedy, with his propensity to pessimism, was fearful
about the treaty's prospects in the Senate. He wanted to obtain a
large majority to pave the way toward further agreements. To help
get this majority, he agreed to four national security "safeguards" put
forward by the Joint Chiefs of Staff as conditions for their support
of the treaty. These required the president to commit himself to (1) a
vigorous underground test program; (2) high-level maintenance of
U.S. weapon laboratories; (3) continued readiness to resume atmospheric testing; and (4) improving our national technical means for
detecting Soviet treaty violations. Reassured by the safeguards and by
forecasts (some from me) that Plowshare (peaceful nuclear explosion)
experiments would be permissible under the treaty, a number of senators who had been leaning against voted in favor. The Senate "consented" to the treaty by a margin of 80 to 19 on September 24, 1963,
after what Dean Rusk characterized as "a classic and sober debate,"[3]
and it entered into force on October 10.

For John Kennedy it was a Pyrrhic victory. Instead of representing, as he had wished, a step toward an end to all testing, the vote

represented to many a validation of continued testing, albeit underground. Without the frightening mushroom clouds and radioactive fallout from atmospheric tests, there was no longer any significant public concern to act as a brake. Testing after the test ban continued at a rapid rate.

Emphasis on the Safeguards

Even before the Limited Test Ban Treaty entered into force, conservative members of Congress began to press for specific measures to implement the four national security safeguards. On September 24, 1963, the day after the Senate vote, Representative Craig Hosmer, who had been a leading opponent of the treaty, wrote President Kennedy a letter on this matter. He noted that the president's assurances about the safeguards had been general in nature. He called attention to the resistance of some prominent scientists—he mentioned Eugene Wigner and Leo Szilard—to an extensive underground testing program on the grounds that this would set back the cause of peace. He noted "with apprehension" that some members of the administration seemed to share this thinking. Hosmer then went on to set forth some "specifics" he thought necessary to implement the safeguards. They included building a community at the Nevada test site; developing a new testing site for high-yield tests; adding laboratory facilities and personnel; readying a complete new missile range for atmospheric tests; equipping additional Pacific islands for testing; construction of test diagnostic ships; building a fleet of twelve new planes for gathering radioactive air samples; and making extensive additions of test detection facilities. Hosmer estimated the cost of his specifics at $1 billion in capital outlays and $250 million annually in operating costs. These amounts were far in excess of any being contemplated by the administration.

Hosmer's letter was referred to me and I answered it on October 17. I enclosed a message the president had sent to Congress the day before requesting an additional $17.5 million for the AEC's weapons laboratories for the current fiscal year. Having received my letter, Hosmer wrote the president again, showing in tabular form a comparison of the $1 billion he estimated was needed and the $17.5 million the administration had requested. He said that the comparison raised doubts that the safeguards were "being taken seriously by those who may be advising you."

Pressure for vigorous implementation of the safeguards continued into President Johnson's term. On March 25, 1964, the Joint Senate–House Republican Leadership issued a statement requesting that Johnson reaffirm Kennedy's commitments. Senate Minority Leader Everett Dirksen personalized the request by pointing out that it was he who had read Kennedy's statement pledging the safeguards on the Senate floor during the test ban debate, and that he had done so at the late president's request. The statement by the Republican leaders also requested that President Johnson provide a "six-month report" on the safeguards steps being taken, noting that "some members of Congress have questioned whether or not a sufficient portion of the overall defense budget is being expended in this field."

President Johnson replied by making public a letter that Secretary McNamara and I had sent to him. As to safeguard 1 (a vigorous underground testing program), our letter stated that the United States had conducted more than twenty underground tests in the eight months since the signing of the test ban treaty, including the "highest yield nuclear device ever detonated in the continental United States." As to safeguard 2 (the maintenance of modern laboratory facilities), we indicated that during the fiscal year then in progress the government would spend about $350 million on weapons laboratory research and over $25 million on improving laboratory facilities. Regarding safeguard 3 (readiness to resume atmospheric testing), we stated that the United States was proceeding on schedule with development of a capability involving "minimum reaction time." As to safeguard 4 (improving U.S. ability to monitor Soviet tests), our letter described the various improvements in detection techniques already achieved or planned, including the placement in orbit in October 1963 of two instrumented satellites designed to detect nuclear explosions in deep space.

There the matter rested for the moment, but President Johnson was on notice that there were forces in Congress more interested in a vigorous testing program than in further restrictions on testing. This may well have reinforced his own tendency to be quite skeptical about the value of test bans, including the Limited Test Ban Treaty.

The FY1965 Testing Program

The U.S. underground testing program for the fiscal year beginning July 1, 1964 came under review at a White House meeting on June 16.

At President Johnson's request I gave an overview of the tests planned for the year: 45 to 55 in the weapons development category, 8 in the Plowshare category, and 12 in the weapons effects and detection category, a total of 65 to 75. The president asked why so many more tests were planned than had been conducted in the current fiscal year (45). I explained that the AEC had refrained from testing during the summer of 1963, a sensitive period in the test ban negotiations. McNamara added that much of the increase was in test detection experiments, a category that had only originated as a result of the test ban treaty and Safeguard 4.

Bundy asked [CIA Deputy Director Marshall S.] Carter how the rate of Soviet testing compared to our own. Carter said we had detected only three Soviet tests since the treaty. The president wanted to know why there was such a difference between their rate of testing and our own. Bundy replied that the Soviets used to say they couldn't afford an underground testing program. No other explanation was offered.

Rusk said that, from a foreign policy point of view, it was desirable to carry on a vigorous program of underground tests. We didn't know what Soviet plans were; they might break out of the test ban treaty and resume atmospheric testing. Another possibility was that we and the Soviets might move toward a comprehensive test ban, implying that it was desirable to get in a full underground test program while this was still permitted.

U.S. underground testing continued at a high level during the Johnson years. In the five years 1964–68, there were 140 announced underground tests.[4] During the same period the United States announced 25 Soviet tests. (The rate of Soviet testing picked up markedly during the 1970s, for a while exceeding that of the United States.)

A Matter of Interpretation

Unexpressed at the June 16 meeting on the AEC's testing program was a difficulty imposed by the Limited Test Ban Treaty. Besides banning nuclear tests in the atmosphere, outer space and under water, Article I of the treaty also prohibits underground tests that cause "radioactive debris to be present outside the territorial limits" of the testing nation. This language became very troublesome to us in the AEC. We had had ample opportunity to foresee the problem, since these words had been in the draft treaty submitted by the United

States in August 1962. In all honesty, we had been asleep at the switch, and the problem did not become manifest until after the treaty was signed.

The difficulty centered on the phrase "causes radioactive debris to be present . . ." Did this mean a minute trace of radioactivity that could barely be measured by the most sensitive instruments? The AEC opposed this interpretation—it would have handicapped us severely in our conduct of both weapons tests and Plowshare experiments. We pointed out that interpreting the phrase as prohibiting the export of the most minute detectable amount of radioactivity caused the treaty to be self-amending, its meaning changing with each advance in detection capability. Stimulated by Safeguard 4, such advances were occurring at a rapid pace. In addition, the cessation of atmospheric testing had greatly reduced the levels of man-made background radiation, thus making more noticeable any small increment of radioactivity from an underground event. We argued for a more realistic, *de minimus* interpretation, one that would permit nuclear explosions if radioactive debris crossing a national border were present only in very minute quantities, bearing no foreseeable relationship to human health.*

The AEC's position, while logically strong, was legally weak. As the ACDA pointed out, there was nothing in the text of the treaty to indicate that the presence of small amounts of debris was to be accepted, nor had any other signator advocated such a standard. ACDA noted further that in testifying for the treaty before the Foreign Relations Committee, I had myself said that it would not permit tests resulting in "*detectable* amounts of radioactive debris . . . outside of our continental limits." The ACDA favored a strict interpretation of the treaty's words. They feared that to adopt any other standard would impugn the good faith of the United States in seeking arms control agreements and injure our reputation as a country that took its treaty obligations seriously.

One reason why the AEC was reluctant to accept a strict interpretation was that underground testing was a relatively new and inexact discipline. We could not predict with precision what consequences would follow a given explosion. In trying to make up our minds

---

*Allan Labowitz narrates that this interpretation was first articulated by George Ball, who appeared to improvise it in response to a question at a news briefing. (Private conversation, June 13, 1986.)

whether to conduct any given test, therefore, we were caught between two imperatives. On the one hand, we did not want to violate the test ban treaty. On the other hand, we were under an injunction (Safeguard 1) to conduct a vigorous underground testing program.

Soon after the test ban treaty entered into force, President Kennedy took steps to lift some of the burden of decision from the AEC's shoulders. On October 31, 1963, he established a procedure for the review and approval of any underground explosion "which by its nature could reasonably give rise to domestic or foreign charges of a violation of the Nuclear Test Ban Treaty . . . even though the sponsoring agency believes that the charges would prove to be unfounded." The AEC was instructed to "make every effort" to avoid such explosions. If after careful study, however, we believed a particular suspect explosion—whether weapons test or Plowshare experiment—should remain in the program, we would have to submit the proposal to a committee chaired by the national security adviser, with high-level representation from State, Defense, AEC, CIA, the Joint Chiefs, and ACDA. (This group became known as the "269 Committee," because the National Security Action Memorandum that established it bore that number. Its formal name was "Review Committee on Underground Nuclear Tests.") If the committee approved the explosion, it would pass along its recommendation to the president, who would have to give his personal approval before the project could go forward.

Despite all precautions and scrutiny, the feared event, an alleged treaty violation by a U.S. test, soon came to pass.

The Venting of PIKE

In the first of the AEC biweekly reports I sent to President Johnson, just five days after President Kennedy's assassination, I wrote:

On October 7, 1963, the underground nuclear test program was reoriented to comply with the provisions of the Limited Test Ban Treaty. . . . Since the treaty, the AEC has conducted all underground test detonations at depths that provide reasonable assurance of containing radioactive debris. Based on past experience, there is high assurance that the next five events will not produce measurable radioactivity.

My prediction was borne out in the next four tests. But the fifth was another matter. My diary for March 13, 1964, contained the following laconic note:

The PIKE event in Nevada vented.

The following day:

There is much concern over the venting of PIKE from the standpoint of possible violation of the Test Ban Treaty.

On March 17:

Charles Johnson (White House) called to say that people there were getting worried about PIKE. I asked whether we should talk to Bundy about it. He said he would let me know after the morning staff meeting if this seemed to be called for. If we decided we had a problem there would then be time enough to get the president involved. He urged us to make sure we had a good review of what happened.

The following day, March 18:

The danger of PIKE having violated the Test Ban Treaty seems to have passed.

But on March 20:

It appears that a small amount of radioactivity crossed the Mexican border in the vicinity of Yuma, Arizona.

This information came from an elaborate investigation we launched immediately following PIKE. Radiation monitors and automatic recording instruments were used to measure radiation levels along the fallout trajectory. Six aircraft were used to track the radioactive cloud. In addition, the air force flew forty-four tracking sorties. The increase of radioactivity in Las Vegas, Boulder City, Yuma, and elsewhere in Arizona, while measurable, was slight and considered not to be hazardous. It was concluded that air masses that might have contained suspect material entered Mexico and then returned to the United States. We could not verify this absolutely, however, because we could not fly tracking sorties on the Mexican side of the border. (Subsequently, radioactive contamination was found in milk samples ten miles on the U.S. side of the Mexican border.)[5]

In response to questions from the White House and the ACDA, the AEC was at pains to point out that a number of previous tests similar to PIKE had not vented. The difference in this case was that a crack had developed as a result of a local weakness in the geological structure. We promised to be more careful about our geological evaluation in the future and, if possible, to conduct tests only when the wind was blowing away from Mexico. Yet, there could be no guarantees.

On April 7:

> I called Bundy to make sure the president understood the venting situation in Nevada. I pointed out that it was our national policy (Safeguard 1) to conduct these tests. Despite all precautions, once in a while one of these unforeseeable incidents might occur. The president and everyone else concerned should understand that fully. Bundy agreed to put this before the president.

The Soviet Union did not make a big issue of the PIKE incident, although a Tass news dispatch and a formal diplomatic note made it clear that they had taken note of it. In all likelihood the Soviets tempered their response because they understood full well that such mishaps might happen in their own program also and they did not want to establish too high a standard of accountability.

With the passage of time we were able to improve our techniques so as to assure that nuclear weapons tests were fully contained underground. As we shall see later on, however, the PIKE episode would further weaken our ability to defend the Plowshare program against the onslaught of its critics.

JFK's Hopes Unfulfilled

An abiding consideration driving the AEC's underground testing program was the possibility mentioned by Dean Rusk at the June 16, 1964, meeting: that the United States and the Soviet Union might agree on a treaty putting an end to all tests. In President Kennedy's view, such a measure was the single device on the international scene that offered greatest promise of leading humanity toward a safer world. He believed that a comprehensive test ban had the potential for preventing the spread of nuclear weapons capability to additional nations and, by limiting qualitative improvements, of arresting the nuclear arms race between the superpowers. As to the Limited Test Ban Treaty, what it seemed likely to achieve by itself was just that—limited. Its major direct effect was to drastically reduce radioactive fallout from nuclear tests. But it could not wholly eliminate fallout—nonsigners China and France might still test in the atmosphere. Some thought that the LTBT would discourage proliferation by making it more technically difficult and costly for additional countries to enter the nuclear club. Considering, however, that the particular nations thought to be on the threshold of a weapons capability all had considerable industrial prowess, it seemed unlikely that any would be dissuaded by the rigors of underground testing.

Fully aware of these limitations, both Kennedy and Khrushchev had stated on more than one occasion that the Limited Test Ban Treaty would only fulfill the hopes they both had for it if it led to further steps; if, by generating what Khrushchev called "a fund of confidence," it could lead the major powers to take some national security risks in order to achieve genuine and significant arms control and, ultimately, disarmament.

The hope of using the Limited Test Ban Treaty as a springboard to a more significant agreement was expressed in its preamble, where the parties proclaimed their aim "to achieve the discontinuance of all test explosions of nuclear weapons for all time," and their determination "to continue negotiations to this end." On November 27, 1963, five days after Kennedy's death, the UN General Assembly took note of this preambular statement and urged in a near-unanimous vote that negotiations for a comprehensive test ban proceed at the ENDC "with a sense of urgency." The United States and the Soviet Union both voted for the resolution but promptly made it clear to the delegates that they were still far apart on the issue of verification. For the United States, Ambassador Adlai Stevenson asserted that on-site inspection was still needed to "make it possible to dispel doubts as to the nature of certain seismic events." The Soviet delegate countered by stating that his government "would not be prepared to accept *any* inspections inasmuch as they are not necessary." Thus the earlier Soviet offer of three on-site inspections per year, which Khrushchev had always explained as a political gesture to placate President Kennedy and the U.S. Senate, was formally withdrawn.

If all that stood in the way of a more comprehensive test ban agreement was verification, Brazil's foreign minister, João Augusto de Araujo Castro, had a suggestion. He proposed to the General Assembly a gradual approach beginning with the prohibition of those underground tests already verifiable by national technical means (seismic monitoring, satellite reconnaissance, and other methods of gathering intelligence without on-site inspection). The threshold would then be lowered progressively as further improvements were made in the techniques of verification. The fact that neither superpower endorsed this eminently practical idea was considered an indication that each of them in fact wanted to continue testing, and that the verification issue was to some extent a smoke screen. There were suspicions, indeed, that if push came to shove the United States would itself not have welcomed on-site inspection.[6]

Obedient to the General Assembly's request, the ENDC took up the test ban issue when it resumed its work in January 1964. As we have noted, President Johnson's message of January 21, 1964, to the committee included in its panoply of proposals one for a comprehensive test ban "under effective verification and control." A week later the Soviets also advocated a comprehensive treaty but insisted that "no special international control need be organized to detect underground tests. . . ." The Brazilian delegate repeated the suggestion that had been made by his foreign minister at the General Assembly and received support from several of the other delegations. The superpowers responded by restating their positions. Then, in June, Soviet Deputy Foreign Minister Valerian Zorin told the ENDC that his government had decided to drop demands for the rapid extension of the Limited Test Ban Treaty to include underground tests.[7] At the conclusion of the ENDC sessions in September, the neutral Eight submitted a joint memorandum in which they expressed regret that no progress had been made toward a comprehensive test ban.

On July 30, 1964, President Johnson issued a statement in observance of the first anniversary of the signing in Moscow of the Limited Test Ban Treaty. The only benefit of the treaty that he mentioned was that a "year without atmospheric testing has left our air cleaner." His statement placed greatest emphasis on the fact that, because of the four national security safeguards, the treaty had not impaired the military strength of the United States. He reported that "the Joint Chiefs of Staff had reviewed the . . . [safeguards] program and agreed that satisfactory progress is being made under it." No reference was made in the president's statement to any hope for a comprehensive test ban.

From time to time in formal messages, Johnson would in future years espouse a comprehensive treaty. It was my impression, however, that these expressions were pro forma, put forward primarily to affect world opinion, and without personal conviction or enthusiasm. It is jumping a little ahead in our story, but I believe it will be helpful in understanding the president's attitude if I narrate here part of a conversation I had with him on December 27, 1966. It took place at his Texas ranch, to which some agency heads had been invited for individual discussions about their budgets for the next fiscal year.

> At one point the president asked me whether the Limited Test Ban Treaty was interfering with progress in the Plowshare program. I said that it was. He said that he questioned the value of the treaty and asked me to give him some arguments in defense of it. I explained the hopes that the treaty would lead to a decrease in international tensions and to a slowing of nuclear weapons proliferation. The president seemed not at all impressed by these arguments. In connection with the AEC's budget request for a supplemental test site area, I explained to him that it would probably be desirable to complete tests on the antiballistic missile before we signed any comprehensive test ban treaty, and that these tests might require another four or five years. The president accepted this and didn't seem convinced of the value of a comprehensive treaty. In fact, he expressed doubt as to the entire value of the ACDA and skepticism about its accomplishments.

On December 21, 1964, prospects for a comprehensive test ban were considered briefly at a meeting of the Committee of Principals.

> General Wheeler thought the Chinese would not go along with a CTB, and McNamara said that India, Germany and others would not sign unless China did. Recalling the need for the four safeguards to get the Limited Test Ban through the Senate, Bundy predicted it would be hard to get Senate approval of a comprehensive ban. McNamara expressed the view that the LTB was working to the advantage of the Soviets because underground tests were enabling them to close the gap in weapons

technology. [This argument implied a need for a more comprehensive treaty.] I disagreed with McNamara, arguing that the United States also was making much progress with underground tests; also that they enabled us to keep our weapons laboratories viable and healthy.

The variety of views within the administration about the whole question of test bans seemed inherent in the variety of missions performed and constituencies represented by the several agencies. A similar situation had existed in the Kennedy administration. The major difference between the two administrations seemed to derive from the attitudes of the two presidents. President Kennedy, an ardent test ban advocate, had been able through skilled and energetic leadership to overcome internal opposition and bring the matter to the negotiating table, although, as we have observed, what he came away with was far less than he had sought. With President Johnson being indifferent at best, his administration's support of further limitations on testing was mainly rhetorical. A comprehensive test ban seemed more remote at the end of 1964 than it had for several years past.

Notes

1. Seaborg, *Kennedy, Khrushchev and the Test Ban.*
2. Testimony to Senate Committee on Foreign Relations, *Hearings on Promoting a Comprehensive Test Ban Treaty*, p. 107.
3. Address at Barnard College, 22 January 1964, quoted in *Documents on Disarmament: 1964*, p. 10.
4. Includes four tests in the VELA program for improving test detection capabilities. Data from U.S. Department of Energy, "Announced United States Nuclear Tests."
5. Congressional Research Service, "Soviet Compliance with Arms Control Agreements," pp. 12 ff.
6. Newhouse, *Cold Dawn*, p. 14.
7. Mastny, *Disarmament and Nuclear Tests*, p. 27.

18
1965: More Debates, More "Violations"

International Debate

Beginning in 1965, consideration of a comprehensive test ban came more and more to be linked to the debate about a nonproliferation treaty. Nonnuclear weapon states were by that time in growing rebellion against the apparent desire of the superpowers to achieve a "naked" treaty, one separate from any nuclear disarmament measures. At the ENDC, India's Ambassador Trivedi attacked "the unrealistic and irrational proposition that a non-proliferation treaty should impose obligations only on non-nuclear countries while the nuclear powers continue to hold on to their privileged status by retaining and even increasing their deadly stockpiles." Leaders of other delegations voiced similar feelings. In September 1965 the neutral Eight at the ENDC issued a formal memorandum stating their collective view that "measures to prohibit the spread of nuclear weapons should . . . be coupled with or followed by tangible steps to halt the nuclear arms race."[1]

A comprehensive test ban was the one measure that the neutrals seemed most willing to accept as a reasonable quid pro quo. Here, however, they ran into the impasse created by the sharply divergent views of the United States and the USSR on how such a pact should be verified. In an effort to forge a compromise that both superpowers might accept, the neutrals lined up behind a proposal offered by UAR Ambassador Hassan for a so-called threshold test ban. This was substantially the same proposal as had been introduced in 1964 by the foreign minister of Brazil. It would have extended the Limited Test Ban Treaty to encompass all underground tests generating seismic signals greater than 4.75 on the Richter scale,* this being the level that was thought to be verifiable without on-site inspection. At the same time there would also be a moratorium on tests below the threshold to give scientists additional time to explore the technical problems of verification.

While supporting the UAR proposal, the neutrals were quite critical of those attitudes of the superpowers that stood in the way of a fully comprehensive test ban. Trivedi, for example, chided the United States for its unwillingness to accept "insignificant theoretical risks." The Soviets were criticized for refusing to countenance technical discussions on the need for inspection.

When the ENDC reconvened on July 27, 1965, President Johnson informed the delegates that "a truly comprehensive test ban treaty" was one of the objectives he had instructed the U.S. delegation to pursue "with all the determination and wisdom they can command."[2] In his opening statement Foster noted that there had been major progress in the detection and identification of seismic events.[3] (The "identification" problem was that of determining whether a particular detected underground event was an explosion or an earthquake. Identification requires the recording of a clearer signal than is needed for detection purposes alone.) Foster described a prototype array of 525 instruments that the United States was building in Montana. This was expected to improve greatly the ability to filter out background noise (caused by continuous vibrations of the earth) from the true signal emitted by a seismic event. He estimated that the Montana array would have a signal-to-noise ratio at least ten times greater than that of the quietest single-instrument station. He urged establishment of a worldwide system of such arrays in order to reduce greatly the number of unidentified seismic events. He thought the number could be reduced still further by the use of ocean-bottom seismometers to locate events near shorelines. Nevertheless, it was the U.S. estimate that, for the next several years at least, there would be about forty-five unidentified seismic events per year in the Soviet Union and, for this reason, it was our contention that on-site inspections would continue to be necessary. Foster indicated our willingness to work out inspection arrangements that minimized "intrusiveness."

---

*U.S. experts estimated that this threshold would correspond to tests in the range of 30 to 40 kilotons, depending on the surrounding medium. For reference, note that the Hiroshima bomb yielded somewhat less than 20 kilotons and that the Threshold Test Ban Treaty signed in 1974 prohibited underground tests yielding more than 150 kilotons.

The Swedish delegation submitted a memorandum recommending an international "detection club" involving the collection and distribution of data by several suitably located stations coordinated by some international body.[4] This idea was included in a joint memorandum unanimously endorsed by the neutral Eight on September 15, 1965.[5] The memorandum appealed to the nuclear powers "to suspend forthwith nuclear tests in all environments" and stressed the "advantages that would accrue from international cooperation in the work of seismic detection."

At the General Assembly in September, Ambassador Goldberg again pointed to the "substantial improvement in seismic detection capabilities" that had resulted from U.S. research. He said the United States would invite a large number of UN members to visit the Montana test detection site in October. On December 3, the General Assembly voted 92 to 1 (Albania), with France and all Eastern bloc nations except Romania abstaining, for a resolution urging all nations to suspend nuclear tests and requesting the ENDC to continue working for a comprehensive test ban "with a sense of urgency."[6] The United States voted for the resolution but, as Foster explained, this did not mean we had changed our view that some inspection would be required for an effective test ban.

Internal Debate

The lukewarm support that the United States gave to a comprehensive test ban in international discussion reflected a considerable divergence of views on this subject within the Johnson administration. When the Gilpatric Committee Report was formally presented to President Johnson on January 21, 1965, former test ban negotiator Arthur Dean announced the committee's recommendation that a comprehensive test ban be a prime objective of U.S. policy. As an indication of how strongly the committee felt about this, he stated that this policy decision should be made firmly so that a comprehensive test ban treaty would move forward *"without opposition in the government."* (Emphasis added.) Dean, who had been Kennedy's principal test ban negotiator, would have had vivid recollections of the uphill battle fought for test ban proposals during the Kennedy years. Nevertheless, the idea of muzzling opposition in advance was a startling one. Lacking a firm presidential commitment, it had no chance.

On August 25, 1965, test ban policy was discussed by the Committee of Principals at a meeting attended by Vice President Humphrey.

Dr. Robert A. Frosch of the Advanced Research Projects Agency, Department of Defense, presented a briefing on our improving capabilities for detecting and identifying Soviet underground tests without inspection. He indicated that the number of seismic events in the Soviet Union that could not be positively identified as either a nuclear test or an earthquake had shrunk from about 80 per year to about 30 per year.

Joint Chiefs Chairman Wheeler suggested that we be conservative in public descriptions of our seismic detection capability. [The greater this capability appeared to be, the more difficult it would be to defend the U.S. position that on-site inspections were needed for an underground test ban.] [Herbert] Scoville [ACDA assistant director for science and technology] presented a very optimistic assessment of the ability of photographic intelligence to supplement seismic methods in further reducing the number of unidentified seismic events.

Fisher reported that, in view of the dim prospects for a nonproliferation agreement at the ENDC, there was increasing emphasis there on a comprehensive test ban treaty as a means of preventing proliferation. He thought the reduction in unidentified events described by Dr. Frosch should make it possible for the United States to reduce the number of onsite inspections we would demand in a comprehensive test ban. On the other hand, he doubted there was time to clear a changed position within the government, including the Congress,* before the adjournment of the ENDC, expected in from two to four weeks. Vice President Humphrey agreed that the necessary clearances for a totally new U.S. position could not be obtained in so short a time. Nor did he feel there was any need for a change; it was "better to stay with a sound position than to change for the sake of change." McNamara agreed that this was not the time for the United States to put forward a new proposal.

Llewellyn Thompson doubted that the Soviets wanted a comprehensive test ban treaty. He added that, if there were such a treaty to which the Chinese did not adhere, there was a possibility that the Chinese would test weapons for the Soviet Union.

---

*Fisher might well have had in mind that the Joint Committee on Atomic Energy, in hearings held August 16, had expressed great skepticism about the value of a comprehensive test ban.

> Rusk thought it was not to our advantage to change our policy on a comprehensive test ban, considering (1) that there might be a national emergency [presumably over Vietnam] by the time Congress returned in January 1966, and (2) that the Soviets seemed not to be interested. He felt we should stay where we were unless the Soviets indicated they would accept some inspection. Bundy agreed with the others that this was not the time to change our test ban position in Geneva. If we could get together privately with Moscow and agree on an appropriate number of onsite inspections, that would be another matter.

The upshot of this meeting seemed to be that the United States found itself locked into a position—insisting on inspections in a comprehensive test ban—that was increasingly difficult to defend on technical grounds but that could not easily be changed for reasons of domestic and international politics. It was also becoming more apparent that, whatever arguments were used (for example, about difficulties of verification), the opposition of the Joint Chiefs of Staff to test ban proposals had a simple and clear basis—they believed continued testing was essential to the maintenance and further development of our nuclear deterrent.

The conclusions reached by the Principals were soon put to the test in Geneva. On September 7, Foster rejected the UAR's threshold test ban proposal. The Soviet Union accepted it, causing us some diplomatic embarrassment.

Diplomatic Ping-Pong

In 1964 the United States had experienced a period of discomfiture after the PIKE test vented and apparently caused radioactive debris to cross the Mexican border. In 1965 it was the Soviet Union's turn to squirm. On January 15:

> The Soviets conducted an underground test at 6 A.M. today of about 150 kilotons, of which about 10 percent vented, as measured by acoustic signals.

In subsequent days, more information became available. On January 19, the AEC upgraded its estimate of the blast's force to the "intermediate range," two hundred kilotons to a megaton. It was obviously the largest Soviet underground test yet. A Swedish scientific expert was quoted as saying that the signals received "almost surely came from the first known underground explosion of an H-bomb."[7] High-flying U.S. planes were reported to have picked up small quantities of radioactive material over the northern Pacific, and in our January 19 announcement the AEC reported detecting "a certain amount of venting." We added: "The amounts of radioactivity measured to date will not produce measurable exposure to persons."

This event, quite obviously an accident, as PIKE had been, set in motion an almost ludicrous sequence of meetings and diplomatic exchanges. The crux of it was that some on our side wanted to exploit this situation in order to make the Soviets pay the maximum price in public embarrassment. I tried to tilt the scales toward a moderate response because I feared the repercussions of too severe an accounting on our own test program and on Plowshare. There was another reason. Three days before the Soviet test we had conducted a reactor safety experiment at the Nevada Test Site as part of AEC's program to deveop a nuclear-powered rocket for space exploration. This experiment, known as KIWI, involved the deliberate destruction of a nuclear reactor. It was conducted to obtain data on the safety effects of such an accident. During the experiment portions of the reactor vaporized and released some fission products into the atmosphere. The AEC made it quite clear in its public discussion of the incident that a reactor was not a nuclear explosive and that therefore KIWI could not be considered a violation of the test ban treaty. Nevertheless, we felt that if the Russians were pressed too hard on their accidental venting they would make counteraccusations about KIWI.

On January 19, a special meeting of the Committee of Principals was called to consider how we should react to the Soviet incident.

> McCone described the evidence: 6 to 8 seismic signals from the Semipalatinsk area indicating an underground test of about 300 kilotons—AEC's initial estimate had been 150 kilotons; accompanying accoustic signals indicating that about 15 kilotons had vented; appearance of radioactive debris over Japan at about the predicted time.
>
> It was decided that there should be a press release, accompanied by a background briefing for key press people. I argued for stating that this was not a violation of the Limited Test Ban Treaty, but all the others opposed such a statement. McCone argued strenuously that it was indeed a violation. All the others

felt it should not be regarded as a violation but that it would not be good tactics to make this concession in our news release.

On January 21:

George Ball called to say that the Japanese had detected fallout estimated to be twice as great as that from the Chinese test of last October. Ball thought this might change a routine story into one much more dramatic and hoped the AEC could do something to keep the lid on. He thought we might make calls to individual reporters explaining the event as being due to Soviet inexperience in underground testing. (This was without doubt a correct assessment.) He and I agreed that the Japanese measurements might not be accurate.

Before the president entered the room at the meeting later that day on the Gilpatric Committee Report, Rusk reported that he had called in Dobrynin to ask for an explanation of the venting. He had told the ambassador that it was important to the United States to know whether it had been an accident or whether the Soviet Union had changed its attitude toward the Limited Test Ban Treaty. Dobrynin had answered that he himself knew nothing about the event and that, because the top Soviet leaders were in Warsaw, it might take some time to get an answer. He had expressed confidence, however, that there was no change in Soviet policy.

Just as I had feared, Dobrynin called on Llewellyn Thompson the following day to demand an explanation of our January 12 KIWI excursion, which the Soviets alleged might be a treaty violation. According to Thompson's report, Dobrynin at first stated that the Soviet request was "not related to the inquiry which Secretary Rusk had made of him regarding an atomic event said to have taken place in the Soviet Union." A little later, however, he said that "in fact there may have been some similarity between the two events in that both may have been accidents."

The game of diplomatic ping-pong was now on in earnest. On January 25, it was back to the Soviet explosion; Dobrynin delivered the Soviet reply to Rusk's official inquiry. It read as follows:

This January 15th, an underground nuclear explosion was indeed carried out in the Soviet Union. This explosion was carried out deep underground. The quantity of radioactive debris that leaked into the atmosphere was so insignificant that possibility of its fallout outside the territorial limits of the Soviet Union should be excluded. Thus, the underground explosion that was carried out does not affect the provisions of the treaty barring nuclear weapons tests in the atmosphere, in outer space and under water.

Later that day:

> Rusk read me this message over the telephone and asked me what I thought about it. I said my off-hand reaction was to regard the fallout as a not very significant amount and not a violation of the test ban treaty and to let it go at that. I pointed out once more that we were very serious about needing some breathing room for our own tests. Rusk thought the Soviets might have denied the spread of debris in ignorance that the Japanese had discovered some. He asked what I thought of making public the Soviet statement. I said it would not reflect well on them to have "excluded the possibility" of fallout when the Japanese had already found radioactivity on the ground.

The United States did not in fact publish the Soviet statement. Later that afternoon, however, the Principals met to consider how we should respond to their response to our inquiry about their test.

> Foster distributed a draft note that was almost ridiculously severe. It said that we could not accept the Soviet statement that the amount vented was insignificant in view of the debris collected in Japan; that the United States viewed the matter as "of the utmost seriousness"; and that a repetition would "jeopardize the existence" of the test ban treaty. The draft note requested "as a matter of urgency a detailed explanation from the Soviet Union as to how this incident occurred," and assurance "that steps are being taken to prevent its repetition."
> I said it would be very unfortunate if we sent such a severe note because it could lead to consequences that might seriously restrict our own testing program. [I think this may well have been part of ACDA's intention.] I suggested that we issue instead a brief press release. I just happened to have had a draft release prepared, and I distributed it. The group edited my draft and it was released from the State Department immediately following the meeting.

The release summarized the Soviet response to our inquiry and merely added that "the United States is continuing its own evaluation of the facts involved."

On January 26, it was again KIWI's turn. The AEC responded to the Soviet inquiry by denying that reactor safety experiments or reactor accidents could be classified as nuclear explosions falling under the provisions of the test ban treaty. We went on, nevertheless, to give a very full account of the KIWI experiment, its purposes, and its results.

It seemed as though this whole fracas might now subside. Anyone who thought that, however, failed to reckon with our ever-vigilant news media. On February 17:

> At 4 P.M. my assistant, Arnold Fritsch, received a phone call from George Herman of CBS News saying that they had a "scoop." They had found out from an official source that the recent Soviet test was an *atmospheric test* in direct violation of the test ban treaty and that the AEC knew this was the case and was covering up. Walter Cronkite intended to use this item in that night's broadcast at 7 P.M. Fritsch did his best to persuade Herman that the item was not true. At 4:05 P.M. I told Bundy what was happening. He was not concerned; we could knock it down after the broadcast. I told him my only worry was that such a broadcast might upset the president. Bundy didn't think it would. At 4:10 P.M. I informed Foster. At 4:35 P.M. Foster called back. He had talked to a close friend of Cronkite who said that the information came from reporter Daniel Schorr, who had obtained it from "a highly informed source." Foster said he told Cronkite's friend that the informed source was in fact misinformed. Foster believed that Cronkite was not going to use the item. I passed this along to Bundy and Llewellyn Thompson.

At length the matter came to rest. On November 19, 1965, the State Department announced, "on the basis of discussions with the Soviet government," that the venting from the Soviet test had been a result of "miscalculation" and that the United States had asked the USSR "to take precautions to assure observance of the limited test ban treaty."

Notes

1. *Documents on Disarmament: 1965,* p. 425.
2. Ibid., p. 281.
3. Ibid., pp. 281ff.
4. Ibid., pp. 390ff.

5. Ibid., p. 425f.
6. Ibid., p. 623f.
7. Mastny, *Disarmament and Nuclear Tests,* p. 53.

19
1966: A Threshold Treaty Rejected

Geneva

When the Eighteen Nation Disarmament Committee reconvened following a long recess it was customary for the U.S. president to send a message. Kennedy began this practice; Johnson continued it. Accordingly, the Committee of Principals met on January 21, 1966, to consider ACDA's draft of the message Johnson would send on January 27.

The draft outlined a seven-point U.S. program. A nonproliferation treaty headed the list. Following were renewed U.S. proposals for such measures as a comprehensive test ban, a complete cutoff of fissionable materials production, the demonstrated destruction of nuclear weapons, a freeze on the development of strategic nuclear delivery vehicles, and a halt in regional nonnuclear arms races.

At the Principals meeting General Andrew J. Goodpaster, representing the Joint Chiefs of Staff, objected to including a comprehensive test ban in the list of recommended measures. He argued that continued testing was needed to meet the Defense Department's requirement for an effective antiballistic missile (ABM) using hot X-rays as the killer mechanism.* He was quickly put down, Foster, others, and I contending that advocacy of a test ban was U.S. policy and that this session of the ENDC was not the occasion to make new policy.

The key word here was "advocacy." As will be evident shortly, I in fact agreed with Goodpaster that some further tests were necessary to solve the hot X-ray problem—the Soviets were believed to have

---

*Nuclear explosions can produce high energy electromagnetic radiation (similar to light waves but of much greater energy) that could penetrate the outer shields of incoming nuclear warheads and thus destroy them.

made substantial progress in this direction in their 1962 test series. What we were telling him, however, was that, in the ongoing propaganda contest over arms control between the United States and the Soviet Union, it would be poor tactics for the United States to back off at that time from its previous public espousal of a comprehensive test ban.

The message sent by President Johnson aimed to show that the U.S. position on testing was flexible and reasonable. It stated that the United States indeed favored extending the Limited Test Ban Treaty to cover underground tests, and continued: "For such an extension, the United States will require only that number and kind of inspections which modern science shows to be necessary to assure that the treaty is being faithfully observed." The Soviet position remained as before; in his message to the committee, on February 1, Premier Kosygin said that the USSR "would agree to barring underground tests, but only on the basis of the use of national systems of detection."

At this point, Sweden's ENDC delegation, headed by Alva Myrdal, entered the debate as a formidable third force.[1] The Swedes had previously argued that a comprehensive test ban was much to be preferred to a nonproliferation treaty, not only as a means of arresting the nuclear arms race, but even as a way of preventing proliferation. They believed that U.S. insistence on on-site inspection was the chief obstacle to a comprehensive test ban. They took issue with our position on technical grounds. This was something the Russians, who insisted that the issues were entirely political, had seldom done.

Mrs. Myrdal began the 1966 debate in Geneva by questioning whether on-site inspections would in fact be of much use in uncovering clandestine tests. In raising this question she had considerable support, including some from U.S. investigators.* She then maintained that the growing capability for detecting a clandestine test by national technical means was probably already sufficient to deter any potential evader. In case there was doubt about this, however, she had a proposal. If there was a suspected violation, and if the country on whose territory the event occurred could not or would not provide

---

*In 1959 a panel headed by Robert F. Bacher of the California Institute of Technology concluded that on-site inspection would have an exceedingly small chance of proving that a suspicious event had occurred, especially if the perpetrator was bent on concealment (Kistiakowsky, *A Scientist at the White House,* p. 6). The following year testimony on this matter before the Joint Committee on Atomic Energy led a number of Congressmen to conclude that the chance that an on-site inspection would uncover evidence of a violation was near zero (Jacobson and Stein, *Diplomats, Scientists and Politicians,* p. 253).

a satisfactory explanation, the other side could issue a "challenge for inspection." If the nation under suspicion would not then invite inspection, this could serve as grounds for abrogation of the treaty by the complaining party. In Myrdal's view, such a threat of withdrawal would be a decisive enforcement tool.[2]

Adrian Fisher, replying for the United States, found that the Swedish approach had some merit but that it did not accord fully with the technical realities. Citing U.S. research, he maintained that there were in the Soviet Union each year about forty-five significant seismic events—which he defined as those registering 4.0 or more on the Richter scale—that could not be identified by national means as either earthquakes or explosions. (As indicated in the last chapter, Defense Department officials in charge of seismic research estimated this number as only thirty.) Nor did he feel that the notion of inspection challenges was politically sound. He was not optimistic that the Soviet Union would respond cooperatively to challenges, as it had repeatedly and dogmatically asserted that national technical means were sufficient for identification. Furthermore, a challenge was in reality an accusation, and a treaty that depended on accusations for its enforcement was not likely to reduce international tensions. For those who contended that the United States ought to be willing to take some risk and sign a test ban treaty with insufficient verification provisions, Fisher offered Aesop's warning: "Beware lest you lose the substance by grasping at the shadow."

The Soviets also disagreed with Myrdal's proposal. Roshchin characterized it as "aimed at pushing through in a disguised form the idea of international inspections." His explanation revealed the deep national roots of the Soviet attitude toward on-site inspection:

> States and peoples, especially those which more than once within the lifetime of one generation have borne the heavy consequence of foreign aggression, cannot and must not show unconcern and complacency in questions of their security. They will certainly not assume an obligation to open their territories to inspection for which there is no necessity.[3]

Almost six months later, on November 22, 1966, Foster again defended the U.S. position before the General Assembly's First Committee.[4] Noting that it was the third anniversary of John F. Kennedy's death, he stated that the United States continued Kennedy's quest for an "effective" comprehensive test ban. He acknowledged that there had been improvements in verification techniques. Notwithstanding, he said that the signals presented to remote seismometers by some earthquakes were still indistinguishable from the signals of man-made explosions. Consequently, he saw "no alternative to some on-site inspection to fill the gaps in our information."

Washington

While loyally and skillfully presenting the offical U.S. position before international bodies, the ACDA sought to moderate it in Washington. The agency first attempted to persuade the Committee of Principals that the United States should accept a threshold test ban. On January 17, 1966, Foster circulated a proposal for a ban on all underground tests having an explosive force above 4.75 on the Richter scale, with enforcement to be by national technical means alone. With one all-important difference, this was the same as the proposal that had been introduced by the United Arab Republic and supported by the Soviet Union and a majority of the delegations at the ENDC. The difference was that the UAR proposal included also a moratorium on all tests below the 4.75 threshold, during which technical work on verification techniques would be pursued. Foster knew well that, after the bitter experience of August 30, 1961, when the Soviet Union suddenly and without warning broke an informal three-year moratorium with a massive and long-prepared series of atmospheric tests, no U.S. Congress would accept an unpoliced moratorium, nor would any president ask them to do so.

On January 19, I conveyed to Foster AEC's largely negative views about his proposal for a TTB. I maintained that the additional restraints the proposed treaty would impose on near-nuclear-weapon states were insignificant and "would contribute only marginally to discouraging proliferation." On the other hand, the threshold limitation "would, without question, impose serious inhibitions on the achievement of some goals of AEC's weapons development program." I mentioned in particular the Defense Department's requirement for a high-yield, high-altitude ABM warhead. To develop this warhead would require tests yielding in excess of 500 kilotons, whereas 4.75 on the Richter scale corresponded to tests of only about 30 kilotons. It was our view that if a TTB was in force, the United States might be constrained to tests even below 30 kilotons to avoid risking inadvertent violations. Finally, I contended that, in the absence of on-site inspection, the proposed treaty would lead to international controversy and recrimination. I pointed out that magnitude determination by seismography was not precise; it might vary by as much as 0.5 magnitude units on either side of an average value. This could result in sharp disputes as to whether a specific event violated a threshold test ban.

My letter, and perhaps other responses as well, must have caused some dismay within ACDA, such that, at the Principals meeting on January 21:

> Foster opened the meeting by saying that, regrettably, he had been forced to defer consideration of a threshold test ban treaty. However, he said he hoped to bring it up later, "in view of its many virtues."

True to his word, Foster circulated the TTB proposal again in late spring. On June 16, I submitted AEC's written comments, repeating substantially the same points I had made in January. The Principals met on the issue the following day, June 17. The specific agenda item was a proposed ACDA letter to the president suggesting "a Presidential proposal [to the ENDC] for a new test ban agreement extending the Limited Test Ban Treaty to cover verifiable underground tests."

> Fisher said that the two major issues were: could such a treaty be verified, and was this the most fruitful arms control initiative for us to be working on? McNamara then summarized the points in my letter of January 19 and said that they "carried some force." Rusk asked about the possibility of cheating under a threshold treaty and [CIA Director] Raborn said the possibility was strong. I said that, of the objections to the proposed treaty, the fact that it would prevent production of the needed ABM warhead was the most serious. Rusk asked whether this problem could be solved by raising the threshold from 4.75 to 5.0. I replied that it might be possible under such a higher limit to develop a crude ABM but not the one that the Department of Defense said it needed. [A 5.0 threshold was considered to allow tests yielding about 80 kilotons as against about 30 kilotons for a 4.75 threshold. This colloquy provides an illustration of how the major powers sometimes try to tailor arms control proposals to fit their weapons programs.]

Vice President Humphrey asked what the objective was of a threshold test ban. Fisher replied that the purpose was to turn down the arms race from the megaton level to the tens-of-kilotons level. The vice president observed that a country like Israel would be quite satisfied with bombs of from 20 to 50 kilotons, implying that a TTB would not affect the proliferation problem. Rusk observed that the ratio of the effect of a TTB to that of the Southeast Asian situation was like the ratio of a popgun to a megaton explosion.

Early in July, Rusk sent a memorandum to the president on the threshold test ban issue. Having expertly summarized the arguments pro and con, he described the existing situation:

No consensus was reached at the Principals' meeting on the desirability of making a proposal for a threshold test ban at this time. It is suggested that you may wish to discuss this personally with the Principals.

Thus we were in mid-1966 in roughly the same situation with a threshold test ban as with a nonproliferation treaty. The bureaucracy being deadlocked, it would take active presidential involvement to move either matter forward. As far as I know, however, no active effort was made by anyone in the administration to engage the president's interest in the TTB. It is doubtful, for example, that Rusk, believing that the TTB had only "popgun" significance, pushed the president further after sending his memo. Nor did the president, to my knowledge, accept Rusk's suggestion to discuss a TTB with any of the Principals. Other issues soon pushed the idea to the sidelines, and it was not seriously discussed again during Lyndon Johnson's presidency.

Sequels

In the atmosphere of detente fostered by SALT I, there was to be further discussion of test limitations. A team of U.S. experts went to Moscow for technical discussions in the spring of 1974. A Threshold Test Ban Treaty was rapidly negotiated and it was signed by President Nixon and Chairman Brezhnev during the summit meeting in July 1974. Under the treaty both sides undertook: (1) not to conduct underground tests yielding more than 150 kilotons; (2) not to interfere with each other's national means of verification; and (3) to exchange detailed data on all tests and test sites in order to facilitate verification.

The Threshold Test Ban Treaty was expected to go into effect on March 31, 1976, and both sides claim to have observed it from that time forward. Ratification was delayed, however, because of the need to deal with the problem of peaceful nuclear explosions (PNEs). Beginning in the fall of 1974, negotiators labored more than a year to arrive at terms whereby PNEs of more than 150 kilotons might be allowed, but they concluded that the verification problem—to assure that the explosions were indeed peaceful ones from which no military benefits could flow—was too difficult. Accordingly, a further agreement, the Peaceful Nuclear Explosions Treaty, was signed in May 1976. Under its terms, individual PNEs were required to be within the 150-kiloton limit imposed by the Threshold Treaty. In addition, each side was to have the right to observe grouped PNEs by the other side that had an aggregate yield greater than 150 kilotons, and no grouped PNEs could yield more in total than 1.5 megatons.

The Threshold and PNE treaties were submitted together to the U.S. Senate in July 1976. During hearings before the Foreign Relations Committee, the Threshold Treaty was repeatedly decried as a sham by those favoring a comprehensive test ban, on the basis that the "ludicrously high" limit of 150 kilotons would have no adverse effect on the work of weapon designers. In consideration of such views and the upcoming presidential election, the committee took no action on the treaties in 1976. They have never been resubmitted to the Senate.

The Reagan administration has indicated at various times, such as in the president's address to the UN General Assembly on September 22, 1986, that it might be willing to resubmit the TTB and PNE treaties to the Senate if certain verification problems were solved.

Notes

1. The discussion in the following paragraphs is based in part on an internal AEC memorandum by Warren Heckrotte of the Livermore Laboratory, who was a member of the U.S. delegation at the ENDC.
2. U.S. ACDA, "Negotiations on a Comprehensive Test Ban, 1965–1967."
3. *Documents on Disarmament: 1966*, p. 530.
4. Ibid., pp. 751–56.

The Nonproliferation Treaty was opened
for signature on July 1, 1968, in Washington, London, and Moscow. Shown at the
ceremonies in the East Room of the White
House are, from right, President Johnson,
Secretary Rusk, ACDA Director William
Foster, British Ambassador Sir Patrick
Dean, and Soviet Ambassador Dobrynin.
In his remarks, the president announced
that agreement had just been reached between the superpowers to enter into arms
limitation talks "in the nearest future."
To Johnson's keen disappointment, these
talks did not begin until more than a year
later, after he had left office.

Y. R. Okamoto

The high point of the Glassboro (New Jersey) summit meeting—June 23 and 25, 1967—occurred at luncheon on June 23, when, at President Johnson's invitation, Secretary NcNamara made an impassioned plea, here being conveyed to Premier Kosygin by the interpreter, that the two powers abstain from large-scale deployment of defensive systems lest this set off another round in the nuclear arms race. Soviet spokesmen have since confirmed that this presentation by McNamara had a strong effect on Kosygin and others in his party, leading in a very important way to SALT I and the ABM Treaty.

OPPOSITE PAGE

A large part of the time at Glassboro was spent by President Johnson and Premier Kosygin in earnest head-to-head conversation, with only an interpreter and a photographer present in addition to the principals. The pictures taken at Glassboro were not posed "photo opportunities." White House photographer Yoichi Okamoto was allowed to stay in the room while the substantive conversations were taking place.

John Palfrey's departure from the Atomic Energy Commission on June 30, 1966, left two vacancies on the commission. These were filled by the appointment of Wilfrid I. Johnson (left) and Samuel N. Nabrit, shown receiving the oath of office on August 1, 1966, from W. B. McCool, secretary of the commission, as the president and Vice President Humphrey (background) look on. Nabrit served only a year, to be replaced after a further year's delay by Francesco Costagliola.

The members of the Atomic Energy Commission changed several times during the Johnson presidency. Robert Wilson left the commission on January 31, 1964, and was replaced by Mary I. Bunting, shown with the author and the president. Dr. Bunting served for only a year, to June 30, 1965.

The author

The members of the Atomic Energy Commission at the outset of the Johnson presidency are shown here with the president. From left, James T. Ramey, Robert E. Wilson, the president, the author, John G. Palfrey, and Gerald F. Tape.

Y. R. Okamoto

On October 10, 1966, Soviet Foreign Minister Gromyko visited the White House to discuss the main provisions of a nonproliferation treaty. Shown here, seemingly quite pleased with the situation, are Ambassador Dobrynin, Gromyko, Secretary Rusk, the president, and Ambassador-at-Large Llewellyn Thompson. Immediately afterward, Rusk and Gromyko went to the State Department for further talk, after which Gromyko told reporters: "It looks like both sides are striving to reach agreement."

President Johnson and the author each turning a screw on the plaque declaring the Experimental Breeder Reactor No. 1 to be a National Historical Landmark. This reactor at the National Reactor Testing Station in Idaho had produced the world's first usable electricity on December 20, 1951. During the ceremony on August 26, 1966, President Johnson spoke of relations with the Soviet Union, saying, "[W]hile differing principles and differing values may always divide us, they should not, and they must not, deter us from rational acts of common endeavor."

While a senator, Vice President Hubert Humphrey had been a leading advocate of arms control and one of the authors of the legislation establishing the Arms Control and Disarmament Agency. He and the author are shown together as he addresses the annual joint conference of the American Nuclear Society and the Atomic Industrial Forum, Washington, D.C., November 15, 1965.

Y. R. Okamoto

Shown with President Johnson are Secretary Rusk (back to camera) and William S. Foster, director (right), and Adrian S. Fisher, deputy director, of the Arms Control and Disarmament Agency. Although the ACDA nominally reported directly to the president, it was a rare occasion when ACDA leaders had such direct contact as this with President Johnson. He appeared to have had a dim view of the ACDA and preferred to consult on arms control matters with such senior advisers as the secretary of state, secretary of defense, and national security adviser

President Johnson and his Cabinet, plus certain other officials, meeting at the White House, October 20, 1964. The main topics of discussion were three unsettling events that had occurred in distant places during the preceding few days. These were China's first nuclear test, the unexpected ouster of Nikita Khrushchev, and the electoral loss of the incumbent Conservatives in Britain to a Labour party thought to be less friendly to U.S. policy. Around the table, from left, John A. Gronouski, postmaster general; Adlai E. Stevenson, ambassador to the UN; the author; Robert S. McNamara, secretary of defense; Orville L. Freeman, secretary of agriculture; W. Willard Wirtz, secretary of labor; Donald Hornig, White House science adviser; Walter Heller, chairman, Council of Economic Advisers; Luther H. Hodges, secretary of commerce; Dean Rusk, secretary of state; President Johnson; C. Douglas Dillon, secretary of the treasury; Budget Director Kermit Gordon; James E. Webb, NASA administrator; and Sargent Shriver, director of the Peace Corps.

President Johnson addressing the UN General Assembly on December 17, 1963. At this early stage in his administration, when his stand on international issues was still a subject of uncertainty and concern, the president spoke reassuringly to the delegates, saying: "The United States wants to press on with arms control and reduction."

A private chat in the Oval Office.

In June 1954 J. Robert Oppenheimer, head of the World War II atomic bomb project at Los Alamos and later chairman of AEC's influential General Advisory Committee, was stripped of his security clearance following extended hearings before a three-man AEC personnel security board. This decision caused much bitterness in the American scientific community. It had been President Kennedy's intention to express how many in the nation felt about Dr. Oppenheimer by honoring him with a public presentation of the AEC's Enrico Fermi Award. President Johnson carried out Kennedy's intention on the originally scheduled date, December 2, 1963, ten days after the assassination. At the White House ceremony are, from left, the author, the president, Dr. Oppenheimer, Peter Oppenheimer, Mrs. J. R. Oppenheimer, Mrs. Johnson, and, in foreground, AEC Commissioners Robert E. Wilson, James T. Ramey, and John G. Palfrey.

While Lyndon Johnson as president had problems getting along with Robert Kennedy and some others close to the Kennedy family, as vice president he had very good relations with President Kennedy. The two are shown during a visit to Los Alamos Scientific laboratory, December 7, 1962. In the car, from left, are Norris Bradbury, director of the laboratory, and New Mexico Senator Clinton P. Anderson, an influential member of the Joint Committee on Atomic Energy.

Wolfe

On the evening of August 20, 1968, Soviet Ambassador Dobrynin had the uncomfortable task of informing President Johnson that, even as they spoke, Soviet and other Eastern bloc armed forces were invading Czechoslovakia. This was a heavy blow to the president because a summit meeting for launching arms limitation talks was to have been announced the next morning. Walt Rostow, who was present, states that, despite the president's disappointment, he was very gentle with the ambassador, even to the extent of expressing sympathy for the latter's difficult mission.

Y. R. Okamoto

President Johnson and President-elect
Nixon held an earnest conversation in the
Oval Office on November 11, 1968, six
days after the latter's election. According
to the account in Nixon's memoirs, Johnson said he wanted to do everything possible to help the new administration
succeed, adding: "The problems at home
and abroad are probably greater than any
President has ever confronted since the
time of Lincoln."

20
1967 and Beyond:
Testing Tested

Where you stand is where you sit.

—A Washington adage

A Personal Dilemma

Sporadic discussion on a comprehensive test ban continued into 1967 both at the ENDC and in Washington. On July 11, ACDA Director Foster stated once again that the United States was prepared to accept a comprehensive test ban provided there was adequate inspection. As noted in the last chapter, I had been among those who argued in January 1966, over military objections, for including a restatement of this long-standing U.S. position in President Johnson's pending message to the ENDC. Yet, on August 4, 1967, I found myself writing to Secretary Rusk that, because of changed circumstances, a complete test ban should not at that time be pushed by the United States.

I told Rusk that underground tests would be necessary for a longer period than had previously been thought. A Soviet antiballistic missile (ABM) system, along with associated radars, was being deployed in a ring around Moscow. Opinions differed, but some in our government thought this system potentially capable of defending a large area of the western USSR. The president and the Congress had accordingly decided that the U.S. response should be to develop "a complete new generation of weapons for the strategic offensive forces."* I continued:

---

*This U.S. reaction to Soviet deployment of defensive weapons should be carefully noted by those who question how the Sovet Union might react to deployment of the U.S. Strategic Defense Initiative.

Both development and proof tests* are required for these high-priority systems. Additionally, since these new systems will constitute the major U.S. response to the new Soviet ABM deployment, it is vitally important that there be assessments of their vulnerability to nuclear attack. This requires exposure of components and asemblies to large fluxes of neutrons, gamma rays and X-rays that can only be provided by nuclear detonations. The development of the techniques for carrying out these nuclear effects tests within the constraints of the Limited Test Ban Treaty has been an important achievement of recent times.

Having expressed my official view as a tester of weapons, I added a few words testifying to my personal discomfort with the situation:

I had personally hoped that the necessary underground testing associated with the development of the DOD weapons systems could be accelerated so that the results would be available at an earlier time; however, I cannot find a way, despite a great deal of personal attention to the problem. I realize the advantages of taking steps beyond the present Limited Test Ban Treaty as soon as it is feasible.

These two paragraphs were expressive of a personal dilemma in which I frequently found myself while AEC chairman. At all times, then and since, I have strongly believed that judicious arms control agreements, most especially a comprehensive test ban treaty, are essential to secure a tolerable future for humankind.[1] Yet, in my official position, I felt obligated on occasion to point out the technical need for certain types of tests. This was especially true when, as in this case, it was national policy to develop major new weapons—there is no way to do this without testing. It was a clear instance of the old Washington adage, "Where you stand is where you sit."†

---

*The term "proof tests," as used in the 1960s, meant tests to determine whether a newly developed weapon would work as it was designed to do. More recently, this term has been used to designate tests of old, stockpiled, off-the-shelf weapons suspected of having deteriorated to an unacceptable degree. The need to perform tests of this latter description in order to maintain confidence in the viability of our deterrent force is frequently offered as an argument against a comprehensive test ban. While I was AEC chairman (1961–71), no such tests were conducted. I doubt that very many, if any, were conducted through the remainder of the 1970s.

†I did not always allow the conditions of my employment to prevail over my personal convictions. When the debate on whether to deploy the Safeguard ABM system was raging during the Nixon administration, for example, word reached me repeatedly that the president wanted me to make speeches in favor of deployment. This was not a part of my official duties and I was unwilling to do it, an attitude that did not add to my standing within the administration.

Curtains for the Comprehensive

Foster did not contest my technical arguments about the need for protracted underground testing, but he was apprehensive about the consequences of having abruptly to abandon the pro-test ban position previously avowed by the United States. As he wrote to me on May 20, 1968, "any public retraction . . . would seriously jeopardize our chances of persuading countries to sign and ratify the nonproliferation treaty." In order to cope with this dilemma, Foster proposed a set of tactical maneuvers to be used when the ENDC reconvened in the summer of 1968. He described these in a memorandum to Rusk:

> 1. The U.S. will attempt to focus attention on other measures, such as halting the production of fissionable material for weapons, demonstrated destruction of nuclear weapons, and seabed arms control. This should help to deflect attention from the comprehensive test ban.
>
> 2. In commenting on the comprehensive test ban, the U.S. delegate will reiterate our past statements that our information on seismic capabilities indicates that a comprehensive test ban cannot be adequately verified without some onsite inspections. If we are pressed on this point, the U.S. will reiterate our willingness to undertake technical discussions on test ban verification problems, provided the Soviet Union would also participate. [Foster could have confidence that the Soviets would, as in the past, refuse to take part in such discussions.]
>
> 3. The Soviets probably have their own nuclear weapons testing requirements which tend to diminish their interest in a comprehensive test ban. If the U.S. continues to stipulate that we would not accept a comprehensive test ban without onsite inspections and the Soviet Union continues to maintain that such inspections are not necessary, pressure from other countries to reach agreement on a comprehensive test ban can probably be kept within manageable proportions for the time being. If the Soviets ever do agree to onsite inspections of some sort, we would have to enter into negotiations, but these negotiations could be quite protracted.

Foster's memorandum concluded with this warning, reminiscent of the one given at the June 16, 1964, meeting by Secretary Rusk (chapter 17):

> Meanwhile, I believe those underground explosions designed to satisfy priority security requirements should be carried out as early as

possible in the knowledge that at some future time foreign policy considerations may well require the cessation of all nuclear explosions which cannot be justified as peaceful.

Foster's warning provided an illustration of a paradox that has been noted by George Rathjens, among others.[2] This is that one of the effects of arms control negotiations has been to speed up the arms race, as each military establishment hastens to rush to completion any weapon developments that seem "threatened" by a pending agreement.

Having offered a strategy to ward off a comprehensive test ban at Geneva, the ACDA apparently felt it unnecessary to alter the content or tone of U.S. public pronouncements. On July 13, 1968:

Adrian Fisher called to say that he was going to recommend that President Johnson advocate a CTB in his message to the ENDC at its reconvening next week. I told Fisher that the AEC had seen the draft of this message and that we had problems with it. It was decided that I would write the president a memo stating AEC's point of view.

In my memo I told the president:

We feel that it would be a mistake to reiterate at this time our previously stated aim to "seek to achieve the discontinuance of all test explosions of nuclear weapons for all time." We feel strongly that this is unrealistic in view of the absolute necessity for underground testing in order to meet our announced commitments in the field of strategic weapons.

AEC's position apparently prevailed. President Johnson's message to the ENDC of July 16, 1968, contained no mention of a comprehensive test ban. Diplomatic embarrassment from this omission followed soon after. On July 29, the Swedish delegation at the ENDC presented a report by seismic experts from ten countries indicating that it was possible without on-site inspection to distinguish large- and medium-sized earthquakes from nuclear explosions.

Howard Hughes Objects

From these levels of high policy, we descend now to an improbable episode illustrating the impact that private wealth can have on national purpose. The AEC had scheduled a weapons test called BOX-CAR for April 24, 1968, at the Nevada Test Site. Yielding more than a megaton, it was to be, by a slight margin, the largest test ever conducted within the United States. On April 18, Foster called me to express his concern that the timing of the test might have an unfortunate impact on the UN debate on the Nonproliferation Treaty, which was to start the same day. I told Foster we would look into the possibility of changing the date. Not satisfied with this answer, Foster appealed to higher levels. The next day Dean Rusk called me. He wanted an unequivocal assurance that we would definitely postpone the shot. I agreed to delay it for a couple of days.

Meanwhile, the White House, members of Congress, and the AEC were being deluged with an avalanche of telegrams, letters, phone calls, and other communications protesting the proposed test on various grounds: it would contaminate underground water supplies; wreck Boulder Dam; cause earthquakes; vent radioactive debris into the atmosphere; damage buildings in Las Vegas, and so on. These were all hazards that we had looked into. We thought all the fears except that about earthquakes were baseless. There was some reason for concern about follow-on seismic events (see below) but we felt this was being greatly exaggerated. Accordingly, we issued a reassuring press release on April 19.

It soon became apparent that most of the protests had been instigated and orchestrated by eccentric billionaire Howard Hughes and his associates, even to the extent of offering generous financial support to organizations if their members would join the chorus.* By this time in his life, at the age of sixty-three, Hughes was a highly neurotic, drug-ridden recluse who never left his Las Vegas apartment, received no visitors, and commanded his considerable economic empire by written or telephoned instructions to subordinates who never saw him.[3] The impending BOXCAR test apparently stirred his anxiety as no other event in his life, and he resolved to pull out all the stops

---

*I would not wish to leave the impression that the Hughes organization instigated all the opposition that was expressed about this test. There were indeed some protests from other sources as well. The (St. Louis) Committee for Environmental Information, a long-standing critic of nuclear testing, called for a postponement of the test because of possible seismic damage, earthquake triggering in California, and release of radioactivity. The Women's Strike for Peace, citing the concerns of the St. Louis Committee, also called for a postponement (of indefinite duration). The Women's International League for Peace and Freedom called for cancellation on grounds that the test would be dangerous and produce tension. The Federation of American Scientists, SANE, and the United World Federalists called for postponement of all tests until after consideration of the nonproliferation treaty by the UN General Assembly.

in an effort to get it cancelled. Not the least of Hughes's concerns was that such powerful tests would scare away tourists from Las Vegas and imperil his huge investments there. But he also apparently had genuine, deeply felt fears, such as that underground tests would contaminate "underground substances" and pollute "the very bowels of the earth on which we live."

On April 22:

> I received a telephone call from Senator Howard Cannon (Nevada). Cannon said that one of Hughes's men had called him over the weekend to let him know they were protesting the shot and asking for a ninety day moratorium so that top engineers and scientists could study its possible effects. Cannon said he had answered that this subject had already been studied to death. He asked whether it was OK for him to say that this device was very little larger than some previous shots and that the effects had been very thoroughly studied in the past. I said those were the facts, adding that no such deeply buried device had ever vented and that there was no problem with the water. I then called Nevada's other senator, Alan Bible, to reassure him. He said he had also been getting a terrific amount of mail.

When it became apparent that his attempts to gain a postponement through pressures directed at the AEC and Congress were getting nowhere, Hughes decided to write directly to President Johnson, with whom he had had some prior association. He began writing on the evening of April 24. According to his associates, it took him all night and half the next day to compose the letter so that, when he finished it at midday on April 25, there was no time left to deliver it to the White House before the test on the twenty-sixth. Accordingly, it was dictated over the phone to a lawyer in Clark Clifford's law office (Hughes had been a client of Clifford's), who hand-delivered it to the White House. President Johnson first saw the letter early in the evening of the twenty-fifth.[4]

Hughes's letter to the president said in part:

> Based upon my personal promise that independent scientists have definite evidence, and can obtain more, demonstrating the risk and uncertainty to the health of the citizens of southern Nevada . . . will you not grant even a brief postponement of this explosion to permit my representatives to come to Washington and lay before

whomever you designate the urgent, impelling reasons why we feel a 90-day postponement is needed? . . . I am certainly no peacenik. My feelings have been well known through the years to be far to the right of center. It is not my purpose to impede the defense program in any way and I can positively prove that if my appeal is heeded the nuclear testing program will proceed more rapidly than at present. . . . The AEC technicians assure that there will be no harmful consequences, but I wonder where those technicians will be ten or twenty years from now. There are some sheep lying dead in nearby Utah. [The killing of the sheep had nothing to do with nuclear testing. It had resulted from some army testing of nerve gas.]

The president apparently took this letter very seriously. He directed Walt Rostow, Science Adviser Donald Hornig, and me to report immediately on the substantive issues. Meanwhile, the test would have to be reauthorized by him before it could proceed. I did not get this message right away, being on my way home from a trip to Mexico City when the president issued his instructions. When I arrived home shortly after 11 P.M. on April 25, I received a phone call from Hornig asking me to help him prepare a memo for the president summarizing the arguments for allowing the next day's test to proceed. We worked on the memo over the telephone until well after midnight.

The president returned from a state dinner for King Olav of Norway at about midnight to find a memo from Rostow awaiting him. Rostow wrote: "I see nothing in Hughes' letter that raises questions which the AEC has not confronted with as much responsibility as could be expected."

Hornig's memo was delivered to the president at 8 A.M. on the twenty-sixth. Hornig was not so unequivocal as Rostow in his support of the test.[5] He pointed out that the largest previous test at the Nevada Test Site had caused no damage in Las Vegas, but this one's yield would be 50 percent greater. He acknowledged that "[t]he earth shock may be felt for a distance of 250 miles, perhaps as far as Los Angeles. Cracked window panes and plaster damage in Las Vegas cannot be ruled out. . . . AEC has set up to pay any legitimate damage claims promptly." He continued:

The AEC has investigated the possibility of triggering earthquakes very carefully and consulted the most knowledgeable people. There is no likelihood of this occurring, but it cannot be absolutely excluded. . . . As to venting, none of the large deep underground tests to date have vented at all. It is nearly impossible. It is clearly unfortunate that the test coincides with the opening of the UNGA. However, a postponement would probably make it coincide with some other point in the debate. A complete cancellation seems in-advisable—the test will furnish a calibration point for later tests of the ABM warhead. I recommend that we do not change the test plans.

On April 26:

When I called him at 8:35 A.M. Hornig told me that the president had decided to let the shot proceed. It went at 10 A.M., Wash-ington time, with no untoward events—no venting and about as much seismic effect in Las Vegas as we had predicted. I called Rostow and asked him to inform the president.

That evening, at a reception for King Olav at the Norwegian Embassy:

The president told me that he was pleased with the way the test had gone. I thanked him for allowing it to go forward under the difficult circumstances. The president then said he had this letter from Howard Hughes that required an answer and that he would like me to draft a reply for him. He referred to my ability to "find people frothing at the mouth and then quietly devastate them," and he wanted a reply in this vein.

I sent over my draft answer on May 2. It was another ten days or so before the letter was sent, with some revisions by White House staff. Addressed to "Dear Howard," the letter's main points were that the AEC had given safety assurances, that these assurances had proven to be correct, and that the Nevada site would continue to be the principal location for the underground tests. The tone was respectful, but firm.

The president's letter at first infuriated Hughes, both because of its tardiness and its content.[6] Brooding further about it, however, Hughes somehow managed to interpret the letter as an invitation to bribery. He thereupon sent his chief lieutenant, Robert A. Maheu, to the LBJ ranch, with instructions to offer the president of the United States a million dollars for a change of policy toward nuclear testing! There were different versions of what went on at the ranch. Maheu, not daring to carry out his instructions literally, apparently implied a link between a relatively modest contribution to the Johnson Library and the future of nuclear testing in Nevada. The president was interested in the former but apparently refused to discuss the latter.

Hughes's fixation about nuclear testing did not end with BOX-CAR. He continued to seek changes in U.S. testing policy, taking particular aim at tests scheduled for December 9, 1968, September 16, 1969, and March 26, 1970. In the process he sought to "influence" President Johnson (again), Hubert Humphrey, Robert* and Edward Kennedy, and Richard Nixon. All three tests went forward as scheduled.

That wealth brings influence is a commonplace. That anyone would have sought to carry this influence to the extremes Hughes attempted is to be explained only in terms of his peculiar combination of arrogance, daring, and dementia.

Sequels

The conflict with apparently needed weapon tests essentially spelled the end to the comprehensive test ban's chances during the Johnson administration. There were to be no further serious negotiations of a CTB until President Carter announced it as a primary goal of his administration early in 1977. Tripartite (U.S., U.K., USSR) negotiations followed, during which the Soviets agreed for the first time to accept a system of on-site inspections. The system was to be based on challenges and voluntary responses, along the lines Alva Myrdal had suggested at the ENDC, with appeals as necessary to the UN Security Council. By the end of 1978, the negotiating teams were virtually agreed on the terms of a treaty. It foundered, however, in the face of a weakening political will to proceed on both sides,† and became moribund following the Soviet invasion of Afghanistan.

---

*According to Drosnin (p. 258ff.), Pierre Salinger had approached Hughes's lieutenant, Maheu, saying that Robert Kennedy agreed with Hughes about delaying tests in Nevada—he had already spoken out against testing in public speeches—and asking for a contribution for Kennedy's presidential campaign. Hughes offered $25,000 and Salinger indicated he would pick up the check in Las Vegas following the California primary on June 4, 1968. This of course never happened—Robert Kennedy was shot on June 4.

†President Carter was induced to withdraw U.S. support for a CTB in a White House meeting with Harold Agnew and Roger Batzel, directors of the Los Alamos and Livermore weapons laboratories, respectively, during the summer of 1978. According to an administration official who was present at the meeting, the main argument used by the laboratory directors against a CTB was that the U.S. stockpile of nuclear weapons could not be guaranteed as reliable in the absence of nuclear testing. (Letter from Hugh DeWitt, Livermore Laboratory, June 18, 1985.)

At a National Security Council meeting on July 19, 1982, President Reagan formally decided to end U.S. participation in international efforts to achieve a comprehensive test ban. The administration has given various reasons for its position, some of which seem more genuine than others. It has been argued that such an agreement could not be verified, but this point has been disputed in the scientific community. Another argument has been that periodic nuclear tests are needed to ensure the continued reliability of the weapons stockpile. Experience indicates that other methods will adequately, if not perfectly, achieve this objective. I think the true basis for the administration's position lies in a belief that development of ever more effective nuclear weapons is essential to maintaining a credible deterrent against perceived Soviet aggressiveness, expansionism, and perfidy. Specifically, it has been acknowledged that a nuclear test ban would interfere with the development of exotic new weapons, such as those contemplated for the Strategic Defense Initiative.[7]

In August 1985, Chairman Gorbachev announced that, in an effort to obtain a comprehensive test ban, the Soviet Union would unilaterally cease testing for six months. When this moratorium expired in February 1986, the Soviets indicated it would be extended for an additional six months. Then in August 1986, it was again extended, this time until the end of the year. Along with its moratorium, the Soviet Union has indicated that it would adopt a much more forthcoming attitude toward on-site verification if the United States would agree to a test ban. The official U.S. reaction has included dismissal of these Soviet moves as propaganda. Mixed in with such statements has been a more candid argument, to the effect that continued testing will be necessary as long as the security of the United States and its allies depends on nuclear weapons.

Notwithstanding the administration's opposition, there has lately been renewed interest in the United States among opinion leaders, citizen groups, and members of Congress in a comprehensive test ban. In February 1986 the House of Representatives adopted, by a near party-line vote of 269 to 148, a resolution urging that the United States enter into negotiations for a CTB. The Senate had earlier adopted a similar resolution. In August 1968 the House voted to cut off funds for all tests yielding more than one kiloton. In October 1986, the House voted to cut off funds for all nuclear tests for one year beginning January 1987. In order not to tie President Reagan's hands at his summit meeting with Chairman Gorbachev at Reykjavik later that month, however, the House lifted this restriction in exchange for the president's commitment to discuss step-by-step reductions in nuclear testing with the Soviets. In the preliminary skirmishing before the blow-up of the Reykjavik meeting, the Soviets are reported to have modified their insistence on a total ban on nuclear tests and to have adopted the U.S. approach—step-by-step reductions.

I am participating wholeheartedly in the movement for a CTB. I believe that such an agreement offers the simplest and most attainable method for halting dangerous qualitative improvement in nuclear arms, for strengthening the nonproliferation regime, and for providing momentum toward further progress in arms control and, eventually, disarmament. As I wrote in 1983:

> The benefits of a CTB far outweigh the risks. If we had been able to negotiate a CTB with the USSR in 1963, when it was necessary to settle for a Limited Test Ban, we and the rest of the world would be much better off. We are negotiating today at a higher and more dangerous level. It would be to our great advantage to achieve a CTB now before we proceed to an even higher and still more dangerous level.[8]

Notes

1. See, for example, chapter 22, "Still Needed: A Comprehensive Test Ban," in my book, *Kennedy, Khrushchev and the Test Ban*, pp. 292–301; also, "Seaborg proposal: Support a comprehensive test ban," *Chemical and Engineering News*, June 13, 1983, p. 2.
2. Oral presentation to public forum on "Peace in a Nuclear Age," McLean, Virginia, November 3, 1985.
3. This story has been told from the Hughes perspective by Michael Drosnin in his book, *Citizen Hughes*, which is based on correspondence and memoranda in Hughes's own handwriting.
4. Drosnin, *Citizen Hughes*, p. 208f.
5. Papers of LBJ; Peace, General; PC1, Box 3, LBJ Library.
6. Drosnin, *Citizen Hughes*, pp. 220ff.
7. Smith, "The Allure of Nuclear Testing," p. 670.
8. *Chemical and Engineering News*, June 13, 1983, p. 2.

Part VI

Drawing Nearer to the NPT

In the end, the miseries and burdens which the nuclear arms race imposes upon the nuclear powers may be the most effective deterrent in dissuading others from walking into the same trap.

Freeman Dyson
Weapons and Hope

21
Proliferation Threats

I am not really thinking of nuclear arms, but if 20 or 30 ridiculous little countries are going to have nuclear weapons, then I may have to revise my policies.

—The Shah of Iran
1975

Dire Predictions

Beneath the lid the international community was attempting to place on the spread of nuclear weapons, the proliferation cauldron continued to bubble. The Chinese, whose first nuclear test in October 1964 had added so greatly to the pressures and anxieties, stimulated further concern with additional tests; by mid-1967 they had conducted six. Briefing the Joint Committee on Atomic Energy on July 14, 1967, CIA Director Richard Helms estimated that "with continued testing [the Chinese would] be able to develop a thermonuclear weapon in the ICBM weight class with a yield in the megaton range by about 1970." The French program was also proceeding apace. Though lagging behind the Chinese in thermonuclear weapon design, they had developed higher-yield fission devices. Helms testified that France had an operational strategic force of about sixty Mirage IV aircraft with a stockpile of nuclear weapons.

Even before the entry of France and China into the nuclear club, there had been pessimistic forecasts about the dangers of proliferation. Among the most famous was the statement made to newsmen by President Kennedy in March 1963: "I see the possibility of the president of the United States having to face a world in which 15 or 20 or 25 nations may have these weapons. I regard that as the greatest possible danger and hazard." Proliferation has been described as Kennedy's "private nightmare." It was this concern more than any other that seemed to motivate his quest for a test ban.

There were many other dire appraisals to match Kennedy's. In October 1964, Secretary McNamara warned in a Chicago radio interview that decreasing costs would enable "tens of nations" to develop nuclear weapons in ten to twenty years. In its July 19, 1965, issue, *U.S. News and World Report* published an interview with me entitled "Worldwide Race for A-Bombs—Can It Be Stopped?" Asked, "Could a lot of other countries build atomic bombs if they set their minds to it?" I answered:

> Oh yes. A large number have the potential, over a period of years and on the basis of the scientists they have and the materials they could acquire in one way or another. I'm speaking of such countries as Japan, India, West Germany, Sweden, Italy, Canada, Israel, and maybe—over a little longer period of time—Brazil, Switzerland, Spain, Yugoslavia, and Egypt.*

A principal factor in these alarming estimates was the increasing availability of plutonium. The prospective supply was significantly increased during the mid-1960s by enhanced prospects for nuclear power plants, which produce plutonium as a by-product of routine operation. A milestone event pointing in this direction occurred on December 12, 1963, when the Jersey Central Power and Light Company announced a contract with the General Electric Company for the construction of a 515 electric megawatt nuclear power station costing $68 million. This was the first time a utility had chosen a nuclear power plant over an alternative fossil-fueled plant—in this case one burning coal—based wholly on its economic competitiveness. Similar decisions by other utilities followed and, before long, a large-scale shift to nuclear power was in full swing. More than half the new steam generating capacity announced by U.S. electric utilities during the years 1966–68 was nuclear. By the end of the Johnson administration more than one hundred large-scale nuclear power plants were operating, under construction, or in the planning stages in this country. Similar expansion was occurring abroad. In a survey published in November 1965, the prestigious International Institute for Strategic Studies (London) estimated that by 1970 Canada's power reactors could produce enough plutonium for 224 Nagasaki-type

---

*After this issue appeared I received a phone call from the ambassador of one of the countries I had named. He said his foreign office had asked him to thank me for mentioning his country as a potential nuclear power, since this had done a great deal for its prestige.

bombs, and that by 1972 India could produce enough for 230, West Germany for 170, Japan for 92, Italy for 120, Sweden for 32, and Czechoslovakia for 30. (The institute's estimates were based on a requirement of five kilograms of plutonium for each bomb.)

The possibility of proliferation was enhanced by the fact that entering the "nuclear club" was not really a very costly matter. In March 1966 testimony before the Joint Committee on Atomic Energy, I estimated the cost of a "Class B membership"—one involving one or two bombs—at $25 million to $100 million, and that of a capability such as China seemed to be developing at about $1 billion.[1]

My estimates were in line with those made public in October 1967 by UN Secretary-General U Thant. As requested by the General Assembly, he had appointed a group of experts to study the financial costs of acquiring nuclear weapons. The experts estimated that to produce ten 20-kiloton plutonium devices in ten years would cost $104 million; to produce one hundred such devices in ten years would cost $188 million. (To these costs would of course have to be added those of delivery systems.) The experts warned, moreover, that these already moderate costs would decrease further as the technology became more familiar and weapons-grade plutonium more abundant. They estimated that by 1980 the amount of nuclear power produced would involve "the production of plutonium sufficient for thousands of bombs each year."[2]

Summing up the prevailing pessimism, a Washington observer commented that "coping with the proliferation problem required the services of only two men—one to count and the other to wring his hands."[3] The pessimism may well have been overdrawn. To begin with, the chemical processing and fabrication of plutonium is a very formidable, hazardous, high-technology task. In addition, reactor-grade plutonium contains a considerable proportion of unwanted Pu-240, which further complicates the undertaking.

The dire forecasts were based also on a common tendency to confuse capability with intention. The fact that many nations could produce nuclear weapons did not mean that in the reality of their political and economic situations they would choose to do so. National attitudes toward this question were influenced by widely varying circumstances, which, in addition to the known incentives, might also include some powerful disincentives to "going nuclear." Among these were the fear of preemptive attack; the likelihood that neighbors would follow suit; a probable loss of political respectability; and the

potential erosion of any existing relationship with a superpower bene-
factor. The task, as McNamara had said, was "to create international
restraints and an international climate which would make it possible
for these countries [those who could build nuclear weapons but had
not done so] to decide for themselves that the acquisition of nuclear
weapons [was] not in their individual national interests."[4]

U.S. policymakers may have had a tendency to repose too much
confidence in the ability of collective actions, such as UN resolutions
and a nonproliferation treaty, to dissuade all potential nuclear weapon
states at once, despite their widely varying circumstances. Still, there
was some recognition, in the words of the Gilpatric Committee Report, of the importance of applying "influence on individual nations
considering nuclear weapons acquisition." It was with this in mind
that I was dispatched during 1967 on fact-finding and persuasion
missions to a number of potential proliferation hot spots.

Australia

Australia and India were among the nations most seriously disturbed
by China's growing nuclear prowess. Along with Commissioner Gerald F. Tape and others from the AEC, I visited both countries in
January 1967, on a trip that also included Pakistan and Thailand. As
though to emphasize the importance he attached to the mission, President Johnson supplied us with a military aircraft and crew. (He also
encouraged us to bring our wives, which two of us did. Lyndon
Johnson was a very considerate boss.)

On January 6, in Sydney:

> At dinner, Sir Leslie Martin (Australian AEC member and
> scientific adviser to the Department of Defense) told me that
> the Government of Australia was struggling with the decision
> of whether to produce a nuclear weapon. He added that they
> had not previously told the U.S. government about this internal
> debate—for example, President Johnson had not been told dur-
> ing a recent visit—although both Prime Ministers Menzies and
> Holt had considered informing us.

This same theme was echoed in discussions I had with members
of the parliamentary committees that had responsibility for nuclear
energy matters. Several members raised the possibility that Australia
would eventually have to construct nuclear weapons to protect its

national security. The chairman of one of the committees, William Wentworth, expressed the view that Australia should support a nonproliferation treaty only if it contained adequate guarantees against nuclear agression; otherwise such a treaty would be detrimental to friends of the United States and helpful to its enemies. Views such as Wentworth's tended to focus attention again on the puzzling statement made by President Johnson in October 1964 promising to give "support" against "nuclear blackmail" to any nation that asked for it.

Upon my return I reported on Australia's internal debate in a letter to the president. I believe this is what my hosts expected and wanted me to do. Later in 1967 Australia asked for further consultation with the United States about the nonproliferation treaty, and a team composed of Howard Brown (AEC assistant general manager), Herbert "Pete" Scoville (ACDA assistant director for science and technology), George Bunn (ACDA General Counsel), and Allan Labowitz (my assistant for disarmament) journeyed there for that purpose.* As Labowitz recollects,[5] the Australians were genuinely concerned about their security on a regional basis, being a far less populous country than some potentially hostile neighbors (for example, Indonesia) and they were considering acquisition of nuclear weapons as a possible deterrent to hostile actions by such neighbors.

Australia signed the Nonproliferation Treaty on February 23, 1970, and deposited its instrument of ratification on January 23, 1973. This decision provides an excellent illustration of the disincentives that have dissuaded many nuclear-capable nations from becoming nuclear-weapon countries. Australia's calculation was that its acquisition of nuclear weapons would (1) possibly deprive the nation of the protection of the United States through the ANZUS alliance by demonstrating outright opposition to U.S. diplomacy; (2) stimulate proliferation in East and Southeast Asia; and (3) be "costly and lengthy, with no assurance when completed that it would be relevant to the kind of threat that might by then have materialized."[6]

India

From Australia our group proceeded to Bangkok, Thailand, for a one-day visit. The visit to Thailand was not motivated by a concern about

---

*Labowitz recalls participating also in subsequent "sales" visits to Japan, South Africa, and Portugal. He found them all to be "hard sells" and, as we now know, unsuccessful in the case of South Africa.

proliferation but rather by President Johnson's feeling, communicated to me during a meeting at his Texas ranch, that the Thais could benefit from some technical advice about the peaceful uses of atomic energy.

We next flew to Bombay, India. Much of the world's concern about proliferation focused on India. On January 27, 1965, I had attended a luncheon in honor of Jerome Wiesner on the occasion of his departure from his position as White House science adviser.

Wiesner had just returned from a visit to India. He reported that they were seriously considering going into the production of nuclear weapons and that the United States would have to come up with an acceptable alternative (presumably a credible guarantee of India's security) in order to stop them.

Substance was given to Wiesner's warning on September 23, 1965, when eighty-six members of India's Parliament, representing all parties, presented Prime Minister Lal Bahadur Shastri with a letter calling on the government "to make an immediate decision to develop . . . nuclear weapons." Having sustained a bloody nose in frontier clashes with China in 1962, the Indians felt legitimate concern about their security. At the least, the Indian fear was that, unless they emulated China's nuclear program, if only in token fashion, their prestige and influence in Asia would be drastically diminished. Shastri, a determined opponent of nuclear arming, rejected the advice from Parliament. In January 1966, however, he suffered a sudden and fatal heart attack while on a visit to the Soviet Union. His successor, Indira Gandhi, declared on May 11, 1966 that India was not forever committed to foregoing nuclear weapons.

It was against this background that our touring group had a meeting with Dr. Vikram A. Sarabhai, chairman of India's AEC, on January 11, 1967. (He had succeeded the world-famous scientist, Dr. Homi Bhabha, after the latter's death in a plane crash near Geneva a year earlier.) In my trip report to the president I reported on part of the conversation with Sarabhai, as follows:

I emphasized the importance which the United States attaches to the conclusion of a nonproliferation treaty. I particularly explored with him the disturbing reports that India might undertake the development of nuclear explosives on the ground that they were to be used only for peaceful purposes. I stressed the U.S. position that the development of peaceful nuclear explosives was tantamount to the development of nuclear weapons and that it should be left to the nuclear powers to meet the legitimate needs of other nations for the benefits of these highly sophisticated devices. Chairman Sarabhai stated categorically that no such program was in progress or contemplated. However, he maintained that the decision of each nation on whether to develop peaceful nuclear explosives should not be inhibited by a nonproliferation treaty.

At a public ceremony during our visit, Prime Minister Gandhi went further. She said that India should not be prevented by treaty from developing nuclear weapons whenever its national interest required.

We spent a day at Trombay, India's major nuclear establishment twenty-five miles from Bombay. There we were shown the CIRUS research reactor, a large facility built in the late 1950s with technical and financial aid from Canada. (CIRUS stands for Canadian–Indian Reactor Uranium System.) We were also shown a plutonium chemical extraction plant built without foreign aid and in operation since 1965. Our guide told us that they had a lot of plutonium on hand, so much so that storage was a problem. As I wrote in my diary at the time:

> **My impression was that India can easily gather enough weapons-grade plutonium for an atomic bomb, a concern because the CIRUS reactor is not subject to safeguards, even though the Indian agreement with Canada limited the reactor to use only for peaceful purposes.**

Upon my return, I summarized my impressions of the Indian situation in a report to the president:

> I believe that [India] is clearly the leader in peaceful applications of nuclear energy in Asia with the single exception of Japan. It has the capability of mounting a significant nuclear weapons program on relatively short notice, but I saw nothing on my visit to suggest that, at present, it is engaged in any such activities.

Soon after our return home, however, increasingly ominous statements began to be made by Indian officials. In March, India's Minister for External Affairs, M. C. Chagla, stated that India had a "special problem" and would not sign a nonproliferation treaty until it had received a guarantee against "nuclear attack or blackmail." By implication, Chagla was indicating that President Johnson's pledge of support to a threatened nonnuclear country lacked credibility. India's "special problem" was obviously China and, after the Chinese crossed the megaton threshold with their sixth test, on June 17, 1967, Indian Defense Minister S. S. Singh stated in Parliament that the country's security problem had acquired "a fresh sense of urgency."

I believe that Sarabhai tried to resist the pressures in India for development of nuclear weapons. I got to know him very well over a period of years, having met with him on numerous occasions in Washington and at the IAEA in Vienna, as well as in India. I agree entirely with Bertrand Goldschmidt's characterization of him as "a sincere and committed pacifist."[7] But in December 1971 Sarabhai died suddenly, in his sleep, of a heart attack. A little more than a year later, at the beginning of 1973, Indira Gandhi gave the orders to ready a test explosion.[8]

On May 17, 1974, India exploded a nuclear device underground in a desert area bordering Pakistan,* using plutonium produced in the CIRUS reactor and extracted by the processing plant I inspected on January 11, 1967. To this date, India has not proceeded beyond the one explosion, is not thought to have an inventory of warheads, and does not appear to have made any significant moves toward acquiring a nuclear weapons delivery system. At the same time, however, India has not shown any interest in signing the NPT.

India's decision to set off its single explosion appears to have been motivated by a number of factors. The utter rout at the hands of the Chinese in the 1962 border war apparently left the nation in a state of shock. When China achieved nuclear weapon status in 1964, India felt seriously threatened. As one Indian diplomat stated: "China may subject a non-nuclear India to periodic blackmail, weaken its spirit of resistance and self-confidence and thus without a war achieve its major political and military objectives in Asia."[9] India also wanted to gain greater respect from the superpowers. When the nuclear-powered aircraft carrier USS *Enterprise* sailed into the Bay of Bengal during the Bangladesh crisis of 1971, it was interpreted by the Indians, in the light of the Nixon–Kissinger "tilt" toward Pakistan, as an attempt to intimidate India. It was felt that Indian possession of a

---

*India was and is a party to the Limited Test Ban Treaty forbidding nuclear explosions above ground.

nuclear weapon might have prevented the United States from undertaking this bit of "gunboat diplomacy."[10] Also, though India received support from the Soviet Union in the Bangladesh matter, there was fear of a loss of Soviet protection in the event of a USSR–China rapprochement. In general, India seems to have wanted, at slight cost, to create a sense of strategic ambiguity in its region that might shore up its security. Whatever India's 1974 test might have gained along these lines—and the gain may have been substantial—it deprived the country of much of the moral standing previously earned as a leader in movements for international peace and disarmament. This had been a source of prestige and influence, and, by winning for India many friends likely to offer diplomatic—even military—support in an emergency, had added to the nation's security. Whether India gained more than she lost by her 1974 test is therefore open to question.

Pakistan

The final stop on our tour was Pakistan, a nation then much less advanced in nuclear technology than India. There I presented to the government authorities a U.S. check for $350,000 in fulfillment of our commitment under the Atoms for Peace Program to share in the cost of Pakistan's first reactor, a small research unit that was only then achieving its first routine operation.

I found in Pakistan a deep suspicion about the nuclear intentions of India. In introducing me at a lecture I gave at the Lahore Atomic Energy Center, Chairman I. H. Usmani of the Pakistan AEC publicly voiced this mistrust and stated that, if India were to explode a nuclear device, the United States and other nations would share the blame because we provided India with assistance without international controls. In a press conference I held following my lecture I attempted to deflect this criticism by emphasizing that the United States required bilateral safeguards for any nuclear assistance we provided. My remarks were reported in the next day's *Pakistan Times* under the headline: "U.S. Not to Help India Make A-Bomb."

(Pakistan has not signed the Nonproliferation Treaty and is widely believed to be rapidly nearing a nuclear weapons capability.)

Brazil

Later in 1967 I led an AEC–State Department group on a ten-day, six-nation tour of South America, visiting Venezuela, Brazil, Argentina, Chile, Peru, and Colombia, in that order. Once again the president supplied us with a military plane and crew.

The main purpose of the trip was ostensibly to implement the president's pledge, made at a meeting of Western Hemisphere heads of state in April, that the United States would join with Latin American countries in exploring a coordinated regional program for the peaceful uses of nuclear energy. Our trip was also seen, however, as an opportunity to rally support for the nonproliferation treaty.

We felt a particular need to do this in the case of Brazil. Dominant elements there were known to oppose Brazilian adherence to an NPT if it precluded their independent development of nuclear explosives "for peaceful purposes." Because we were convinced that such development made no economic sense and would in fact be tantamount to acquisition of a weapons capability, Brazil's attitude presented a most disturbing situation in our own hemisphere. If Brazil were to carry out its announced intention, for example, what would be the reaction of Argentina, Brazil's rival for nuclear technology leadership on the South American continent?

On July 3, 1967, our delegation met with Brazilian Foreign Ministry officials. It turned out that our hosts were not too well informed on nuclear matters and pertinent U.S. policies. Foreign Minister José Pinto, for example, did not seem to know that the USAEC was a federal agency. The Brazilians also did not seem to understand that if the United States furnished a peaceful nuclear explosions service to other countries under an NPT, as we proposed to do (see chapter 24), we did not intend to include in our price any part of the tremendous research and development costs incurred in connection with our weapons program. I pointed out that this was a main reason why we could provide the service at only a fraction of what it would cost the Brazilians to provide it for themselves. I also explained that nuclear explosives had not yet been developed to the point where they were ready to be used in peaceful applications. The Brazilians had apparently interpreted an overenthusiastic AEC booklet on our own Plowshare program as indicating the contrary. I hoped that the clarification on these points might cause the Brazilians to reevaluate their policies.

In a press conference following our meeting I stressed the importance of a nonproliferation treaty to the final ability of the United States to assist Brazil with peaceful explosives. I was most disturbed to read in the next day's newspapers very distorted versions of what I had said. For example, it was reported that I had advocated withholding all nuclear aid from Brazil. In my subsequent report to the president I attributed the erroneous reporting to the unwillingness of certain Brazilian officials to let the public hear our side of the story.

Later on July 3, I met with a fairly large group of Brazilian military leaders for a frank and full discussion of the potential of nuclear explosives for both military and civilian use on the South American continent. I found this group to be far better informed than the Foreign Office officials. I took the occasion to offer Brazil the opportunity to participate in a joint AEC–Bureau of Mines project exploring the use of nuclear explosives for the in-situ retorting of oil shale. This was a serious offer, but it was also designed to smoke out Brazil's real intentions regarding peaceful nuclear explosives. (Before the beginning of my Latin American trip the AEC staff had reviewed possible applications for peaceful nuclear explosions in Brazil. Attention quickly focused on the oil shale project, which was then in its early stages, because Brazil had a very high proportion of the world's oil shale resources, and also because Brazil's other oil reserves were very limited. We had ascertained that the joint AEC–Bureau of Mines project was unclassified at that stage and that there would be no objection from the Bureau of Mines to adding one or two Brazilians to the project staff for a year or more. We felt that this was an offer Brazil could not refuse if its interest in peaceful nuclear explosives was genuine.) The reaction we got could best be described as a polite brush-off. This was clear evidence to us that the Brazilians' avowed interest in peaceful nuclear explosions was mainly a cover to keep alive a nuclear weapons option.

Israel

Israel was another focus of proliferation concern. Following their joint setback in the Suez debacle of 1956, France had agreed to sell Israel a 24-megawatt materials test reactor, which was later erected at Dimona in the Negev desert. This plant was believed capable of producing enough plutonium for one Nagasaki-sized bomb per year.[11] In addition, Israel was suspected, erroneously I believe, of having obtained supplies of enriched uranium by a 1965 diversion from a fuel fabrication plant in Pennsylvania.*

---

*This suspicion was based on circumstantial evidence. During a routine audit in 1965 of the NUMEC Company enrichment plant in Apollo, Pennsylvania, AEC inspectors were unable to account for some two hundred pounds of enriched uranium. The company, whose chairman was a Zionist, had a business relationship with Israel. These circumstances seemed to point to a clandestine diversion of the missing material to Israel. It is all but certain, however, that the material was lost during complicated chemical procedures that, to save money, were conducted with inadequate care.

On September 27, 1967, at the IAEA's General Conference, I conferred with Ambassador Hassan Tohamy, the United Arab Republic's resident representative in Vienna, about Israel's weapons potential:

> Tohamy expressed with great dismay and apprehension his country's feeling that Israel was making significant progress toward the production of nuclear explosives. The UAR believed that Israel had increased the capacity of its hot laboratory* at Nahal Soreq so that it could process significant quantities of irradiated fuel from the Dimona reactor and recover sufficient plutonium to produce about one nuclear bomb per year. He said he understood this hot lab was not subject to U.S. safeguards despite the $200,000 of U.S. aid given for its construction.† He said he intended to make a strong statement on this from the floor of the Conference, one that would evoke discussion from the floor, unless I could convince him he was wrong, in which case he would make a milder statement. I told him that my visit to Nahal Soreq in September 1966 had convinced me that the hot lab did not have the capability he attributed to it. He said that public statements I had made at the time of my visit had been reassuring but that subsequent developments had again aroused concern. Following overnight checking, we assured Tohamy the next day that the hot lab still did not have the capacity to warrant the concerns he had expressed. Accordingly, Tohamy's speech on September 29 was quite mild—it contained no charges that the facility was being used in a manner inconsistent with IAEA principles.

Speculation that Israel might be engaged in weapons research and fabrication, utilizing plutonium from Dimona, has persisted. At a meeting of the Atomic Energy Commission on July 11, 1969, we discussed sending a team to inspect Dimona. In due course application was made to the Government of Israel for permission to make

---

*A hot laboratory is one designed for the safe handling of radioactive materials. It usually contains one or more heavily shielded enclosures in which radioactive materials can be handled remotely through the use of manipulators and viewed through shielded windows so that there is no danger to personnel.

†The hot lab was not subject to safeguards because it was used primarily for isotope production and because its capacity was too limited to produce significant quantities of plutonium. Safeguards inspections were conducted, however, at the Soreq Research Establishment's research reactor, and the hot lab was visited in the course of these inspections.

such a visit, but it was refused. At the present time, as Lewis Dunn writes, "virtually all U.S. government officials and outside analysts" agree that Israel already has covertly produced a limited number of assembled or nearly assembled atom bombs.[12] (In October 1986, *The London Sunday Times* carried a story that Israel had been secretly building nuclear warheads for twenty years at an underground plant at Dimona and had stockpiled one hundred to two hundred nuclear weapons. The information was divulged by an Israeli technician who had worked at Dimona. It gained credibility because it was accompanied by charts and photographs.[13])

The Centrifuge

A further proliferation danger was that some breakthrough in technology might occur that would bring nuclear weapons more easily within the reach of additional nations. One such possibility was the gas centrifugation process for producing enriched uranium. In this process, the heavier U-238 atoms in uranium hexafluoride gas are spun out by centrifugal force and thus separated from the lighter U-235 atoms, much as milk is separated from cream. The centrifuge was briefly considered as the enrichment method of choice in the early days of the wartime atomic bomb project, but was rejected in favor of the gaseous diffusion method largely because the latter had fewer development problems remaining to be solved at a time when haste was of the essence. It was always recognized, however, that the centrifuge had significant potential economic advantages, particularly for European countries. As compared to gaseous diffusion it would require only a small fraction of the electricity per unit of output. (Electricity was relatively more costly in Europe than in the United States.) In addition, centrifuge plants could operate efficiently on a much smaller scale than diffusion plants, which are intrinsically huge.

In 1953, the AEC began again to study centrifuge technology as a possible economic encouragement to the development of civilian nuclear power. Development work was undertaken also in Britain, West Germany, and the Netherlands. The interest of these countries was in producing enriched uranium for power reactors in a way that would be economically attractive and that would lessen dependence on U-235 supply by the United States. In 1959, the AEC concluded that centrifuge technology had advanced to such an extent that units already developed could be used in U-235 enrichment plants and that the power and space requirements for such plants were so modest as to be amenable to clandestine operation. The AEC at once came under competing pressures. On the one hand, U.S. industry wanted the technology made freely available in order to lessen the fuel costs of future civilian power endeavors. On the other hand, there were those who wanted the centrifuge placed under wraps as an antiproliferation measure. It was economics versus security—a classic dilemma of the nuclear age.

The AEC tilted toward the latter view and embarked on steps to limit spread of the technology. In July 1960, it prevailed on the U.K., West German, and Netherlands governments to impose security classifications on their gas centrifuge programs. At the same time, tight security restrictions were imposed on the industrial firms participating in the AEC's own program, and gas centrifuges and their component parts were placed on the Commerce Department's Positive List to prevent export.

By 1964 there were indications, both at home and abroad, of desires to break free from these restrictions. At a meeting of U.S., British, Dutch, and West German representatives early in the year, the latter two argued for a relaxation of the restrictions, ostensibly because the centrifuge process was useful in a variety of peaceful applications in addition to the separation of U-235. It was only with difficulty that we persuaded them to continue their classification arrangements. U.S. firms working in the field were similarly restive. Thus, when I met with representatives of the General Electric Company and the Allied Chemical Company, who were conducting a joint centrifuge venture, they told me of their frustration in having to explain to their boards of directors that, under existing restrictions, there was no indication they could establish a commercial operation even if their development work was successful. Compounding the AEC's difficulty in determining a policy was the realization that, despite our best efforts to restrict it, the gas centrifuge technology might eventually be acquired by other nations.

In April 1964 I wrote to Messrs. Foster and McNamara, among others, seeking guidance "to assure that the [centrifuge] policy we adopt at this time will best serve our national security interests." Specifically, I asked for their views on "the importance to the United States of maximum delay in the acquisition by an Nth power* of a

---

*The letter "N" has been borrowed from mathematics to describe the indeterminate number of countries that may acquire nuclear weapons in the future. The term "Nth power" is used to designate the next country likely to do so.

capability to produce fissionable materials for atomic weapons use, even in very limited quantities."

Foster's views were strong and unequivocal. He wrote:

> I believe that we should continue to resist all pressures to release controls on the dissemination of gas centrifuge technology. . . . It is important to retard the proliferation of nuclear weapons to *any* additional countries without exception. . . . While I recognize that it is difficult, if not impossible, to prevent the dissemination of any technology, I want to emphasize two points: (a) If we delay such dissemination for several more years, there may be international agreements by then to control the proliferation of nuclear weapons. (b) In any case, U.S. security interests require that we delay such dissemination as long as we can.

McNamara replied in similar vein. He recognized that we could only retard, not prevent, the technology's growth and diffusion. "Even so," he wrote, "the goal of retardation is a worthwhile one." He recommended that we continue our restrictive policies and endeavor to persuade others with significant centrifuge programs to do the same. He also recommended that, in order to dampen the incentive of countries to develop their own centrifuge technology, "the U.S. should leave no doubt that enriched uranium will be available from this country on attractive terms. . . ."

On October 11, 1964, I also discussed our dilemma with Chairman Holifield of the Joint Committee on Atomic Energy:

> At first Holifield said he favored AEC continuing to develop the gas centrifuge technology, but doubted that U.S. industry should be allowed to continue its development work. I told him there was some argument in favor of allowing industry to continue under strong security controls, since this would place it in a strong competitive position in the event foreign countries should develop the process. This could actually aid the non-proliferation concept rather than hinder it; it would discourage other countries because their process would not be economically competitive. After I made these points, Holifield seemed to agree that this was a question that deserved further discussion at an executive session of the JCAE.

Such a session was indeed held, but not until March 9, 1967. Four of the five AEC commissioners were present, signifying the importance we attached to the issue. By this time the proliferation scare had worsened considerably, largely due to the Chinese tests and the reaction to them. As a consequence, the AEC had, albeit reluctantly, come round to the point of view expressed by Holifield more than two years earlier: We believed that private work on the gas centrifuge should be cut off, but that the AEC should continue a strong program. All the JCAE members agreed readily, with the exception of Representative Craig Hosmer. He at first argued vigorously against excluding industry, but in the end he also went along.

Another opinion being expressed on this issue was that of the Soviet Union. The Soviets charged that further work on the centrifuge in Western Europe could lead to West German development of nuclear weapons.[14]

The next task was to break the news to industry. On March 14, 1967, the AEC commissioners (again all but one—Commissioner Samuel M. Nabrit was out of town) met with officers of two of the companies involved, W. R. Grace and Company and Electro Nucleonics, Inc., to tell them that we had decided to terminate centrifuge work in private corporations. Electro Nucleonics took it particularly hard. Their representatives tried to persuade us, as a minimum, to support their work. Later in the day I received a letter from them pointing out that our action would result in about a $10 million loss of stock equity on the open market and hinting that they would hold the AEC responsible. (Subsequently, the AEC helped Electro Nucleonics move from weapons-related work into the biological field, where their experience with and knowledge about the centrifuge found useful applications.)

Centrifuge Sequels

In 1976, in the face of high estimates for future nuclear energy growth, a fourth gaseous diffusion plant was started at Portsmouth. It was thought that there was not enough time to develop gas centrifuge technology to meet the expected large increment in demand from nuclear power plants. A year later, when projections of nuclear power growth were revised downward, this decision was reversed. Work stopped on the additional unit at Portsmouth and construction was authorized on a Gas Centrifuge Enrichment Plant (GCEP), also at Portsmouth, with the expectation that it would be able to provide service at costs equal to or less than that of the gaseous diffusion process. In subsequent years, however, the prospects for economic competitiveness of the GCEP dimmed, largely because electricity costs, which are about 80 percent of total costs in the rival diffusion process, had stopped increasing at expected rates—in fact, in the early 1980s the price of electricity actually declined.

Also, beginning in 1974, the United States began to lose its share of the worldwide enriched uranium market to lower-priced competition from European suppliers, mainly the Soviet Union and a Western consortium (Eurodif) headed by France. Whereas in 1974 we had supplied 100 percent of the enriched uranium needs of the free world, by 1985 the U.S. share had shrunk to less than 50 percent. The Department of Energy therefore decided in 1984 to revamp this country's uranium enrichment strategy in order to save money and recapture market share. On June 5, 1985, after a study of many months' duration, Secretary of Energy John S. Herrington announced decisions:

> To stop work on the GCEP and "end U.S. government involvement in the development of gas centrifuge technology." ($2.6 billion had already been spent on the GCEP project. It was estimated that it would have cost $3.7 billion to $5 billion to complete.)

> To place the Oak Ridge gaseous diffusion plant, which had been in operation for more than forty years, in standby. (It and the plants at Paducah and Portsmouth had been operating at considerably less than capacity.)

> To focus research, development, and demonstration efforts on a new process, atomic vapor laser isotope separation (AVLIS), which, Secretary Herrington said, "has the technical and economic potential for better performance and lower production cost than the [gas centrifuge.]" While this "technology of the Twenty-first Century" is being developed, the gaseous diffusion process is expected to continue to meet the needs of U.S. customers at home and abroad.*

Although gaseous centrifugation as a method of isotope separation has been discarded as economically infeasible for the United States,

---

*If isotope separation by laser proves successful, it might be used to separate plutonium-240 from the plutonium in spent power reactor fuel, making the remainder more suitable for weapons purposes. This would have ominous implications for proliferation as it would greatly increase the quantity of weapons grade plutonium available to non-nuclear-weapons states.

it continues to be employed elsewhere. It is commonly believed, for example, that Pakistan is using this method for its nuclear program.[15]

Notes

1. JCAE, *Nonproliferation of Nuclear Weapons, Hearings,* February–March 1966, p. 67ff.
2. U.S. ACDA, *International Negotiations on the Treaty on the Nonproliferation of Nuclear Weapons,* p. 93.
3. James Schlesinger, "Nuclear Spread," in Kertesz, ed., *Nuclear Non-Proliferation,* p. 27.
4. JCAE, *Nonproliferation of Nuclear Weapons, Hearings,* February–March 1966, p. 75.
5. Private conversation, June 13, 1986.
6. Richardson, *Australia and the Non-Proliferation Treaty,* p. 21.
7. Goldschmidt, *The Atomic Complex,* p. 201.
8. Pringle and Spigelman, *The Nuclear Barons,* p. 379.
9. Quoted in Ganguly, "Why India Joined the Nuclear Club," p. 31.
10. Ibid., p. 32.
11. Willrich, *Non-Proliferation Treaty,* p. 277.
12. Dunn, *Controlling the Bomb,* p. 48.
13. *Washington Post,* October 29, 1986.
14. Roberts, *The Nuclear Years,* p. 75.
15. Craig and Jungerman, *Nuclear Arms Race,* p. 380.

22
Slow Progress
on Safeguards

Background

The December 1966 superpower agreement on Articles I and II still left much to be accomplished before there could be a complete nonproliferation treaty. There had been no serious negotiation, for example, on the matter of verification safeguards.

Lest there be confusion, I should point out that the meaning of the term "safeguards" in the context of a nonproliferation treaty is quite different from its meaning as applied to the four national security safeguards exacted from President Kennedy by the Joint Chiefs of Staff as a price for their support of the Limited Test Ban Treaty. Safeguards in relation to the NPT are a mechanism for detecting on a timely basis any diversion of nuclear materials from peaceful to weapons uses. The techniques currently employed include the checking and cross-checking of accounting records documenting the presence, receipt, and movement of nuclear materials; the submission of accounting reports based on the records; surveillance at key locations by cameras and other instruments; the use of seals and other techniques to assure against unreported movement of material; and—of great importance—the performance of independent measurements and observations by outside inspectors.

Safeguards are designed to *detect* diversion, not to *prevent* it, except insofar as the high risk of detection acts as a deterrent. They serve in essence as a warning system. When the safeguards system

Many of the decisions and events described in this and the following chapter relating to AEC's safeguards policies bear the imprint of Myron B. Kratzer, who was head of the AEC division of international affairs during these years. A profound student of the subject, Kratzer was one of the architects of the IAEA's safeguards system and remains today one of the world's leading experts in this field. I gratefully acknowledge his assistance also in the writing of this chapter and the one following.

indicates that a diversion has taken place, it is then up to interested nations and the international community to take such steps as will prevent the diverted material from being converted into weapons.

Under the Atoms for Peace Program, the AEC initially had applied its own safeguards to the materials and equipment the United States provided to other nations. We felt from the start, however, that international safeguards were intrinsically superior to bilateral safeguards, and we expected the IAEA to assume this responsibility as soon as it achieved the necessary capability. Our reasons for preferring international safeguards were fundamental. In the first place, in a situation where a nation might receive nuclear assistance from more than one source, having each supplying nation apply its own safeguards would result in costly duplication of effort and an untenable burden on the recipient state. Next, the whole world—not only the supplying country—needed assurance that nuclear material was not being diverted; safeguards administered only by the supplying country would lack credibility, especially if the recipients were the supplier's allies. Finally, it was necessary to remove safeguards as a potential factor in the competition for nuclear business; a situation that might arise if suppliers began to woo customers with offers of fewer or less stringent safeguards (or, conceivably, no safeguards at all).

Early History of IAEA Safeguards

Under the IAEA Statute adopted in 1956, IAEA safeguards were to be applied only to peaceful nuclear projects for which the IAEA itself provided assistance, or in cases where IAEA safeguards were specifically requested by a nation or by parties to a bilateral or multilateral agreement. Thus limited, IAEA safeguards activities developed slowly. With the United States supplying nuclear materials and equipment under the Atoms for Peace Program to many nations, the IAEA never took on the supply role that had been envisaged for it by President Eisenhower, a role that would have triggered more rapid development of a safeguards capability. As long as the IAEA lacked this capability, the United States felt compelled to continue its own bilateral safeguards.

In the IAEA's early years, there was strong opposition to staffing and strengthening its safeguards function. The Soviet Union led this opposition, supported by India and several other developing nations. The argument most commonly advanced was that safeguards were an infringement of national sovereignty. (One can only speculate as to whether more was involved. India, for example, objected particularly to extending safeguards to equipment at a time when she seems to have been acquiring the equipment for an independent fuel cycle, thus keeping open a weapons option.)

In spite of the resistance, work on a safeguards system went forward quietly within the IAEA staff, assisted by advisers from the United Sates and other nations. A package of rules and procedures that became known as the First Safeguards Document was approved by the IAEA's Board of Governors in March 1961. It applied only to relatively small reactors, however—those with a thermal output of less then 100 megawatts. In February 1964 the safeguards system was expanded to cover full-scale power reactors. In the interim, the Soviet Union had changed its attitude to one of support for IAEA safeguards. Negotiations then went forward in a much improved atmosphere on a further revision and improvement of the system. At length, in April 1965, the IAEA Board of Governors and General Conference approved a system that is still in use for IAEA safeguards applied outside the NPT. This system is generally referred to by the number of the information circular in which it was first published: INFCIRC/66. It was extended to include chemical processing plants in June 1966 and fuel fabrication plants in 1968.

Tarapur: An Important Precedent

As soon as it became apparent that the IAEA would develop an effective safeguards system, the United States decided to request all its bilateral partners to accept IAEA safeguards as a precondition for further supply of nuclear materials. A key negotiation was with India. Early in 1963, India contracted to purchase two power reactors from the General Electric Company, for construction at Tarapur, a site north of Bombay. This commercial action had been preceded by lengthy negotiations of a U.S.–India Agreement for Cooperation under which: (1) there would be an exchange of unclassified information regarding the design, construction, and operation of the Tarapur plant; (2) the United States would supply enriched fuel for twenty-five years; (3) materials and equipment supplied by the United States were to be used solely for peaceful purposes; (4) the United States would initially apply bilateral safeguards; and, most significantly, (5) the IAEA would, at a suitable time, be requested to enter into a trilateral agreement for the application of its safeguards. This agreement was especially noteworthy because, as Henry D. Smyth, U.S. ambassador to the IAEA, testified,

> [Tarapur] is the first major foreign nuclear power project outside the Euratom complex in which the U.S. government will be a major participant and because the agreement is with India, a Government which has not always been friendly to safeguards and a Government which has such a major world position as a leader of the developing countries, particularly in Asia.[1]

India was at first reluctant to agree to the IAEA safeguards provision, preferring to accept only U.S. safeguards. Their position won some sympathy in the State Department, but the AEC, supported by the Joint Committee, held out for requiring IAEA safeguards and prevailed. There was compromise on one point: India argued that it should not be the only government subjected to IAEA safeguards. Seeing justice in this, we agreed with them that IAEA safeguards should not be applied at Tarapur until they had been widely accepted by other U.S. trading partners. (Critics in Congress and elsewhere argued that this concession was a mistake and that, because of it, IAEA safeguards might never be applied at Tarapur. This fear proved unfounded, however, and IAEA safeguards were initiated at the Indian plant in January 1971.)

The Indian agreement was an important turning point in gaining wide acceptance of IAEA safeguards; it provided a legal, technical, and political precedent that helped to persuade other U.S. trading partners to follow suit. By 1965, the transfer from AEC to IAEA safeguards had been accomplished for twenty of the United States' bilateral agreements, with others to follow soon after. Even with the Indian precedent, however, this was a long and difficult process in some cases.

Sweden Drags Its Feet

One of the last U.S. trading partners to agree to replace U.S. with IAEA safeguards was Sweden. This seemed paradoxical, given the fact that the IAEA's director general, beginning in September 1961, was the Swedish scientist, Sigvard Eklund. It was also a situation that I

took as a personal challenge. Largely because of my Swedish ances-
try,* I had excellent contacts in Sweden, being personally acquainted
with Prime Minister Tage Erlander, with Harry Brynielsson (managing director of Aktiebolaget Atomenergi, the joint government–industry enterprise that ran the country's nuclear energy programs), and
with numerous others prominent in Sweden's scientific, technical, industrial, and political communities. I had a matchmaker's zeal in
wanting to effect a marriage between these two objects of personal
concern, Sweden and IAEA safeguards, and I used every reasonable
opportunity toward this end.

The first bilateral agreement between Sweden and the United States
for cooperation in the civil uses of atomic energy went into effect on
January 18, 1956. It was one of the so-called research agreements
under which the United States, under U.S.-administered safeguards,
supplied a limited amount of enriched uranium to fuel research reactors. During 1963, consultations began between the U.S. and Swedish governments with a view to replacing this agreement with a broader
one that would include the supply of a greater quantity of enriched
fuel for power reactors.

In January 1964, I wrote to Brynielsson emphasizing the importance the AEC attached to having the new agreement provide for
IAEA safeguards. I suggested, in fact, that a trilateral U.S.–Swedish–
IAEA agreement to this effect be signed at the same time as the new
U.S.–Swedish bilateral. Had Sweden agreed, it would have represented the largest nuclear power program under IAEA safeguards in
a single country. To my disappointment, the Swedish government
demurred, giving as its primary reason that the IAEA safeguards system still had certain deficiencies that they hoped would soon be
overcome.

I had another opportunity to work on my Swedish contacts during
the second UN Conference on the Peaceful Uses of Atomic Energy,
held in Geneva during the summer of 1964. On September 3 and 4,
I hosted a cruise for representatives of many nations aboard the *Savannah,* the world's first—and, to date, only—nuclear-powered cargo
and passenger ship. Along with my guests, who included officials or

---

*My mother and my paternal grandparents were born in Sweden. I was born and spent my
childhood in a Swedish section of Ishpeming, Michigan. I learned the Swedish language from
my mother before I learned English.

representatives of fifteen national nuclear energy organizations,* I flew to Sweden from Geneva the afternoon of September 3 and spent the night aboard the *Savannah,* preparatory to cruising on September 4 from Hälsingborg to Malmö. We were joined for the cruise by a large group of Swedish industrialists. I took the opportunity to urge again on the Swedes, during a conversation at which Eklund was present, the desirability of having IAEA safeguards replace U.S. safeguards in the new U.S.–Swedish bilateral. Most of the Swedes appeared to resist the idea, although this sentiment was not unanimous— some electric utility representatives favored it.

The next day, September 5, I continued my campaign in Stockholm, meeting with Prime Minister Erlander and with Olof Palme, then a member of the Cabinet and the Senate.

> I explained why the United States and Eklund wanted Sweden to transfer from U.S. to IAEA safeguards. I described the IAEA's safeguards system and said it would not interfere with the development of nuclear power in Sweden. I suggested that the prime minister agree at least to a six-month trial on one reactor. Erlander thought he could get his cabinet to agree to that.†

In November 1965 I saw Prime Minister Erlander again, at a dinner in his honor given by the Swedish ambassador in Washington. I again urged that Sweden adopt IAEA safeguards and he again spoke encouragingly.

In spite of all the encouragement we received from Erlander—and I am convinced he personally was favorably disposed—the best we could obtain when the new power bilateral was signed on June 28, 1966, was a provision recognizing the desirability of IAEA safeguards

---

*Among the guests were IAEA Director-General Eklund, Andronik Petrosyants (chairman of USSR State Committee for the Utilization of Atomic Energy), Gunnar Randers (managing director, Institute for Atomic Energy, Norway), Oscar A. Quilhillalt (president, National Atomic Energy Commission, Argentina), I. H. Usmani (chairman, Pakistan Atomic Energy Commission), Homi J. Bhabha (chairman, Indian Atomic Energy Commission), and Sir William G. Penney (chairman, United Kingdom Atomic Energy Authority).

†Immediately following this meeting, my wife and I hosted a luncheon for thirty-six relatives. It took place in Skansen, part of a Stockholm park where there is a reproduction in miniature of the salient physical features of Sweden, including some characteristic dwellings. Among these is the home, Laxbrostugan, of some of my mother's ancestors. It was physically transported to Skansen as an exemplar of the typical home of the late seventeenth century in the Bergslagen region northwest of Stockholm.

and agreeing "promptly" to begin negotiations with the IAEA for their application. But when, more than three years later, on September 16, 1969, I had another meeting with Erlander,* the transfer to IAEA safeguards still not having taken place, I had to remind the prime minister that this inaction was not consistent with Sweden's pledge that something would be done promptly.

Meanwhile, Sweden's nuclear power program was growing apace, and the 50,000 kilograms of U-235 we supplied under the bilateral agreement of June 1966 were no longer adequate. Accordingly, on October 22, 1970, an amendment to the agreement was signed, increasing the amount we supplied to 122,300 kilograms. We used the opportunity to request Sweden to reaffirm its intent to adopt IAEA safeguards. Active negotiations were then initiated that led finally to a trilateral (U.S.–Sweden–IAEA) safeguards agreement. When it was signed in Vienna on March 1, 1972, however, I did not have the satisfaction of participating. I had left the government the year before.

My Swedish contacts gave me different explanations from time to time for their delay in accepting IAEA safeguards on U.S.-supplied material. At bottom I think the basic reason was that they were reluctant to give up the devil they knew for one they did not know. They had become used to U.S. safeguards and regarded them as acceptable. They expected the United States to continue to apply safeguards in an unburdensome manner and to be reasonable in dealing with any problems that arose. They did not know what to expect from the IAEA and may have feared that agency inspectors could make life difficult. In spite of some allegations that have been made recently, I am convinced that Sweden was *not* trying to conceal any activity leading to the production of weapons.[2]

The Euratom Exception

Notwithstanding its strong convictions about the desirability of a universal system of international safeguards administered by the IAEA, the AEC reluctantly agreed that the six countries in the European Atomic Energy Community (Euratom) should be allowed to apply Euratom, rather than IAEA, safeguards.

---

*Also present at this meeting was Ingvar Carlsson (under secretary of state, prime minister's office), who would succeed Olof Palme as prime minister following the latter's assassination in February 1986, and Bo Aler, who was slated to succeed Brynielsson as head of Sweden's atomic energy program.

Euratom came into existence on January 1, 1958, to foster development of the peaceful atom in its member countries: Belgium, France, Italy, Luxembourg, the Netherlands, and West Germany. It was decided at the outset that the existence of Euratom would not affect the members' ultimate freedom of decision on whether to employ atomic energy for military purposes. Safeguards were introduced, however, to ensure that nuclear materials declared to be for peaceful use would not be diverted to military use. The existence of Euratom safeguards was thought to eliminate the need for any foreign or international controls on the territories of the member countries. Indeed, the possibility of avoiding such controls was said to have been a decisive factor in inducing some countries to accept the Euratom treaty.[3]

The Euratom countries explained a part of their distaste for the intrusion of foreign inspectors as a fear of espionage, particularly industrial espionage. Nuclear-generated electricity and other peaceful uses of the atom were seen as fields of enormous commercial opportunity. The Euratom countries, especially France and West Germany, intended to compete vigorously for the new markets and did not wish to be disadvantaged by the loss of industrial secrets to potential competitors. There was also some fear that IAEA inspections, if carried out by personnel from the Eastern bloc, could lead to breaches of military security. On this latter point, Dr. Francis Perrin, high commissioner of the French AEC, was very specific. In a conversation with me in November 1964,

> Dr. Perrin said that the chief reason why France objected to IAEA safeguards was the possibility of the inspector coming from "a country like Russia," to which they felt they could not openly object. He said that a country like Israel could easily require that the safeguards inspectors not be Arabs, but it would not be that simple for the French to object to Russians.*

But the most important Euratom objection to IAEA safeguards may have been political. "Eurocrats" in the community—those who supported the movement for a united Europe—thought it important that Euratom retain the ownership and control of fissionable material,

---

*One of the provisions of the IAEA safeguards system is that the host country has the right to disapprove in advance any inspector designated by the IAEA. Nationality is probably the most frequent reason for such disapproval.

including safeguards control, because they regarded this prerogative as an important demonstration of the community's supranational character. This point of view had much support in our State Department.

Between 1954 and 1958, the United States had sold nuclear materials directly to the future Euratom countries through bilateral agreements. After Euratom was established, however, procurement for the entire organization was centralized in a Euratom Supply Agency, and in 1958 a United States–Euratom Cooperation Agreement was signed to recognize this new reality. Thereafter, as bilaterals with individual Euratom countries expired, we "folded them in" to the United States–Euratom agreement. It stipulated that safeguards would be applied by Euratom itself, with only loose oversight by the United States. Nor did the agreement contain the provision for future transfer to IAEA safeguards that was found in our bilateral agreements with other countries. Indeed, in the first draft IAEA was not even mentioned. When this draft was being discussed there was criticism, by the Joint Committee among others, that such an arrangement would "undermine the IAEA." The State Department, on the other hand, defended the proposal in the interest of European unity. A temporary resolution of the issue was reached through a cosmetic change by which the agreement, in its final form, made a passing mention of the IAEA. Thereafter, Euratom safeguards ceased to be a source of controversy for several years. During this period, AEC's continuing review found that the Euratom system was a good one— not equal to that employed by the United States under its bilaterals, but fully equal to the IAEA safeguards of that period. In answer to criticism from other nations that Euratom safeguards constituted "self-inspection," we pointed out that the system in fact had an "adversarial" character in that nationals of France, West Germany, and Italy, who were competing for nuclear business, were inspecting each other's reactors. A number of countries, including the Soviet Union, did not accept this argument.

Article III: Beginnings

It was our favorable findings on the effectiveness of Euratom safeguards that allowed AEC in intragovernment discussions during 1965 to concur, with some reluctance, in a proposed NPT Article III mandating that all non-nuclear-weapon signatories accept IAEA "or equivalent" safeguards on all their nuclear activities. (The phrase "or equivalent" was recognized as a reference to Euratom.) This was far better than the alternative some were proposing—no safeguards at all—and was thought to keep the door open for later change to a stronger provision based more exclusively on IAEA safeguards. The AEC suggested a further provision whereby nuclear-weapon parties also would be required to accept IAEA or equivalent safeguards, but on their peaceful nuclear activities only. Upon learning that this was unacceptable to the British, the AEC agreed to a weaker provision, again for the nuclear-weapon signatories only, requiring them merely to "cooperate in facilitating" the application of IAEA safeguards. We also concurred in a *fall-back* provision whereby the same weak provision—"cooperate in facilitating"—would be applied as well to the non-nuclear-weapon parties if, and only if, it appeared that a U.S. proposal for mandatory safeguards was proving a primary obstacle to acceptance of the treaty as a whole.

What was our astonishment and dismay, then, when we learned, shortly before the U.S. draft nonproliferation treaty was to be introduced in August 1965, that ACDA Director Foster proposed to include this weak fall-back provision in the draft treaty's *first submission,* making no distinction between weapon and nonweapon parties. On August 13, I wrote to Foster conveying AEC's unhappiness about this apparent breach of our understanding and urging that every effort be made to have the mandatory provision reinstated for the non-nuclear-weapon countries—they should be *required* to have IAEA or equivalent safeguards. On the same day I phoned Foster in Geneva telling him that my letter was on the way and again emphasizing the AEC's concern about what had happened.

> Foster said it was the fall-back provision or nothing as far as our allies on the ENDC—Italy, Canada, and the U.K.—were concerned. He said he had made it clear that the United States was accepting the deletion of mandatory safeguards under protest and that it was the very definite intention of our delegation to give aggressive support to the basic idea of IAEA safeguards in speeches, discussions, etc. I asked whether it might not be possible to have a neutral—say Sweden, Mexico, or Brazil—propose an appropriate amendment to our draft treaty—thereby achieving the purpose of the amendment without ourselves being blamed by our allies. He thought this was a possibility and that Sweden might be the one to do it. Again he assured

me that what the United States had put down in this initial draft would not be our last word and that the U.S. delegation could be depended on to push for mandatory safeguards.

And so it was that the draft treaty introduced by the United States on August 17, 1965, contained the following Article III, from the AEC's point of view a miserably weak provision:

Each of the States Party to this Treaty undertakes to cooperate in facilitating the application of International Atomic Energy Agency or equivalent international safeguards on all peaceful nuclear activities.

Nor did Foster's statement to the ENDC when he tabled the U.S. draft bear out his promise of an "aggressive" support of mandatory safeguards. Far from it. "We have drafted the [safeguards] provision in its present form," he said, "to take account of the views of countries who do not seem prepared at this time to accept IAEA safeguards in all applicable circumstances." He did, however, extend the invitation I had suggested for intervention by a neutral country by adding: "The United States will be especially interested to receive suggestions from the non-nuclear members of this committee as to means of strengthening this provision."

Alva Myrdal, Sweden's brilliant and dedicated representative, rose to the bait, not at the ENDC, but at the meeting of the UN General Assembly that began later in September. On October 7, Myrdal told the UNGA's First Committee that there were no intractable control problems in a nonproliferation agreement in view of the IAEA's recently strengthened safeguards system. She recommended that *all states* participating in such an agreement place their peaceful nuclear programs under IAEA safeguards. At the same meeting, Foster himself delivered a strengthened endorsement of IAEA safeguards. He criticized the Soviet draft treaty introduced on September 24 for its lack of any provision for safeguards. He pointed out that the numerous nuclear power plants scheduled for construction around the world would soon be producing large amounts of plutonium. To allay suspicion that some of this material might be used to produce weapons he believed the time had come to accept IAEA safeguards on "all civil uses of atomic energy."

But Foster's support of mandatory safeguards appeared to be more bark than bite; he was still unwilling to press our allies in the ENDC by proposing a strengthened Article III. His position was summed up in a statement to the First Committee on October 18: "We recommend as strong a provision on this subject as is possible in the light of the views of all those interested in acceding."[4] In correspondence with me early in 1966 Foster asked, in the same vein, whether failure to obtain a strong safeguards article should be allowed to prevent agreement on "an otherwise acceptable treaty." I replied: "We are not convinced that any nonproliferation treaty that does not call for mandatory safeguards on non-nuclear-weapon signatories could be 'an otherwise acceptable treaty.'" We at AEC began to feel some kinship with those critics of ACDA who felt that pursuit of "agreement for agreement's sake" made that agency too willing to compromise on fundamentals.

Unexpected Allies

Help for AEC's position soon arrived from a new and powerful source. On January 18, 1966, during his speech on the Senate floor introducing SR 179 (the so-called Pastore Resolution "commending" President Johnson's efforts in behalf of a nonproliferation treaty—see chapter 15), Joint Committee Chairman John Pastore included some very strong comments on the subject of safeguards. Referring to the U.S. draft treaty's Article III, Pastore said he "would not accept that noncommittal phrasing." Instead he strongly recommended that when the U.S. delegation returned to Geneva on January 27, it be given specific instructions to replace the draft Article III with "clear, explicit, definite, unequivocal language" committing nonweapon parties to accept "IAEA or similar international safeguards on all of their nuclear activities." Because of the influence of the Joint Committee on the Senate as a whole, Pastore's comments were interpreted as implying that there might be difficulty in obtaining a two-thirds vote in the Senate for any nonproliferation treaty that did not have a strengthened Article III.

The new situation created by Pastore's comments was considered at the meeting of the Committee of Principals on January 21. This was the meeting at which General Goodpaster challenged continued U.S. espousal of a comprehensive test ban in President Johnson's forthcoming message to the ENDC (see chapter 19). After the test ban discussion had been concluded,

I suggested that the president's message also contain some favorable reference to IAEA safeguards, such as a recommendation that "the nonproliferation treaty provide for specific undertakings toward this end." I was immediately challenged by Foster. He opposed the addition of such a statement on the grounds that it would lead to problems with "countries such as Italy." A spirited discussion followed, during which I alluded to Pastore's strong statement on the Senate floor three days earlier and added that his views were shared by many other members of both houses.

Allan Labowitz, who was at this meeting, recalls that at about this point Dean Rusk leaned back and said, "Well, I guess I owe John Pastore this one." Rusk then indicated that the foreign secretary of Canada was due in Washington the following day and that, he, Rusk, would bring up the matter of IAEA safeguards in their discussions.[5] (Both Canada and Italy took the position that if there were to be mandatory IAEA safeguards they should be imposed on nuclear and nonnuclear nations alike.)

Following the Principals meeting on January 21, it was decided that the president's message would indeed mention safeguards, and in language that tilted rather far toward AEC's point of view. It came out as follows:

I urge agreement that all transfers of nuclear materials or equipment for peaceful purposes to countries which do not have nuclear weapons be under IAEA or equivalent international safeguards. At the same time, the major powers should accept in increasing measure the same international safeguards they recommend for other states.

Article III was again considered by the Principals on February 28. Sensing that the tide had turned in favor of AEC's position, I sought to press the advantage:

I claimed that the U.S. had been too quick to adopt the fallback provision in introducing its draft treaty. I saw no reason why we had to compromise so readily on Article III at a time when the jury was still out on Articles I and II. I recommended that our delegation in Geneva seek to strengthen the article and that they seek instructions from Washington if such efforts failed. [I wanted to be sure that the AEC would have an opportunity to be heard as the negotiations proceeded.] Foster said that the delegation had made a strong attempt to get a stronger Article III but that they had to fall back in order to get Western concurrences in Geneva. Rusk said stronger safeguards were needed if a treaty was to succeed in preventing proliferation. But McNamara, who came in late, seemed to accept the weaker Article III as necessary, citing Italian opposition to strengthening it.* Rusk then said he would approach Italian Foreign Minister Fanfani to try to get him to modify his position.

The following day it was my turn to testify at the Joint Committee's hearings on the Pastore Resolution. Here I found myself in the uncomfortable position of trying to defend the U.S. draft treaty's Article III against the relentless questioning of Pastore and Representative Craig Hosmer, both of whom knew quite well where I really stood on the issue. A few excerpts will indicate the tenor of this rather miserable experience:

> Representative HOSMER. What I am getting at is this: You have laid great stress on the necessity . . . to have international inspection. However, the drafts of the treaty proposed so far do not bind the signatories to international inspection. They go no further than to indicate that they will in the future cooperate toward such an end. Now is that a fatal mistake?
> Dr. SEABORG. No, I don't think that is a fatal mistake. . . . I think our policy is to get the strongest safeguards provisions that we can and still get the treaty. . . .
> Senator PASTORE. When you say the best safeguards that we can get, it strikes me almost anything will do provided it is the best we can get under the circumstances. Now is that exactly the case? What kind of safeguards do we need, and are we approaching that. . . ?
> Dr. SEABORG. I think it is frankly too early to know. . . .
> Senator PASTORE. Do you think we will know at the proper time?
> Dr. SEABORG. Yes, I think we should be in a position to know. I don't know that we could know definitely for the indefinite future whether they are going to be effective. . . .
> Senator PASTORE. How will the Congress ever know when the treaty comes up here if you fellows don't know? . . . Now take a look at article III of the draft proposal. [Reads the article.] Do you think that is good enough?

---

*McNamara had taken this position in writing on February 24, when he wrote to ACDA Deputy Director Adrian Fisher that he was prepared to support the draft treaty's weak Article III if that was necessary to obtain a treaty.

Dr. SEABORG. I could think of interpretations of that language, yes, that would be good enough. [At this point Hosmer laughed aloud, for which he was rebuked by Pastore.] Let me amplify by saying I would like to see it stronger, obviously.[6]

This episode only served to confirm the impression that any treaty that came to the Senate with the fall-back Article III would be in deep trouble. Yet, not everyone agreed. For example, McNamara's position, as expressed at Principals, was echoed by Henry D. Smyth, U.S. ambassador to the IAEA, who told me on March 17 that, though he had originally believed a strong Article III was necessary, he now felt that a nonproliferation treaty with a compromise Article III, or without any Article III, was better than no treaty at all. I told Smyth that the AEC did not agree with him. Our feeling was that a treaty without adequate safeguards might be worse than nothing. It would raise false hopes and, after it proved ineffectual, the floodgates of proliferation might open, with incalculable consequences.*

On July 1, 1966, I wrote to Secretary Rusk commenting on a proposal the State Department had circulated embodying some further revisions of the U.S. draft treaty as a whole. I noted the absence of any strengthened Article III among the proposed revisions. I pointed out that the time was ripe for such an article. I noted, particularly, that there was no evidence of any Soviet objection. There was, in fact, evidence of Soviet assent. On March 3, 1966, Tsarapkin had stated at the ENDC:

> Some representatives of non-aligned States . . . raised the point that it might perhaps be appropriate, for the fulfillment by non-nuclear States of a treaty on non-proliferation of nuclear weapons, to take advantage of the control arrangements (safeguards) worked out by the International Atomic Energy Agency. In this respect we should like to announce that the Soviet Union would be prepared to examine this problem.[7]

Tsarapkin did go on to say, however, that "it would be more appropriate to concentrate [first] on solving the main problems . . . , namely, defining basic obligations in Articles I and II.

---

*By this time the AEC's militancy on the subject of IAEA safeguards was becoming notorious within the government, so much so that Dean Rusk was able to evoke amusement at a Principals meeting by referring to the NPT as "Dr. Seaborg's treaty." Playing along with the gag, I said I would accept the treaty as being mine only if it contained proper safeguards.

On July 28, 1966, Adrian Fisher at last presented at the ENDC a statement of U.S. policy that was all the AEC or the Joint Committee could have wished. The United States advocated, he said,

> a system under which the non-nuclear weapons States undertook to accept IAEA or equivalent international safeguards on all their peaceful activities. Such international safeguards would effectively provide clear evidence to the non-nuclear weapon States that other non-nuclear weapon States were not developing weapons under the guise of peaceful application of nuclear energy. Such reassurances would of course be essential to the continuing stability of the non-proliferation treaty and the permanent realization of its objectives.

A month later Foster cabled to Rusk that the U.S. position had been accepted by our allies on the ENDC. Still there was not in 1966 any formal submission of a strengthened Article III that would give effect to this policy.

An Opening to the East

In September 1966, it was time again for the annual General Conference of the International Atomic Energy Agency, an event that is to the IAEA what a meeting of the General Assembly is to the United Nations. Once more I journeyed to the grand old imperial city of Vienna as head of the U.S. delegation to attend formal plenary sessions in the Hofburg, fabled winter palace of the Habsburgs, and also to meet and talk with delegates from other countries at the numerous social functions that took place during conference week. (This was no place to be if one wanted to lose weight. Fortunately, this has never been one of my problems.)

On September 21, the opening day of the conference, I had lunch at the Swedish Embassy, a brief contact with my ancestral roots. There I talked with the USSR's chief delegate, Igor D. Morokhov. I stressed my familiar theme that in a time of political difficulties continuing contact between scientists in our two countries was all the more important. Morokhov said he agreed. (In recalling this conversation now I am reminded poignantly of the exchange of visits between U.S. and Soviet nuclear scientists in 1963: our visit to the Soviet Union in May that contributed to the favorable atmosphere leading to the Limited Test Ban Treaty, and their return visit in November, so tragically interrupted.) After the day's conference session I attended a reception by the Government of India. From there I taxied to a reception at the Czech Embassy, where Morokhov and I resumed our conversation. The subject turned to safeguards:

> I urged that the Soviets follow our example and place one or more power reactors under IAEA safeguards. He said that would be useless because the Soviets didn't use any of the reactor-produced plutonium for weapons. I tried to explain to him that this would nevertheless be an important step in mollifying the non-nuclear weapon countries. He said that the USSR's main concern was West Germany and that *if the United States could convince West Germany to put her power reactors under IAEA safeguards, then the Soviet Union would arrange to have Eastern European countries do the same.* He seemed very earnest about this discussion and suggested that we pursue the matter further during the remainder of the Conference.
>
> Morokhov then complained about our having furnished a "ton" of plutonium to Euratom without IAEA safeguards. I tried to explain to him the protection afforded by the supranational character of Euratom safeguards but, as previously, this seemed to make very little impression. Morokhov went on to say that the prevention of proliferation would require much stronger safeguards than the IAEA now had and he seemed to doubt that the IAEA framework would ever be sufficient. I said I thought it would be sufficient and that to start another organization would take too long.

I do not know what happened overnight among the Eastern bloc delegations, but in the general debate the following morning the Polish representative (Wilhelm Billig) rose to announce that his country would put its civilian power reactors under IAEA safeguards if West Germany would do the same. Then in the afternoon the Czech representative (J. Neumann) said the same on behalf of his country. At that evening's diplomatic reception, I again spoke to Morokhov:

> He asked me, with a twinkle in his eye, whether the Polish and Czech proposals would be embarrassing to the United States and I assured him they would not. I asked whether the proposals should be taken seriously and was assured that they should.

I was quite enthusiastic about the Polish and Czech offers. They seemed to offer an opening that might lead eventually to universal acceptance of IAEA safeguards. On my return from Vienna, therefore, I tried to stir interest and enlist support within the administration. On October 11:

> I brought up the Polish–Czech offer with [White House Science Adviser Donald] Hornig. He asked if it was workable or just a gimmick. I said I thought it should be taken seriously and that we should be doing something about it. I called Walt Rostow. Referring to the Polish-Czech offer, I said I hoped it would be taken seriously. He was noncommittal.

On October 13, I wrote to Secretary Rusk:

> This is the first time that any member of the Soviet bloc has specifically offered to accept continuous inspection of nuclear facilities within its territory. Such an offer was generally recognized in Vienna as offering great possibilities for progress toward a universal system of safeguards and toward nonproliferation. I recognize that the coupling of this proposal to a similar action by West Germany raises grave problems for the countries in the Euratom complex, especially West Germany. The complications obviously are of concern to the United States. But the serious consequences of flat rejection should also be of concern to us. My fellow Commissioners and I strongly feel that this proposal . . . warrants our most careful study and consideration.

I received no encouragement from any quarter. It seemed apparent that the State Department, in particular, was not about to override the strong objections of the Euratom countries to IAEA inspection.

At year's end there was movement of another sort. On December 23, I was able to write to Rusk, based on reports from the U.S. delegation to the UN, of "a strong impression that the Soviets would accept mandatory safeguards [in an NPT] so long as it did not require them to accept safeguards upon any activities within the USSR, and did not appear to preserve Euratom safeguards as an equivalent to IAEA safeguards." There seemed little problem in meeting the first condition. Although Soviet unwillingess to accept on-site inspection stuck in the craw of many members of Congress, it was really not a vital consideration in a nonproliferation treaty, which would be concerned primarily with activities within nations that did *not* have nuclear weapons. To meet the second condition, however, given the State Department's strong political support of Euratom, would take some doing.

There was no overt connection between the Polish-Czech offer in September 1966 and the Soviet change of position in December, but George Bunn, who on several occasions negotiated with the Soviets about safeguards, believes they were of a piece.[8] Prior to September 1966, the Soviets had consistently opposed inspection both in their own territory and that of their allies. But Bunn speculates that when the satellites made this proposal—and he believes it did originate with them—the Soviets saw the opportunity to get safeguards applied in West Germany and leaped at it. But if the satellites indeed originated the September proposal, what motivated them? Bunn has what he acknowledges is a hunch that the idea originated with the German Democratic Republic. (The GDR was not a member of the IAEA, but they associated themselves with the proposal in other forums, so that actually it was a Polish-Czech-GDR offer.) In Bunn's speculation, the GDR's motive was to gain additional recognition for itself. This was at a time when they were being rejected in almost every such effort; for example, they had been denied entry into both the UN and the IAEA. The GDR might well have thought that if they entered into a safeguards agreement with the IAEA to implement the September 1966 offer, IAEA membership might follow.

Notes

1. JCAE, *International Agreements for Cooperation, Hearings,* September 1963–June 1964, p. 27.
2. For example, Larsson, "Build a Bomb!", pp. 55–83.
3. Polach, *Euratom,* p. 95.
4. *Documents on Disarmament: 1965,* p. 477.
5. Private conversation, June 13, 1986.
6. JCAE, *Nonproliferation of Nuclear Weapons, Hearings,* February–March 1966, pp. 58–60.
7. *Documents on Disarmament: 1966,* p. 87.
8. Private conversation, November 21, 1986.

23
The Superpowers Agree

I want to make it clear, very clear, to all the world that we in the United States are not asking any country to accept safeguards that we are unwilling to accept ourselves.

—Lyndon B. Johnson
December 2, 1967

A Step Backward

When the U.S. and Soviet negotiating teams met in New York early in October 1966 to work out a revised text for Articles I and II (their previous suggestion having been rejected by the American side at the Camp David meeting of October 1 and 2), they also tried to reach agreement on the text of Article III.[1] On October 10, the U.S. team (Foster, Bunn, and Samuel de Palma) handed the Soviet team (Roshchin, Roland Timobayev, and Velodya Schustov) a very simple draft providing, in effect, for mandatory IAEA "or equivalent" safeguards on all non-nuclear-weapon states. The Soviets adamantly refused to accept the "or equivalent" concept because that meant Euratom safeguards. Instead they let it be known that their preference was for a treaty without any safeguards article.

Foster was aware that there were elements in the State Department that would have been glad to accept the Soviet position; it would insure a treaty and remove pressure from our allies. However, he was by now a staunch advocate of safeguards. (I think I did not appreciate at the time how fully ACDA had become an ally of the AEC on this issue. One reason I did not appreciate it was that the AEC was shut out from viewing a lot of the cable traffic—largely, I think, out of concern that we would reveal everything we learned to the Joint Committee in keeping with our legal obligation to keep the committee "fully and promptly informed.") Foster therefore continued to press in the negotiations for an Article III with meaningful safeguards.

After lengthy bargaining with the Soviets, Foster recommended to Washington late in November 1966 that the United States agree to mandatory IAEA safeguards on all non-nuclear-weapon states. Based on the tenor of the negotiations, he felt confident that the Soviets would agree to that. On November 30, his impression was confirmed. The Soviet delegation, quite evidently under new instructions, stated that they indeed favored—in fact, they insisted on—the formulation Foster had recommended.

Anticipating an adverse reaction, the State Department bureaucracy was unwilling even to communicate the concept of mandatory IAEA safeguards to the allies, especially at a time when the latter were already burdened with the consideration of the proposed Articles I and II. Subsequently there was a sympathetic review in the State Department of all the problems the allies were having, and it was decided that the next step for the United States should be to attempt to ease, rather than toughen, safeguards requirements. I first encountered the results of this new, softer position on February 1, 1967:

> Looking at the most recent restatement of the proposed Article III, I noticed that the weakening words "as soon as practicable" had been added. I called Bill Foster to protest. He said, sardonically, "That was a bow to the distinguished people in this building." [The ACDA was quartered in the State Department's headquarters building.] He said that the Europeanists in State felt there was a need for a transition period, particularly to protect Euratom. I argued that the transition period should not be open-ended, as the words "as soon as practicable" would make it; there needed to be some kind of deadline. Foster added that the new language had not been tried out on the Soviets and he didn't know that he could sell it to them. I predicted it would also give us trouble on the Hill, but Foster said he had already talked to Pastore and Holifield of the Joint Committee and that they recognized the difficulties. He asked that I send him a letter expressing AEC's concerns, which I agreed to do.

My letter pointed out that the phrase "as soon as practicable" might allow "countries such as India" to avoid safeguards for an indefinite period, during which they might progress toward a weapons capability. I agreed that Euratom should be allowed a "reasonable period of time" to adjust to IAEA safeguards, but argued that this should be accomplished "through subsidiary understandings in the form of public declarations rather than in the treaty itself."

New German Resistance

The concessions being fostered in the State Department were directed most of all to the West Germans, whose eventual adherence to a nonproliferation treaty seemed in doubt. The Federal Republic was now under new leadership. In November 1966, Chancellor Erhard's government had fallen apart and new elections had been held. As a result, the Christian Democrats, under Kurt-Georg Kiesinger, and the Social Democrats, under Willy Brandt, had formed a coalition, with Kiesinger as chancellor and Brandt as vice chancellor and foreign minister. This new government immediately shifted its emphasis in nuclear matters from NATO defense arrangements to the adverse effect a nonproliferation treaty might have on German industry. Early in 1967 Kiesinger is reported to have remarked to Vice President Humphrey that the NPT negotiations were the most difficult aspect of U.S.–FRG relations. At about the same time there was an intelligence report that the West Germans had no intention of signing the NPT.[2]

With specific relation to safeguards, the main concern the Germans expressed was the potential for industrial espionage. In an interview with *Die Welt* on February 18, 1967, Brandt suggested that inspectors "only be accepted from countries which subject themselves to safeguards."[3] This would have ruled out inspectors from the Soviet Union. It might also have excluded inspectors from the United States and the United Kingdom, potential rivals of Germany in the competition for nuclear markets, if we did not subject our own facilities to safeguards, although by April 1967 the Germans were probably aware of the likelihood of a U.S. offer voluntarily to accept IAEA safeguards. The particular facet of her industry that Germany probably wanted most to protect from espionage was identified by Brandt in another Bundestag statement on April 27, 1967, when he noted that German scientists were "working with prospects of success on the development of the second generation of reactors, the so-called fast breeders."[4]

The German preference was clearly to retain Euratom safeguards, which Brandt characterized as "very effective." The only problem, as he saw it, was to define the relationship between the Euratom system and any new international regime that might be introduced. Secretary

Rusk made some blunt comments about the German attitude in a TV interview on February 10, 1967. He speculated that there could be groups in other parts of the world who might also wish to put together "a little family group that would inspect itself." He then added: "I have no doubt at all that the safeguards in Euratom insure that the activities in Euratom will not be abused. The problem is, how do we persuade 120 other nations that this is the case? We have not found an answer to this question yet."[5]

On March 6, 1967, we learned that the State Department had decided to propose a compromise solution. Secretary Rusk was about to write to President Johnson recommending that Article III allow Euratom safeguards to remain indefinitely, subject only to verification of their adequacy by the IAEA. I immediately phoned the secretary to express AEC's disagreement. In this conversation and a following letter I contended that it was premature to give up on IAEA safeguards. I argued that the West Germans could be induced to accept them if assured, first, that they would not be required to accept inspectors from Eastern bloc countries or from potential commercial rivals not themselves subject to safeguards, and, second, that the United States would continue to assure adequate fuel supplies for West Germany's peaceful nuclear program. I pointed out further that, on a technical basis, IAEA verification of Euratom safeguards would require rights of access for IAEA inspectors as intrusive as those granted to the Euratom inspectors themselves. Next, I noted that efforts to achieve even the slightest degree of Soviet recognition of the Euratom safeguards system had uniformly failed.

Three days later Joint Committee Chairman Pastore proposed essentially the same plan as Rusk's, but with greater specificity, in a speech on the Senate floor. (George Bunn states that it was Adrian Fisher who suggested to Pastore that he make this speech and who supplied its basic ideas.)[6] Pastore proposed that Euratom be permitted to retain its full safeguards responsibilities without time limit, subject, however, to its undertaking "to develop equivalent technical standards for safeguards systems under which International Atomic Energy Agency inspectors would be authorized to verify Euratom's system."[7]

Proponents of Euratom's cause now apparently pointed to me as a chief remaining obstacle and on March 21 a deputation of West Germans—part industrial, part diplomatic—descended on me. Their proposal was brazen and simple: The NPT should be allowed to go forward without an Article III—no safeguards at all! My answer to them was equally simple: An NPT without safeguards would be worthless. It was a short meeting.

On March 31, we sent our allies the new safeguards proposal that resulted from the administration and congressional initiatives earlier in the month. It provided that Euratom safeguards would be allowed to continue for a period of three years, during which there were to be negotiations between IAEA and Euratom to come up with a system for IAEA verification of the effectiveness of Euratom safeguards. At the end of the three-year period, either there would be an agreement, in which case Euratom safeguards could continue under its terms, or, failing an agreement, each individual non-nuclear-weapon state would have to accept IAEA safeguards. The AEC lined up behind this proposal. Although the Euratom countries did not reject it outright, several of them had difficulties with it. They pointed out that it gave the IAEA no incentive to adjust its safeguards to the particular needs of Euratom countries. The agency need only pretend to negotiate for the three years and then it could impose its safeguards regardless of any objections. In discussions among themselves and with U.S. representatives, Euratom personnel referred to the three-year transition idea as "the guillotine clause." The Soviet Union added its flat rejection just before the ENDC reconvened on February 21, saying that it would not consent to any arrangement that excused West Germany from true international controls for three years.

A Holding Action

As 1967 progressed, more and more discordant voices were heard on the safeguards issue. Japan expressed its opposition to Euratom "self-inspection," widening the breach among our allies. Walt Rostow stated his view that the United States was moving too far, too fast on the NPT and was not giving adequate consideration to the political problems it might create for our allies.[8] Meanwhile, West German officials continued to raise objections and, in my view, deliberately to obstruct forward movement on the NPT. I pressed various State Department officials to lean on the Germans, but to no avail.

Early in April 1967, ACDA fashioned still another safeguards proposal, a compromise between its previous "guillotine" proposal and the approach advocated by Senator Pastore. It called for Euratom and IAEA to reach an agreement within three years on verification of the former's safeguards system by the latter. The proposal did not specify what would befall if the required agreement were not reached. Even so, the Euratom nations were critical of the new draft, and the Soviet Union rejected it.

The Six Day Arab–Israeli War in June 1967 tended to stiffen the backs of the Euratom countries by calling attention once again to the unreliability of Mideast oil supplies and the importance of nuclear energy to Europe's future.

Despairing of his ability to come up with anything soon on safeguards that the various factions would accept, Foster began to sound out the Soviet delegation in Geneva about submitting a joint draft treaty that, for the moment, would have no text for Article III. After some hesitation, the Soviets agreed to the idea. On August 24, 1967, in Geneva, the two nations presented separate but identical treaty drafts. The safeguards article, in its entirety, read:

ARTICLE III

(International Control)

As Adrian Fisher noted, the blank article was put in the treaty drafts "to make it plain we hadn't given up on it."[9] The drafts did contain, moreover, the following two preambular paragraphs, which survived unchanged through all successive modifications into the treaty's final formulation:

[The Parties to this Treaty]

Undertaking to co-operate in facilitating the application of International Atomic Energy safeguards on peaceful nuclear activities.

Expressing their support for research, development, and other efforts to further the application, within the framework of the International Atomic Energy safeguards system, of the principle of safeguarding effectively the flow of source and special fissionable materials by use of instruments and other techniques at certain strategic points.

The first of these paragraphs echoed the safeguards clause in the first U.S. draft treaty, but significantly omitted the words "or equivalent," indicating how far the United States had at this point moved toward insisting that safeguards under the treaty be those of IAEA, not those of Euratom or any other "equivalent."

The second preambular paragraph resulted from some negotiations between ourselves and the West Germans. Anticipating that the final treaty probably would require IAEA safeguards, the Germans urged that these take a form that would minimize disturbance of production processes and violation of industrial secrecy. This could best be done, they thought, by concentrating measurements at certain strategic points in the flow of nuclear materials and by using instruments to make these measurements whenever possible, thereby minimizing the need for inspectors. The German position was supported by other nonweapon states advanced in nuclear energy, as indicated by a resolution adopted by the Conference of Non-Nuclear-Weapon States in October 1968.

The Foster-Roshchin Draft

In Geneva the two delegations held fast to their respective positions through the summer of 1967, each being under instructions not to budge. The Soviets insisted on mandatory IAEA safeguards on all non-nuclear-weapons states. Despite its unpopularity with the allies, the U.S. team was holding out for a variant of the guillotine proposal requiring all non-nuclear-weapons states to accept either IAEA or IAEA-verified safeguards within three years.[10]

To help break this impasse, Roshchin suggested that as a first step a group of "experts" from each side sit down and discuss the matters at issue, but without any negotiating authority. George Bunn headed the U.S. team. From this process there emerged in rather short order a text on which both delegations agreed. The first and critical sentence read as follows:

> Each non-nuclear weapon state party to the Treaty undertakes to accept safeguards, in accordance with the Statute of the IAEA and the Agency's safeguards system, as set forth in an agreement to be negotiated and concluded with the IAEA, for the exclusive purpose of verification of the fulfillment of its obligations assumed under this Treaty with a view to preventing diversion of nuclear energy from peaceful uses to nuclear weapons or other nuclear explosive devices.

A subsequent paragraph of the article provided that agreements with the IAEA could be concluded either individually or "together with other states," thus providing for a Euratom-IAEA agreement.

The agreement on this text was still among the "experts" only. Their governments had not seen it. There now followed an artful maneuver. Since each delegation had been ordered not to depart from a previous position, each decided to transmit the agreed text to its government as a suggestion emanating from the other side. Thus, Foster sent it to Washington as a "Roshchin draft," and recommended it. Roshchin sent it to Moscow as a "Foster draft," and recommended it. Foster did take the wise precaution of letting Rusk in on the scheme. (Bunn relates that the arrangement nearly got blown out of the water when Llewellyn Thompson, now ambassador in Moscow, expressed interest to Gromyko about the "Roshchin draft." Whereupon Gromyko asked whether it wasn't a "Foster draft." This was duly reported by a very puzzled Thompson and there might have been awkward consequences for all concerned except that Rusk, having been preinformed, protected them.)

The agreed text was duly submitted to the North Atlantic Council in August 1967 as a "Roshchin draft." (There would have been difficulties if it had appeared to be a U.S. suggestion in view of an earlier Rusk promise to Brandt not to change the existing U.S. proposal without prior consultation.)

An Anniversary Present

A key step toward softening the opposition to IAEA safeguards was taken on December 2, 1967, when President Johnson announced that the United States would accept the application of IAEA safeguards to all its peaceful nuclear activities at the time that such safeguards were generally applied to other nations under the NPT. The actual announcement was the culmination of a series of prior suggestions and events.

In September 1960 the United States had offered to place four small reactor facilities under IAEA safeguards. These were the Piqua (Ohio) Nuclear Power Facility, the Experimental Boiling Water Reactor at Argonne National Laboratory, and two research reactors at Brookhaven National Laboratory. The offer was made at the IAEA General Conference just before the critical vote on whether or not to adopt the agency's safeguards system. Our purpose was to show U.S.

support and sway opinion in favor of the system. The U.S. offer was accepted by the IAEA Board of Governors early in 1962. In 1964, shortly after the IAEA system was expanded to include large reactors, the United States offered to include also the Yankee Atomic Power Plant at Rowe, Massachusetts, one of the largest civilian reactors then in existence.

Before the decision on Yankee was implemented I wrote to my counterpart in the Soviet Union, Andronik H. Petrosyants, asking whether the USSR "might not wish to join us in offering civil power reactors to be placed under IAEA safeguards." I suggested that we offer Yankee and that they offer a plant of similar capacity, the Voronezh reactor in central Russia. I maintained that the experience the IAEA would gain if we did this would strengthen its safeguards system. Petrosyants rejected the suggestion on the curious ground that there was no need to strengthen the IAEA system since it did not lead to disarmament. It seemed apparent that the Soviet Union still had real difficulty in opening its facilities to the prying eyes of foreigners— a mind-set of centuries cannot be changed overnight.

The United States went forward on its own. An agreement was signed with the IAEA on June 15, 1964, renewing the understanding with respect to the two Brookhaven reactors and Piqua, and adding Yankee. The first IAEA inspection of Yankee began on November 16, 1964. In April 1966 the United States offered also to make available the Nuclear Fuel Services, Inc., plant at West Valley, N.Y., in order to help the IAEA expand its range of safeguards operations to include chemical processing plants.* The first inspection of West Valley began on August 7, 1967, and ended six weeks later. Ten IAEA inspectors participated in this round-the-clock training exercise.

As we have seen, the original U.S. motivation for placing these reactors under IAEA safeguards had been to help the agency establish its system, develop its techniques, and train its personnel. When the safeguards issue loomed as an obstacle to acceptance of a nonproliferation treaty, however, the focus of American interest began to change. We now wanted to use our own acceptance of IAEA safeguards as leverage to win such acceptance from others. At a meeting of the

---

*The material placed under IAEA safeguards at West Valley included irradiated fuel from the Yankee plant. Chemical processing plants provide a far more difficult safeguards challenge than do reactors. In the vast majority of reactors fissionable material is bound up in discrete, easily counted fuel rods. In chemical processing plants the fissionable material is present as a liquid diffused through a maze of complicated machinery.

Committee of Principals in February 1966, Secretary Rusk sought to broaden the U.S. commitment. He asked this challenging question: Could not the United States accept what it was asking non-nuclear-weapon states to accept; would we not be willing to place *all* our own peaceful nuclear facilities under IAEA safeguards?

No immediate action was taken on Rusk's suggestion, but a seed had been planted. On April 25, 1966, Secretary McNamara wrote to me conveying the same suggestion as a formal proposal. He argued that it "would in no way imperil U.S. security but would place us in a much better position to appeal for international safeguards for . . . crucial non-nuclear states." Noting that IAEA did not have adequate resources to conduct the numerous inspections that would be required, McNamara suggested that the United States grant the agency $4 million to recruit and train an adequate number of inspectors during the ensuing four years.

At the outset, AEC staff reacted negatively to McNamara's proposal. They noted that the U.S. example in placing five reactors under safeguards had not yet led to matching offers from others.* Further, the staff argued, the contemplated action would: (1) place a financial and manpower burden on the IAEA; (2) dissipate U.S. leverage to influence other countries to submit facilities to safeguards on a matching basis; (3) embarrass the British, some of whose reactors produced both electricity for civilian use and plutonium for military purposes; (4) create security difficulties by bringing foreign inspectors into contact with U.S. personnel who had access to classified information; and (5) prevent the United States from making military use of the plutonium produced in power reactors. There was also serious doubt whether the U.S. government had the legal authority to require privately owned facilities to undergo international inspection. For all these reasons, the staff felt that the United States stood to lose more than it would gain by acceptance of the McNamara proposal. They favored instead an approach under which the United States would offer to place a few additional nuclear power plants under IAEA safeguards, or offer to match other nuclear-weapon states on a plant-for-plant or megawatt-for-megawatt basis.

As 1967 proceeded, the staff's objections began to seem less significant when weighed against the problems the Article III impasse

---

*Later in 1966 the United Kingdom would offer its Bradwell Nuclear Power Station.

was creating in NPT negotiations and interallied relations. Complaints were being made by the Italians, Belgians, West Germans, and Japanese that the application of safeguards would create commercial disadvantages for their nascent nuclear industries. The competitor mentioned most often was the Soviet Union, but it was clear to us that they were actually more concerned about competition with the United States and that they diplomatically refrained from saying so. We tried to respond to these complaints by pointing out that IAEA inspectors would be under instructions not to interfere with operations. It was difficult to make this argument convincingly, however, because at that time (early 1967) there had been little prior experience in the application of safeguards to large commercial facilities. (There had been, in fact, only the single experience—with Yankee.)

My own feeling was that the arguments about commercial disadvantage may have been somewhat contrived; that they may in fact have been a surrogate for resistance to the main provisions of the NPT. The requirement that they renounce nuclear weapons into the indefinite future was a serious domestic political issue in several of the industrial countries. It was not quite respectable, however, for any of them to acknowledge this. It was perfectly respectable, on the other hand, to argue that the proposed safeguards provision threatened to disadvantage them in the legitimate development of their industries.

In this situation the ACDA came forward with an adroit strategy. On February 18, 1967, Foster circulated among the Principals a proposal that the United States offer the IAEA the opportunity to apply its safeguards to all U.S. peaceful nuclear activities, with the provisos (1) that the offer would be made only after it was clear that it might significantly facilitate acceptance of Article III; and (2) that it would be effective only after entry into force of an NPT with mandatory safeguards.

Our allies may not have been entirely sincere in objecting to the NPT just because it imposed discriminatory safeguards. They had themselves chosen to make their stand on this ground, however, and meeting their objections head on in the manner proposed by ACDA seemed to offer the allies no further basis for opposing the treaty.

On February 21, I met with Herbert Scoville, ACDA assistant director for science and technology, to convey AEC's assent to the proposal. He and I agreed, however, that before any commitment was made the plan should be tried out on the North Atlantic Council and the Joint Committee on Atomic Energy. Soon after, these probes were in fact made, with favorable reactions in each case. Additional impetus came from the British, who on March 27 let it be known that they would follow the U.S. example insofar as strictly civilian nuclear facilities were concerned.

A key factor not yet tested was whether U.S. industry would consent willingly to being offered up for international inspection. On March 23, all AEC commissioners, along with representatives from ACDA and State, met with leading industry figures in Rowe, Massachusetts, the site of the Yankee nuclear power plant. It was particularly helpful that officials of Yankee and Nuclear Fuel Services, Inc., were able to testify at this meeting that their own experiences with safeguards had been favorable. Other meetings and correspondence with industry followed. Based on these interchanges, I wrote to Rusk and Foster stating the AEC's conclusion that the contemplated U.S. offer would be "generally supported."

On April 6, 1967, a memorandum from Foster, concurred in by Rusk, McNamara, and myself, recommended to the president that he approve a public statement of the offer, to be released whenever it might be most helpful to the NPT negotiations. President Johnson approved the recommendation on April 9. At my suggestion, the public announcement was made on December 2, 1967, at ceremonies marking the twenty-fifth anniversary of the event that launched the nuclear age: the achievement by Enrico Fermi and his associates—beneath the grandstand at the University of Chicago's football stadium—of the world's first sustained, controlled nuclear chain reaction. The president's remarks, transmitted to us celebrants in Chicago by closed-circuit television,* included the following:

> We are now engaged in major effort to achieve . . . a [non-proliferation] treaty, in a form acceptable to all nations. . . . We do not believe that the safeguards we propose in that treaty will interfere with the peaceful activities of any country. And I want to make it clear, very clear, to all the world that we in the United States are not asking any country to accept safeguards that we are unwilling to accept ourselves. So I am, today, announcing that when such

---

*In recognition of the national origin of Enrico Fermi, there were also remarks by the Italian prime minister in what I believe was the first use of a transatlantic satellite TV hook-up.

safeguards are applied under the treaty, the United States will permit the International Atomic Energy Agency to apply its safeguards to all nuclear activities in the United States—excluding only those with direct national security significance.

Two days later the British followed with a matching announcement.

Separate But Identical Drafts

Even before the U.S. offer was formally announced, knowledge that it was impending created a favorable atmosphere in U.S. negotiations with other industrial countries. In late October 1967, the Euratom countries accepted the "Roshchin draft" submitted to them in August, subject only to what appeared to be minor changes in wording. One of these changes, however, was to be a source of further difficulty. It involved the very first sentence of Article III, which, in the Roshchin draft, began as follows:

> Each non-nuclear weapon state party to the treaty undertakes to accept safeguards in accordance with the Statute of the IAEA and the Agency's safeguards system, as set forth in an agreement to be concluded with the IAEA, for the exclusive purpose . . .

The allies wanted to dissociate "IAEA" a little more from "safeguards" in order not to diminish the future role of Euratom safeguards. They therefore suggested rephrasing this opening as follows:

> Each non-nuclear weapon state undertakes to accept safeguards, as set forth in an agreement to be negotiated and concluded with the IAEA in accordance with the Statute of the IAEA and the Agency's safeguards system, for the exclusive purpose . . .

Foster handed the revised text to Roshchin on November 2, 1967. A week later the Soviets responded. They accepted all the minor changes suggested by the allies except that in the first sentence. They wished to adhere to the prior version, the one in the Foster-Roshchin text.

The alternative opening sentences were considered by the North Atlantic Council at a meeting on November 24 during which Belgium, West Germany, and Italy again expressed their strong preference for the revised version. The United States was far from being exercised about the differences in the two texts, which appeared to have little practical effect, if any. On the other hand, we wanted to maintain the support of the allies. Therefore, we refused to accept the version preferred by the Soviets, and when the ENDC adjourned on December 18, 1967, there was still no agreement on Article III.

During this period the West Germans began to backtrack and raise other difficulties. On November 20, 1967:

> I received a call from Henry Smyth, U.S. ambassador to the IAEA. He said he had talked to Foster in Geneva and that the latter was very disturbed by developments. According to Foster, the Germans had produced a very long list of new demands that had to be met to obtain their adherence to the NPT. Smyth said both he and Foster were convinced that the Germans were doing everything they could to delay completion of the draft treaty. He asked if I could do anything from the Washington end to help matters. I said I would try.

A few days later, before a Cabinet meeting, I told Rusk and Katzenbach, in separate conversations, that I thought the Germans were being unreasonable and that their demands had begun to seem clearly aimed at blocking the treaty. I suggested that they consider dealing with the Germans in a firmer manner.

On December 29, 1967:

> I met with John Hall, IAEA deputy director general, back home on vacation. He said Director General Eklund wanted me to know that he had spent a half-hour alone with Willy Brandt in Bonn and found him very friendly to the NPT. It was Eklund's view that if Secretary Rusk would clamp down a little on Bonn, the Germans would go along with the NPT.

As we have seen, there was a great reluctance in the administration, from President Johnson on down, to treat the Germans other than with kid gloves. In any case, the difficulties at this particular time, the exact nature of which I do not recall, were soon ironed out, and the United States was again able to negotiate with the Soviets on behalf of a united alliance.

During the following weeks Secretary Rusk met a number of times with Foreign Minister Gromyko and urged the Soviets to reconsider their rejection of the U.S.-backed draft language for Article III. (Gromyko was in the United States attending the UN General Assembly.) *The New York Times* reported that the negotiations were pushed by President Johnson who, hard pressed on Vietnam, was said to want a "peace" achievement for the forthcoming presidential campaign.[11] A target date for achieving U.S.–USSR agreement was January 18, 1968, when the ENDC was set to reconvene. (It had become customary for the major powers to present important proposals on the opening day of ENDC sessions.) In order to help persuade the Soviets, Fisher was authorized to present a statement of "Guiding Principles," previously agreed to by our European allies, that conveyed our understanding of how the IAEA and Euratom would interact if the Soviets accepted our language. They read:

> 1. There should be safeguards for all non-nuclear-weapon parties of such a nature that all parties can have confidence in their effectiveness. Therefore safeguards established by an agreement negotiated and concluded with IAEA . . . must enable the IAEA to carry out its responsibilities of providing assurance that no diversion is taking place.
> 2. In discharging their obligations under article III, non-nuclear-weapon parties may negotiate safeguards agreements with the IAEA individually or together with other parties; and, specifically, an agreement covering such obligations may be entered into between the IAEA and another international organization the work of which is related to the IAEA and the membership of which includes the parties concerned.
> 3. In order to avoid unnecessary duplication, the IAEA should make appropriate use of existing records and safeguards, provided that under such mutually agreed agreements IAEA can satisfy itself that nuclear material is not diverted to nuclear weapons or other nuclear explosive devices.

Fisher promised to make the principles public at the same time as an agreed Article III in order to assure that they would be part of the negotiating history on which future interpretations of the treaty would be based.

President Johnson was scheduled to deliver his State of the Union message to a nationwide audience on the evening of January 17. The White House was in contact with Geneva up until the last possible moment, hoping that a last minute deal on safeguards would make it possible for the president to announce U.S.–Soviet agreement on a complete nonproliferation treaty. The most that could be offered by the U.S. delegation before the president mounted the podium was expressed in the following passage in the speech:

> On the basis of communications from Ambassador Fisher this afternoon, I am encouraged to believe that a draft treaty can be laid before the conference in Geneva in the very near future. I hope to be able to present that treaty to the Senate this year.

What was happening in Geneva at this eleventh hour was described by Fisher in subsequent congressional testimony:

> Pursuant to instructions, on Wednesday evening [January 17] around 5 o'clock Geneva time, I went to Mr. Roshchin and said we were prepared to agree to the revised duration clause [one stating that the treaty would run for twenty-five years, with a conference to be held then as to its extension] if they would accept our November 2 formulation for the safeguards article. . . . [This was the one that contained the revised first sentence the allies wanted.] He told me he couldn't let me know until 10 o'clock the next morning. . . . I told him 10 o'clock in the morning would be 4 A.M. Washington time, that we were prepared to table a treaty on the basis I had proposed but that if he were to propose any changes I would have to say "no" since the notion of getting any changes in instructions at 4 A.M. was a little hard. . . . On that happy note, Wednesday ended. At 10 the next morning Roshchin asked me to come to his villa. I did. He indicated that they accepted the proposition we had made: that is; the November 2 safeguards formulation, with my agreeing to state publicly that safeguards . . . must enable IAEA to provide assurance that no diversion is taking place.[12]

At 4:25 A.M., Washington time, on January 18, 1968, word of the agreement reached the White House. That afternoon, Geneva time, the United States and the Soviet Union laid before the ENDC separate but identical drafts of a complete nonproliferation treaty.*

---

*Adrian Fisher makes clear in his oral history interview (p. 27) that it was the Soviets who did not want to call it a joint tabling, adding: "Precisely why they felt that way I'm not sure."

Article III

Although some of the terms of the identical draft treaties of January 18, 1968 were to undergo considerable change before the NPT reached its final form, Article III survived virtually intact. It is therefore worth considering briefly some of its main features.

The principle obligation is set forth in the first sentence, the one to which the Soviets had initially objected: each non-nuclear-weapon party "undertakes to accept safeguards as set forth in an agreement with the International Atomic Energy Agency." Thus, the safeguards applicable to any given party need not be identical to the IAEA safeguards already in use or those negotiated with other countries. But the agreements must be "in accordance with the Statute of the International Atomic Energy Agency and the Agency's safeguards system." Thus, the safeguards have to be acceptable to the IAEA; this assured the Soviets and others that there would be no special leniency for Euratom countries.

The safeguards have as their exclusive purpose to verify that there is no diversion of nuclear energy from peaceful purposes "to nuclear weapons or other explosive devices." "Other explosive devices" can refer only to peaceful nuclear explosives, and since these also have a "peaceful purpose" there is a superficial contradiction. It has never caused any difficulty, however.[13] Diversion for PNE purposes is clearly covered, as well as diversion for weapons purposes.

The required agreements can be concluded either individually or "together with other states"; this allowed for a collective Euratom–IAEA agreement.

All parties to the treaty undertake not to supply nuclear materials to any non-nuclear-weapon state unless the materials are subject to safeguards. In this way even states that do not sign the treaty have to accept safeguards on any material they receive from parties to the treaty.

Safeguards are to be designed in such a way as not to interfere with international cooperation in, or peaceful uses of, nuclear energy. This implied that the IAEA would continue on the course, originally urged by West Germany and expressed in the Preamble, of devising and implementing safeguards involving maximum "use of instruments and other technical devices at strategic points in the flow of nuclear materials, with a view to restricting the safeguards operations to the necessary minimum."

Negotiation of safeguards agreements with the IAEA was to begin within 180 days of the treaty's entrance into force, or when the party involved ratified the treaty, whichever was later. Each agreement was to enter into force within eighteen months of the commencement of negotiations. Thus, there would be ample, but not unlimited, time for any nation to adjust itself to the coming of safeguards.

Implementation

Long before the NPT entered into force, on March 5, 1970, it was recognized that the existing IAEA safeguards system, as set forth in INFCIRC/66, did not accord in all respects with the arduously negotiated criteria set forth in the treaty. Accordingly, on that same date, the IAEA established a Safeguards Committee for the purpose of producing a new guide to be followed in negotiating IAEA safeguards agreements under the NPT.* Some fifty IAEA members sent representatives to the eighty-two meetings held by the committee.[14] In March 1971 the committee completed its assignment, producing a volume entitled "The Structure and Content of Agreements between the Agency and States Required in Connection with the Treaty on the Non-Proliferation of Nuclear Weapons," the so-called "blue book" (INFCIRC/153). This guide, a most impressive accomplishment, has been followed in all IAEA safeguards agreements with NPT parties, including that with Euratom.

Negotiations on the Euratom–IAEA safeguards agreement did not begin until November 1971, and the agreement was not signed until April 1973. All Euratom members delayed their ratifications of the NPT until after the latter date. The fact that there would be this delay in ratification was announced by Euratom countries when they signed the treaty. This gave Euratom increased bargaining power in its negotiation of a safeguards agreement with IAEA. Some other industrialized countries, notably Japan, also delayed their ratifications pending the outcome of the Euratom negotiation.

The U.S. safeguards offer was not implemented until December 9, 1980, when a U.S.–IAEA agreement entered into force. The condition laid down by President Johnson—that the offer would be implemented only "when safeguards [were] applied under the treaty"—

---

*The committee's first chairman was Kurt Waldheim, later to be secretary-general of the United Nations and president of Austria.

was not satisfied until 1976, when agreements between the IAEA and all the Euratom countries plus Japan had entered into force. At that time the already-negotiated U.S.–IAEA agreement was submitted to, and subsequently approved by, the IAEA Board of Governors. The U.S. Senate approved it on July 2, 1980. Under terms of the agreement and a protocol thereto, the United States submits a listing of its non-military nuclear facilities to the IAEA. The IAEA can at any time select any or all of the listed facilities for either one of two treatments: the complete application of safeguards, including inspections, or a lesser treatment, without inspections, requiring only the maintenance of IAEA-prescribed records, submission of design information, and possible submission of reports. The IAEA has selected only a limited number of facilities for the full safeguards treatment—lack of manpower prevents more extensive inspection—changing the plants selected from time to time so as not to burden some enterprises more than their competitors. As of October 1986, the plants subject to the full treatment were the Westinghouse Fuel Fabrication Plant in Columbia, South Carolina; Unit 4 at the Florida Power and Light Company's Turkey Point Plant; and Unit 1 of Jersey Central Power and Light Company's Salem Nuclear Generating Station.

As of the end of 1986, all five nuclear powers had agreed, at least in principle, to the application of IAEA safeguards to at least some of their peaceful nuclear facilities. The only general across-the-board offers are those of the United States and the United Kingdom. In the case of France and the Soviet Union the agreements are limited to facilities selected by the respective countries. The agreement with France, which became effective in September 1981, covers major components of a fuel reprocessing plant. Under the agreement with the Soviet Union, which entered into force February 21, 1985, the IAEA applies its safeguards to one research reactor and one light-water cooled power reactor. (This agreement is one more refutation of the idea, so often advanced by U.S. opponents of a comprehensive test ban, that the Soviets will not under any circumstances agree to on-site inspection on their territory.) The People's Republic of China announced during the IAEA General Conference in September 1985 that it was entering into safeguards negotiations with the IAEA. As of the end of 1986, no agreement with China had been submitted to the IAEA Board of Governors for its review.[15]

The scope, content, financing, staffing, and adequacy of IAEA safeguards have continued to this day to be subjects for some lively controversies. To address these issues would exceed the limits of this book. My general conclusion is that IAEA safeguards have been remarkably successful, considering all the difficulties—notably including political difficulties.

Notes

1. Information on this negotiation from George Bunn, private conversation, November 21, 1986.
2. George Bunn, as above.
3. *Documents on Disarmament: 1967,* p. 94.
4. Ibid., p. 211.
5. U.S. ACDA, *International Negotiations,* p. 70.
6. Private conversation, November 21, 1986.
7. Quoted in Barnes, "The Nuclear Non-Proliferation Treaty," p. 389.
8. Barnes, "The Nuclear Non-Proliferation Treaty," p. 390.
9. Transcript, Adrian Fisher Oral History Interview, 10/31/68, by Paige E. Mulhollan, Tape 3, p. 22, LBJ Library.
10. Information in this section supplied mainly by George Bunn, private conversation, November 21, 1986.
11. Barnes, "The Nuclear Non-Proliferation Treaty," p. 407.
12. House, Committee on Foreign Affairs, *Hearings on Arms Control and Disarmament Act Amendments, 1968,* February 1968, p. 62.
13. Myron Kratzer, private conversation, December 1, 1986.
14. Szasz, "International Atomic Energy Safeguards," in Willrich, ed. *International Safeguards,* p. 77.
15. Information in this paragraph based on conversation with J. Christian Kessler of the ACDA staff, September 5, 1986.

Part VII

Conflicts about Peaceful Explosions

They shall beat their swords into plowshares and their spears into pruning-hooks.

Isaiah 2:4

Beat your plowshares into swords, and your pruning-hooks into spears.

Joel 4:10

24
The Perils of Plowshare

Through the Plowshare program the United States can aid almost all nations in the world . . . in a way that no amount of United States dollars can equal.

—John S. Foster, Livermore Director
June 1963

Background

During the Suez crisis of 1956 personnel at the Livermore weapons laboratory began studying the use of nuclear explosives to build an alternate sea-level canal across Israel. This was done at the suggestion and under the leadership of Harold Brown, a division leader at Livermore, who, twenty years later, would be President Carter's secretary of defense. Early in 1957 the inquiry was expanded to consider the peaceful use of nuclear explosives on a broad scale. Prospects were brightened by data obtained in September 1957 from RAINIER, the first underground nuclear test explosion.

Greatly encouraged by the preliminary studies at Livermore and by RAINIER, the AEC established a formal program for peaceful nuclear explosives (PNEs)* late in 1957, placing it at first in the Division of Military Application. This was logical in the sense that PNEs and nuclear weapons employed basically the same technology, but it was not very smart public relations. Later, in 1961, we recognized this error and established a separate Division of Peaceful Nuclear Explosives.

Enthusiasm for PNEs became international after a series of U.S. reports presented to the second UN Conference on the Peaceful Uses of Atomic Energy (Geneva, 1958) described their potential economic

---

*As is customary, the acronym PNE is used in this text to designate either or both of peaceful nuclear explosives and peaceful nuclear explosions. The meaning intended in each use of the acronym should be clear from the context.

benefits in glowing terms. The nuclear test moratorium from 1958 to 1961 prevented further experimental explosions, but afforded ample time for Livermore to conduct desk studies of a wide range of applications. The picture that emerged from this work was that PNEs offered exciting prospects in three major categories. These were: (1) massive excavation and earth-moving projects, such as the digging of canals and harbors; (2) releasing relatively inaccessible natural resources, such as natural gas trapped in tight geologic formations; and (3) experiments in pure science, such as using the intense burst of neutrons in a nuclear explosion to produce rare isotopes and even new heavy elements. In all three categories it appeared that PNEs either could do what could not be done at all by other methods or could achieve the same results more economically.

It was the excavation applications that most stirred the world's imagination. The list of contemplated projects was a long one. Aside from the canal across Israel, a partial list, as it emerged in the late 1950s, included a new sea-level canal across the Isthmus of Panama; shortening and straightening the Santa Fe Railroad in the Mojave Desert; connecting the Mediterranean with the Qattara Depression, a below sea-level area in western Egypt, to produce hydroelectric power; excavating a harbor in North Africa; providing an irrigation canal on the upper Ob River (USSR); diverting the Pechora River to provide irrigation and raise the level of the Caspian Sea (USSR); removing overlying material to expose a molybdenum deposit in northeast Siberia; removing rapids to make South American rivers more navigable; creating a harbor near ore deposits on the remote northeast coast of Australia; building a sea-level canal across the Isthmus of Kra (Thailand) to shorten the sea lanes between the Mideast and the Far East; and increasing the flow of irrigation water from the Niger River (Africa).

Politics and the Canal

Most seriously advanced of all the excavation proposals was that for a new sea-level canal to supplement or replace the Panama Canal, whose aging system of locks was considered vulnerable and which could not, in any event, accommodate very large vessels such as supertankers and U.S. aircraft carriers. The routes initially considered suitable for a nuclear-excavated canal included two in Panama, one in Colombia, and one through Costa Rica and Nicaragua. Preliminary studies favored a sea-level route in eastern Panama, near the Colombian border.

The canal project originated as one of the desk studies at Livermore. When published in 1958, the study aroused the strong interest of the Panama Canal Company, the U.S. government corporation that operated the waterway. The company studied the matter further and submitted its affirmative findings to President Eisenhower in 1960.

Early in the Kennedy administration political considerations gave the project an added sense of urgency. Nationalist elements in Panama, with apparent encouragement from Castroite agents, began in forceful and menacing terms to express their dissatisfaction with the 1903 treaty under which the United States operated the canal and governed the Canal Zone. They objected particularly to the lack of Panamanian sovereignty over the Zone. President Chiari of Panama came to Washington in 1961 to negotiate treaty changes with President Kennedy. Though these talks were inconclusive, Kennedy did agree that Panama's flag should fly side by side with our own at designated places in the Zone. Undoubtedly prompted by the political unrest, President Kennedy directed the AEC in May 1962 to undertake a five-year program that would establish the need, location, costs, and problems of building by nuclear means a second canal across the isthmus.

The unrest continued into President Johnson's term, and on January 7, 1964, Panama presented him with his first foreign crisis. Some American students in the Canal Zone had violated the Kennedy–Chiari agreement by raising the American flag in front of their high school. Bloody riots ensued and Panama severed diplomatic relations with the United States. President Chiari then sought to use the crisis as leverage to pry basic treaty revisions from the United States.

On January 17, 1964, I attended a meeting of the heads of regulatory and other non-Cabinet agencies during which the president asked Thomas C. Mann, assistant secretary of state for Latin American affairs, to report on the situation in Panama. (This may seem a strange group for a discussion of the Panama matter and, strictly speaking, it was not a discussion—we were not asked for our views, nor did we volunteer any. Johnson had a way of using Cabinet or other high-level gatherings as audiences to hear presentations on issues that were concerning him, whether or not a majority of those present had responsibilities in the particular field. In this he was very unlike Kennedy, who seldom assembled even his Cabinet, preferring on any problem to meet only with those who might have something of importance to contribute. Kennedy's procedure was far more efficient in conserving his own time and that of others. But Johnson apparently felt the need to use sympathetic groups as sounding boards and sources of support and presumably gained some personal benefit from such meetings.)

> Mann described the trouble and how it began with the incident involving American students. He indicated that 45 Communists had been identified among the rioters; 13 of them were alleged to have been trained in Cuba. He said that although the crowd came at them in waves the Panamanian police fired over their heads. Some people were hit by ricocheting bullets, however. [The point of this, as Johnson would write later, was that the "Panamanian authorities made little effort to maintain law and order."[1]] Mann said that this incident increased the urgency of starting a sea-level canal somewhere other than in Panama. The president indicated that the trouble must have been planned ahead of time and that the Panamanians had used the flag-raising incident as a pretext. He said he had telephoned President Chiari, saying that he would send the best men in our government down to talk with him on honorable terms but that the United States would not agree to revise the treaty with a pistol at its head. The president said that Chiari had agreed to negotiate and then had broken the agreement; we would not let them get away with such outrageous behavior. The president said he had been up until 1:00, 2:00, and 2:30 A.M. since the Panama crisis broke and that he hoped for a sensible solution.

After the phone conversation between Presidents Johnson and Chiari, a small delegation headed by Mann paid Chiari a visit. The latter then quickly restored order and on April 3 agreed to resume diplomatic relations. Thereupon, President Johnson appointed Robert B. Anderson, who had been secretary of the treasury under Eisenhower, as special ambassador to begin treaty negotiations. On December 18, 1964, politically fortified by his overwhelming election victory, Johnson announced two decisions. The first was to press forward with plans for a sea-level canal. The second was to seek an "entirely new treaty" that would recognize Panama's sovereignty over the Canal Zone while allowing the United States to operate and protect the canal for a fixed number of years.*

The president's first decision had been anticipated by Congress which, on September 22, 1964, authorized an Atlantic–Pacific Interoceanic Canal Study Commission (CSC) with a mandate to

> make a full and complete investigation and study . . . considering national defense, foreign relations, intercoastal shipping, interoceanic shipping . . . for the purpose of determining the feasibility of, and the most suitable site for, the construction of a sea-level canal connecting the Atlantic and Pacific Oceans; the best means of constructing such a canal, *whether by conventional or nuclear excavation,* and the estimated cost thereof (emphasis added).

Robert Anderson was named chairman of the CSC. This group continued in existence for six years and had considerable influence over the AEC's Plowshare program.

The Canal vs. the Test Ban

Events in Panama and the establishment of the CSC dictated that the AEC move as quickly as possible on its nuclear excavation experiments to determine the feasibility of nuclear excavation of a new Panama canal. Before we could proceed very far with this undertaking, however, we ran into a stern new reality in the form of the 1963 Limited Test Ban Treaty. At the time the treaty entered into force, in October 1963, the AEC had had time to conduct only one excavation experiment. This was SEDAN, a 100-kiloton device, which was detonated in Nevada on July 6, 1962. It involved excavation of a crater 1,280 feet in diameter and 320 feet deep.

The treaty provision of greatest concern was the one prohibiting any nuclear explosion that "causes radioactive debris to be present outside the territorial limits of the State under whose jurisdiction or control such explosion is conducted." I have already discussed (chapter 17) the controversy over how this clause was to be interpreted

---

*It was not until 1978 that, after heroic efforts by U.S. negotiators Sol Linowitz and Ellsworth Bunker, two treaties with Panama were finally signed and managed by a one-vote margin to pass the Senate. Under one of the treaties ownership of the canal passes to Panama in 1999. The other treaty guarantees the canal's neutrality after the change in ownership. By the time the treaties were signed the question of a new canal had become moot. It had been determined that the economics of supertanker operation did not require passage through the canal.

and the difficulties that a strict interpretation caused for the AEC's underground weapons testing program. The issue was to cause even greater problems for Plowshare.

It was not for lack of effort on AEC's part that Plowshare had been saddled with this burden. Throughout the course of the test ban negotiations (1958–63) the AEC had succeeded in having peaceful nuclear explosions exempted from each successive draft treaty submitted by the Western side. The first U.S. test ban proposal, for example, submitted at Geneva on January 30, 1959, would have exempted PNEs under an arrangement by which the nuclear explosives would have been drawn from an internationally supervised depository. The Soviet counterproposal was that there should be full external and internal preinspection by the other nuclear side before a nuclear device could be used for a peaceful explosion. The Eisenhower administration was willing to assent to external, but not to internal, inspection. (The latter, it was thought, would reveal too much about our nuclear weapons.) The Soviet proposal also stipulated that there should be parity between the superpowers in the number of peaceful detonations allowed. The United States objected to this provision because it would have given the Soviet Union a veto over the number of our peaceful explosions.

After the intensive review of U.S. test ban policy ordered by President Kennedy at the outset of his administration, the U.S.–U.K. draft treaty of April 21, 1961, substantially accepted the Soviet position on internal inspection* and indicated willingness to seek revision of the Atomic Energy Act to make such inspection possible. The draft did not accept the Soviet "one for one" formula. The concession on inspection implied considerable hardship for the AEC, because it meant that we could use for Plowshare only obsolete devices that were bulky and high in fallout. Nevertheless, I went along with the concession at this time because of my sympathy with President Kennedy's zealous pursuit of a test ban treaty. There were those in the AEC community who disagreed strongly with my position.

The Soviets indicated at Geneva that the revised U.S. position on PNEs was acceptable, although they still maintained that such explosions were "superfluous and even dangerous." (They were soon to

---

*The U.S. proposal was that British and Soviet representatives would be allowed to examine, but not copy, blueprints of U.S. devices. They could inspect but not handle the parts. They could be present when the device was reassembled and exploded, and they would be allowed to install instruments and receive data.

change their tune on this as their own ambitious PNE program took shape.) No formal agreement was registered on this point, however, because negotiations continued on other parts of the treaty. On August 27, 1962, the United States and United Kingdom submitted two new draft treaties, one for a comprehensive and one for a limited test ban treaty. The provisions for PNEs in the two treaties were identical: Such explosions could be carried out if agreed to unanimously by the United States, United Kingdom, and USSR, or if performed in accordance with an annex to the treaties that was to be submitted later. It was awkward and embarrassing to have to acknowledge that the annex could not be presented along with the rest of the draft treaties because it had not yet been possible to get agreement on its contents within the U.S. government.

In February 1963 the ACDA circulated within the administration a draft PNE annex that it hoped would fill the gap. It specified that the side conducting a PNE would invite all other parties to the treaty to observe preparations, instrumentation, and actual firing, and to inspect the nuclear device both externally and internally. I felt it necessary to argue strongly against this draft. Since April 1961, when President Kennedy had agreed to internal inspection, the Plowshare experimental excavation program had progressed to the point where it absolutely required thermonuclear devices of very advanced design. These could not safely be subjected to Soviet inspection. The AEC therefore felt strongly that the concession Kennedy had offered, which I had previously supported, should be rescinded.

Argument on these matters continued within the administration for the next several months. In the course of this debate I suggested an alternative to ACDA's annex whereby each side would be limited to an annual quota of PNEs, and there would be a 50 kiloton limit to the yield of each explosion. Foster opposed these ideas and the Committee of Principals was unable to reach any conclusion, favorable or otherwise.

I next took up the Plowshare matter directly with Foster. I pointed out to him the importance of considering the point of view of the Congress. On the one hand, it was clear that Congress would not permit disclosing to the Soviets any of the advanced explosives needed to make reasonable progress in excavation technology. On the other hand, vigorous objection could be expected from members of the Joint Committee on Atomic Energy if adequate provision were not made for Plowshare in a test ban treaty. Because Foster personally objected to both my PNE quota and yield limit ideas, I offered two new suggestions: (1) prohibit in all PNEs diagnostic instrumentation of the kind needed to obtain weapons data, and (2) require the nation conducting the PNE to make debris samples available for the other nuclear side to analyze. These new suggestions were considered by the Principals on June 14, 1963. They received very little support. It was becoming evident that the AEC's enthusiasm for Plowshare was not widely shared, whereas there was considerable concern about the adverse diplomatic consequences that could arise if a PNE seemed to violate a test ban treaty.

On July 3, 1963, a week before Averell Harriman departed for the Moscow test ban negotiations, the AEC conducted a briefing at the State Department for him, George Ball, and about fifteen others. Our purpose in this briefing and in a subsequent memorandum was to suggest some liberal criteria under which Plowshare cratering detonations might be allowed in a limited test ban treaty.

But Harriman never had the opportunity really to engage the Soviets on this subject. As soon as he broached it in Moscow he found them opposed to making any special provision whatever for PNEs. They argued that making an exception for PNEs would detract from the treaty's worldwide political value (undoubtedly a valid point), and that the right to conduct underground tests under a limited treaty already afforded latitude for some types of PNEs (but unfortunately, from our point of view, not for most excavation projects).

After his return from Moscow, Harriman told me of a private conversation with Khrushchev at a Soviet–American track meet, in which the latter had said that the two sides "should have no difficulty in agreeing on such matters when the subject had been more carefully explored, and when tensions were relieved by a test ban and reduced by other understandings. Peaceful uses [of nuclear explosions] would then meet popular approval." Convinced that the Soviet views were not unreasonable, Harriman persuaded President Kennedy to give up on a PNE exemption clause in return for a Soviet concession on another matter important to us. This was a clause permitting withdrawal from the treaty if a party decided that "extraordinary events, related to the subject matter of this Treaty, have jeopardized the supreme interests of its country." The U.S. delegation included this provision because it felt that the Senate, preoccupied with China's nuclear development, would insist on it. This was probably a miscalculation. When the first Chinese test came, a year after the treaty entered into force, not a single senatorial voice was raised in favor of exercising the withdrawal option.

Upon his return from Moscow, Harriman conveyed to me his conviction that in due time it would be possible to amend the treaty in order to liberalize the rules for Plowshare projects.*

In my Senate testimony for the treaty I drew a distinction between the actual construction of a new trans-Isthmian canal and experiments to develop excavation technology. I said that the former "probably could not be done under the present treaty limitations"—the isthmus was too narrow, borders were too close. As to the experiments, I testified as follows:

> Our present considerations lead us to believe that excavation experiments or projects which have a downwind distance of several hundred miles from the project site to a territorial limit probably can be conducted and that these experiments will be sufficient to develop the excavation technology.

On the basis of my and other similar testimony, the Senate Foreign Relations Committee stated to the Congress its understandinng that "the Plowshare program . . . will not be seriously inhibited by the Treaty." I am convinced that these assurances helped win support for the treaty from several senators who might otherwise have opposed it. This conviction caused me considerable personal discomfort in ensuing months and years as concern about violating the treaty began to impede the program. Certainly I had not intended to deceive any senators—yet there might have been an appearance that I had done so.

A Mound Instead of a Crater

In late September 1963, the AEC sought presidential approval for Project SCHOONER, a 100-kiloton cratering experiment in hard rock at a site in southwestern Idaho. It was to be a follow-on to SEDAN in a five-year program to demonstrate excavation technology. Within

---

*I have learned since that information about the progress of the negotiations was deliberately withheld from the AEC so that we, abetted by the Joint Committee, would not intercede vigorously in favor of PNEs and possibly imperil the treaty that President Kennedy so ardently wanted. Having Harriman come to see me after his return was apparently part of this arrangement. (George Bunn, private conversation, November 30, 1986.)

a few days Bundy informed us that a memorandum was afloat in the White House arguing that the entire excavation program should be terminated because it was inconsistent with the Test Ban Treaty. In view of this agitation, and considering that the treaty, although ratified by the Senate, had not yet entered into effect, Bundy felt that it was an inopportune time to ask the president to rule on so large an explosion as SCHOONER. (The 269 Committee review procedure had not yet been established.) Accordingly, the AEC withdrew its request for approval and decided to reorient its efforts toward a number of smaller-yield experiments. The first of these was to be SULKY, estimated to yield only 0.1 kiloton.

We requested approval for SULKY from the 269 Committee on January 15, 1964. In my letter to Bundy, the committee's chairman, I made clear that SULKY represented "about the smallest-scale experiment from which useful cratering information [could] be obtained," and that if we were to be able to continue a meaningful program, "a way must be found to carry out such experiments." Although acknowledging a "theoretical risk" that SULKY might give rise to detectable radiation across our borders, I felt that the risk was minimal. I called attention to the Foreign Relations Committee's statement to the Senate, largely based on my testimony, that "the Plowshare program . . . will not be seriously inhibited by the Treaty."

I repeated these arguments at the 269 Committee's meeting on February 7. In the discussion I was supported by Defense, opposed by State and ACDA. Four days later, Bundy phoned:

> He said that unless I had an objection he proposed to issue a memorandum saying that, in view of the delicacy of the U.S.–USSR relationship, President Johnson had decided to defer consideration of SULKY, without prejudice, until next winter. The expectation was that the intervening time could be profitably used for a review of the possibilities for assuring that there would be no release of detectable radiation across a national border. I said I had no objection so long as this was only a postponement and did not preclude the shot.

Actually, I did have an objection. I confided to my diary that "this decision was a mistake."

On February 25, I caught flak from the other direction. I testified before the JCAE, which just happened at this time to be conducting its authorization hearings on the Plowshare budget for the next fiscal year. Here I was cast in the role of defending the administration's position in delaying cratering explosions before a group of staunch Plowshare adherents. As I understated in my diary: "I had some difficulty." Another unpleasant result of this appearance before the JCAE was that we were forced to reveal the existence of the 269 Committee that had reviewed SULKY. For reasons I found difficult to understand, the administration had tried to keep the existence of this group secret, despite the AEC's obligation under the Atomic Energy Act to keep the JCAE "promptly and fully informed."*

In due course SULKY was resubmitted and approved. The experiment took place on December 18, 1964, at the Nevada Test Site. In order to be sure of not violating the test ban treaty, the AEC buried the device at an overly conservative depth. As a consequence we ended up with a mound instead of a crater. Even so, some radioactivity was detected off-site. The amount was small and quickly dissipated, long before it could reach a national border.

SULKY was not a total loss. We obtained useful information from it. What we had chiefly lost was time. To still the clamor of its opponents and ease the impatience of its friends, Plowshare needed a relatively quick success. We had hoped through the series of experiments of which SULKY was a part to demonstrate nuclear excavation technology convincingly to skeptics in the United States and elsewhere. As 1964 ended we were a long way from having done that.

Impatient Friends

The impatience of Plowshare's congressional supporters was again in evidence at a hearing conducted by the Joint Committee on January 5, 1965. I did much to bring on these expressions of impatience when I told the committee in my prepared testimony that we would need five more years to develop the necessary explosives and cratering techniques before nuclear excavation of a sea-level Panama Canal could begin. Even then, I added, the economics of the nuclear approach would have to be weighed against that of conventional construction. I also touched on difficulties being encountered by the program on a

---

*Bundy speculates that both Presidents Kennedy and Johnson had withheld information about this committee because of a desire to stay in control of the review and approval process. Certainly they did not want to share control with a group as aggressive as the Joint Committee (private conversation, January 22, 1986).

number of other fronts, eliciting this volley from Senator Clinton P. Anderson of New Mexico:

> Senator ANDERSON. My only point, Doctor, was that some years ago we talked about the great possibilities of Plowshare to use it to build harbors. Now, you have a good answer why we can't build harbors.
> Dr. SEABORG. Yes.
> Senator ANDERSON. To use it to dig canals. Now we find many years before we can do that.
> Dr. SEABORG. Yes.
> Senator ANDERSON. To use it for extracting oil from shale and there is no progress. I am just wondering where Plowshare is going or is it going backward?[2]

Next it was the turn of the committee chairman, Senator John O. Pastore of Rhode Island. He first exacted an acknowledgement from me:

> Chairman PASTORE. [A]s you sit there, Dr. Seaborg, do you ever envision the use of nuclear explosives for the building of a sea-level canal without some modification of the nuclear test ban treaty?
> Dr. SEABORG. I do not.

Pastore then followed with a veiled threat:

> Chairman PASTORE. I think if we ruled out removing oil from shale and remove from this whole scene the use of nuclear devices to build a canal I think myself we have weakened the whole spirit and initiative and impetus to Plowshare. . . . For instance, if they [the Panamanians] decide to build a canal next to the existing canal . . . I think that is the end of your Plowshare program. [The proximity of cities would have made it impossible to use nuclear excavation along that route.]
> Dr. SEABORG. Yes, except that—
> Chairman PASTORE. I mean the end of it in the spirit that [the canal is] the one thing that has given this thing life and the one thing that has more or less enthused this committee to provide the money for Plowshare. Once you have ruled that out, I am afraid interest is going to drop off. I am perfectly willing to double, treble or quadruple the appropriation if we are going to use nuclear devices for

the building of a canal. If we are not, I would like to take a second look at the size of the budget. That is all it amounts to.*

Later in the day:

I met with Dr. Gerald Johnson [Livermore Laboratory associate director for Plowshare].**We talked about the hearing today and Jerry was somewhat discouraged. I told him I thought there was nothing unusual about the Committee members' attitude today, and that they would be surprised to learn that he was in any way discouraged about Plowshare's future. I told him that we were depending on him to carry on with his usual enthusiasm. . . . By the time he left he indicated he would try to continue with the same interest.**

The International Road to Salvation

At this point, I, among others, felt that AEC's best chance of engendering enough enthusiasm for PNEs to make revision of the test ban treaty possible was to develop cooperative projects with other countries. AEC did its best to stimulate international interest and enthusiasm. During April 1964 we conducted a Plowshare Symposium to which nine nations sent representatives. At about the same time we declassified essentially all information on the *effects* of peaceful nuclear explosions. (We had no choice but to continue to protect information on the *design* of the explosives, because they incorporated advanced weapons technology.) At the third UN Conference on Peaceful Uses of Atomic Energy, held in Geneva during the summer of 1964, the AEC directed attention to Plowshare with a major scientific paper, an exhibit, and a film. There were encouraging signs of interest. Even the Soviet Union, still a missing piece in the puzzle, seemed to be coming round. Based on bits of intelligence that came our way, I was able to report in a letter to Under Secretary of State George Ball on February 12, 1965, that "the Soviet attitude towards . . . nuclear excavation has materially improved since the period prior to the execution of the Limited Test Ban Treaty."

---

*AEC budgets had to undergo an additional hurdle not faced by other departments. Before the budgets could even be considered by the appropriations committees of the House and Senate, they had to be "authorized" in a separate action by the JCAE.

In this same letter to Ball I proposed that a program of international cooperation in PNEs be initiated as soon as possible. The State Department's reply, signed by Secretary Rusk, concurred in the concept of international cooperation but recommended a cautious step-by-step approach. As a first step, Rusk suggested that "a few initial experiments with international participation . . . be conducted [in this country] under substantially the present constraints as to permissible radioactive debris." He held out the hope that eventually "this course of action could lead to such amendment of the treaty or other appropriate international understanding as might be necessary to permit major excavation projects." I answered on April 7, suggesting that the very first step should be to initiate discussions with the USSR, because we believed the Soviet attitude would "have an important bearing on the evolution of the program." I then set forth what AEC had in mind when it proposed international cooperation:

> It has been our position from the beginning in suggesting international cooperation that when the time comes for foreign applications we would supply the nuclear explosive and arm and fire it [in the cooperating country] under U.S. custody and security. . . . [A]rrangements could be worked out with the other country to allow it to share in the control of the timing of the detonation to insure the safety of its public.

I urged that the proposed cooperative program be initiated "very soon . . . to derive the maximum benefit from the favorable foreign attitudes that have been expressed as of late towards this technology."

At this moment prospects for Plowshare appeared to be brightening. But a week later another cloud, a radioactive one, crossed the horizon.

Another Venting of Another Shot

On April 14, 1965, we conducted a Plowshare experiment called PALANQUIN at the Nevada Test Site. It involved detonation of a 4-kiloton thermonuclear device buried at a depth of 280 feet in an emplacement hole drilled to 615 feet. The purposes were to explore cratering mechanisms in hard dry rock such as might be encountered in Panama, and to investigate emplacement techniques that would reduce the amount of radioactivity released to the atmosphere.

It was our expectation, based on earlier experiments, that a large fraction of the radioactive debris would go down the hole and that very little would reach the atmosphere. Also, following the experience of SULKY, we expected PALANQUIN to create a fully contained mound rather than a crater. (The purposes of PALANQUIN, unlike SULKY, were such that we would have been satisfied with a mound.) Our expectations proved wrong in both respects. The dust cloud from the explosion rose to a height of eight thousand feet, and contained higher-than-expected levels of radioactivity. This air mass moved northward rather slowly, dispersing laterally as it traveled. As I reported to the president, the radioactivity was much less than that following the errant Soviet test of January 15, 1965, and well below any possible health hazard level, even close to the test site. Worrisomely, however, the radioactivity was sufficient to be readily detectable by properly equipped aircraft should the cloud drift into Canada.

On the afternoon of April 15, the radioactive air mass was located east of Spokane, the next morning over Butte, Montana. To our relief, it appeared then to drift to the southeast. Still, there remained some risk that parts of the cloud might follow a different path and cross the border. On April 17, we issued a low-key press release, hoping thus to soften the impact of any possible test ban violation. All seemed calm for a few days. On April 24, I had lunch at the Soviet Embassy with Ambassador Dobrynin and some Soviet scientists. It was a pleasant, entirely social occasion; there was no mention of PALANQUIN.

But on April 29, the calm was broken. Dobrynin delivered a Soviet aide-mémoire to the State Department, asking for more information than had been given in AEC's meager press release. The Soviet note, adopting an unusually testy tone, said in part:

> [T]he assertion of the Atomic Energy Commission [in its press release] that the fallout of radioactive debris is within the boundaries of the U.S.A. is unconvincing because the Commission does not control the air streams . . . and there is reason to believe that with the conduct of this explosion there took place a violation of the Treaty barring nuclear weapon tests in three environments.

Then, on May 5:

> **Indications are that some radioactive debris from PALANQUIN, a few counts of barium-140, have been detected by our Air**

Force over Bermuda; we are victims of our own sensitive detection equipment!

"You're Another!"

On May 4, the diplomats produced the U.S. answer to the Soviet
inquiry. The first part of the reply described PALANQUIN, its purposes, and all the precautions taken. No acknowledgement was made
of any escape of radioactivity from the United States, nor was there
any claim that there had been none. And then, pursuant to the old
legal dictum, "If you have a weak defense, attack!", our government
chose to revive the issue about the escape of radioactivity from the
Soviet weapons test regarding which there had been so much diplomatic give-and-take earlier in the year (see chapter 18):

> In this connection the Government of the United States believes it
> necessary to revert to consideration of a very much larger nuclear
> explosion conducted in the Soviet Union on January 15, 1965, . . .
> which resulted in many times as much radioactive debris being re-
> leased to the atmosphere. . . . If the Soviet Government were more
> forthcoming in response to the request of the United States Govern-
> ment for further information concerning the January 15 Soviet test,
> the United States Government might be better able to conclude that
> there was no intention on the part of the Soviet Government to
> violate the terms of the [test ban] Treaty.

The U.S. note concluded by saying that the Soviet test had caused
"grave concern"; that a repetition could "jeopardize the very existence of the Treaty"; and that the U.S. regarded the treaty as of
"utmost importance."

I considered this product of U.S. diplomacy to have been mis-
chievous and damaging, as had been the Soviet note that prompted
it. The spectacle of two great nations playing the child's game of
"You're another!" over two obviously accidental events was far from
edifying. (Unfortunately, this pattern of accusation and counterac-
cusation has persisted to the present day.)

The exchanges that followed PALANQUIN were certainly not
helpful to the future the AEC had in mind for international cooperation in PNEs, with major Soviet participation. This cause was to
sustain one more blow in 1965. In late September, following my at-

tendance at the IAEA's annual General Conference in Vienna, I visited the United Arab Republic. One of the principal topics discussed in my meeting with their officials was the Qattara Depression Project, which envisaged nuclear excavation of a fifty-mile canal or tunnel from the Mediterranean to the depression, a drop of fifty meters. The force of the falling water was expected to power a 165-megawatt electric generating station at the depression end. This project had been broached by the UAR to U.S. delegates at two international conferences in the autumn of 1964. AEC Commissioner John Palfrey, while in the UAR later in 1964, had mentioned the possibility of a visit by U.S. Plowshare experts to discuss the project in greater technical detail. This was done in accordance with State Department advice that it was appropriate in discussions with other governments to mention U.S. interest in cooperative PNE endeavors. During my visit UAR officials requested that Palfrey's suggestion be implemented. I reported all this in a letter to Bundy on November 26, 1965. I expressed the AEC's view that a visit by Plowshare experts to the UAR was desirable "at this time." I asked whether he had any comments. Indeed he had:

> I think it is clear that such a visit at this time would inevitably focus considerable attention on the project and encourage the belief that the U.S. was prepared to support it. I do not believe we have yet really thought through all the political, economic, and arms control implications that would be involved in either encouraging or undertaking this project.

Evident in Bundy's response, which was clearly inconsistent with what Rusk had told us earlier, was a persistent skittishness in the administration about risking the future of arms control endeavors on the as yet unproven prospects of PNEs. This had been evident earlier when the Gilpatric Committee Report recommended that "Plowshare must not be allowed to stand in the way of a comprehensive test ban." I should add, in passing, that the administration's uncertainty and internal conflicts about Plowshare might have been resolved more readily by the exercise of presidential leadership. But President Johnson was preoccupied elsewhere. There was now to occur, in connection with another Plowshare project, a prolonged imbroglio in which the administration's internal bickering and indecision reached new levels.

Notes

1. Johnson, *The Vantage Point*, p. 181.
2. JCAE, *Plowshare*, January 5, 1965, p. 22.

25
CABRIOLET, or How Not
to Run a Government

1965

While promoting the use of peaceful nuclear explosions abroad, the AEC was attending at home to the requirements of the Atlantic–Pacific Interoceanic Canal Study Commission. That body, established in September 1964 in the aftermath of the crisis in Panama, was preparing a report to the president for which the AEC was to supply technical data. Our effort to fulfill this duty required a series of six nuclear cratering experiments. First in line was to be CABRIOLET, in which a 2.7-kiloton explosive would be detonated at a depth of 170 feet in hard, dry rock at the Nevada Test Site. From this experiment we hoped to obtain basic technical information about cratering and the subsequent distribution of radioactivity that would be applicable to excavation of a trans-Isthmian canal.

Authority to conduct CABRIOLET was first requested in November 1965 in the form of a letter to McGeorge Bundy in his capacity as chairman of the 269 Committee. We sought approval to make the shot on or about March 1, 1966. If it were done much later we would be into the cattle-grazing season and might run the risk of contaminating milk supplies with iodine-131 fallout.

The explosive device we had in mind for CABRIOLET was specifically designed to minimize radioactivity. Even so, we frankly acknowledged in our application to the 269 Committee that there would be a 50 percent chance, after about two days, of a minuscule amount of radioactivity being detected at the Canadian border. This of course raised the question of whether we would be in violation of the Limited Test Ban Treaty and again brought into focus the question whether the treaty was to be interpreted literally, forbidding the export of the most minute detectable amount of radioactivity, or, as AEC contended, "reasonably," allowing export of small amounts that would not affect human health.

Even if AEC's interpretation of the treaty were not accepted— and in truth it had very little support inside the government—we urged that CABRIOLET be approved because, if it were not conducted, the ill effects on the canal undertaking and on all future excavation projects would outweigh the diplomatic embarrassment of a technical treaty violation.

The ACDA, Plowshare's persistent antagonist, was quick to disagree. A week after AEC's formal submission to the 269 Committee, Foster wrote to Bundy that it was "an inopportune time to conduct an event which could very well create accusations of our not living up to our treaty commitments." He felt that there were diplomatic tides stirring that could lead to a clarification of the treaty's meaning within a few months. Better to wait than to risk diplomatic embarrassment. Deputy Secretary of Defense Cyrus Vance weighed in with an even more severe opinion. He recommended that CABRIOLET be postponed and that the entire Plowshare program be reviewed. In light of the Vietnam War, Vance thought it unwise to open another propaganda front on which the U.S. could be attacked. In the State Department some staff favored going ahead with the experiment; others were opposed.

1966

When the 269 Committee met at the beginning of March 1966 to consider CABRIOLET, ACDA once again urged that all excavation experiments be postponed until doubts about interpretation of the Limited Test Ban Treaty were resolved by suitable amendment. AEC responded that the wait for a treaty amendment would inevitably be a long one and would eliminate all possibility of our providing needed technical data to the Canal Study Commission before June 30, 1968, when that group was required to submit its report to the president. As an alternative to a formal treaty amendment, we suggested trying to reach an informal modus vivendi with the Soviet Union. Intelligence information indicated that the Soviets were by this time embarked on an ambitious PNE program of their own.

On March 28, we received a letter from the Joint Committee on Atomic Energy, Plowshare's staunch defenders. Chairman Chet Holifield warned that if cratering experiments were not permitted "the entire Plowshare program would have to be reevaluated." Plowshare appeared now to be threatened by friend and foe alike.

On April 1, with time running out if we were to conduct CABRIOLET before the 1966 grazing season, I had a brief talk with Dean Rusk before a Cabinet meeting. He said he was reluctant to recommend approval in view of the 50 percent chance that some radioactivity might cross the border.

Walt Rostow, newly installed on April 1 as national security adviser, telephoned on April 11 to discuss CABRIOLET from his White House perspective.

> He was sure I knew that McNamara was against it. Also, Rusk was getting enough noise in the diplomatic field to make him feel that something might conceivably happen in the next six months to clear up the whole Plowshare concept and this caused him to want a postponement. The question now really was whether I wanted to take it up with the president when he returned from Texas. The president had said he would be glad to meet with me so I could argue my case. I said I would like to discuss it further with him, Rostow, before deciding whether to go to the president.

The next day, AEC Commissioner John G. Palfrey and I had lunch with Rostow. He endorsed Rusk's suggestion that we hold off for six months while seeking an understanding with the Soviet Union on what constituted a violation of the test ban treaty. We expressed doubt that the Soviets had any incentive to reach such an understanding—they were proceeding with their test program under a liberal interpretation of the treaty while we were hobbling ourselves with a strict one. (We had evidence of three or four Soviet explosions that had "caused radioactive debris to be present" across the Chinese border.)

Following our lunch with Rostow, I wrote to Rusk reviewing all the arguments in favor of CABRIOLET. I pointed out that "hunting atoms at international borders [had] become a scientific stunt." Playing this game, we were hindering ourselves. We had managed to conduct only two small cratering experiments since the test ban treaty. I told him that CABRIOLET was the cleanest shot we could fire. It would yield at most 2 picocuries of radiation at the Canadian border after two days. Against this minor risk one had to consider that

CABRIOLET was crucial to the canal project. I maintained that no canal route outside the present Canal Zone was economically credible without nuclear excavation. If we wanted to build a canal through a country politically more dependable than Panama, for example, Colombia, we had to go forward with Plowshare experiments.

Continuing AEC's "full-court press," Commissioner Palfrey and I met with Rusk in his office three days later:

> We reviewed the intelligence evidence regarding Soviet PNEs. We also emphasized my 1963 Senate testimony in which I indicated it would be possible to conduct some excavation experiments under the treaty. Rusk didn't appear to have understood this. He had evidently been under the impression that we had promised only that fully contained Plowshare experiments could be conducted, not excavation experiments.
>
> Rusk concluded that he couldn't give a "yes" or "no" answer. He said this was a matter that would have to be taken to the president.

Picking up on his last comment, I sent Rusk on May 12 a draft memorandum that he might send to the president explaining CABRIOLET. But the secretary was evidently not satisfied with our presentation. On May 28, he wrote to me suggesting that "an additional period of perhaps two or three months, during which we could look into Soviet intentions, make a comprehensive intelligence community assessment of Soviet progress in nuclear excavation, and have our staffs work together on other aspects of the memo, would be worthwhile in terms of putting a more complete and fully rounded paper before the president." I replied on June 2, assenting to "active pursuit of discussions with the Soviets," but pointing out that if we were to conduct CABRIOLET in November 1966 (after the grazing season but before the winter) we needed approval by August.

On June 20, the AEC conducted an intelligence briefing that presented evidence that the Soviets were indeed carrying on a substantial PNE program. Both Rusk and Under Secretary Ball attended the briefing.

Events in Geneva now provided the AEC with another argument. On August 9, Adrian Fisher unveiled at the ENDC an AEC-originated proposal that the nonproliferation treaty provide for a peaceful nu-

clear explosions service by nuclear-weapons states for other states.*
(See chapter 27 for greater detail about the events in Geneva.) We
were now able to contend that disapproval of CABRIOLET would
mean in effect that excavation projects, the main focus of foreign
interest in PNEs, would have to be excluded from this service. We
claimed that the United States had a moral obligation to develop
excavation technology in order to honor its new commitment.

On August 24, I called Rusk reminding him of our previous meetings and correspondence and of our need for an early decision if
CABRIOLET was to go in November. He said he would check. A
week passed during which we heard nothing. On September 2, I wrote
despairingly in my diary: "Perhaps we should give up on the excavation part of Plowshare." But Rusk had indeed been checking, eliciting in the process a sharp and well-reasoned diatribe from Foster.
In this memorandum the ACDA director met head-on some of the
points AEC had been making. He argued as follows: (1) I had myself
testified at the 1963 test ban hearings that the criteria for treaty violation would be detection and identification of radioactive debris,
not health standards. (This was a telling point. At the time of the test
ban hearings I had failed to anticipate the situation that would arise
later from the improved detection capability.) (2) The president had
stated on July 5, 1966 that the United States intended "to live up to
the test ban treaty religiously and scrupulously follow it." (3) The
potential for violating the treaty would increase with the more powerful excavation experiments scheduled to follow CABRIOLET.

Notwithstanding Foster's formidable intervention, Rusk recommended to the president, on September 16, that he allow CABRI-
OLET to proceed. The secretary wrote:

This problem has been considered fully and carefully over a considerable period of time at the highest levels of government. It is my
view that the advantages of proceeding with CABRIOLET outweigh
the risks.

---

*Representatives of various non-nuclear-weapon states at the ENDC, particularly the UAR, had
complained of the injustice of a treaty that would deny their countries the benefits of peaceful
nuclear explosions. In response, several AEC staff members, following up on proposals I had
made for a peaceful nuclear explosions service to be provided by the United States on a bilateral
basis, came up with the idea of having such a service provided in the context of the NPT. It
was part of AEC's effort to remove every possible excuse for nations not to join the NPT.

Diminishing the force of his recommendation, however, Rusk communicated to the president in the same memorandum the contrary views of ACDA's prestigious General Advisory Committee, headed by John J. McCloy. The committee stated that its members were unanimously opposed to CABRIOLET because they considered it prejudicial to nonproliferation and a "conscious violation of the test ban treaty."

The president went along with Rusk, as he was wont to do. On September 19, on the basis of informal approval from the White House, I sent a teletype message to Nevada authorizing "all necessary preparations for project readiness." But the needed formal approval did not come through. On October 11, I called Rostow to ask where things stood. To my consternation and amazement he said that the president was having various people "take a fresh look at it." What had happened, as I later found out, was that, after the decision to proceed had been made, the president's own Science Advisory Committee, at a regular meeting, unanimously recommended that he disapprove the experiment. At this point President Johnson, undoubtedly confused and probably exasperated by the conflicting advice he was getting, took an administrative step that, in my recollection, had no precedent. He decided to submit this dispute within his administration to "binding arbitration!" He designated as sole arbiter the newly appointed under secretary of state, Nicholas Katzenbach, and indicated he would accept Katzenbach's recommendation.*

On October 18, Katzenbach conducted a meeting about CABRIOLET that was attended by representatives of State, Defense, Budget, CIA, the White House, ACDA, and AEC. The familiar, tired arguments were presented on both sides, resulting in the usual rhetorical gridlock. Next followed a period of more than two months during which we received no indication which way the wind was blowing. Then, on December 20, word came from Rostow that, pursuant to Katzenbach's recommendation, the president had authorized CABRIOLET. We scheduled it for February 1, 1967, concerned, as we had

---

*Katzenbach had been deputy attorney general under Robert Kennedy. When Kennedy resigned in September 1964 to run for the Senate, the president is reported to have said: "I'm not going to pick that fellow Katzenbach [for attorney general]. He would be reporting to Bobby every night." (Transcript, Kenneth O'Donnell Oral History Interview, 7/23/69, by Paige E. Mulhollan, Tape 1, p. 68, LBJ Library.) The position was left vacant for over four months, Katzenbach serving as acting attorney general. Johnson finally relented and appointed him attorney general in January 1965. When Katzenbach moved over to the State Department late in 1966 he was succeeded as attorney general by Ramsey Clark.

been a year earlier, about getting it in before the grazing season. I wrote in my diary on December 20: "We have waited a long time for this." Little did I know that we were to wait a time longer. The CABRIOLET comic opera had more than another year to run.

1967

For technical reasons CABRIOLET, scheduled to go on February 1, 1967, was set back to February 10. At 11 A.M. on February 9, I received a call from Rostow. He said the president had approved the statement the AEC proposed to issue following the next day's test. But at 2:30 P.M.:

> Rostow called again to say that the president had changed his mind; he had decided to *cancel* CABRIOLET for the present! [So much for binding arbitration!] Rostow said I should issue the operational orders and then drop by to see him and he would explain; he did not want to do so over the phone.
>
> Ten minutes later [Commissioner Gerald F.] Tape and I were in Rostow's office at the White House. He gave us a number of reasons for the cancellation. One was the ongoing negotiations on the Nonproliferation Treaty and the Latin American nuclear-free zone treaty, in both of which peaceful nuclear explosions were an important issue. Another reason had to do with diplomatic pressures over the continued bombing of North Vietnam during a period when it seemed to some that fruitful peace negotiations could occur.
>
> Apparently there had been meetings among the president, Rusk, McNamara, Rostow and others in which it was decided that the risk of an incident with CABRIOLET was too great to be taken on at this time.

I spent the better part of February 10 calling some of Plowshare's strong supporters to explain what had happened. Some took it rather well, but not the Joint Committee on Atomic Energy. In its report on the AEC's fiscal year 1968 appropriations, which was issued shortly after the postponement, the committee expressed "its deep concern that planned Plowshare experiments have not been conducted." Referring to the U.S. offer to provide nuclear explosive services to other nations, the report stated: "It is abundantly clear that if we do not actively pursue the development of this technology we will not be able to make it available to anyone—even ourselves." The committee went on to say that it was also "disturbed by the overly strict interpretation which the Executive Branch continues to place upon the Limited Test Ban Treaty."

This latest postponement of CABRIOLET led to deep discouragement within the AEC family, particularly at Livermore. Michael May, the laboratory director, went so far as to suggest that we now abandon the excavation applications of Plowshare and concentrate instead on the fully contained explosions for deep mining of minerals and liberation of entrapped oil and natural gas. Such projects would at least not be subject to the risk of venting and possible treaty violation. The other commissioners and I felt, however, that we had no choice but to press on with cratering experiments. The excavation application seemed the best hope of keeping Plowshare alive, and we still deeply believed in the ultimate promise of the program. So we sought once more to gain approval for CABRIOLET.

On February 28, Tape and I met again with Rostow at the White House.

> We pointed out [just as we had the previous year] that it would be necessary to reach a decision to shoot early in March if we were to get CABRIOLET done before the grazing season began. Otherwise the device, which was already emplaced, would have to be destroyed. It would cost about $1.4 million more to execute the experiment later in the year with a new device. Rostow said he would bring all this to the attention of the President.

The White House was not to be stampeded by this cost-based argument. On March 17, I received a note from Rostow saying: "The President has requested that you review the problem of the rescheduling of CABRIOLET and submit a recommendation to him by April 15, 1967, as to whether CABRIOLET should be rescheduled for the Fall of 1967." Offered no better choice, I recommended that it be rescheduled. On May 1, Rostow called.

> He said we were cleared to proceed with the planning of both CABRIOLET and BUGGY, next in the planned series of cratering experiments. There was no commitment as to actually conducting the explosions—we were merely to plan—and there was to be no public announcement.

By October 10 preparations for CABRIOLET were far advanced and I applied for authority to conduct the test. I requested that approval be granted at least two weeks prior to November 16, the target readiness date. Once again it was a question of conducting the experiment before the onset of winter.

Now Plowshare's opponents and proponents approached the battlements once again. On October 17, Foster wrote Rostow recommending that CABRIOLET be disapproved, because of feared diplomatic repercussions. He said, in part:

> The reason given for postponing CABRIOLET last February was to avoid complicating discussions of the non-proliferation treaty and the treaty on denuclearization of Latin America. A more critical stage in their international consideration will occur in November, when both treaties are expected to be the focus of General Assembly discussion. If CABRIOLET is carried out at that time and, as seems probable, the U.S. is charged with violating the Limited Test Ban Treaty, the U.S. will be in the position of demonstrating its unwillingness to accept arms control restrictions imposed on it by existing international obligations at the very time we are asking other nations to undertake new treaty commitments of their own.

Canal Study Commission Chairman Anderson intervened on behalf of CABRIOLET on October 20. He wrote to Rostow that he understood ACDA was again opposing the experiment "in spite of assurances given us last spring. If you feel there is any likelihood that the president will not approve it for execution as requested by the AEC, I would like to discuss it with the president before the decision is made." There evidently was such a likelihood, and Anderson made his arguments to the president on October 25.

Assailed by strong representations from both sides, the president deferred decision until the interested parties could all be brought together with him to discuss the issues face to face. The meeting took place on November 28, the November 16 target readiness date having slipped by in the meanwhile.

Tape and I attended for the AEC. Others present included Rusk, McNamara, Fisher, CIA Director Helms, Budget Director [Charles L.] Schultze, Katzenbach, Robert Anderson, Science Adviser Hornig, and Rostow.

The President opened the meeting by saying that CABRI-
OLET presented him with a difficult decision. He asked Rusk to
summarize the situation. Rusk said that what was involved
seemed very clear: it was a matter of balancing the Plowshare
program against the Limited Test Ban Treaty. [I would not have
wanted him to put it exactly that way.] Estimates were that there
was a 50-50 chance that radioactive debris from the explosion
would be detected at a national border. As to this estimate,
Rusk said that in his experience scientists were not always correct. He recalled that in 1962 scientists had substantially under-
estimated the effects a U.S. atmospheric test [STARFISH] would
have on the upper atmosphere.[1] There was still controversy
about how much radioactivity at a border would constitute a
violation of the treaty, but clearly a significant amount of radioactive debris would be a serious matter. Another serious
question, Rusk said, was whether CABRIOLET was worth doing
if nothing more would be done afterward.

The president asked me to comment on Rusk's remarks. I
recalled that assurances had been given to the Senate by me
and others during the test ban hearings that some Plowshare
explosions, including excavation experiments, would be permitted under the treaty. It was my opinion that these assurances
had been necessary to ratification because influential Senators
(I named Senators Anderson, Jackson and Fulbright) seemed to
want to be assured on this point before they would vote for
the treaty or urge others to do so. As to whether CABRIOLET
was worth doing if nothing followed, I said it was not—a planned
program of cratering experiments would have to follow for
CABRIOLET to be of any value.

I commented at some length on whether CABRIOLET would
violate the test ban treaty. I called attention to a letter Rusk
himself had written to the Joint Committee prior to ratification
in which he said that the U.S. government would interpret the
treaty as broadly as the Soviets did. I pointed out that the Soviets
had conducted 14 tests that led to craters, that radioactive debris had been detected beyond Soviet borders after at least four
of these, and that on two of these the amount of debris exceeded anything that could possibly take place with CABRIOLET.

The president then asked me the direct question: Could
there be a treaty violation if CABRIOLET was conducted? I said
I did not think this possible if we used the sensible and reasonable "de minimis" interpretation of what constituted a violation
or adopted the philosophy of the Rusk letter. The president

next asked me whether I thought CABRIOLET was as important as the Limited Test Ban Treaty. I said that the treaty was much more important but that since CABRIOLET could be conducted without violating the treaty it was not necessary to choose between the two.

I next pointed out the relationship of CABRIOLET to non-proliferation. We had offered PNE services to non-weapon countries in an effort to dissuade them from developing nuclear explosives on their own. CABRIOLET was needed to develop the technology so we could make good on our offer. I mentioned my visits to Brazil and India and how much importance these countries attributed to PNEs.

Anderson emphasized the importance of Plowshare techniques to mankind. He felt postponement of CABRIOLET would mean the end of the excavation program. At that point Panama would know there was no alternative to an improved, conventionally built canal in Panama and would therefore be more difficult than ever to deal with, whereas Colombia might feel we had been dealing with them in bad faith.*

Hornig pointed out that CABRIOLET was a test of only 2.7 kilotons, whereas digging a canal would require megatons. We would need to revise the treaty to do that, so why not seek a revision right away? Rusk suggested we at least get an agreement with the Soviets on interpretation of the existing treaty before we did CABRIOLET. I answered that this would require years. We had been trying to get such an agreement for two years without success. I added that the Soviets had no incentive to make such an agreement with us since they were carrying out Plowshare-type tests under their own permissive treaty interpretation without an agreement.

The president next asked Katzenbach for his opinion. Katzenbach, whose decision as arbiter had favored going ahead with CABRIOLET, now seemed to argue against it! He said that, even based on what the AEC had said about how the treaty should be interpreted, CABRIOLET could violate it. I argued that if we interpreted the treaty as liberally as the Soviets did CABRIOLET would certainly not violate it. But Katzenbach made the point that the Soviets had never publicly stated these more liberal criteria. I derived some comfort from the fact that the president then joined me in making the point that the Soviets

---

*It was generally agreed that a proposed canal route in Colombia could be utilized only if nuclear excavation was employed.

had nevertheless used the criteria in deciding to conduct their cratering experiments.

With the president's agreement I read aloud the strong statements made in the Joint Committee's authorization report for fiscal year 1968 expressing the committee's displeasure at the failure to conduct cratering experiments. The president then adjourned the meeting. While he announced no immediate decision at the meeting, we were encouraged. His interventions during the discussion had seemed sympathetic.

On December 19, Bromley Smith, executive secretary of the National Security Council, called from the White House to say that President Johnson had decided to go ahead with CABRIOLET, with the understanding, however, that this decision did not constitute approval of any follow-up program until CABRIOLET had been evaluated. "In view of the agony of all the considerations," Smith asked me to stay in close touch with Rusk on how the details of CABRIOLET were to be handled to minimize "unpleasant aspects." Further, the shot was not to be scheduled until late January so that any announcement or leak about final preparations would come after the State of the Union message and after the resumption of ENDC negotiations, scheduled for January 18. In short, CABRIOLET was to be treated as a guilty secret.

1968

On January 18, 1968, I called Rusk.

I said we had set January 24 for CABRIOLET, subject to his specific concurrence. He said he didn't understand why he had been given this role. I told him it was part of the final approval process established by the president that he, Rusk, was to approve the date lest maladroit timing lead to some diplomatic fallout. Rusk then said that he did approve the date.

I then called the head of AEC's division of peaceful nuclear explosives, John Kelly, to say that they could begin cementing the device in place. On January 25, AEC publicly announced that it planned to conduct CABRIOLET the following day. On January 26:

CABRIOLET went at 11 A.M. I was present in the Situation Room and heard the countdown and description of the shot. It created a crater about 400 feet across and 125 feet deep. The wind was right, blowing away from Mexico, and a snowstorm in northern Nevada apparently brought down much of the debris. The snowstorm was a stroke of good luck! No radioactivity attributable to CABRIOLET was detected by the Canadians.

Due to the repeated postponements CABRIOLET cost about $5 million, nearly three times the originally estimated cost. In addition, the several postponements resulted in a significant and highly prejudicial delay in the ability of the AEC to report to the Canal Study Commission on the feasibility of a nuclear-excavated canal. The consequences of this were yet to be faced.

Note

1. For more on this incident, see my book *Kennedy, Khrushchev and the Test Ban,* p. 156.

26
The End of the Story

Unfortunately, neither the technical feasibility nor the international acceptability of such an application of nuclear excavation technology has been established to date.

—The Canal Study Commission
Final Report, 1970

The Treaty of Tlatelolco

The right of nations to carry out their own peaceful nuclear explosions, and to develop their own explosives for that purpose, was the principal bone of contention in the negotiations leading to the Treaty for the Prohibition of Nuclear Weapons in Latin America.[1]

This treaty, known as the Treaty of Tlatelolco after the district of Mexico City where most of the deliberations took place, was noteworthy as the first international agreement to ban nuclear weapons from an inhabited region. (Previous treaties had banned them from Antarctica and outer space.) The idea was first broached by Brazil late in 1962 following the Cuban missile crisis, which had aroused intense concern throughout Latin America. In February 1967 a text was submitted to the UN General Assembly, which endorsed it in December 1967. The treaty entered into force on April 22, 1968.

Under the treaty's principal terms, each Latin American party renounced the right to acquire nuclear weapons and to station nuclear weapons on its territory. Each Latin American party further agreed to place its nuclear facilities under the jurisdiction of a control organization established to administer the treaty, and also under International Atomic Energy Agency safeguards. To enforce these provisions the treaty provided for a system of challenge inspections much like that which Alva Myrdal was proposing at the ENDC for a comprehensive test ban treaty.

Nations outside Latin America subscribed to the treaty through a pair of protocols. Under Protocol I each outside state having a dependent territory in Latin America agreed to preserve the nonnuclear status of the area. Under Protocol II nuclear weapon powers agreed not to station nuclear weapons in Latin America and not to use nuclear weapons against any of the Latin American parties to the treaty.

All Latin American nations have signed and ratified the treaty except Argentina, which has signed but not ratified, and Cuba, which has neither signed nor ratified. The instruments of ratification for Brazil and Chile, however, indicate that those countries will not consider themselves bound by the treaty until all eligible Latin American states have signed and ratified. The United States, the United Kingdom, the Netherlands, and France (the states having dependent territories in Latin America) have signed Protocol I, and all have ratified it except France. All five nuclear weapons powers have both signed and ratified Protocol II. Mainland China's adherence marks the first time it has joined the other nuclear powers in an arms control agreement. The U.S. adherence marks the only time this country has accepted any legal restriction on its right to use nuclear weapons.

Initial discussions and drafts of the Treaty of Tlatelolco did not mention PNEs. By March 1965, however, Brazil was insisting that the treaty allow peaceful explosions in Latin America, and both Panama and Nicaragua were seeking assurance that the treaty would not interfere with the possible use of nuclear explosives to excavate a trans-Isthmian canal. Still there was no proposal that the treaty allow any Latin American party to develop its own nuclear explosives. The evolving draft treaty began to give encouragement to such indigenous development in May 1966, when tentative approval was given to a definition of a nuclear weapon that included the idea of intent: A nuclear explosive was to be considered a weapon only if it was "intended to be used for a military purpose." Both the United States and the United Kingdom promptly indicated their disapproval of the proposed definition. The British stated that a peaceful nuclear explosive was in effect a weapon—in the existing state of technology there could be no possible distinction. The United States agreed with the British on this and, with an eye to Plowshare's future, urged that the treaty ban all nuclear explosions in Latin America, *except* where a Latin American country obtained PNE service from an existing nuclear weapon state.

Brazil mounted a determined campaign to hold the line against the U.S.–U.K. views. Brazil's attitude was mirrored in conversations other U.S. officials and I held in Washington with Brazil's foreign minister, Sérgio Corrêa da Costa, on September 13, 1967. Though these talks focused on the nonproliferation treaty, the Brazilian position carried over also into the Tlatelolco negotiations.

> I mentioned that the United States could help Brazil with peaceful nuclear explosions under proper circumstances. Da Costa mentioned a specific excavation project—the construction of a 5 to 7 kilometer canal linking the Amazon River basin with the River Platte basin. It was his hope that the U.S. would provide assistance in performing the necessary feasibility studies on this project. He did not mention our providing the explosion service, however, which was what we had in mind. As I had done when I visited Brazil two months earlier [chapter 21], I explored in some detail Brazil's expressed interest in building its own nuclear explosives for peaceful purposes. I pointed out that it would be an enormous economic burden for Brazil to take this path, whereas the United States could furnish the service through an appropriate international organization at our direct cost, without any charge for research and development. I emphasized that we had been working on this technology for at least 20 years and still had at least five years to go before we would have the proper kind of explosives. This was by way of indicating what Brazil would have to face if it tried to go it alone. Da Costa nevertheless clung to the position that Brazil wanted to build its own nuclear explosives for peaceful purposes "as a matter of principle."

From this conversation and other indications (see under "Brazil" in chapter 21), it was hard not to conclude that the "principle" involved was that Brazil wanted to keep alive its option to develop and manufacture nuclear weapons. Such an attitude on the part of a nation in our own hemisphere was, of course, very disquieting. Other Latin American nations followed Mexico's lead in disagreeing with Brazil on this issue. A factor in determining their position undoubtedly was a fear of losing Anglo–American support for the pending treaty.

Those who opposed Brazil prevailed to the extent that the notion of intent was dropped from the treaty's definition of a nuclear weapon, which in the final text (Article 5) was construed to be "any device capable of releasing nuclear energy in an uncontrolled manner and which has a group of characteristics that are appropriate for use for warlike purposes."

The final treaty contained so many compromises as to seem self-contradictory. On the one hand, Article 18 authorized parties to carry out peaceful nuclear explosions. On the other hand, Article 1 prohibited indigenous development of nuclear weapons, which were so defined (Article 5) as to include peaceful nuclear explosives. Despite the contradictions, the treaty's provisions lent themselves to an interpretation that was satisfactory to the United States. Under this interpretation, with which a majority of Latin American nations agreed, until nuclear explosives for peaceful purposes could be developed that had characteristics making them unsuitable for military use, there could be peaceful nuclear explosions in Latin America only when carried out on a service basis by an existing nuclear-weapon state. Brazil and Argentina demurred from this interpretation of the treaty, stubbornly insisting on the technically invalid position that there already were fundamental differences between peaceful nuclear explosives and nuclear weapons.

This controversy was to be carried over into subsequent debates on the Nonproliferation Treaty (see chapter 27).

Last Craters

The successful detonation of CABRIOLET on January 26, 1968, set the stage for the execution of two other cratering experiments during that year. In neither case was there major opposition from within the government. BUGGY went off on March 12. It involved the simultaneous detonation of five low-yield (about 1 kiloton) nuclear explosives in a row. It created a ditch-like crater 860 feet long, 280 feet wide, and 68 feet deep. As with CABRIOLET, the explosion was set off in hard rock, the medium most likely to be encountered in a trans-Isthmian canal. Again there were no problems of radiation crossing the border. (After seeing a film of BUGGY, I commented somewhat testily in my diary: "This and CABRIOLET should have been approved for execution long ago.")

On December 8, 1968, SCHOONER was successfully detonated at the Nevada Test Site, creating a crater 850 feet in diameter and over 240 feet deep. Its purpose was to extend cratering technology in hard rock to encompass higher yields, approaching those that would be required for actual construction of a canal. (SCHOONER's yield was 300 kilotons, as compared to CABRIOLET's 2.7.) It released in the atmosphere the highest levels of radioactivity recorded in the United States since the test ban treaty. The radioactive debris seemed to stay well within U.S. borders, however; there appeared to be no question of a treaty violation. What was our astonishment, then, when on January 21, 1969, the first full day of the Nixon administration, the Soviet chargé d'affaires in Washington delivered an aide-mémoire stating that SCHOONER had caused a "two to fivefold increase in fallout in the regions along the Baltic, Volga, Northern Caucasus, and Crimea." The following day I explained to Nixon assistant Robert F. Ellsworth that this corresponded to an absurdly small amount of radioactivity.

> I said that if their techniques were similar to ours, involving the passage of large amounts of air through filter papers, followed by chemical identification of products, the background against which they were measuring the "two to fivefold increase" probably corresponded to something like 0.1 picocurie of radiation per cubic meter of air. I said that this illustrated the absurdity of interpreting the test ban treaty as forbidding such infinitesimal amounts of radioactivity.

I then portrayed for Ellsworth the situation of the Plowshare program as we saw it. It was an attempt on my part to gain the new administration's sympathetic support. Although President Nixon himself later indicated that he had a special prejudice in favor of Plowshare, time was running out. Completion of BUGGY and SCHOONER still left the AEC's cratering program far behind what was required by the Canal Study Commission for its report to Congress. This was evident in a letter I received from CSC Chairman Anderson on August 23, 1968. He noted that the CSC had twice asked Congress for an extension of its study time, originally set to end June 30, 1968. Their "final reporting date" was now December 1, 1970. It was the commission's intention to render a report on that date "with or without a final determination of the feasibility of nuclear excavation." The need for a decision on U.S. canal policy would not permit further postponement. In order to meet the CSC's schedule the AEC would have to bunch the three remaining projects in its experimental program into one fiscal year, and this at a time of budget retrenchment. Anderson was aware that this would be very difficult to accomplish; he urged us, nevertheless, to do our best.

As it developed, we were unable, despite President Nixon's favorable prejudice, to obtain administration approval for even one further cratering experiment. I reported this to the CSC late in 1969, and added a final despairing argument:

> [I]t is our view that, given the authorization and funds, the problems regarding technical feasibility can be solved within a relatively short time. Each step we have taken . . . has resulted in lowering the potential risk involved. . . . [O]ur increased understanding of the cratering mechanisms has increased our belief in the potential benefits of this undertaking for mankind. . . . We believe that if for any reason a decision to construct an interoceanic canal is delayed beyond the next several years, nuclear technology might . . . provide a realistic option.

But the CSC had given up. In a report to President Nixon on December 1, 1970, it effectively closed the book on a nuclear-excavated canal, with these words:

> One provision of the law required us to determine the practicability of nuclear canal excavation. Unfortunately, neither the technical feasibility nor the international acceptability of such an application of nuclear excavation technology has been established to date. It is not possible to foresee the future progress of the technology or to determine when international agreements can be effectuated that would permit its use in the construction of an interoceanic canal. Hence, although we are confident that some day nuclear explosions will be used in a wide variety of massive earthmoving projects, no current decision on U.S. canal policy should be made in the expectation that nuclear explosive technology will be available for the construction.[2]

Obiter Dicta

The demise of nuclear excavation was a heavy blow to the Plowshare program, whose hopes for the future rested so heavily on the foreseen opportunities to perform excavation projects as a service for other nations. I would not wish to leave the impression that the delays or denials of CABRIOLET and other experiments bore sole responsibility for this unhappy denouement. Without doubt they hastened the outcome, but there were some serious objections to nuclear excavation that might well have prevailed in any case.

The original attraction of the technology was based to a large extent on cost estimates that showed nuclear means of excavation as having an enormous economic advantage over conventional methods. The advantage rested principally on the amount of energy released per unit weight of explosive. Nuclear explosives gave truly a "bigger bang for a buck." As of 1970, it was estimated that ten kilotons of TNT would cost almost fifteen times as much as an equivalent thermonuclear explosive. At the two-megaton level the cost of TNT was about seventeen hundred times greater. (The cost of a nuclear explosive increases very little with its yield.) Another important factor in the cost comparisons was that the Plowshare program was given virtually a "free ride" insofar as research and development costs were concerned. Such costs—and they were huge—were virtually all charged to the weapons program. This applied not only to the "R&D" costs of developing the explosive. Also involved was the fact that much of the data used by Plowshare scientists to sketch out the phenomenology of peaceful explosions was provided by underground weapons tests.

Another advantage of nuclear excavation was speed. The job could be accomplished in a fraction of the time required by alternative methods and would thus avoid many of the dangers that had contributed to the more than six thousand deaths sustained during the thirty years of construction on the Panama Canal. (One should, of course, recognize that many of those deaths had been from yellow fever and malaria.) It also seemed possible to complete with nuclear explosives some projects that could not be accomplished at all by conventional means—the digging of a harbor on the remote northwest coast of Australia, to give one example.

It was these advantages that motivated us in the AEC to pursue the nuclear excavation experimental program so tenaciously—we truly believed that the program could lead to enormous and otherwise unobtainable benefits for mankind. The opportunity to turn the menacing technology of nuclear explosions into something so beneficial was irresistible, especially for those of us who had worked in the wartime atomic bomb project.

The lure of the program perhaps made us less than completely objective in weighing the arguments against nuclear excavation. We have already noted the diplomatic argument advanced within the administration—that cratering explosions, even on an experimental level, could lead to accusations that the United States had violated the Limited Test Ban Treaty. We never succeeded in putting this problem to rest.

Then, there was the matter of the cost estimates, which had seemed so favorable. As of 1960 it was estimated that a nuclear interoceanic canal would cost only one-third as much as one dug conventionally. When similar estimates were made ten years later, however, the best nuclear route was estimated to cost $200 million *more* than the best conventional route. The difference in the two sets of estimates lay almost entirely in the costs of the nuclear alternative—they had skyrocketed, basically because cost factors overlooked in the first estimates began to be taken into consideration.[3] For example, there would be the costs—political and social as well as economic—of evacuating forty-three thousand inhabitants, for as long as a year during construction, from a sparsely inhabited area of sixty-five hundred square miles along the canal's path.[4] In order to operate the new canal, there would be costs for new towns; for high-level bridges or canals; for harbors, piers, and warehouses; for security personnel and their housing. (A conventionally built alternative would escape many of these costs because its route would presumably lie alongside that of the existing canal.) Also, if the existing canal were to be abandoned, that part of Panama that depended on it would suffer economic and political consequences that could not be ignored.[5]

Noneconomic problems also abounded and some of these might have been insuperable. It was estimated that three hundred nuclear explosions aggregating 200 megatons in explosive power—twenty times as much as had been expended in all previous wars—would have been necessary for nuclear excavation of a sea-level canal.[6] The potential for blast damage and radiation from explosions of such magnitude was sobering indeed. Fear was also expressed that the aftershocks caused by a big explosion might trigger a major earthquake. Most competent geologists considered this risk to be extremely small, but there could be no absolute assurance. Added to all the other difficulties was a warning from biologists: A sea-level canal ran the risk of doing serious damage to aquatic life by mixing Atlantic and Pacific species.[7]

In the final analysis it was radiation that aroused the greatest concern. Although we in the AEC were confident that this hazard could be controlled, it weighed so heavily on many minds that there was grave doubt a majority of the parties to the Limited Test Ban Treaty would ever have approved amending the treaty to permit the canal project to go forward.

All these factors together cast such a pall of uncertainty and concern that the U.S. nuclear excavation program would probably have been doomed even if CABRIOLET and its follow-on experiments had been approved and had taken place on schedule.

Extracting Natural Gas

Before we consign the U.S. Plowshare program to its place in history, we should consider briefly another application to which considerable importance was attached at one time. This was the use of nuclear explosions to release natural gas trapped in relatively impermeable rock strata far beneath the surface. A nuclear device was thought able to fracture the rock formations, thereby freeing the gas so that it would flow into accessible wells. Attention focused on this application in the late 1960s because natural gas, a very clean, hence desirable, fuel, appeared to be diminishing in supply and was rapidly increasing in cost.*

In 1965, the El Paso Natural Gas Company proposed a cooperative project with the AEC and the Interior Department to examine the phenomena involved in the use of nuclear explosions to recover gas. An experimental explosion, called GASBUGGY, took place on December 12, 1967, on one of the company's leases in New Mexico. It involved a 29-kiloton explosive buried at a depth of 4,240 feet. (There had been little difficulty gaining approval from the 269 Committee since the explosion would be fully contained—there was virtually no possibility that escaped radioactivity would cause accusations of a treaty violation.)

GASBUGGY seemed highly successful. A rate of production several times greater than that of neighboring wells was achieved, although, because the gas was slightly radioactive, none of it was sold commercially. A second experiment, equally successful, followed in September 1969. Its purpose was to extend GASBUGGY experience to greater depths and different types of rocks. Named RULISON, this

---

*It was predicted by the *Oil and Gas Journal* that, if conventional production methods were continued, U.S. gas reserves would not be able to meet demands after 1974 (AEC Annual Report for 1969, p. 200). This estimate was, of course, grossly in error. The outlook for natural gas supply in the United States today is much more favorable.

second experiment involved explosion of a nuclear device more than eight thousand feet deep near Grand Valley, Colorado. The industrial sponsor in this case was the Austral Oil Company. Resulting natural gas production was copious. Amounts of radioactivity in the gas were very small but there was some and, again, none of the gas was sold commercially. A third experiment, RIO BLANCO, was held in 1973 in Colorado. It was considered a failure because the chimneys formed by the three vertically stacked nuclear explosives failed to link up as planned.

Despite early successes, the gas stimulation application soon faded from the scene. A prime reason was the concern about radioactivity in the gas, however modest the amounts. Popular apprehensions were reflected in an amendment to the Colorado state constitution requiring a referendum on each further nuclear explosion proposed to take place in that state. And finally, with the passage of time, the focus of attention in energy matters shifted to various nonnuclear technologies. As explained by a U.S. representative, A. J. Hodges, at an IAEA technical committee meeting in November 1976:

> In the U.S.A. research into energy sources such as solar, geothermal, fusion, and synthetic coal-derived fuels is receiving increased government attention and support. Industrial companies have found that much of their available capital and technical effort is required in shorter-range extraction, conversion, and exploration technologies. These developments, together with the increasing world-wide awareness of the importance of the environment, have favoured the extension of conventional technologies over the potential use of nuclear explosions for peaceful purposes.

RIO BLANCO proved to be the last Plowshare explosion. Following it, Plowshare in all its manifestations gradually disappeared from the AEC budget. (In 1957 the amount budgeted for Plowshare was over $150 million; in 1970, approximately $13.7 million; in 1973, $7 million; in 1977, $1 million; in 1978, almost nothing.) In total the United States conducted forty-one Plowshare explosions. Most were conducted in the years 1962 to 1968. During each of these years there were four or more tests. Thereafter, the program dwindled rapidly. There were only two explosions in 1969, one in 1970, one in 1973, and none since.[8] By 1979, Dr. Gerald Johnson, erstwhile Plowshare chief at Livermore, was quoted as saying that he was "firmly convinced that PNEs have no practical economic utility in the United States now, or in the foreseeable future."[9]

The Soviet Program

The Soviet Union's PNE program began later than that of the United States. They did not begin their testing program until 1968 but proceeded with vigor thereafter. Their early projects included:

Construction of a water reservoir in a dry riverbed for storing heavy spring runoff.

Stimulation of oil recovery from a geologic formation that had been previously depleted.

Snuffing out of runaway oil and gas fires when they could not be controlled by ordinary means (two projects).[10]

In contrast to U.S. abandonment of Plowshare, the Soviet Union has continued a relatively vigorous PNE program, having conducted some seventy explosions between 1973 and mid-1986. As late as August 1983, Yevgeniy G. Zhvakin, scientific attaché at the Soviet Embassy in Washington, emphasized to me in conversation that the Soviet Union considered PNEs to have considerable future importance.

The majority of the peaceful explosions the USSR has conducted have been in salt formations near petroleum supplies, the purpose being to create storage for condensed gas or liquid hydrocarbons. Explosions of this type often have been conducted consecutively, in clusters of as many as six to eight, with individual yields of about 20 kilotons. Other purposes for which the Soviets have conducted PNEs have been to stimulate oil and gas recovery and to create cavities for the disposal of oil field wastes. Still another use has been for deep seismic sounding. In this application explosions are conducted at great depths and about five hundred kilometers apart in order to obtain information about the earth. There have been about ten explosions for this purpose. In the early 1970s the USSR announced at the IAEA the commercial availability of their method of using nuclear explosions to extinguish gas well fires. I am not aware that anyone has taken advantage of this service as yet.[11]

The contrasting attitudes adopted by the United States and the USSR in recent years toward peaceful nuclear explosions represent an unusual divergence in their approaches to an aspect of nuclear technology. Several explanations for this come to mind. One is that the Soviets have the advantage of a wider territory over which to disperse radioactivity and therefore need have less concern about violating the Limited Test Ban Treaty. They also, until recently at least, have had a population less sensitized to fear of radiation than ours, and one not given to protesting government activities. Thus, there may have been less concern about utilizing oil or gas slightly contaminated with radioactivity. Finally, the economics of natural resource industries in the USSR may be quite different than in the United States.

Two recent events may alter the approach of the USSR toward continued use of peaceful nuclear explosions. First, the Chernobyl accident in April 1986 may cause attitudes toward radioactivity in the Soviet Union to become more like those in the United States, thus inhibiting certain PNE applications. Secondly, as of the end of 1986, the Soviets had conducted no peaceful nuclear explosions since Chairman Gorbachev announced a unilateral moratorium on nuclear tests in August 1985. This is an indication that the Soviets would make no attempt to retain their PNE program should there be a comprehensive test ban, as advocated by the Soviet regime and the overwhelming majority of other governments throughout the world.

Notes

1. For some of the discussion in this subsection I am indebted to the account in Richard L. Williamson's Ph.D. dissertation, "Peaceful Nuclear Explosions: Implications for Arms Control," American University, 1976.
2. *Report of the Atlantic–Pacific Interoceanic Canal Study Commission,* 1970, vol. 1, p. 1.
3. Williamson, "PNE's: Implications for Arms Control," p. 31.
4. Ibid., p. 30.
5. Stratton, "Sea-Level Canal: How and Where?," pp. 514ff.
6. Inglis and Sandler, "Non-Military Uses of Nuclear Explosives."
7. Ibid., p. 47.
8. Williamson, "PNE's," p. 14f.
9. York and Greb, "The Comprehensive Test Ban," p. 29.
10. Seaborg and Corliss, *Man and Atom,* p. 190f.
11. Much of the information in this paragraph derives from a telephone conversation with Milo Nordyke of Livermore Labortory, June 13, 1986.

Part VIII

The NPT:
A Shaky Start

I consider this treaty to be the most important
international agreement limiting nuclear arms
since the nuclear age began. It is a triumph of
sanity and of man's will to survive.

Lyndon B. Johnson, July 9, 1968
(letter transmitting NPT to the Senate)

27
Rounding Out the Treaty

What benefit is non-proliferation today if we anyway have to face holocaust?

—Alva Myrdal
1966

A New Cleavage

The first three articles of the draft nonproliferation treaty (Articles I
and II setting out the basic obligations of nuclear-weapon states not
to transfer, and nonweapon states not to acquire, nuclear weapons;
and Article III prescribing safeguards) pretty well encompassed what
the United States and the Soviet Union hoped the final treaty would
be. These articles would not have restrained either nation from doing
anything it had seriously contemplated.

The superpowers might have thought that, once they reached
agreement on the articles of importance to themselves, they could
easily win acceptance from other nations. That, after all, was the way
things had gone with the Limited Test Ban Treaty. In the case of the
Nonproliferation Treaty, however, matters would take a different turn.
The nonnuclear countries were not about to accept without resistance
a pact that they believed to be highly discriminatory against them.
Through the latter part of 1966 and all of 1967 international debate
on the treaty was therefore dominated by efforts of nonweapon countries* to obtain some redress of what they considered the imbalance
in the superpowers' proposals. These efforts were accompanied by an

---

*A note on semantics. From time to time herein I, and others cited, refer to "nonnuclear" or
"nonweapon" countries or states or powers. Purists will be quick to point out that this is not
strictly accurate. Almost all of these countries had some nuclear activities so they were not, strictly
speaking, "nonnuclear." Similarly, they all had weapons of some sort, so the term "nonweapon" does not literally apply. The technically correct designation, used in the Nonproliferation
Treaty and other formal documents, was "non-nuclear-weapon" country or state or power.
This has seemed to me and others a little too cumbersome for repetitive use; hence, our inexact
abbreviations.

outpouring of resentment and bitterness so exceptional as to reflect what one scholar described as "a new cleavage in the international system."[1] Whereas the system had previously been divided into military blocs built along ideological lines, it now seemed to be splitting into nuclear weapon "haves" and "have-nots." In this new situation the United States and the Soviet Union found themselves in unaccustomed alliance as they sought to fend off the demands of the non-weapon countries.

To some extent what the nonnuclear countries gave vent to in their pronouncements seemed like an unfocused expression of indignation. Some of them resented particularly the implication, referred to by the Nigerian delegate to the ENDC, "that the desire of hitherto non-nuclear states to acquire nuclear weapons is only a matter of prestige."[2] On the contrary, they wished it known that they had legitimate fears that needed to be addressed in any treaty. This being the case, they resisted what India's Trivedi described as "the unrealistic and irrational proposition that a non-proliferation treaty should impose obligations only on non-nuclear countries, while the nuclear Powers continue to hold on to their privileged status or club membership by retaining and even increasing their deadly stockpiles."* The French defense minister, Messmer, sympathizing with the non-nuclears, characterized the treaty as an attempt "to castrate the impotent."[3]

The complaints of the nonweapon countries emanated from all points on the political compass. From within NATO came the comment of Italian Foreign Minister Fanfani that the nuclear powers wanted to deal only with "the limited problem of future proliferation" but not with "the extremely serious and urgent problem of those who have exploded nuclear devices." Fanfani's criticism was echoed by the Federal Republic of Germany. Though not a member of the ENDC, the FRG found repeated occasion to argue that the treaty would impose restrictions only on the countries without nuclear weapons and that "more comprehensive solutions" were needed. Most surprising of all, Romania split with the rest of the Soviet bloc, threatening not to sign the proposed treaty unless the nuclear powers ceased all testing and undertook complete nuclear disarmament.

---

*Trivedi had a marvellous linguistic gift. He apparently was aware of it, for the story is told that on one occasion he corrected the grammar of the U.K. representative at a meeting of the IAEA Board of Governors. Trivedi and Sweden's Alva Myrdal were probably the most eloquent spokesmen for the non-weapon countries.

The most vehement and insistent critics of the "naked" treaty proposed by the superpowers were found among the nonaligned nations. The record of the ENDC from mid-1966 to mid-1968 teems with their bitter complaints. Alva Myrdal, in a paper written for a London symposium, expressed a prevailing view:

> The non-aligned nations . . . strongly believe that disarmament measures should be a matter of mutual renunciation. Therefore, they have refused to subscribe to the judgment that the most urgent disarmament measure in our time is an international treaty merely on non-proliferation, which would leave the present five nuclear-weapon parties free to continue to build up their arsenals. . . .

The nonnuclear nations referred repeatedly to the UN General Assembly's Resolution 2028 of November 19, 1965, which instructed the ENDC to follow five main principles in negotiating a nonproliferation treaty. They emphasized particulary the second and third principles, which read as follows:

> (b) The treaty should embody an acceptable balance of mutual responsibilities and obligations of the nuclear and non-nuclear Powers;
> (c) The treaty should be a step towards the achievement of general and complete disarmament and, more particularly, nuclear disarmament; . . . *

In pressing their criticisms and demands, the nonweapon countries focused on particular gaps in the early treaty drafts of the superpowers. To remedy these deficiencies they sought certain specific assurances. These related to:

> Their right to pursue peaceful nuclear activity without fear of discrimination or competitive disadvantage.

---

*The remaining three principles were:
(a) The treaty should be void of any loop-holes which might permit nuclear or non-nuclear Powers to proliferate, directly or indirectly, nuclear weapons in any form;
(d) There should be acceptable and workable provisions to ensure the effectiveness of the treaty;
(e) Nothing in the treaty should adversely affect the right of any group of States to conclude regional treaties in order to ensure the total absence of nuclear weapons in their respective territories.

Their right to develop and detonate nuclear explosives for peaceful purposes.

Their right to expect that the superpowers would requite the non-nuclears' sacrifice by agreeing on certain arms control and disarmament measures for themselves, or that they would at least negotiate vigorously and in good faith toward such ends.

These sought-after assurances provided the bases for Articles IV, V, and VI, respectively, of the final Nonproliferation Treaty.

Article IV: Technical Assistance

A primary concern of certain nuclear have-nots was that a nonproliferation treaty not stifle their opportunity to pursue such peaceful nonexplosive nuclear applications as the use of nuclear reactors to produce electricity and the use of radioisotopes and radiation in medicine, agriculture, industry, and research.

Perhaps the most vehement expressions along these lines emanated from West Germany. Having experienced a near-miraculous recovery from the ravages of World War II, to the point where its industrial output ranked third in the world, the Federal Republic had great ambitions for its budding nuclear industry. Contributing to German disquiet was an abiding suspicion that the United States was putting its common interests with the Soviet Union in gaining an NPT above the common interests of the Western alliance.[4] This suspicion had been stimulated by the manner in which the test ban had been negotiated "at the summit" in Moscow, sidestepping the established multilateral forum for test ban negotiations.[5] George McGhee, who was U.S. ambassador to Bonn during the Johnson years, has noted that there was a widely held view in Germany that we had made a secret deal with the Soviets about the NPT: "They'd help us in Vietnam if we could get Germany to sign the Treaty." McGhee acknowledges that we probably did not keep the Germans adequately informed about our negotiations with the Soviets about the NPT. His explanation was that "there was nothing really to discuss [with our allies] until the Russians indicated they were willing to make concessions, which they hadn't previously. As soon as the Russians gave this indication, then we did talk with the allies." He might have added that these negotiations were so secret that organs of the United States government—including the AEC—sometimes did not know what was occurring.[6]

West German antagonism to a nonproliferation treaty found expression, often exaggerated, in internal political debate. In February 1967, former Chancellor Konrad Adenauer referred to the NPT as "a Morgenthau plan raised to the 2nd power."* A month later, Adenauer declared that if Germany adhered to such a treaty it would be signing its own death warrant.[7] Finance Minister Franz Josef Strauss, a powerful right-wing leader, said that an NPT would be a "super-Versailles" for Germany and threatened to resign if Germany signed. German resistance was stiffened by Russian threats. On February 9, 1967, Chairman Kosygin said at a press conference in London that the Federal Republic would "have to join the agreement on nonproliferation whether it wants to or not." He then added a grim warning: "We will not allow the Federal Republic of Germany to have nuclear weapons and we will take all measures to prevent it getting nuclear weapons. We say it with utter resolution." A week later Chancellor Kiesinger said in a television interview:

> We have been addressed very rudely by Mr. Kosygin. I have replied that whether we sign such a treaty depends only on our own sensibility and conscience. . . . There are very important problems. For example, we must not be hindered in the peaceful use of nuclear energy. Neither our research nor the benefit which our economy derives from such peaceful development of nuclear energy must be obstructed.[8]

Addressing the Bundestag, Foreign Minister Willy Brandt emphasized that the West German government and others were seeking to ensure that the NPT did not "further widen the already existing technical gap between the nuclear powers and the non-nuclear countries."

(Stated West German objections to the NPT, whether focusing on having to renounce the MLF; or, later, on dangers of industrial espionage in safeguards inspections; or, still later, on competitive disadvantages in peaceful activities, were all in some degree rationalizations for a reluctance to formally forswear the possibility of ever acquiring nuclear weapons. This concern, felt particularly by

---

*During World War II, U.S. Secretary of the Treasury Henry Morgenthau, Jr., had proposed a postwar settlement that would have eliminated most of Germany's heavy industries, making it primarily an agricultural country.

politicians of the right, but really quite general among West German politicians, did not seem at any time to be widely shared by the population. The various objections to the NPT advanced by West Germany were given added weight by the Soviet Union's intention— sometimes expressed, sometimes implied—to ratify the NPT only when the Federal Republic did so.)

A principal German argument was that knowledge gained through the research, development, and production of nuclear weapons would be applicable also to peaceful endeavors and would confer on the nuclear-weapons powers industrial and commercial advantages vis-à-vis Germany. Brandt discussed this question with the president and others during a visit to Washington on February 18, 1967, and apparently received strong assurances. Following these conversations, Secretary Rusk said at a news conference that the actual industrial spin-off from weapons programs was "infinitesimal." Three days later President Johnson added further reassurances in his message to the reconvening ENDC. The president said:

> A nonproliferation treaty must be equitable as between the nuclear and the non-nuclear-weapon countries. . . . I have instructed our negotiators to exercise the greatest care that the treaty not hinder the non-nuclear powers in the development of nuclear energy for peaceful purposes. . . . [W]e recommend that the treaty clearly state the intention of its signatories to make available the full benefits of peaceful nuclear technology—including any benefits that are the by-product of weapons research.[9]

Following these exchanges, the matter of weapons "spin-off" ceased to be a major issue in the treaty negotiations. There remained, however, a need to find appropriate treaty language for the principle of nondiscrimination enunciated by the president. Here the lead was taken by Alfonso García Robles, Mexican under secretary for foreign affairs. In suggesting language for the NPT, García Robles borrowed from the recently concluded Treaty for Prohibition of Nuclear Weapons in Latin America, in whose negotiation he had played the foremost role.* In March 1967 García Robles proposed at the ENDC that the NPT contain an Article IV conveying assurances about peaceful uses. The language he put forward formed the basis for that

---

*In 1982 Garcia Robles would share the Nobel Peace Prize with Alva Myrdal.

adopted in the identical Soviet and U.S. drafts of August 24, 1967, in which Article IV read as follows:

> Nothing in this Treaty shall be interpreted as affecting the inalienable right of all the Parties to the Treaty to develop research, production and use of nuclear energy for peaceful purposes without discrimination and in conformity with Articles I and II of this Treaty, as well as the right of the parties to participate in the fullest possible exchange of information for, and to contribute alone or in cooperation with other States to, the further development of the applications of nuclear energy for peaceful purposes.

When this language was proposed initially, there was some concern within the AEC about the import of the words "fullest possible exchange of information," the more so as a subsequent amendment expanded them into a more comprehensive "fullest possible exchange of equipment, materials and scientific and technological information." By some interpretations the language seemed to imply an almost unlimited obligation. This impression was reinforced by a speech that Ambassador Goldberg made in the General Assembly at about this time in which he said in effect that the United States would make available all its information and technology to any non-nuclear-weapon state that joined the treaty. This speech, which neither the AEC nor the ACDA had had an opportunity to review, promised far more than was legally or politically realistic. For example, the AEC wanted to insure that no one would interpret Article IV as implying an increased obligation on our part to disseminate uranium enrichment technology, whether of the gaseous diffusion or the centrifuge variety. To bring expectations into accord with reality, therefore, the AEC persuaded the State Department to instruct the U.S. delegation to the UN that the draft Article IV would not "override the Atomic Energy Act, contravene existing U.S. export policies, . . . oblige U.S. to meet all requests and demands, or remove all discretion as to the nature of our cooperation and the parties with whom we deal."

When these clarifications were made known at the UN and the ENDC, the limitations of the draft Article IV became apparent to the nonnuclear countries, and they began to press for more significant concessions. Mexico now proposed language that would make it a positive *duty* for the nuclear-weapon parties to aid the nonweapon parties in their development of peaceful applications. The Mexican justification of this startling proposition included the following:

We believe that if, as a contribution to international peace and security, the non-nuclear powers renounce for all time certain activities and experiments which, but for the Treaty, they might carry
out, it is only fair that they should receive in return as their authentic
right any scientific and technological benefits derived from the experiments and activities they renounce.[10]

Both the UAR and Sweden agreed with the Mexican approach.
Italy went even further. On August 1, 1967, Foreign Minister Fanfani
suggested an agreement "under which the nuclear Powers would
transmit periodically to the non-nuclear States signatories to the treaty
an agreed quantity of the fissile materials they produce." Under Fanfani's concept the material would be supplied at less than market
price.[11]

Though all were willing to concede that the basic obligations imposed by Articles I and II were discriminatory against the nonweapon
countries, it now began to appear that some of the Article IV proposals being put forward to redress the balance were themselves excessive. The Italian proposal, in particular, received scant
consideration. The Mexican concept of "duty," while greeted with
sympathy, was nevertheless declared by several Western representatives, including Fisher, to be too sweeping. A compromise was forged,
however, whereby the identical U.S. and Soviet drafts of January 18,
1968 retained the August 1967 formulation of Article IV and then
added the following:

Parties to the Treaty in a position to do so shall also cooperate in
contributing alone or together with other States or international organizations to the further development of the applications of nuclear
energy for peaceful purposes, especially in the territories of non-
nuclear weapons States Party to the Treaty.

This new sentence clearly deepened the obligation to provide assistance. And it did something else. As Mason Willrich has pointed
out,[12] the phrase "parties in a position to do so" introduced a new
category of *contributing states,* broader than the previous "nuclear-
weapon states." The phrase was never defined, but it presumably
included not only nuclear-weapon states but also nonweapon states
advanced in nuclear technology, such as Canada and West Germany.
Recipient nations, on the other hand, continued to be defined as "non-

nuclear-weapon States," a category that also included Canada and West Germany. This was, at the least, confusing.

The confusion did not last long. As finishing touches were placed on the treaty at the UN, the powerful numerical presence of the Third World in that body was brought to bear, and when the treaty emerged in its final form on May 31, 1968, some all-important words had been added to Article IV. Those to whom contributing states were to contribute were now described as "non-nuclear-weapon States Party to the Treaty, *with due consideration for the needs of the developing nations of the world*" (emphasis added).

Thus, Article IV had veered significantly from its original intent, which had been to assuage the concerns about discrimination felt by technically advanced nonweapon countries like West Germany. As it emerged finally, the article had become an instrument obligating developed nations to provide technical assistance in the peaceful uses of atomic energy to less developed ones. At this point, one might conclude that the ransom being exacted by the nonnuclear nations for their adherence to the NPT was getting a bit out of hand. Nations for whom the nuclear weapons option had never existed and who therefore were giving up nothing were being given a claim on potential benefits of the peaceful atom.[13]

The implementation of Article IV has in large part devolved upon the International Atomic Energy Agency. The agency administers a technical assistance program funded by voluntary contributions from member states. By contrast, support of safeguards, the IAEA's other major responsibility, is funded from a "regular" budget for which member states are assessed proportional shares. Some developing countries have argued in the past that these funding arrangements place the technical assistance program at a disadvantage. Others, however, point to the fact that IAEA expenditures for technical assistance have been growing step-by-step with those for safeguards. Moreover, since 1981, contributions to the technical assistance budget have been guided by indicative planning figures that the contributing nations are meeting. This procedure seems to assure that the technical assistance budget will continue to keep pace with that for safeguards.

Another controversy about technical assistance has concerned the fact that the IAEA may not under its charter discriminate in its direct grant of funds between those who have signed the NPT and those who have not, even though Article IV specifies that there should be such preference given. On the other hand, the United States and other advanced countries can and do give preference to parties to the treaty when they support through contributions in kind (materials, equipment, services of experts, and fellowships) so-called footnote a. projects, namely, meritorious projects not financed by the IAEA because of insufficient funds but declared by the agency's staff to have technical merit.[14]

Article V: Peaceful Nuclear Explosions

In the U.S. nonproliferation treaty draft of August 17, 1965, and the March 21, 1966 amendments thereto, the main prohibitions (Article I and II) referred to "nuclear weapons." Non-nuclear-weapon states would not manufacture or receive them; nuclear-weapon states would not transfer them. Another article of the draft treaty provided a paragraph for a definition of "nuclear weapons," but left it blank. A definition could not be supplied largely because there was a disagreement within the U.S. government on how to handle peaceful nuclear explosions. Predictably, the disputants were the ACDA and the AEC, and the issue was the survival of Plowshare. The ACDA wanted to define nuclear weapons as including all nuclear explosives, whatever their purpose, thereby blanketing both weapons and peaceful explosives in the prohibitions of Articles I and II. The AEC wanted peaceful explosives to be dealt with separately. We proposed (1) that the prohibitions of Articles I and II apply to "nuclear weapons and other nuclear explosives," and (2) that there then be a separate article dealing with the "other nuclear explosives," one that would permit nuclear weapons states, without transferring custody of the explosives, to provide a PNE service for other states. (As mentioned earlier, we felt that the future of the Plowshare program rested on our ability to carry out such an international service.)

In this instance AEC's position prevailed within the administration and, on June 30, 1966, an informal memo was sent to the Soviet delegation at the ENDC to ascertain their attitude toward providing for a peaceful nuclear explosions service in the Nonproliferation Treaty. Little came of this probe, but at least it did not provoke an openly hostile reaction. (Sometimes in dealing with the Soviets no reaction is a good reaction.) Accordingly, on August 9, Adrian Fisher formally presented the U.S. proposal to the ENDC.

Immediate reaction in Geneva was sparse and mixed. Canada endorsed the suggestion on August 25 and announced that it would not seek to develop its own peaceful nuclear explosives. India and Brazil, however, continued to hold out for the right of each nation to conduct its own PNEs.

The United States expanded on its concept of an international peaceful nuclear explosions service in March 1967, when Foster presented to the ENDC five principles which, in the U.S. view, should guide this activity. These had been worked out primarily by AEC staff. Most significant were the following:

> Service should be provided under appropriate international observation but the explosive should remain in the custody of the nuclear-weapon state performing the service.

> Means should be provided for nonnuclear states to request the service through an international body.

> Costs should be kept as low as possible and in any case should not include the costs of research and development.*

The identical U.S. and Soviet draft treaties of August 24, 1967, gave effect to the U.S. position on peaceful explosives in two ways. Articles I and II precluded the transfer and acquisition of "nuclear weapons *or other nuclear explosive devices.*" In addition, the principles espoused by the U.S. in March 1967 were stated in a paragraph in the draft treaties' Preamble.

In ensuing sessions of the ENDC a controversy arose about why statement of these principles was confined to the Preamble. The British opposed any change in this respect on the basis that having an article about peaceful explosives in the body of the treaty might provide a loophole that could undermine its stability. This argument was not strong enough, however, to withstand the general tide of revolt that was sweeping the ENDC in 1967. Consequently, the revised U.S. and Soviet drafts of January 18, 1968, contained a new Article V that, using virtually the same words, converted the previous pream-

---

*The remaining principles were:
There should be full consultation among nuclear and nonnuclear parties to the Limited Test Ban Treaty about any amendment to that treaty necessary to carry out feasible projects.
The conditions and procedures for international collaboration in accomplishing PNE projects should be developed in full consultation with non-nuclear-weapon states.

bular statement of principle into a binding obligation. After some further amendment in May 1968, the final text of Article V read as follows:

> Each Party to the Treaty undertakes to take appropriate measures to ensure that, in accordance with this Treaty, under appropriate international observation and through appropriate international procedures, potential benefits from any peaceful applications of nuclear explosions will be made available to non-nuclear-weapon States Party to the Treaty on a non-discriminatory basis and that the charge to such Parties for the explosive devices used will be as low as possible and exclude any charge for research and development. Non-nuclear-weapon States Party to the Treaty shall be able to obtain such benefits, pursuant to a special international agreement or agreements, through an appropriate international body with adequate representation of non-nuclear-weapon States. Negotiations on this subject shall commence as soon as possible after the Treaty enters into force. Non-nuclear-weapon States Party to the Treaty so desiring may also obtain such benefits pursuant to bilateral agreements.

The last sentence in the article, regarding the possibility of bilateral arrangements, resulted from strong U.S. representations instigated by the AEC. Our argument was that, in order to preserve the viability of such Plowshare projects as the Panama Canal, we must not be saddled with the need to await multilateral approval of each undertaking. The bilateral option was resisted at first by Sweden's Alva Myrdal, who felt that PNE projects should proceed only under international auspices. She eventually relented when assured by the United States that, even when conducted under bilateral arrangements, such projects would be subject to international observation. (In November 1970, a few months after the NPT entered into force, negotiations were carried out and a paper was developed at the IAEA on the nature and terms of such "international observation.")

Article VI: Disarmament

What the rebellious nonnuclear nations sought most clamorously in the Nonproliferation Treaty was some pledge that the superpowers would take steps to bring a halt to their bilateral nuclear arms race, recognized generally as a threat to all nations. In May 1965 Sweden became the fourth member of the ENDC, following Canada, India, and the UAR, to suggest that any agreement to halt the spread of nuclear weapons must be linked to an agreement by the nuclear-weapon powers to stop weapons production. In September the neutral Eight at the ENDC joined in a declaration that "measures to prohibit the spread of nuclear weapons should . . . be coupled with or followed by tangible steps to halt the nuclear arms race and to limit, reduce, and eliminate the stocks of nuclear weapons and the means of their delivery." The Eight reaffirmed this position in another memorandum the following August. Alva Myrdal of Sweden expressed the nonnuclears' impatience on this subject most aptly when she asked: "What help is non-proliferation today if we anyway have to face holocaust?"

The superpowers seemed startled by the vehemence of these expressions by the nonweapon states. Secretary Rusk acknowledged as much in these words during his Senate testimony on the Pastore Resolution in February 1966:

> I would say, Mr. Chairman, that the interest on the part of the non-nuclear states as registered in the last few months is, surprisingly, not so much aimed at the question of assurances and guarantees as it is aimed at a clear demonstration that those who have nuclear weapons are proceeding on a path of disarmament.

Within the administration it was Robert McNamara who seemed most sympathetic to the point of view of the nonnuclears. Speaking in March 1966, he said: "Since the Nonproliferation Treaty is essentially an act of self-denial on the part of potential nuclear states, we cannot expect [them] to accept these restraints upon themselves unless we take steps . . . ; we too must be willing to accept both restraints and obligations." But McNamara's was neither the prevailing nor the official American view. At the ENDC and elsewhere, the United States and the Soviet Union joined hands to fend off the demands for a linkage of nonproliferation with disarmament. Foster presented the case in a blunt and forceful manner. Speaking early in 1966, he pointed out that the Big Three had themselves suffered discrimination through the restrictions they had accepted in the Limited Test Ban Treaty (a dubious point). He argued that it was the nonnuclear states that had most to gain from restricting proliferation and that, by insisting on a link to disarmament measures, they might block progress toward a treaty and thus hurt themselves. The Soviet Union joined with the

United States in this position. Although agreeing with the nonaligned nations that nuclear disarmament was urgently needed, the Soviets stated that they did not wish to "tie up a series of measures in a single package or to make agreement on any one of these measures dependent on the implementation of other measures."

Both the U.S. and the Soviet drafts of 1965 had contained in their preambles brief statements of intent regarding disarmament. These were merged in the identical treaty drafts of August 24, 1967, to read as follows: "The States concluding this Treaty . . . Declaring their intention to achieve at the earliest possible date the cessation of the nuclear arms race. . . ."

The nonaligned and other nonnuclear countries were by no means satisfied with these declarations. Ambassador Trivedi of India expressed the views of many by saying that when principle (c) of the UN resolution of November 19, 1965, spoke of the NPT being a step towards nuclear disarmament, it "was meant not merely as a pious preambular platitude, not just as an insubstantial incantation to be repeated occasionally as a simple magic charm, but as envisaging a concrete programme of specific action." West German Foreign Minister Brandt stated his country's feeling that

> the moral and political justification of a nonproliferation treaty follows only if the nuclear states regard it as a step toward restrictions of their own armaments and toward disarmament and clearly state they are willing to act accordingly.[15]

Canada also made strong statements along these lines.

The superpowers nevertheless continued to resist the coupling of nonproliferation with disarmament. At the UN, Ambassador Goldberg insisted that the nonweapon states had the most to lose from proliferation. He referred to various disarmament proposals the United States had made during the years, implying that we would continue to press for such measures, but argued that to insist on linking them with the NPT risked defeat of the treaty. The British adopted a compromise position. Disarmament Minister Lord Chalfont agreed that it would be "unnecessary as well as imprudent" to insist on disarmament before signing an NPT. He believed, however, that the treaty should reflect an intention by the nuclear-weapon powers to move toward disarmament and that the nonnuclears should be provided with a "means of redress" if progress was too slow to suit them.

The tide of revolt on the disarmament issue ultimately ran so strongly that the superpowers felt obliged to give ground in order to save the treaty. The identical U.S. and Soviet drafts of January 18, 1968 retained the preambular declaration about the "intention to achieve at the earliest possible date the cessation of the nuclear arms race." In addition, however, there was a new Article VI in the body of the treaty, which read:

> Each of the Parties to this Treaty undertakes to pursue negotiations in good faith on effective measures regarding cessation of the nuclear arms race and disarmament, and on a treaty on general and complete disarmament under strict and effective international control.

In accepting this undertaking by the superpowers merely to pursue negotiations in good faith, the nonnuclear states tacitly agreed with the British contention that it was unrealistic to insist that the superpowers agree on actual disarmament measures as a precondition to an NPT. For their part, the superpowers advanced beyond the "pious preambular platitudes" so ridiculed by Trivedi. In the March 1968 revision of the draft treaty their obligation was made even stronger with the addition of the words "at an early date" after the words "pursue negotiations in good faith." Also, Alva Myrdal succeeded in her efforts to have added to the Preamble the following paragraph advancing her favorite cause, a comprehensive test ban:

> Recalling the determination expressed by the Parties to the 1963 [Test Ban] Treaty in its preamble to seek to achieve the discontinuance of all test explosions of nuclear weapons for all time and to continue negotiations to this end.

The British suggestion that the nonnuclears be provided a "means of redress" if progress was too slow was also implemented. The August 1967 identical drafts had provided that a single review conference be held five years after the treaty's entry into force "to assure that the purposes and provisions of the Treaty [were] being realized." The March 1968 revision added a provision that additional review conferences, "with the same objective," could be held at five year intervals if decided upon by majority vote. Such review conferences could cover all aspects of the treaty, but it was commonly understood that their main purpose would be to monitor the compliance of the nuclear-weapon states with Article VI. What has transpired in the three review conferences held thus far will be briefly noted in the next chapter.

Notes

1. Barnes, "The Nuclear Non-Proliferation Treaty," p. 384.
2. Quoted in Young, *A Farewell to Arms Control?*, p. 93.
3. Young, "The Control of Proliferation," p. 11.
4. Sommer, "Bonn Changes Course."
5. Bader, *The United States and the Spread of Nuclear Weapons*, p. 50f.
6. Transcript, George McGhee Oral History Interview, 7/1/69, by Paige E. Mulhollan, tape 1, p. 14, LBJ Library.
7. *Documents on Disarmament: 1967*, p. 144.
8. Ibid., p. 91.
9. Ibid., p. 98.
10. Ibid., p. 397.
11. Mastny, *Disarmament and Nuclear Tests, 1964–1969*, p. 76.
12. Willrich, *Non-Proliferation Treaty*, p. 130.
13. Young, "The Control of Proliferation," p. 13.
14. Information in this paragraph and the one preceding supported by phone conversation with Linda Gallini, ACDA, July 7, 1968.
15. *Documents on Disarmament: 1967*, p. 93.

28
Approval Amid Doubts

If we had known in 1968 how little the nuclear powers would do . . . to meet their end of the Nonproliferation Treaty bargain by controlling their arms race, I would have advised my government not to sign the treaty.
—A distinguished former diplomat[1]

Security Guarantees

When the ENDC adjourned on March 14, 1968, the superpowers had failed to obtain the desired unanimous support for their jointly drafted Nonproliferation Treaty. Despite all the concessions made in successive drafts, the most recent of which had been submitted but three days earlier, only seven ENDC members publicly endorsed the treaty. Aside from the superpowers themselves, this number included Britain, Canada, and the three dutiful Soviet satellites: Bulgaria, Czechoslovakia, and Poland. Brazil, India, and Italy were known to have strong objections to particular aspects of the treaty. At a recent meeting of Eastern bloc nations in Sofia, Romania had withheld its approval. Mexico, Sweden, and the United Arab Republic were believed to favor the treaty but without sufficient enthusiasm to declare themselves formally. The attitude of France, the member that never attended an ENDC meeting, was still unknown. Among nations outside the ENDC, the misgivings of West Germany, whose assent to the treaty was one of the Soviet Union's main goals, had been widely publicized. There were also rumblings of discontent from such important nations as Australia, Japan, and Pakistan.

A major source of dissatisfaction with the successive drafts of the treaty had been the lack of any provision guaranteeing the security of non-nuclear-weapon countries against nuclear attack or blackmail. As the UAR's Ambassador Khallaf told the ENDC, "It is inconceivable that the non-nuclear States which under the treaty would renounce nuclear weapons could quite simply agree by the same act to reserve to nuclear powers the privilege of threatening them or attacking them with those same weapons." This feeling was particularly acute among the nonaligned countries, which, unlike U.S. and Soviet allies, did not have the protection of a superpower's nuclear umbrella. As already noted (chapter 11), President Johnson had committed the United States to a sweeping but vague form of security guarantee after the first Chinese test in October 1964. The president's assurance had been repeated by Ambassador Goldberg at the UN in September 1965. Then, in his message to the ENDC of January 27, 1966, the president had stated once again: "the nations that do not seek the nuclear path can be sure that they will have our strong support against threats of nuclear blackmail." The repetition of this pledge caused alarm among some in the administration and in Congress. Thus, in testifying on the Pastore Resolution in February 1966, Secretary McNamara tried to pull back a little. He stated that, though some kind of a security guarantee had been discussed with other nations, the administration had no intention of making the United States a policeman of the world.

In February 1966 the Soviet Union weighed in with an alternative approach to a security guarantee when Premier Kosygin offered to add to the Soviet NPT draft a clause "on the prohibition of the use of nuclear weapons against parties to the treaty who have no nuclear weapons on their territories."[2] This proposal, obviously designed to call attention to the presence of U.S. nuclear weapons on the soil of several NATO countries, was of course unacceptable to us. It was, however, welcomed by several delegations at the ENDC who were particularly attracted by the idea of incorporating a security guarantee into the treaty itself. Then on November 17, 1966, the UN General Assembly adopted a draft resolution that included a call to the nuclear powers to give assurance against the use or threatened use of nuclear weapons against nonnuclear powers. The vote was 103 to 1 (Albania), with Cuba and France abstaining. A week later the UNGA, again by overwhelming vote, requested the ENDC "to consider urgently" the Kosygin proposal.

By 1967 the clamor for a security guarantee had grown to such proportions that the main issue seemed to be whether the assurance should be a part of or separate from the Nonproliferation Treaty. The UAR, India, and Romania were among the leading proponents of the former approach. India went so far as to suggest that a U.S.–USSR guarantee against nuclear attack on nonnuclear countries was *all* that was needed—it could be a *substitute* for a nonproliferation treaty. (This view was presented to a meeting of the U.S. Atomic Energy Commission on April 14, 1967, by my Indian counterpart,

Vikram Sarabhai, and the Indian ambassador to the United States, B. K. Nehru. It fell to me on this occasion to argue the inadequacy of the Indian approach.)

In August 1967, Foster presented the U.S. position to the ENDC. The security guarantee problem, he said, was too complex to be dealt with in a nonproliferation treaty, and added: "We have been exploring action which could be taken in the context of the United Nations. . . ." This exploration bore fruit the following spring. On March 7, 1968, the United States, the United Kingdom, and the USSR submitted to the ENDC a proposal that security assurances related to nuclear intimidation take the form of a Security Council resolution that each of the three would support. The resolution would first note the security concerns of states wishing to subscribe to the NPT. It would then recognize that any nuclear aggression, or any threat thereof, created a situation requiring immediate action by the Security Council, "especially its permanent members."

The weaknesses in this formulation were quickly apparent. It added nothing, except perhaps a note of urgency, to the Security Council's existing obligations. Nor did it add anything to the obligations of the United States as a member of the council. A further consideration was that each nuclear-weapon state at that time, except China, was a permanent member of the Security Council and could therefore veto any proposed Security Council action directed at itself. (No one raised the suggestion, as Bernard Baruch had when presenting the Baruch Plan in 1946, that the veto power be suspended.) The resolution seemed therefore to be directed primarily at, and to be effective only against, China. This doubtless had a reassuring effect on nations like India that felt particularly threatened by China, but it was far from resolving the broad issue of nuclear aggression.

Despite its obvious shortcomings, the proposal for a Security Council resolution gained support from some ENDC members.*

---

*George Bunn recalls a diplomatic effort to move beyond the Security Council resolution. During the summer of 1965 the Soviets at Geneva asked whether there couldn't be something in the text about nonuse of nuclear weapons against non-nuclear-weapons states that were parties to the treaty. They seemed willing to drop the anti-NATO qualification in the Kosygin proposal about not having nuclear weapons on their territories. Bunn, after talking to his Soviet counterparts, worked out a suggested treaty provision: There would be no use of nuclear weapons against any non-nuclear-weapons state "except in defense against an act of aggression in which a state owning nuclear weapons is engaged." This proposal was cabled home by Foster. It got nowhere in the U.S. government, however. It appears to have been shot down on the basis of a reluctance on the part of the Joint Chiefs of Staff to accept any limitation on the use of nuclear weapons. But, as indicated in chapter 26, the United States did accept a limitation on its use of nuclear weapons in the Treaty of Tlatelolco. (George Bunn, private conversation, November 21, 1986.)

Approval by the UN

It was understood that the General Assembly would consider the draft Nonproliferation Treaty when it reconvened on April 24, 1968. If the treaty was approved, the security guarantee matter would then be brought before the Security Council.

Strategy for the General Assembly debate on the NPT was discussed at a White House meeting I attended on March 27, 1968.

> Foster said the Soviets would like to "railroad" the NPT through the UN but that the United States was resisting such tactics, preferring to allow the dissident nations time to talk themselves out. He hoped for UN approval later in the spring. The United States was working hard behind the scenes to get the support of as many nations as possible, particularly such nuclear-capable ones as Brazil, Israel, Italy and South Africa. [Among these, only Italy had adhered to the treaty as of the end of 1986.]
>
> Foster feared that unwelcome amendments might still be proposed under the guise of obtaining a more equitable balance between nuclear-weapon and non-nuclear-weapon countries. He was also concerned that the Soviet Union might refuse to ratify the treaty until West Germany did. [This fear proved groundless. The Soviet Union ratified on March 5, 1970; West Germany on May 2, 1975.] He suggested we might wait to see what Germany's plans were before submitting the treaty to the Senate. He termed the joint action by the United States, United Kingdom, and USSR on the security guarantee matter a "remarkable achievement."
>
> Foster turned to what the next steps might be after the NPT. He said the Big Three would have an obligation under Article VI of the treaty to move in good faith toward arms control and disarmament measures. He mentioned in particular such steps as a comprehensive test ban, a cutoff of nuclear materials production, strategic arms limitations, and a new item—forbidding nuclear explosives on the seabed. Katzenbach said both UN and Senate approval of the NPT involved some problems but it still might be possible to achieve both in 1968.
>
> Goldberg termed the NPT the greatest accomplishment since the Limited Test Ban Treaty. He thought that Foster's time schedule for approval in the UN might be a little optimistic but that we should do everything possible to avoid delay in final adoption.

The president asked specifically about India, Italy, and Brazil. Foster said India wanted to retain its options and not make a commitment yet. [Former Science Adviser Jerome] Wiesner was to visit their AEC head, Sarabhai, to try to influence them.* Foster added that a high Indian official told him they would eventually sign. [They have not done so.] He said Italy's stand was more difficult to understand and predicted they would come around. [They did.] Brazil presented an entirely different situation. They felt they were a big country that needed peaceful nuclear explosives for industrial development and wanted to produce these themselves. [Brazil has not signed.]†

The UN debate on the Nonproliferation Treaty began in the General Assembly's First Committee on April 24. (It will be recalled that the BOXCAR test had been set back so it would not take place on that day.) In introductory remarks, Goldberg emphasized the U.S. belief that the treaty would enhance the security of all states, particularly those without nuclear weapons. He noted that the treaty contained "the strongest and most meaningful undertaking that could be agreed upon" concerning disarmament [namely, the pledge by the superpowers in Article VI to pursue negotiations in good faith at an early date], and stated that the treaty's "permanent viability" would depend on the success of such negotiations. He urged the General Assembly to take favorable action during its current session, warning: "Time is not on our side."

Soviet Deputy Foreign Minister Vasiliy V. Kuznetsov also made introductory comments. He observed that the negotiations leading to the treaty had not always proceeded smoothly. A "certain imprint of compromise" had resulted, but this had not sacrificed the heart of the matter, which was to block "all forms of access to nuclear weapons" by nonnuclear nations. He then assured the delegates that the Soviet Union was willing to negotiate on disarmament and listed a number of desirable measures. His list was virtually the same one Foster had unfurled at the White House meeting on March 27.

---

*Wiesner had visited India in 1964, as described in chapter 21.

†Brazil's status is somewhat ambiguous. It has signed and ratified the Treaty of Tlatelolco committing it not to acquire nuclear weapons. However, it has made its ratification conditional on the effective ratification by all other Latin American states, and Cuba and Argentina have not ratified. Moreover, as noted in chapter 26, Brazil interprets that treaty to permit indigenous development of peaceful nuclear explosives. The United States disputes Brazil's interpretation and there is question (chapter 21) about the sincerity of Brazil's interest in PNEs.

Following the introductory comments by the superpowers, representatives of non-nuclear-weapon states paraded to the UN microphones to voice essentially the same complaints they had expressed previously at the ENDC. The treaty did not provide an "acceptable balance of mutual responsibilities" as between the nuclears and non-nuclears (Japan, Pakistan); it did not sufficiently liberalize the international flow of nuclear materials and information (Australia, Italy, Japan, Nigeria, Pakistan); it failed to require safeguards on the peaceful nuclear activities of nuclear-weapon states, giving them potential industrial and commercial advantages (Australia, Brazil, India, Japan, Nigeria); it lacked any tangible commitment to ending the nuclear arms race (Ethiopia, Romania, South Africa).

The tripartite security guarantee resolution that was before the Security Council for action was also mentioned in the General Assembly debate. Some gave it faint praise—"a step in the right direction"—but no one thought it adequate. One deficiency noted was that it was intended to apply only to parties to the NPT whereas the UN Charter required that all states threatened with aggression be treated equally. It was noteworthy that the nations making this comment, namely, India and South Africa, did not intend to sign the NPT.

While giving voice to their various criticisms, some of the non-nuclear-weapon countries nevertheless urged that the NPT be approved. The Ethiopian delegate declared that it was a choice "between making a little progress or no progress at all." Australia, announcing it would vote to approve the treaty but might not sign right away, said it was the "only agreement in immediate prospect." Alva Myrdal concluded that, once this treaty was signed and out of the way, attention could then turn to other agreements that meant more, such as a comprehensive test ban.

On May 31, the United States and the Soviet Union took account of the various comments by submitting to the UN's First Committee one more revised version of the NPT. It was the seventh draft of the treaty to be presented formally for international consideration. The most significant change was the addition to Article IV of the clause, mentioned above, directing that in the provision of technical assistance for peaceful uses there be "due consideration for the needs of developing areas of the world." Otherwise, the revisions were minor. There was a new paragraph in the Preamble "recalling" the principles of the UN Charter limiting the use of force. The right of parties to acquire nuclear materials and equipment for peaceful purposes was given greater emphasis in the language of Article IV. Article V was reworded to emphasize obtaining peaceful nuclear explosion assistance through an international body over obtaining such assistance by bilateral agreement; both options remained open, however.

On June 12, 1968, a resolution commending the revised treaty was adopted by the General Assembly. The vote was 95 to 4, with 21 abstentions. After the vote was taken, President Johnson told the assembly that the treaty was "the most important international agreement limiting nuclear arms since the nuclear age began." The secretary-general of the United Nations, U Thant, was less grandiloquent. He thought that the treaty represented "the maximum area of agreement now obtainable." A week later the Security Council approved the tripartite resolution on security guarantees by a vote of 10 to 0, with five abstentions (Algeria, Brazil, France, India, Pakistan).

Final Hurdles Cleared: Too Late for LBJ

Having gained approval by the General Assembly, the Treaty on the Nonproliferation of Nuclear Weapons was opened for signature on July 1, 1968, in Washington, London, and Moscow. It was signed on that day by the Big Three and more than fifty other countries.* Significant among the countries that did *not* sign on July 1 were Australia, Argentina, Brazil, the People's Republic of China, France, West Germany, India, Italy, Israel, Japan, Switzerland and South Africa. This list included a majority of the "threshold" nuclear-capable states we were most interested in enlisting. Several countries delayed because they wanted to have a clearer view of the terms of their safeguards agreements with the IAEA before committing themselves.

President Johnson transmitted the treaty to the Senate on July 9, "urgently" recommending its ratification. On the following day, the Senate Foreign Relations Committee, chaired by J. William Fulbright of Arkansas, began its hearings. (Senate members of the Joint Committee on Atomic Energy were also invited to participate in the hearings.) Administration witnesses were Dean Rusk, William Foster,

---

*Until the treaty entered into force on March 5, 1970, there was a two-step procedure for accession. A nation first signified its intent by "signing" the treaty. Subsequently, after necessary legislative processes in some countries, the nation would deposit its instrument of ratification, becoming at that point bound by the treaty's terms. For a nation wishing to adhere to the treaty after its entry into force, only the single step of ratification has been available.

Deputy Defense Secretary Paul H. Nitze, General Wheeler and myself. Our prepared testimony explained the history, content, and advantages of the treaty. My own testimony concentrated on IAEA safeguards and the provision for a peaceful nuclear explosions service.

Many, if not most, of the questions asked by senators sought reassurance that the treaty and/or the accompanying security guarantee resolution did not have certain undesirable effects. For example, we were asked over and over again whether the treaty in any way altered U.S. obligations to NATO, and whether it had any inhibiting effect on U.S. defenses. Particular attention was focused on whether the security guarantee resolution committed the United States to military adventures without congressional scrutiny. (Rusk was at pains to point out that the guarantee was merely a reassertion of a responsibility the Security Council had had all along under the UN Charter.) The fact that West Germany did not sign the treaty on July 1 aroused curiosity: Were they trying to exact a price for their signature, for example, a pledge that U.S. troops would remain on station in Germany? Senators also wanted to explore the significance of the fact that neither France nor China seemed likely to sign. The then hot question of whether the United States should deploy the thin Sentinel ABM system arose again and again in the hearings; although it did not relate directly to the treaty. After apparently satisfactory reassurance was given on all points, Senator Pastore remarked that "being against this treaty is like being against the Ten Commandments."

Some witnesses nevertheless found it possible to speak in opposition. Dr. Robert Strausz-Hupe of the University of Pennsylvania, who had also testified against the Limited Test Ban Treaty, expressed alarm that negotiations with the Soviet Union seemed to be getting a higher priority than strengthening the Western alliance. He saw advantages in our supplying our allies with defensive nuclear weapons, something the treaty would not allow. Representative Craig Hosmer felt that proliferation was not necessarily bad, that the treaty's inadequate safeguards would not prevent it in any case, that the treaty enlarged the role of the United States as a world policeman, and that it would lead to further arms control negotiations that the Soviets would use to obtain strategic advantages. Edward Teller favored approving the treaty only if an exception were made allowing us to transfer defensive nuclear weapons to our allies. (One can already see

in some of the testimony on the NPT evidence of the increasing preoc-
cupation with nuclear defense.)*

Those who opposed the treaty appeared to make little impression.
As the Foreign Relations Committee hearings ended, all indications
were that the treaty was headed for certain and swift committee and
Senate approval. There seemed a strong chance that it might enter
into force while Lyndon Johnson was still president. But the misfor-
tune that dogged this ill-starred presidency was soon to strike again.
On August 19, Soviet and other Eastern bloc armed forces rolled into
Czechoslovakia to snuff out the liberalizing flame of the upstart Dubček regime. There then entered into play that strange American doctrine called "linkage" by which we from time to time deny ourselves
what is in our own self-interest in order to "punish" the adversary
for some misbehavior. Presidential candidate Richard Nixon was
among those who proposed that the punishment for Czechoslovakia
include a delay in ratifying the Nonproliferation Treaty. Nixon stated
that, while he generally favored ratification of the treaty, he opposed
action on it as long as Soviet troops were on Czechoslovak soil.

The Foreign Relations Committee voted on September 17, 1968,
to recommend ratification, but the full Senate voted on October 11
to postpone action. Three days later the Ninetieth Congress terminated its work. White House sources confirmed on November 27 that
President Johnson was considering calling the Senate into special session in December for the specific purpose of ratifying the treaty. He
had directed Majority Leader Mike Mansfield to sound out the views
of Democratic senators. Mansfield's poll indicated that, although the
Senate overwhelmingly approved ratification of the treaty, there was
strong sentiment against a special session unless President-elect Nixon
concurred. Nixon press spokesman Ron Ziegler thereupon stated that
nothing had occurred to alter Mr. Nixon's position on the treaty.

On February 5, 1969, now-President Richard Nixon had a change
of heart. Notwithstanding that Soviet troops were still "on Czechoslovak soil," he recommended ratification of the Nonproliferation
Treaty in a special message to the Senate. He said that such action

---

*Arthur Larson, a former Eisenhower assistant, who testified after Teller, likened the appalling
technical difficulties of missile defense to a suggestion made by humorist Will Rogers during
World War I. Asked what he would do about the German submarine menace, Rogers suggested
that the answer was to raise the temperature of the Atlantic Ocean to the boiling point. When
asked how this could be accomplished, Rogers answered, "Well, that is a technical question for
the scientists" (Senate, Committee on Foreign Relations, *Hearings on Nonproliferation Treaty*,
p. 239f.)

would advance his administration's policy of "negotiation rather than confrontation" with the USSR. The Foreign Relations Committee then conducted a second round of hearings during which substantially the same sorts of questions were asked by virtually the same senators of the same administration witnesses or their replacements. Now that ratification was being sponsored by a conservative Republican president, there were no opposition witnesses. On March 13, 1969, the Senate approved the treaty by a vote of 83 to 15. On March 5, 1970, having been ratified by the requisite number of countries (the Big Three plus forty), the NPT entered into force during special ceremonies in Washington, Moscow, and London.

As of the end of 1986, the NPT had more than 130 parties. It has been pointed out that these parties, together with France,* accounted for "98 percent of the world's installed nuclear power capacity, 95 percent of the nuclear power capacity under construction, and all of the world's exporters of enriched uranium. This means not only that the overwhelming majority of the world's civil nuclear authorities are directly under the treaty's regime, but also that any nonparty seriously interested in developing nuclear power must rely, at least in part, on cooperation with parties to the treaty, whose exports are covered by international safeguards."[3] This has been an impressive accomplishment, one which has generally exceeded expectations, and one for which Lyndon Johnson and his administration deserve much credit.

A Treaty on Trial

Despite the wide acceptance of the NPT, one must not overlook the fact that, by its own terms, this is a treaty on trial. To begin with, it contains, in Article X, a lenient withdrawal clause. Any nation can withdraw on three months' notice "if it decides that extraordinary events, related to the subject matter of this treaty, have jeopardized the supreme interests of its country."† In joining the treaty, therefore,

---

*On June 12, 1968, the French ambassador informed the General Assembly that, although his country would not sign the NPT, it would "behave in the future exactly as the States adhering to the treaty."

†This was the same language as had been inserted into the Limited Test Ban Treaty after some arduous bargaining between Averell Harriman and Andrey Gromyko. True, there is in the case of the NPT an additional requirement, not found in the test ban treaty, that the withdrawing nation provide a "statement of the extraordinary events motivating its action." This is not regarded as a difficult bar to withdrawal, however. As Alva Myrdal commented, there can be no authoritative interpretation of what are proper grounds for withdrawal.

no nation makes an irrevocable commitment. Indeed, the notice period of three months permits a nation that changes its mind to make a rapid turnaround.

Still more serious is the fact that the treaty as a whole is limited in duration to twenty-five years, after which a conference of the parties is to be held to determine, by majority vote, whether the treaty should be extended, and, if so, for how long. This was not the desire of the superpowers. The U.S. draft of August 17, 1965; the Soviet draft of September 24, 1965; and the identical drafts of August 24, 1967, all contemplated a treaty that would be "of unlimited duration." But the smaller nations demurred, and in terms that clearly implied that the duration of the treaty would be held hostage to the performance of the superpowers in keeping their commitments, particularly with respect to disarmament negotiations. As a Swiss representative said, "The non-nuclear-weapon States certainly cannot take the responsibility of tying their hands indefinitely if the nuclear-weapon States fail to arrive at positive results in that direction."

At the time that the superpowers agreed to the limited duration clause, twenty-five years may have seemed a comfortable cushion of time in which to solidify the nonproliferation regime. We must consider today, however, that the deadline, 1995, is fast approaching and that a favorable vote on extending the treaty is far from a foregone conclusion.

The Conference of Nonweapon States

There have been several opportunities since the NPT was signed to sense the attitude of the community of nations toward it. The first occurred at a conference of the world's non-nuclear-weapon states held in Geneva during September 1968. The very fact that the UN General Assembly had called such a conference was evidence that the various compromises fashioned in the NPT and the attendant security guarantee resolution had not stilled the mood of unrest among nonweapon countries.

Perhaps more important than the conference itself was its timing. It had been originally scheduled to take place in Geneva in March of 1968. It was feared that if it was held at that time, before completion of the ENDC and UN votes on the Nonproliferation Treaty, it might be used as a sort of caucus during which the nonnuclears would agree among themselves on a high price for consenting to the NPT. Adrian

Fisher relates that, to forestall this possibility, representatives of the United States (Fisher and UN Ambassador Goldberg) and a heavy-hitting delegation from the USSR met in New York over a weekend with organizers of the nonnuclear conference and

> worked out an arrangement . . . whereby we [the United States and the USSR] would agree to support the conference and participate in its activities, *but* they would agree to delay it until August of 1968.[4]

The security guarantee issue proved to be the dominant focus of discussion at the conference. It was apparent that most of the ninety-two nations represented, eighty-one of whom had already signed the NPT, felt that tying security guarantees to the Security Council's unreliable and veto-bound procedures was insufficient. Nevertheless a Latin American proposal for an international convention to provide more satisfactory guarantees failed by one vote to obtain the required two-thirds majority. The conference's final declaration stressed "the necessity of further steps for an early solution" of the security problem, but offered no specific recommendations.

The only resolution approved by the conference on the security question was one offered by West Germany reaffirming the principles of international law on the nonuse of force, or threats thereof. This had significance in view of the recent Soviet move against Czechoslovakia. Other resolutions urged international agencies to be more generous in funding technical assistance for peaceful uses, recommended steps leading toward further nuclear-free zones, and—with greatest unanimity—called on the superpowers to begin the promised bilateral arms limitation talks.

Review Conferences

A further test of the international community's attitude toward the Nonproliferation Treaty has been provided by three review conferences, held in 1975, 1980, and 1985. The conferences were called for in Article VIII of the treaty in the following language:

> Five years after the entry into force of this Treaty, a conference of Parties to the Treaty shall be held in Geneva, Switzerland, in order to review the operation of the Treaty with a view to assuring that the purposes of the Preamble and the provisions of the Treaty are being realized. At intervals of five years thereafter, a majority of the

Parties to the Treaty may obtain . . . the convening of further conferences with the same objective. . . .

This provision is noteworthy for its inclusion of "the purposes of
the Preamble" among the subjects for review at the conferences. The
identical U.S.–USSR drafts of August 24, 1967, the first to provide
for review conferences, had not included the Preamble as a subject
for review. Others pointed out, however, that the Preamble's declarations on disarmament were more far-reaching than those in the
body of the treaty. The Preamble "recalled," for example, the prior
pledge—in the Limited Test Ban Treaty's preamble—"to seek to
achieve the discontinuance of all test explosions of nuclear weapons
for all time and to continue negotiations to this end." There was a
strong inclination not to allow the superpowers to dodge important
issues by paying lip service to them in the Preamble. It was noteworthy that the British broke ranks with the United States on this issue;
they were among the leaders in urging that the Preamble be included
in review conference agendas.

1975

Antagonism between nuclear-weapon and non-nuclear-weapon states
was the main feature of the first review conference, held in Geneva
in May 1975. The potential for confrontation between the two groups
had been recognized, and the Big Three met in London the weekend
before the conference to concert their positions. Their apparent strategy, as it played out during the meeting, was to concentrate on technical and economic issues such as safeguards, export policies of the
supplying countries, and establishing multinational fuel centers, and
to try to avoid political questions.

Nonweapon countries were divided into two groups: the industrial nations of Europe plus Japan, and the nations that constitute the
Third World—mainly nonaligned countries from Asia, Africa, and
Latin America. The former group expressed some interest in the technical issues, and were generally mild in their criticism of the nuclear-
weapon states. On the other hand, the Third World countries—known
since the mid-1960s as the "Group of 77," although by this time their
numbers had swelled beyond that figure—seemed interested only in
larger political questions. As to these, they were very sharp in their
criticism of the nuclear powers. They made heavy demands, including

an end to all nuclear weapon tests, substantial nuclear arms reductions, a pledge not to attack or threaten nonweapon parties with nuclear weapons, and increased technical assistance in peaceful uses. The reaction of the superpowers to these demands was cold and intransigent. They refused to negotiate on any of the Third World proposals. What is more, they challenged the right of nonweapon countries to criticize their bilateral arms control relationship—the Soviet delegate termed such criticism "unwarranted interference." As though to show disdain for the proceedings, the Soviet Union conducted an underground test just before the conference opened; the United States conducted one a few days later.

Predictably, the first review conference ended in deadlock. By extending the meetings by two days, it proved possible to reach an artificial compromise on a final declaration. This contained a bland summary of the less controversial technical proposals while exhorting the nuclear powers in general terms to carry out their treaty commitments. No one pretended that this report represented a genuine consensus. The Group of 77, in fact, appended an "interpretative statement," stating that they had agreed to the final document only out of respect for its author, conference president Inga Thorsson of Sweden, and that they stood by their political proposals.[5]

1980

"North–South" confrontation again dominated the second review conference, held in Geneva from August 11 to September 7, 1980, this time focusing on both disarmament and nuclear supply issues. The increased emphasis on supply was in response to a trend toward more restrictive trade policies by the industrial nations. The trend had been marked by two outstanding events, both of which occurred in 1978. First was the issuance by the so-called London Club, an informal association of sixteen supplying nations,* of a set of guidelines designed to tighten controls over the export of sensitive nuclear technology, equipment, and materials. Second was the enactment in the United States of the Nuclear Nonproliferation Act of 1978, which called for tighter controls over U.S. export of nuclear materials (particularly plutonium) and sensitive nuclear technology (particularly that

---

*The members of the group were Australia, Belgium, Canada, Czechoslovakia, France, East Germany, West Germany, Italy, Japan, the Netherlands, Poland, Sweden, Switzerland, the United Kingdom, the United States, and the USSR.

related to reprocessing), and included a requirement for renegotiation of existing nuclear supply agreements between the United States and recipient nations.* Less developed countries have felt that the introduction of more restrictive trade policies was a repudiation by the advanced nations of their commitments under Article IV.

Criticism of the major powers' supply actions was very strong at the 1980 review conference, but compromise language addressing these issues seemed to have a fair chance of approval in a final report. The language was never put to the test, however. Even though conclusion of the conference was delayed by a day and a half, it proved impossible to reconcile differences over the arms control issues. Yugoslavia led a group of nations bitterly critical of the failure of the nuclear-weapon parties to fulfill their Article VI obligations. The group focused especially on the test ban issue. Sigvard Eklund, director-general of the IAEA, expressed the general sense of the linkage between the treaty and a test ban when he said:

> The non-proliferation regime can only survive on the tripod of the Nonproliferation Treaty, effective international safeguards, and a comprehensive nuclear test ban treaty. The vital third leg is still missing as it was five years ago.[6]

Had the superpowers shown any receptivity toward the idea of a test moratorium, this might have been accepted as a sufficient evidence of good intentions to still the Third World revolt. In the absence of any such receptivity, the conference adjourned without agreeing on a final report.

1985

On the surface at least, a less confrontational mood prevailed at the 1985 conference, a four-week affair ending in September. According to observers,[7] threats of defection were virtually nonexistent this time. This apparently was due more to a recognition of the NPT's value and a desire to reaffirm its validity than to any increase in satisfaction with the performance of the nuclear powers. Indeed, there was virtual unanimity among the nonweapon states that the Big Three were not in compliance with their obligations under Article VI. Cited by nearly

---

*In enforcing this legislation, the Reagan administration, as a matter of policy, has made exceptions favoring Western Europe and Japan.

all the nations at the conference as the desired first step in fulfilling those obligations was the resumption of trilateral negotiations on a comprehensive test ban treaty. It was pointed out that such a treaty

> would render the development of new nuclear weapons designs practically impossible and would seriously constrain the modification of existing designs. It would also place practical obstacles in the way of would-be proliferators, as governments may hesitate to build a significant stock of untested weapons. Moreover, since a comprehensive test ban would apply to both nuclear-weapons and non-weapon states, it would partly obliterate the politically sensitive aspect of the treaty—its implication that one group of states is permitted to develop and test nuclear weapons, while another is not.[8]

On the test ban issue a split developed between the Soviet Union and the United States, their first serious disagreement on an NPT issue since the treaty was signed. The Soviets clearly indicated their willingness to resume negotiations on a CTBT. The United States, joined only by the United Kingdom, took the position, as stated in the final communiqué, that "deep and verifiable reductions in the existing arsenals of nuclear weapons" were the most important way to satisfy Article VI obligations.

Also evident at the 1985 conference was continued dissatisfaction with the trade policies of the major powers, particularly those of the United States, which were alleged to discriminate in favor of the Euratom countries and Japan. Other nations claimed that such discrimination was a clear violation of Article IV.

Though the 1985 review conference managed to agree on a final report at 5:20 in the morning following its last day, there were clear indications that the consensus was fragile indeed. Thus, despite the apparent strong support that most nonweapon parties have shown for the NPT, one can anticipate that the 1995 vote on the treaty's extension could be critically dangerous if the superpowers do not in the interim take substantial steps toward fulfilling their treaty obligations, particularly those under Article VI.

Notes

1. Quoted in Halsted, "The Spread of Nuclear Weapons," p. 141.
2. Mastny, *Disarmament and Nuclear Tests, 1964–1969*, p. 32.
3. National Academy of Sciences, *Nuclear Arms Control*, p. 244.

4. Transcript, Adrian Fisher oral history interview, by Paige E. Mulhollan, 10/31/68, Tape 1, p. 23f.
5. Epstein, "Retrospective of the NPT Review Conference," p. 15.
6. Quoted in Greb and Heckrotte, "The Long History," p. 39.
7. Albright and Carothers, "Fragile Consensus," and Goldblatt, "Will the NPT Survive?"
8. Goldblatt, "Will the NPT Survive?" p. 38.

Part IX

Toward SALT

There is a tide in the affairs of men
Which, taken at the flood, leads on to fortune;
Omitted, all the voyage of their life
Is bound in shallows and in miseries.

Shakespeare
Julius Caesar, Act IV

29

Arms Limitation:
First Halting Steps

[A]ny disarmament treaty or agreement or procedure that we participate in must be one in which we maintain . . . our favorable differential balance of power.

—Robert S. McNamara
1964[1]

The Verified Freeze

On July 1, 1968, the very day they signed the Nonproliferation Treaty, President Johnson and Soviet Premier Kosygin announced their intention to enter into talks on the limitation and reduction of offensive and defensive nuclear weapons.

The formal arms limitation talks thus announced were to be the first of their kind, but there had been several approaches to this subject matter dating back a number of years. President Johnson himself had made several arms limitation proposals in his first message to the ENDC on January 21, 1964. The proposal that attracted the most attention was that the "United States and the Soviet Union and their respective allies . . . agree to explore a verified freeze on the number and characteristics of strategic nuclear offensive and defensive missiles." The president expressed his conviction that "this initial measure preventing the further expansion of the deadly and costly arms race [would] open the path to reductions in all types of forces from present levels."

Very few specifics of the freeze proposal had been worked out within the U.S. government when the president formally presented it to the world. Behind the apparent simplicity of the idea—let's just freeze!—lurked numerous complexities. (That such complexities exist has, I think, escaped the notice of many who have pushed for a nuclear freeze in the 1980s.) First, it was necessary to define a "strategic missile." This had to be determined separately for missiles that were ground-based, based at sea, and carried on planes. Aside from the weapons themselves, what associated items would be frozen: launching facilities? critical components? How define a critical component? Would replacements of damaged or worn-out items be permitted? If production lines no longer existed for the item being replaced, could something of the same type be substituted? If so, how to define what was the "same type"? How to prevent replacements from being improvements? Would testing be allowed? If not, how to define what was a "test"? How much verification would be by "national technical means"—satellite photography, seismography, intelligence—and how much by inspection? What facilities would have to be opened for inspection? What frequency of inspection: continuing? a specified number? By whom: neutrals? the opposing side? Should there be inspection to verify destruction of weapons? Should weapons not destroyed be counted? And on and on.

A memorandum embodying the U.S. position on many of these issues was circulated by the ACDA to the Committee of Principals on January 24, 1964, three days after the president's message recommending a freeze to the ENDC. A major purpose of the ACDA memorandum was to provide guidance to the U.S. delegation in Geneva, which was receiving many questions from other delegations. One of the more ticklish questions addressed in ACDA's memorandum was how to reconcile a freeze proposal with the new missile launchers that presumably would be needed for the proposed NATO multilateral force. ACDA's suggested answer was that a freeze would not prohibit the MLF facilities if the United States disposed of a "compensating number of national launching facilities." The memorandum specified that the freeze would include all strategic delivery vehicles. This rubric brought strategic bombers as well as land-based missiles within the scope of the proposal.

On April 16, Fisher presented some details of the U.S. freeze proposal to the ENDC. He told the committee that the freeze was intended to apply to ground-based missiles with a range exceeding one thousand kilometers, sea-based and air-to-surface missiles with a range of more than one hundred kilometers, and bombers weighing (empty) more than twenty-seven-and-a-half tons. Worn or damaged missiles could be replaced but no improvements would be permitted. Missile tests and training exercises would be allowed. Verification would involve only the monitoring of airfields, missile launching sites, and critical production steps. There would be no attempt to inspect the levels or deployment of existing armaments.[2]

Despite the U.S. attempt to make the verification procedures relatively unintrusive, the Soviet reaction was negative. Foreign Minister Gromyko in a press interview and Ambassador Tsarapkin at the ENDC advanced similar arguments: Verification of a freeze would require intrusion into the USSR's most secret facilities in all parts of the country. It would thus endanger Soviet security, and without leading to disarmament of any kind.[3]

After these exchanges the freeze idea faded, having had but one brief season in the sun. The United States continued for a while to include it in its list of desirable arms control measures, but with far less emphasis than in 1964. In March 1966 Fisher would point out to the ENDC that American long-range missile forces had almost doubled since President Johnson first proposed the freeze and that Soviet strategic forces had also increased sharply. He therefore regretted that the Soviet Union had not been more responsive two years earlier. The Soviet response was to label the freeze "a long-since discredited and rejected proposal."

John Newhouse has written the following about the freeze episode:

A senior American official closely involved in this affair says that the idea of mutual inventory controls by inspection was really no more acceptable to Americans than to the Russians. In effect, he says, by its proposal, the United States sought to satisfy the rhetorical commitment to arms control while using verification as the means of assuring that nothing would happen. Looking back, this official now says that both the Americans and the Russians had a kind of "let's get together for lunch" attitude toward the subject at that time; each side knew the other was not entirely serious about it.[4]

In contrast to this view, my diary records the following exchange (at a Principals meeting on June 26, 1964), which indicates that there may have been some serious interest, at least on the part of the ACDA:

Rusk asked whether it was true that there had been no Soviet interest in the freeze proposal, to which Fisher replied that he thought their apparent lack of interest could actually mask a real interest.

I am inclined to think that Fisher was deluding himself, since one wonders how the Soviets could have entertained seriously a proposal that would have frozen them into a position of such marked inferiority as they occupied in 1964. The magnitude of the Soviet deficit was revealed in information released by Secretary McNamara on April 14, 1964. (The information was released in answer to charges by presidential candidate Barry Goldwater that McNamara had weakened U.S. defenses.) The data indicated (1) that the United States had approximately 750 operational ICBMs, compared to 188 for the Soviet Union;* (2) that the United States had 192 submarine-based missiles, each with a range of fifteen hundred miles and able to be launched under water, whereas the USSR had "substantially fewer" submarine-based missiles; those they had, moreover, were believed to have a range of five hundred miles or less and to be incapable of underwater launching; and (3) that the United States had on alert 540 long-range bombers, while the Soviets had only half that number able to reach U.S. territory, and that even those, if they hoped to return home, could only reach targets in Alaska and the Pacific Northwest. The Soviets were rapidly narrowing our lead, however, and in 1972 the two sides were able, in SALT I, to agree on what amounted to a five-year freeze on the number of strategic missile launchers.

A Bonfire of Bombers

Another arms limitation idea floated during the Johnson years related to the mutual destruction of bomber aircraft. On January 28, 1964, Tsarapkin presented to the ENDC a Soviet proposal that all the nations of the world join in destroying all their bombers. Foster revealed to newsmen on the same day that the United States had suggested privately to the USSR during the preceding year that the two governments discuss scrapping comparable medium-range bombers—the B-47 on our side and the Badger on theirs. Neither aircraft was in current production and they were considered obsolete. What the United States had in mind was amplified on March 19 when Fisher announced to the ENDC that the United States was prepared to destroy twenty B-47s a month over the next two years, for a total of 480, if the USSR would destroy an equal number of Badgers. Fisher

---

*Not mentioned in the McNamara release was the fact that the Soviet missiles had greater megatonnage than ours. On the other hand, they were relatively inaccurate.

said that such "bomber bonfires" could provide "a graphic example of armament reduction to the entire world." He added that the United States was also ready to match the USSR in destroying further numbers beyond the 480.

Tsarapkin responded the same day, rejecting the U.S. proposal as an effort to pass off the destruction of obsolete bombers as disarmament. He asked the United States instead to respond to the Soviet idea: destroy all bombers everywhere. Fisher pointed out that this would not be acceptable to other nations that depended heavily on bombers for their defense forces. Fisher's point was a telling one and, on April 2, Tsarapkin amended the Soviet proposal. They were prepared now to limit bomber scrapping to the major powers.

President Johnson reendorsed the idea of destroying equivalent numbers of bombers in his message to the reconvening ENDC on June 9. On the same occasion Soviet Deputy Foreign Minister Zorin said that the USSR also gave priority to proposals for the destruction of bombers, and would be "flexible" on the U.S. suggestion. A month later, however, Tsarapkin reverted to the previous adamant position: The bonfires had to include all bombers possessed by the major powers or none. And there, essentially, the matter came to rest.*

"Sixteen Words and One Sum"

The superpowers also flirted briefly during Johnson's term with reductions in military budgets as an approach to arms limitation. The Soviets had advanced this idea repeatedly since Stalin's death. Khrushchev's abiding concern for the welfare of the Russian consumer was undoubtedly a factor in his espousal of military cuts. Late in 1963 he announced a 4.3 percent reduction in planned Soviet military expenditures for 1964, and suggested that the United States follow suit. In his first budget message to Congress, in January 1964, President Johnson announced a small reduction in the U.S. defense budget, from $52 to $51 billion. In real terms (after inflation) the reduction was somewhat more significant, and the Soviet press re-

---

*In his oral history interview for the LBJ Library, Adrian Fisher said of this Soviet proposal: "They're just playing for the galleries and relying on the good sense of the U.S. to keep them from having to put their money where their mouth is. That's a display of confidence in our good judgment which I find truly touching, although sometimes embarrassing. You know, here is the Soviet Union, with China on their borders . . . with a straight face saying, 'Let's get rid of all bombers.' They aren't going to do that" (Transcript, Oral History Interview, 10/31/68, by Paige E. Mulhollan, p. 52, LBJ Library).

ceived it as at least a token response to Khrushchev's challenge. On January 28, Tsarapkin proposed at the ENDC that the recently announced reductions in Soviet and U.S. military budgets be followed up by further mutual cuts amounting to 10 to 15 percent per side. This suggestion was greeted with interest by other delegations in Geneva.

An intrinsic problem that the United States had in approaching arms limitation through budget reductions was that there was no way of knowing from the Soviet Union's announced budget what its military expenditures truly were. Fisher put the matter bluntly at the ENDC on April 9, 1964. He observed that the USSR's published military budget for 1964 consisted of "some 16 words and one sum." He noted further that between 1955 and 1960, a period when the Soviet Union was known to have carried out intensive nuclear armament, its published military budget had *declined* by 15 percent. The inference was clear: The USSR's published military budget could not be believed. Still, the Soviet proposals of reciprocal budget reductions had struck a responsive chord in world opinion; it was difficult for the United States to ignore them.

The Committee of Principals discussed this matter on January 8 and again on February 18, 1964. On January 8:

> Foster suggested establishment of a multilateral international expert committee to study military budget procedures. It could be sold to the Soviets on the basis that if they gave us more information we could react with more confidence to announced reductions in their budget. Rusk said he had brought up the unrevealing Soviet budget with Gromyko and that the latter had felt that the problem was not so difficult; our technical people ought to be able to solve it. Recalling this conversation, Rusk felt that having an expert committee was a good way to probe the Soviets.
>
> McNamara objected to the idea of having the committee be multilateral. He did not feel we should ask the Soviets to expose their budgetary information except to the United States. Bundy agreed. He added that to have such an investigation in an open forum in Geneva could also imply that we intended to make formal agreements with the Soviets on budget reductions, whereas he doubted that Congress would ever accept Soviet-supplied numbers as a basis for budget reductions. [CIA Director] McCone observed, however, that Foster was only suggesting

a study of fiscal *procedures;* he did not see how we could lose by this since we had so much to learn about the Soviets.

Rusk asked whether there were enough questions to ask to make such a discussion fruitful. Both McNamara and McCone felt there were plenty of good technical questions that could be used to probe Soviet procedures. McNamara returned to his criticism of the multilateral approach. He felt that any involvement of the French, Germans, and British would only dilute the information we might get. Therefore, we should first try to get the information on a bilateral basis; if that failed we could then consider doing it multilaterally for the propaganda value. Rusk concluded that we should explore it bilaterally first and then come back to the Principals, but he said he thought there were some advantages to having others, for example, the Nigerians, hear the Soviets admit that they could not give us the information we needed.

The discussion of the budget matter at the February 28 meeting was very brief—it was not the scheduled topic of discussion.

Rusk asked Foster to summarize how things were going in Geneva. Foster said the negotiations were being conducted in "the best atmosphere yet," but then said there had been no agreement, not even on the agenda. The Soviets continued to insist on reductions in military budgets. They were proposing reductions of 20 percent, with the savings to be contributed to the welfare of developing countries. [This play to the galleries was almost too transparent.] Foster said we continued to resist on the ground that there was no way of verifying Soviet reductions.

In December 1964, Premier Kosygin told the Supreme Soviet that the USSR's military expenditures for 1965 were being reduced from 13.3 to 12.8 billion rubles. (The official exchange rate at the time was 1 ruble = $1.11.) He said he was acting after being informed that the United States was also planning a reduction.[5]

Kosygin's information was partially correct: On January 18, 1965, President Johnson sent a special defense message to Congress in which he estimated that defense expenditures for the fiscal year ending June 30, 1965, would be $49.3 billion, $2 billion less than in the preceding year. The president predicted that, barring international complications, defense spending would continue to "constitute a declining portion of our expanding gross national product."

It was not to be. Shortly after this message, the president embarked on his sharp escalation of the Vietnam War and, from that time forward, military spending by both superpowers resumed an upward course. The U.S. military budget increased from $49 billion (1965) to $57.2 billion (1966) to $73 billion (1967). The Soviets in turn announced successive increases of 5 and 8.2 percent. The idea of budget cuts for arms control purposes dropped from sight.

Cutoff and Transfer

We have reviewed in earlier chapters the steps taken by the Johnson administration to reduce the production of fissionable materials and to close down some of the facilities involved. Though President Johnson succeeded to some extent in surrounding these actions with the aura of arms control, they were, as we have indicated, prompted largely by the excess of materials production capacity built up during the 1950s. None of the cutbacks threatened to limit the planned development or production of needed nuclear weapons. There was, however, another proposal regarding fissionable materials production that might have had significant arms-limiting potential. This was to cease entirely the production of fissionable material for military purposes.

The idea had its genesis in President Eisenhower's "Atoms for Peace" address to the UN General Assembly in December 1953. Eisenhower coupled the notion of a complete cutoff in production of fissionable materials with that of contributing some already produced materials to a new international agency that would employ them for peaceful purposes. It was this part of his proposal that led to the establishment of the IAEA. In 1956, Secretary of State John Foster Dulles formally proposed to the UN Disarmament Commission that all future production of fissionable materials be for nonweapon purposes. The Soviet Union rejected the proposal, ostensibly on the grounds that it did not outlaw nuclear weapons. Their real reason probably had to do with the fact that their stockpile of fissionable materials was then much smaller than ours. In 1957 Ambassador Harold Stassen added the other part of President Eisenhower's suggestion to the formal U.S. proposal: In addition to a cutoff of fissionable materials production for military use there should be a transfer of material already produced to peaceful use.

At a meeting of the Committee of Principals on March 1, 1962, it was suggested that, since the ratio of U.S. and Soviet stockpiles of "weapons-grade U-235"* were on the order of five to one in our favor, we should be willing to transfer such material on at least a two-to-one basis. However, General Lemnitzer, chairman of the Joint Chiefs, would not agree even on equal transfers until the results of the next U.S. atmospheric test series were available. On November 20, 1962, two weeks after the test series (Operation DOMINIC) had concluded, President Kennedy approved the concept of offering U-235 transfers in as high a ratio as two to one. In August 1963, the United States formally offered to transfer sixty thousand kilograms of weapons grade U-235 to peaceful use if the Soviets would transfer forty thousand kilograms. These amounts were far more than token quantities. A 1965 ACDA working paper estimated that forty thousand kilograms amounted to about 23 percent of total Soviet production of weapons grade U-235 through mid-1964.

President Johnson's message to the ENDC of January 21, 1964 kept alive the idea of a halt in production of fissionable materials for weapons purposes, although it failed to mention transfer of materials to civilian use. This omission was remedied on February 13 when Foster told the ENDC that the United States was prepared to act quickly on its past offer to transfer weapons grade U-235 to peaceful use in a 60–40 ratio versus the Soviets. An issue then arose within the government as to whether the materials cutoff and transfer proposal should be linked to the freeze proposal. (The freeze was still enjoying its brief heyday.) It was clear that if the two proposals had to be considered as a package the likelihood of either one being adopted was less than if they could be considered separately. The issue was discussed at a meeting of the Committee of Principals on February 28, 1964.

> Rusk said he tended to agree with the Joint Chiefs of Staff that the two proposals should be linked. Foster demurred, saying that President Johnson's message indicated they were separable. [The message had said: "Specifically, this nation now proposes

---

*This was the term used in presentations of the U.S. cutoff proposal at the ENDC and the UN. It should be interpreted to mean the U-235 contained in uranium that has been enriched from its normal (in nature) proportion of about 0.7 percent U-235 to about 90 percent U-235.

five major types of potential agreement:" and then enumerated the
freeze, the cutoff, and three other proposals.] **I agreed with Foster;
I could find no hint of linkage in the president's language.
McNamara said that the language could be subject to either
interpretation, and that he favored linkage. Bundy argued that
linkage would weaken the freeze proposal. Rusk suggested a
third option, which was to proceed with both missile freeze and
production cutoff "in parallel." There was no consensus.**

On December 30, 1964, the United States offered to transfer four
thousand kilograms of plutonium to peaceful use in exchange for a
Soviet transfer of twenty-five hundred kilograms, approximately a
60–40 ratio. In addition, we specified that all U-235 or plutonium
transferred should be placed under international safeguards. The Soviet response was cold. Ambassador Nikolay T. Fedorenko told the
UN Disarmament Commission that the amounts proposed for transfer would not diminish the U.S. nuclear potential, because we had
surplus weapons. In addition, the verification procedures would require the most intrusive controls. It was, the Soviets claimed, another
proposal of "control without disarmament." The neutrals at the ENDC
were most favorably disposed. They thought of the cutoff, however,
not as an isolated measure but as one that should be linked, along
with other "tangible steps," such as a comprehensive test ban and a
freeze of delivery vehicles, to the Nonproliferation Treaty.

To meet the Soviet objection that we were advocating controls
without disarmament, Ambassador Goldberg told the UN General
Assembly in September 1965 that, if the Soviet Union accepted the
idea of the production cutoff and of transfer to peaceful uses on a
60–40 basis, the transferred material should be obtained from the
demonstrated destruction of nuclear weapons chosen by each side
from its own stocks. At the ENDC in January 1966, Fisher enlarged
on Goldberg's proposal by describing in detail the procedures for the
demonstrated destruction of weapons. He noted that to obtain the
suggested amount of fissionable materials a very large number of
nuclear weapons would have to be destroyed. (An ACDA memorandum estimated the number on the Soviet side as more than two
thousand.)

U.S. efforts on behalf of the cutoff and transfer proposal reached
their peak in 1965 and early in 1966. We ceased to press for it thereafter. There were probably two main reasons for our diminished in-

terest. First, most of the energy we had to give to arms control activity began to be taken up by the intensifying negotiations on the Nonproliferation Treaty. Second, the ratio of U.S. to Soviet stockpiles of fissionable materials was diminishing rapidly. As noted earlier, it had been thought in 1962 that our stockpile of weapons grade U-235 was five times that of the USSR. By 1965 the ACDA was estimating that the Soviet stockpile was already half our own, and closing fast. The crossover point, the time when their stockpiles of both U-235 and plutonium might become larger than ours, was thought to be 1970.* From a military point of view, the cutoff proposal was therefore becoming less advantageous, if advantageous at all, to the United States.

Toward More Serious Engagement

While the United States and the USSR batted unacceptable arms limitation proposals back and forth during Lyndon Johnson's first three years as president, both sides continued steadily to add newer and better weapons to their nuclear arsenals. One aspect of the continuing arms race appeared particularly alarming to serious-minded individuals. This was the deployment by the Soviets of an antiballistic missile system around Moscow and rising pressure within the United States to deploy comparable systems for protection of American cities. These developments seemed to imply a much more rapid and destabilizing escalation, because it was clear that each side would have to respond to the other's defensive weapons by building up its own offensive strength. During the last two years of Johnson's presidency, the United States gradually persuaded the Soviet Union to adopt this anxious view of the matter and both sides began to consider entering into serious negotiations leading to restrictions on the buildup of nuclear arms. The beginning steps along this trail, which led in time to the SALT agreements, are considered in chapters 31 through 33. But first we must go on an excursion to the farthest reaches of man's environment—outer space and the ocean floor.

Notes

1. Testimony at Senate hearings on military procurement, 1964, quoted in Larson, *Disarmament and Soviet Policy,* p. 109f.

---

*The United States had the capacity to produce larger quantities than were programmed. The needs of military and civilian programs did not require such full production, however. A considerable portion of our military needs for U-235 was being supplied by retired weapons.

2. Smith, *Doubletalk,* p. 116.
3. Lambert, "Background Information" (unpublished), p. 2.
4. Newhouse, *Cold Dawn,* p. 70.
5. Larson, *Disarmament and Soviet Policy,* p. 246.

30
Outer Limits

I propose that we agree that outer space should be used only for peaceful
purposes. We face a decisive moment in history in relation to this matter.
—Dwight D. Eisenhower
to the Soviet Union, January 1958

Space

On October 10, 1967, I attended a ceremony in the East Room of
the White House signaling the entry into force of the Outer Space
Treaty. (Its full name is "Treaty on Principles Governing the Activities
of States in the Exploration and Use of Outer Space, Including the
Moon and Other Celestial Bodies.") In their remarks for the occasion,
both President Johnson and Ambassador Dobrynin observed that the
date was but three days beyond the tenth anniversary of Sputnik I's
ascent into orbit.

Even before Sputnik the United States had been proposing international controls over activities in space; President Eisenhower had
mentioned the subject several times in his correspondence with Russian leaders. The Soviet Union, on the eve of launching its first satellite, and about to test its first ICBM, was not interested.[1] Their
response followed a by then well-established principle of superpower
behavior in the nuclear arms race: Try to negotiate away the other
fellow's advantage and resist negotiation in areas of one's own
superiority.

President Eisenhower warmed even more to the subject of space
limitations after signing the Antarctic Treaty in December 1959. That
treaty assured that the Antarctic continent would be used for peaceful
purposes only and specifically forbade any nuclear explosions in Antarctica and the disposal there of radioactive wastes. Addressing the
UN General Assembly on September 22, 1960, Eisenhower suggested
that the principles of the Antarctic Treaty might be applied as well

to outer space and celestial bodies. The USSR continued to be coy about the matter. While expressing agreement with the principle that outer space should be used only for peaceful purposes, the Soviets insisted that any formal pact to that effect be linked with agreements on certain outstanding disarmament issues. This was a way of assuring there would be no pact.

When President Kennedy assumed office he wasted no time in reemphasizing the desirability of restricting outer space to peaceful uses, mentioning the subject in both his inaugural address and his first State of the Union message. In September 1963, when the U.S. space program seemed to be catching up or even forging ahead, the Soviet Union announced its willingness to abandon linkage with other disarmament measures and reach an agreement against placing weapons of mass destruction in orbit. The State Department immediately issued a statement welcoming the Soviet announcement. A month later the UN General Assembly passed by acclamation a resolution commending the position of the superpowers and calling on all states to refrain from orbiting weapons of mass destruction, installing them on celestial bodies, or stationing them in outer space.

In 1965 the United States began exploring the possibility of a formal treaty that would give greater substance to the UN resolution. At the same time there was a flurry of diplomatic activity following the display of three new rocket systems at a military parade in Moscow on November 7, 1965. *Pravda* stated that one of the missiles could be fired from space at any target on earth. On November 8, the State Department announced it was studying whether the Soviet Union had violated the intent of the UN resolution by developing an orbital missile. In response, Ambassador Dobrynin stated that the USSR was abiding and would abide by the resolution. The apparent contradiction was explained a month later when *Pravda* asserted its view that the UN resolution did not apply to rockets launched in space so long as they did not complete an orbit around the earth. The USSR offered renewed assurances through diplomatic channels that it did not intend to violate the resolution, so interpreted.*

---

*On November 3, 1967, in the wake of an apparent Soviet test of this new weapon, which he called a "fractional orbital bombardment system" (FOBS), Secretary McNamara issued a statement appraising its advantages and disadvantages. "In our opinion," the secretary said, "the disadvantages are overriding." They included the facts that, as compared to an ICBM, the FOBS would have but a fraction of the payload and would be significantly less accurate (*Documents on Disarmament: 1967*, p. 559). The Soviets apparently came in time to a similar conclusion. After deploying a large number of launchers for the new program, they dismantled them all pursuant to a requirement in the SALT II Treaty (private communication from Center for Defense Information).

On May 7, 1966, President Johnson initiated more intensive negotiations for a formal space treaty with a statement explaining why such a treaty was needed and setting forth what the United States considered its essential elements. On June 16, 1966, both the United States and the Soviet Union submitted draft treaties. Formal negotiations on the drafts began soon after. They were carried out for the United States by our UN ambassador, Arthur Goldberg.

Negotiations continued intermittently in Geneva and New York until early December. According to Goldberg's own account they "went very smoothly and rapidly and were marked by a spirit of accommodation and a willingness on all sides to compromise without sacrificing fundamental principles."[2] The matters on which difficulties arose were, in the main, complicated but not fundamentally important legal issues. The principal substantive provisions were never in controversy.

On December 8, 1966, the superpowers announced that they had reached agreement on a treaty. On December 19, the General Assembly approved it by acclamation. It was opened for signature in Washington, Moscow, and London on January 27, 1967. On April 25, 1967, the Senate gave unanimous approval to the treaty's ratification and, as previously noted, it went into effect on October 10, 1967.

From the point of view of arms control, the principal provision of the Outer Space Treaty is Article IV, which binds parties to the treaty "not to place in orbit around the Earth any objects carrying nuclear weapons or any kinds of weapons of mass destruction, install such weapons on celestial bodies, or station such weapons in outer space in any other manner." Article IV also proscribes any other military use of a celestial body. Other principal provisions of the treaty specify that outer space is "not subject to national appropriation by claim of sovereignty" (Article II); that activities in space must be carried out in accordance with international law (Article III); that astronauts are to be regarded as "envoys of mankind,"* are to be aided if in distress, and returned safely to their countries if they land elsewhere (Article V); and that space shall be explored and used in such a way as to avoid harmful contamination and in a spirit of cooperation and mutual assistance (Article IX).

Speaking at the signing ceremony in Washington on January 27, 1967, President Johnson hailed the event as an "inspiring moment in

---

*Thus the plaque implanted on the moon in July 1969 by astronauts Neil Armstrong and Buzz Aldrin stated: "We come in peace for all mankind."

the history of the human race." In his remarks when the treaty entered into force on October 10, 1967, the president said: "By adding this treaty to the law of nations, we are forging a permanent disarmament agreement for outer space." Regretfully, we must conclude that the president, as was his tendency, overstated the case. What the treaty did chiefly was to prohibit a military action—placing nuclear weapons in orbit—that made little military sense and that neither side seriously contemplated. (The technical drawbacks of orbital weapons were overwhelming. They could hit predetermined targets only on certain days and at certain hours. Moreover, they would be relatively easy to intercept or render inoperative.) What the treaty did *not* do was made amply clear by UN Secretary-General U Thant. In his message of December 19, 1966, congratulating the General Assembly for its unanimous endorsement of the treaty, the secretary-general stated: "I note with regret that the door is not yet barred against military activities in space."

U Thant was, of course, absolutely right. The ICBMs of both superpowers continued to be designed to traverse outer space during a major part of their trajectories. In addition, outer space was becoming increasingly cluttered with reconnaissance satellites and other military hardware. Indeed, at a meeting of the National Aeronautics and Space Council on July 21, 1966, Vice President Hubert Humphrey remarked that 71 percent of the total U.S. payload in space related to activities of the Department of Defense. Currently, the Strategic Defense Initiative of the United States and comparable activity by the Soviet Union threaten to make outer space a principal theatre of the arms race. All this military activity belies the protestations voiced so frequently from 1957 on, including a statement in the preamble of the Outer Space Treaty itself, that outer space should be used exclusively for peaceful purposes.

The Ocean Floor

The rapid advances in military technology being achieved by the great powers aroused a further concern: that there would be an attempt to militarize the bottom of the world's oceans.

Beginning after World War I there had been a trend toward more varied and intensive economic exploitation of the oceans. To assure equity in the use of resources in the sea, and to prevent commercial rivalries from escalating into national conflicts, an attempt was made in 1958 to establish some codes of international behavior in this environment. One outcome of this effort was agreement on conventions distinguishing territorial waters—those acknowledged to fall under the jurisdiction of coastal states—from the high seas beyond. Military considerations were not primary in the 1958 conventions; the focus was on economic equity.

Then, in November 1967, Ambassador Arvid Pardo of Malta introduced in the General Assembly a resolution recommending that study be given to the "reservation exclusively for peaceful purposes of the seabed and the ocean floor." The consequence of Dr. Pardo's initiative was the establishment of an ad hoc UN committee to conduct the needed studies and make recommendations.

It soon became apparent that the superpowers would take divergent paths on this issue. In meetings of the ad hoc committee, the Soviet Union chose to play its by then familiar role of adopting what Alva Myrdal has called "the maximalist approach" designed to win points among the smaller nations.[3] In this case the approach manifested itself in a resolution "solemnly calling upon all states to use the seabed . . . exclusively for peaceful purposes." The United States resisted so sweeping a proposal because we felt a need to protect our continued use of bottom-dwelling listening and communication devices to monitor the activity of Soviet submarines. In view, however, of the Soviet proposal and a general enthusiasm within the UN for taking some action regarding the seabed, we felt under political pressure to make some positive response. The ACDA accordingly came up with the idea that the United States sponsor a measure banning the emplacement of nuclear weapons on the ocean floor. This had the virtue of paralleling the recently adopted Outer Space Treaty.

The ACDA proposal was discussed at a meeting of the Committee of Principals on May 14, 1968.

> Rusk announced the question: should we agree to prohibit weapons of mass destruction on the seabed? If not, who was contemplating such a use of the seabed and why? Turning to [Deputy Defense Secretary Paul] Nitze, Rusk asked whether there were any reasons why the Department of Defense would object to such a ban. Nitze answered that it probably was not in the national interest to narrow *in any way* where weapons could be placed. [Joint Chiefs Chairman] Wheeler amplified Nitze's statement by saying that ocean bottoms might one day be a

desirable place to deploy nuclear weapons. Foster replied that we had made a national commitment to arms control, pronounced by the president himself, and this had also to be taken into account.* He noted that there were alternative proposals before the UN that were much less desirable from our point of view—such formulations as complete demilitarization of the seabed, which was against our interests, and limiting the use of the seabed to peaceful purposes, which was difficult to define. The fact that the Soviet Union was supporting one of these measures gave us a political problem at the United Nations that could not be ignored. Also, Foster said, there was a larger political problem: we were trying to make progress toward a nonproliferation treaty and to do so we had to convince other countries that we were serious about arms control.

Nitze said that Foster had added a dimension to the question posed by Rusk and all could have sympathy with his position. Nevertheless, Nitze thought the present proposal needed further analysis. If we really wanted to limit the arms race, might we not gain more by bilateral discussions with the Soviets on limiting offensive and defensive arms than by negotiations on a variety of multinational restrictions?

Rusk then made a plea for the seabed proposal, and with more vehemence and passion than was his wont. He said that the Soviet Union and the United States already could destroy each other and were even then facing the prospect of moving to higher plateaus of destructive capability. Why in the world would we want to enter still another new environment with nuclear weapons? He thought it would be a futile exercise that would do nothing to increase our security. He saw no reason why the arguments that applied to the prohibition of nuclear weapons in Antarctica and outer space could not be applied as well to the ocean floor.

It was decided that the matter should be studied further.

The Principals discussed the seabed matter again on June 3, having in hand the opinions reached by the Committee of Deputies, who reported that, "except for the Joint Chiefs of Staff," they were in general agreement that nuclear weapons should be banned from the seabed.

---

*John Newhouse reports that the falling out of Wheeler and Foster over the Seabed Treaty affected their future relations and was one of the factors causing ACDA to play a minor role in the formulation of the initial U.S. SALT proposal (*Cold Dawn*, p. 115).

Nitze took issue with the Deputies' statement that banning nuclear weapons on the seabed might save money. On the contrary, he felt that a sea-based nuclear weapons system might itself save money. He then repeated what he and Wheeler had said at the previous meeting: that sea-based nuclear weapons might prove advantageous sometime in the future and therefore should not be foreclosed.

I disputed this point of view, saying that it would never be possible to make progress in arms control if we limited ourselves to banning only those things that might never have any future military advantage. I used the analogy of the Limited Test Ban Treaty. Certainly we couldn't have said in 1963 that there would never be advantages to testing in the atmosphere. Nevertheless, we had to make a determination of *relative* advantage based on many considerations, not all of which were military. This analysis had led the Kennedy administration to the view that, on balance, it was to the advantage of the United States to have the test ban treaty.

[U.S. Information Agency Director Leonard H.] Marks said that a seabed treaty would have great political benefits. Nitze pointed out, however, that a number of nations would probably not be satisfied with our somewhat circumscribed approach—outlawing only nuclear weapons, rather than all military uses, on the ocean floor—and that we might have to go further and further in order to get agreement on a treaty. Foster disagreed strongly. He thought that a treaty based on the proposed American position could be sold at the UN. Rusk agreed with Foster. He thought our limited proposal would be an adequate response to the general desire for action in this field and would take care of 98 percent of the political problem posed for us by the more sweeping Soviet proposal.

General Wheeler took issue with a statement in the Deputies' memorandum to the effect that it was highly unlikely that the Soviets would deploy nuclear weapons on the seabed. He noted that it had also been predicted that they would not orbit a nuclear weapon in space and then they had followed with a fractional orbital bombardment system. Rusk asked whether it was true, so far as we knew, that the Soviets were not currently developing a weapons system for the ocean bed. Helms said this was true. Wheeler objected that we had no verification ability but [Deputy CIA Director Admiral Rufus L.] Taylor took issue with this. He said that overhead reconnaissance gave us this capability to a large extent.

Rusk said he was puzzled by the reluctance of Nitze and Wheeler to support a seabed treaty in view of their past support of the Limited Test Ban Treaty, the Space Treaty, and the Antarctic Treaty. Nitze said contamination of the atmosphere by atmospheric tests was a factor in the Chiefs' support of the test ban. Wheeler added that the decision to support the Test Ban Treaty had been very close among the Joint Chiefs and that we were now paying a heavy penalty for that treaty, especially in the added expense and time required for underground tests. He said that the Chiefs had been disinclined to fight over the Antarctic Treaty [implying that they may have had misgivings even over it!]. They had also not been inclined to argue about the Outer Space Treaty, which seemed easier to verify than a seabed treaty would be.

Rusk asked whether the Chiefs' concerns related to the years immediately ahead or to more distant years—would a treaty be more acceptable if it had a duration clause? Wheeler replied that the present concept of a seabed treaty might be only a first step and that we seemed to be in the process of putting ourselves into a strategic straitjacket. He again emphasized difficulties in verification.

Foster said that all he planned to do on June 17 at the UN ad hoc committee on the seabed was say that we favored placing some restraints on the emplacement of weapons of mass destruction on the ocean bottom. He did not plan to table a treaty draft.

Rusk said that the president had raised the possibility of saying something the next day in a speech at Glassboro State College about the U.S. position on a seabed treaty, but in view of the lack of agreement at this meeting it did not seem possible.

In his Glassboro speech the president's only mention of the deep-ocean floor was as an "opportunity for cooperation" among the nations.

Not long afterwards I had a private session with Dean Rusk in his office. Although it was not the planned subject of our meeting, the conversation drifted in time to the seabed negotiations and Rusk expressed dismay about the attitude of the Joint Chiefs. Passing from the particular to the general, he stated that he was concerned about the growing influence of the military on U.S. foreign policy. He said that he was coming to believe that President Eisenhower had been right when he warned the American people in his farewell address about the possible "acquisition of unwarranted influence, whether sought or unsought, by the military–industrial complex."

In due course the disagreements within the Johnson administration on the seabed matter were resolved; the protreaty position won out. In June 1968 the Soviet Union and the United States presented resolutions expressing their respective points of view to the ad hoc UN committee while at the same time recommending that that body surrender jurisdiction to the ENDC as an organization better suited for discussion of arms control matters. In March 1969 the Soviets submitted to the ENDC a draft treaty providing for complete demilitarization of the seabed. Two months later the United States introduced a more limited treaty prohibiting the emplacement of weapons of mass destruction on the seabed. In addition to their major difference on what was to be prohibited, the Soviet and U.S. treaty drafts differed in their provisions for verification. In a curious reversal of historical roles the Soviet Union contended that all structures on the ocean bottom should be subject to on-site inspection, whereas the United States argued that violations would be easily observable and that *on-site inspection was therefore not necessary.*

At length the Soviets, in a demonstration of apparent reasonableness, came round and adopted essentially the U.S. draft treaty. On October 7, 1969, the United States and the USSR submitted to the Conference of the Committee on Disarmament (CCD)—the new name given to the ENDC after it was enlarged from eighteen to twenty-six members—a joint draft of a "Treaty on the Prohibition of the Emplacement of Nuclear Weapons and Other Weapons of Mass Destruction on the Seabed and the Ocean Floor and in the Subsoil Thereof." The principal obligation of the treaty is described in its lengthy title. Parties are permitted to undertake verification using their own means or those of other parties, provided they do not interfere with legitimate seabed activities.

After extensive debate, the final draft was approved by the General Assembly on December 7, 1970. The treaty was opened for signature on February 11, 1971, and entered into force on May 19, 1972. This was just one more example—to add to the Nonproliferation Treaty and the SALT I agreements—of a treaty incubated during Lyndon Johnson's presidency that came to fruition during that of his successor.

Notes

1. U.S. ACDA *Arms Control and Disarmament Agreements,* p. 48.
2. Statement to Senate Foreign Relations Committee, March 7, 1967, in *Documents on Disarmament: 1967,* p. 120.
3. Myrdal, *The Game of Disarmament,* p. 98.

31
Ascent to Glassboro

I think you must realize that following the deployment by you of an anti-ballistic system I face great pressures . . . not only to deploy defensive systems in this country, but also to increase greatly our capabilities to penetrate any defensive weapons which you might establish.
—President Johnson to Premier Kosygin
January 1967

First Stirrings

The goal of the U.S. nuclear buildup in the 1940s and 1950s was to maintain clear strategic superiority over the Soviet Union. In view of the USSR's superiority in conventional arms, this appeared necessary to deter Soviet adventurism, particularly in the direction of Western Europe. Different reasoning emerged in the early 1960s. Following the Soviet Union's massive buildup after the Cuban missile crisis, a consensus grew in this country that it would be increasingly difficult to maintain nuclear superiority in any meaningful sense.[1] Agreements that would limit nuclear arms on both sides then began to commend themselves as an alternative to continuing the arms race. About the time of the Limited Test Ban Treaty (1963), for example, Secretary of Defense McNamara began making statements warning against the dangers of an uninhibited arms race. The issue was drawn more sharply a year later when it became clear that the Soviets were about to deploy an antiballistic missile (ABM) system around Moscow, and perhaps around other cities as well. This development stimulated a vigorous controversy within the U.S. government. The Joint Chiefs of Staff, supported by a growing sentiment in Congress, attempted to obtain production authority for the NIKE-X ABM system, which had entered development in 1963. NIKE-X was first conceived as a countermeasure to the developing Soviet system, but later there was disagreement as to what its role should be, for example, whether to defend U.S. cities and/or Minuteman silos against the Soviets, or merely to protect against a highly unlikely attack by the Chinese.

McNamara stated his views on this question, and gave an indication of solutions to come, in testimony before the Joint Committee on Atomic Energy in March 1966. The crux of what he had to say was the following:

> We have spent over the past four or five years about $2 billion on the development of an anti-ballistic missile system. It is, we believe, the most sophisticated system in the world today. However, we believe it cannot protect this Nation against what I would call a sophisticated attack.* . . . It *can* defend . . . against the kind of attack that Communist China might direct against us in the decade between, let us say, 1975 to 1985.[2]

But McNamara was unable to still the clamor for U.S. deployment of an extensive ABM defense against Soviet attack. At one point it was contemplated having ABM batteries defending fifty American cities.[3] President Johnson was especially sensitive to pressures emanating from his old colleagues in the Congress. He was beginning to feel that he had to propose an ABM system to the country, lest failure to do so hurt Democratic candidates in the 1966 and 1968 elections. (An unidentified administration official was reported to have said that the president "could be crucified politically . . . for sitting on his hands while the Russians provide a defense for their people.")[4]

Differing points of view on missile defense were presented to the president at a climactic meeting in Austin, Texas, on December 6, 1966. The Joint Chiefs were present, as were McNamara and Deputy Secretary of Defense Cyrus Vance. The Chiefs requested authority to mount a full deployment of NIKE-X to defend U.S. cities against Soviet attack. McNamara, beating a strategic retreat, suggested a compromise whereby funds to meet the Chiefs' request would be included in the president's pending budget for fiscal year 1968, but would not be spent until there had been opportunity to explore limitation of strategic arms with the Soviet Union. The president, himself not an enthusiast for ABM deployment, agreed with McNamara.[5]

In order to assure that President Johnson held to the position reached at Austin, McNamara arranged for the president to meet in

---

*An inference of this statement was that the Soviet ABM system need not be a cause of concern; it also could not ward off such a sophisticated attack as the U.S. could launch.

January 1967 with the White House science adviser (Donald F. Hornig) and his predecessors (James R. Killian, George B. Kistiakowsky, and Jerome Wiesner); and with the director of defense research and engineering (John S. Foster) and his predecessors (Harold Brown and Herbert York). York describes what happened:

> We were asked that simple kind of question which must be answered after all the complicated ifs, ands, and buts have been discussed: "Will it [the NIKE-X] work and should it be deployed?" The answer in relation to defending our people against a Soviet missile attack was "No;" there was no dissent from that answer. . . . There was also some discussion of this same question in relation to a hypothetical Red Chinese missile threat. In this latter case, there was some divergence of views, although the majority view (and my own) was still "No."[6]

Strengthened in his beliefs, President Johnson wrote to Premier Kosygin on January 27, 1967, stating the situation quite directly and eloquently:

> I have directed Ambassador [Llewellyn] Thompson as a matter of first priority to discuss with you and appropriate members of your Government the possibilities of reaching an understanding between us which would curb the strategic arms race. I think you must realize that following the deployment by you of an anti-ballistic missile system I face great pressures from the Members of Congress and from public opinion not only to deploy defensive systems in this country, but also to increase greatly our capabilities to penetrate any defensive systems which you might establish. If we should feel compelled to make such major increases in our strategic weapons capabilities, I have no doubt that you would in turn feel under compulsion to do likewise. We would thus have incurred on both sides colossal costs without substantially enhancing the security of our own peoples or contributing to the prospects for a stable peace in the world.

The president concluded by suggesting that, after Thompson had made an initial exploration with Soviet officials, it might "prove desirable to have some of our highest authorities meet in Geneva or another mutually agreeable place to carry the matter forward."[7]

This message bore the imprint of what McNamara and Rusk had been saying for some time. It is hard to imagine a better statement of the case.

The Kremlin as Hamlet

After the president's letter came a period of many months during which the Russian leadership periodically made affirmative statements about the desirability of arms limitation talks but refused to commit itself to the extent of naming a place and a date. It was evident that there was disagreement within the Kremlin. Just as our Chiefs of Staff were most reluctant to forego their plans for deployment of the NIKE-X, Soviet military leaders probably did not want to give up their own ABM plans. The feeling might have been even stronger on their side because Soviet military doctrine seemed to emphasize defense far more than did our own. As James Reston wrote: "The Soviet government is the victim of its own history. Napoleon and Hitler have made it psychopathic about defense."[8]

The first public response from the Soviets came on February 9, 1967, when Kosygin told a London press conference that the Soviet ABM system was justified because "a defensive system, which prevents attack, is not a cause of the arms race but represents a factor preventing the death of people."* Dean Rusk has characterized Kosygin's view of the matter as "the naïveté of the first look."[9] Evidence that the Soviet leadership was in considerable disarray on this subject appeared on February 15, when *Pravda* published an account of the London press conference. The article attributed to Kosygin a statement he had not made, to the effect that the Soviet government was willing to discuss questions related to both offensive and defensive weapons in the interest of averting a "further arms race."[10] Additional evidence of disarray came in reports leaked to the Western press that the *Pravda* article had embarrassed Soviet officials and that a clarifying article would soon be issued. But it never appeared.[11] Then, on February 27, a month to the day after receiving the president's letter, Kosygin wrote in reply that the Soviet government was "prepared to

---

Documents on Disarmament: 1967, p. 60. Kosygin's statement was remarkably similar in tone to statements President Reagan has made in behalf of his Strategic Defense Initiative. It seemed difficult for Kosygin then, or Reagan more recently, to acknowledge the paradox that, where nuclear weapons are involved, defensive deployments can appear just as threatening as offensive ones.

continue the exchange of views on questions related to strategic rocket-nuclear weapons." He said they would be in touch with Ambassador Thompson about this. "Nor do we exclude the possibility," Kosygin continued, "of holding in the future, as you suggest, a special meeting of our appropriate representatives for a more detailed discussion of this entire problem."

In his eagerness, President Johnson appeared to make more of Kosygin's reply than its contents warranted. On March 2, he announced that the Soviet leader had agreed to bilateral discussions on "means of limiting the arms race in offensive and defensive nuclear missiles." The president said that the talks would take place in Moscow, a gratuitous assumption since the Russians later expressed a preference for Leningrad. (When the talks actually began, in 1969, it was in Helsinki.) Johnson even went so far as to name the U.S. delegation. It was to be headed by Ambassador Thompson and would include John T. McNaughton, assistant secretary of defense for international security affairs; Harold Brown, former director of defense research and engineering; Raymond L. Garthoff, deputy director of the State Department's bureau of politico-military affairs; and an unnamed general.

A Revealing Meeting

In preparation for the expected talks, State and ACDA—a rare collaboration—prepared a "Proposal on Strategic Offensive and Defensive Missile Systems." It was discussed by the Committee on Principals on March 14, 1967. The meeting was noteworthy for its indications of just how unready President Johnson's principal lieutenants were for the talks he was seeking so eagerly; also for the recalcitrant position adopted by the Joint Chiefs of Staff.

> Fisher said the plan was a simple one that stopped far short of the USSR's expressed desire for complete disarmament. [Foy D.] Kohler [deputy under secretary of state and former ambassador to the Soviet Union] stated that the plan had essentially been agreed to by all members of the Committee of Deputies. He noted that it depended for its verification on our own national capabilities. Rusk observed that there were a couple of places where the paper suggested that the United States make concessions even before the Soviets had said "No" to our preferred

positions. He thought we should at least feel the Russians out before making any concessions.

General Wheeler set forth several requirements the Joint Chiefs believed should be met in any arms limitation negotiations. (1) They wanted a plan that would maintain the strategic superiority of the United States at all times. (2) They wanted our negotiators to insist on onsite inspection at the outset and, if this was not accepted, to limit negotiations to fixed land-based systems [the easiest to verify by national technical means]. (3) They did not wish to bargain away the possibility of the United States deploying an ABM system in the future. (4) They wanted any agreement formalized as a treaty. (5) They thought such a treaty should allow us to withdraw if there were hostile actions interfering with our means of verification, other deterioration of our ability to verify, or any attempt to deceive.

McNamara found the situation frustrating. He was convinced that strategic arms limitation was desirable, but also felt that we shouldn't agree to anything we couldn't check. That didn't leave very much. [Science Adviser] Hornig agreed: some arms limitation steps should be taken. The question was how to begin. [CIA Director] Helms said he felt "queasy" about our ability to carry out the unilateral verification called for by the plan.

Walt Rostow said that much depended on the nature of the Talinn system. He thought we should somehow learn more about it.* McNamara suggested we might use an inquiry about Talinn to open a dialogue with the Soviets. This dialogue could include some exchanges about our respective verification capabilities, perhaps even showing each other reconnaissance photographs. Rostow thought that the proper time to table a paper might be after such a dialogue. Neither he nor McNamara thought we should be putting forward a written plan at this time.

Fisher pointed out that we had already been talking to the Soviets for a long time and that what we should be talking to them about now was holding down defensive missiles. Kohler agreed with Fisher. McNamara doubted we were very close, that is, within a year or two, to an agreement with the Soviets on any of these matters.

---

*Talinn was a Soviet defense system using an advanced surface-to-air missile and was deployed extensively in the northwestern parts of the USSR. Most in the U.S. intelligence community thought it was designed only to combat high-flying aircraft, but some thought it also had an ABM potential. If the latter interpretation was correct the strategic balance and the impending negotiations could have been affected.

> Rusk made the challenging observation that, as time went by, we would find ourselves in a situation where we would not be able to make progress in these matters "in bits and pieces"; we would have to take a dramatic big step within a few years if we hoped to arrest the arms race.

Some of the stipulations laid down by the Joint chiefs at this meeting seemed designed to put obstacles in the path of any arms limitation agreement. Certainly, the Soviets were not about to give formal assent to lasting American strategic superiority, especially after the USSR's own massive buildup since the Cuban missile crisis had brought it near to strategic parity. To insist that an agreement allow future development of an American ABM system contravened the whole history of the time; it was precisely our alarm about the Soviet ABM deployment that had led the United States to seek arms limitation talks. Finally, the requirement that any agreement must take the form of a treaty was a reminder that the Joint Chiefs could probably muster enough support in the Senate to deny any treaty they did not like the two-thirds vote needed for ratification.

There were indications that the Joint Chiefs' Soviet counterparts were playing a similar role. Thus, on March 31, the army journal *Red Star* carried an article emphasizing the "very great national" and "strategic" role of antimissile weapons.[12] This article was taken as an indication that the prodefense position had won out within the Soviet military and that they were opposed to any negotiations that might lead to a slackening of their ABM development and deployment.

Selecting the Site

Weeks passed after Kosygin's letter of February 27, 1967, and the Soviets still would not name a date—evidence that serious debate continued in the Kremlin. On May 19, the president wrote again to Kosygin. This time he attempted to lure the Soviet leader by drawing a connection between strategic arms talks and the still-gestating nonproliferation treaty—known to be a high priority goal of the Soviet government. "These two enterprises are not explicitly linked," the president wrote, "but I am sure you are conscious that our task of persuading the non-nuclear powers to accept a nonproliferation treaty would be greatly eased if you and we could demonstrate concurrently our will and ability to begin to bring the nuclear arms race under better control. I hope, therefore, your government will find it possible to respond positively to our proposals to enter into serious discussions on the ABM and ICBM problem."[13]

Still the Soviets hesitated, and on June 13 Ambassador Thompson had to tell a Washington news conference that the time and place for the missile talks had not yet been established. A complication was added on June 17, when the Chinese conducted their first thermo-nuclear test, a blast in the megaton range. Indications were that a second such test was imminent. In briefing the Joint Committee on Atomic Energy a month later, CIA Director Helms estimated that the Chinese had already completed the development of a medium range ballistic missile and that they would have an ICBM capability before 1972. The heightened Chinese threat gave both the U.S. and Soviet armed forces an additional reason to insist on proceeding with their ABM plans.

In late June 1967 Premier Kosygin announced he would attend the upcoming meeting of the UN General Assembly. In his memoirs, Lyndon Johnson conjectures that Kosygin's main purpose in coming to New York was "to boost Arab morale and shore up Soviet prestige with its Arab friends."[14] (The USSR's standing in the Arab world had suffered as a result of its inability to prevent Israel's victory in the Six Day War, June 5–10.) Kosygin also let it be known, however, that he would welcome a chance to confer with the president.

It is significant of the atmosphere of those times that Kosygin felt he could not risk censure by Arabs, North Vietnamese, or Chinese by coming to or near Washington, even to Camp David. Nor would he assent to the U.S. suggestion that the meeting take place at Maguire Air Force Base in New Jersey, which offered many logistical advantages. For his part, Johnson would not agree to come to New York, Kosygin's preference, probably out of concern about the by now inevitable antiwar protestors. To help solve the dilemma, the president turned to an old friend, Governor Richard J. Hughes of New Jersey, asking him to suggest a place that was approximately halfway between Washington and New York, convenient to a major airport and a major highway, and remote from potential demonstrators. The quiet little college town of Glassboro, New Jersey, was selected on June 22, 1967, less than 24 hours before the meeting was scheduled to begin.

Notes

1. National Academy of Sciences, *Nuclear Arms Control,* p. 25.
2. JCAE, *Nonproliferation of Nuclear Weapons, Hearings,* February–March 1966, p. 99.

3. The fifty are listed in Coffey, "The Confrontation," p. 79.
4. *The New York Times,* December 27, 1966, quoted in Coffey, "The Confrontation," p. 76.
5. National Academy of Sciences, *Nuclear Arms Control,* p. 37.
6. York, *Race to Oblivion,* p. 194.
7. Johnson, *The Vantage Point,* p. 479f.
8. *The New York Times,* January 22, 1967.
9. Private conversation, March 13, 1986.
10. Intelligence Memo: "Soviet Military Policy in 1967," p. 17, National Security File, Country File, USSR, Box 223, LBJ Library.
11. Kolkowicz et al., *The Soviet Union and Arms Control,* p. 19.
12. Intelligence Memo: "Soviet Military Policy in 1967," p. 17, National Security File, Country File, USSR, Box 223, LBJ Library.
13. Johnson, *The Vantage Point,* p. 480f.
14. Ibid., p. 481.

32
The Summit

MCNAMARA: We react to you, and we must maintain a certain nuclear strength regardless of what is said around the table.
KOSYGIN: And we react to you—so that's an agreed point.
MCNAMARA: Yes, you are no different from us—you must react to us. What an insane road we are both following.
KOSYGIN: How well you speak!

Friday

The approach of the Glassboro get-together, President Johnson's only summit meeting with a Soviet leader, produced great excitement. For its part, the White House was determined to capture for history every detail of the proceedings and a presidential secretary, Marie Fehmer, was assigned to take detailed notes. As shown below, these notes (from President's Daily Diary, June 23, 1967),[1] reveal much about the president's nervousness and apparent dyspepsia before Kosygin arrived, about the personal encounter between the two leaders, and about the intensity of the discussions, particularly when McNamara attempted to persuade Kosygin that cooperation in controlling defensive missiles was preferable to competition in building them.

10:45 Motorcade arrived at the stone house, "Hollybush"—many, many television cameras—850 accredited press covering this day. Great air of excitement. President went directly in the house followed by advisors. House is Victorian—old; and dining rooms; two conference rooms have been cooled by addition of air conditioners last night. President went first to parlor, then back into Center Hall where he posed for pictures with the Hugheses [New Jersey Governor Richard J. Hughes and his wife] and the Robinsons [Dr. Thomas E. Robinson, president of Glassboro State College, and his wife]. Mrs. Hughes asked the President if Kosygin's daughter was coming with him and the President said he didn't know.

10:50 [President to] rest room. House built in 1845. Two Presidents before have visited the house, Theodore Roosevelt and Taft.

10:55 President to screened side porch—off front of house—to chat privately with Ambassador Thompson. He stood without his glasses because television cameras were covering him all this time, and held his hands behind his back. The President's face was tense— and his hands would open and close—clenching them into a fist and then releasing them.

10:57 McGeorge Bundy joined on the porch*—to tell the President that the Russians were running late 20 minutes because they had been held up in traffic. He also reported that they refused to speed up the pace, and hence would be delayed at least another 20 minutes.

10:59 Secretary Rusk joined on the porch.

11:00 The President out the side of the porch—to shake hands with the crowd—great cheers, wonderful crowd. Secretary Rusk, McGeorge Bundy, and Secretary McNamara stood quietly and watched from the sidelines. President called Governor and Mrs. Hughes to join him as he "worked the crowd."

11:03 President walked in front of house with Ambassador Thompson and Governor Hughes, posed at front door of house with Governor and Mrs. Hughes, Dr. and Mrs. Robinson.

11:05 Back in house—asked M. F. [Marie Fehmer, the note taker] for water and Titralac [an antacid medication].

11:11 [President] back to bathroom.

11:22 The President out the front door of the house—to greet Chairman Kosygin as car pulled up. Posed briefly for photos, then moved into the conference room. The President offered the Chairman a drink of water. He accepted. All members of the party were in the room at this time. The President asked through the interpreter—"How long did it take to drive?" and "Did you get to see some of the country?" The two men evidenced serious faces. The President looked intently at the Chairman, hands free. Kosygin had hands in pockets, removing them to point at the President when he talked to him. Kosygin uses hands a lot to emote. Smiles came on their faces when the Chairman mentioned the pollution in New York. The President said, "That's why Ambassador Thompson chose to live in Moscow." The Chairman congratulated the President on being

---

*Bundy had been called back into the White House to act, as he describes it, "as traffic manager on the Six Day War."

a grandfather—at this point the men had a common ground and they smiled and shook hands. The Chairman said, "I have been one for 18 years, and I have no regrets." Chairman Kosygin is 3–4 inches shorter than the President. The President told the Chairman that McGeorge Bundy was here today and that he had asked him to help on Middle East problems—at this point the two men began to move toward the door of the study—and the President spotted Bundy. He introduced Bundy to the Chairman.

11:30 [President] to study with Chairman Kosygin and two interpreters. Private meeting.

1:30 The President and the Chairman came to the dining room followed by other members of the party. The President asked M.F. for help in seating the chairman and then asked for some vodka. The President asked the Chairman what he would like to drink and the Chairman said, "Whatever you're having," and the President said "I'm having what you're having—vodka." The two men grinned at each other, and both downed quickly—Russian fashion—a serving of vodka—Chairman Kosygin had brought a special bottle of Russian vodka to share with the President.

Luncheon The President, Kosygin, round table to right: Mr. Sukhodrev (Kosygin's interpreter), Secretary McNamara, Mr. Firsov [Kosygin's private secretary], Mr. Watson (Marvin) [White House appointments secretary], Mr. Vorontsov [counselor, Soviet Embassy], Mr. Bundy, Mr. Zamyatin [head of press department of Soviet Foreign Office], Secretary Rusk (across from President), Foreign Minister Gromyko, Ambassador Thompson, Mr. Batsanov [counsellor, Soviet Ministry of Foreign Affairs], George Christian [White House press secretary], General Volkov [security officer for Soviet officials travelling abroad], Mr. Rostow, Ambassador Dobrynin.

1:45 President talking with Dobrynin. At the table, the President began to tell the Chairman—through an interpreter—the story of the jelly in Thailand.* It brought a loud laugh from the Chairman. The President explained to the Chairman about the dinner in Los Angeles tonight and told him what the President's Club was. "We've had one dinner in New York, one in the South, and now one in the West, and I'd give anything if you could go with me because I know you would enjoy it," said the President. McGeorge Bundy leaned over the center of the table and talked to Kosygin about technological development in both countries. Kosygin said he was very much

---

*There apparently were certain standard stories in Johnson's repertory that were well known to White House personnel.

impressed by what he had seen here. Secretary Rusk said he didn't know how the President and Kosygin got along, but he and his counterparts got along real well in their end of the business.* The President told the group at the table that he and the Chairman had talked about grandsons for some time. The President then discussed birthdays with Gromyko—told him his was in 1908 and asked Gromyko when he was born. Gromyko replied that 1908 was a good year for wine. The President smiled, and said that he wished the two countries could agree on everything like they agreed on that—disarmament, arms control, etc.

The President then asked Secretary McNamara to make comments on disarmament, etc. "because sometimes news reports and papers don't always reveal everything, and I think the Chairman would be interested in hearing some of your thoughts in this field." The President continued by saying that he and the Chairman had talked at length about expenditures and how money was going down the drain because the weapon was old by the time they were ready to use it. "I told him that we had the same hopes, but I hadn't found a way for us to all agree on it," said the President. The Chairman said that he would gladly hear what the Secretary had to say. Mr. McNamara began his statement. Early in McNamara's discourse the Chairman interrupted and said, "When you talk on this subject, does Mr. Rusk always agree with you? I want to know the internal spring in this administration." All laughed and the Secretary replied that yes, they did work together—"we've been together for 6 years and never had a disagreement." "That's very bad," laughed the Chairman.† Secretary McNamara continued, saying we were engaged in an arms race advanced beyond any limit. "We react to you, and we must maintain a certain nuclear strength regardless of what is said around the table," said the Secretary. The Chairman said, "And we react to you—so that's an agreed point."

SECRETARY MCNAMARA: "Yes, you are no different from us—you must react to us. What an insane road we are both following."

---

*While Johnson and Kosygin were having their private discussion, the remainder of the two delegations were meeting in another room.

†Walt Rostow tells an illuminating story on the relations of Rusk and McNamara: "In 1965, while we were flying back from the ranch, someone remarked: 'We've been damned lucky to have you two fellows getting on so well,' and Bob spoke up and said: 'It's not due to Dean here, it's due to me.' Which was of course in semi-jest. But then he said something deadly serious: 'I deeply believe that military power is the servant of political purposes and that the secretary of state is the superior officer to whom the secretary of defense is ultimately subservient, and that's the basic reason why we get on.' The other side of it was that Rusk had been a military staff officer and he understood sympathetically the problems of the military" (private conversation June 7, 1985).

CHAIRMAN KOSYGIN: "How well you speak."

McNAMARA: "At some point we should begin to dampen down the expansion of our nuclear arms, and I say this without any suggestion that you should disarm or we should disarm. But we do think that together we can begin to put a lid or limit on weapons."

At 2:15 the door to the luncheon room was closed and M.F. could hear no more. McNamara had closed the door, feeling that the Russians might be getting nervous seeing M.F. take notes.

2:25 From the back stairs, M.F. [was able to continue taking] notes on the conversation: McNamara saying—"I know I haven't made my views clear to many of our own people in this country, and from some of your remarks it is clear that I haven't made my thoughts clear to you either." A further discussion of offensive and defensive weapons—and McNamara saying: "It is a subject which will require more discussion than we have time for today. I would like to continue this discussion with you through Ambassador Thompson. It is a complex subject, and I am sure we can't complete our views in this meeting. Again let me emphasize: 1. I didn't suggest we limit our discussion to defensive weapons; 2. I don't believe that we should limit defensive weapons and continue indefinitely to expand offensive systems. 3. I don't believe this is a question of finding offensive weapons cheaper than defensive weapons. Our basic concern is the security of our people and I think the security of our people can be preserved in ways that will not be contradictory to the security of your people. It is this potentially common ground that I think we should explore. The main point is limited growth of these two [types of] systems. I think continued growth of offensive systems is a great danger to each of us. Development of defensive systems will lead to responses by each of us to offset the other," finished McNamara.

CHAIRMAN KOSYGIN: "Was I then wrong."

McNAMARA: "Very wrong."

CHAIRMAN KOSYGIN: "I have read your statements to the effect that—and this you can't deny—where you consider two points— you said now you have offensive and you have defensive weapons— and then you said that if you look on it budget-wise the offensive weapons are cheaper. Am I wrong?"

McNAMARA: "No, that's true."

CHAIRMAN KOSYGIN: "I have no right to say anything wrong because I am a Prime Minister. I'm not supposed to say anything wrong, so I take what you actually did say, and if you say that offensive weapons are cheaper than defensive weapons—" (This part of discussion not taken—waiter with trays, kitchen noises etc.) This ended the discussion with Chairman Kosygin's closing words to

McNamara, "I guess you'll understand if and when you become a Marxist," and McNamara countered with, "Perhaps I will—if you ever become a capitalist." All laughed. The President then stood and began his toast. . . . The President closed his toast by saying, "I ask you to stand and raise your glass to his Honor, the Chairman, to the Soviet Union, and to peace in the world."

3:10 Lunch ended—and the President retired to a small sitting room with McGeorge Bundy, Walt Rostow, Ambassador Thompson, Secretary Rusk, and Secretary McNamara. The Russian party retired to the conference room.

3:44–4:25 [The president] back into study for private meeting with Chairman Kosygin. At some time during this meeting the President presented the Chairman with an Accutron wrist watch and Gromyko with a world-wide [electric] shaver.

4:35 [The president and the chairman] to the conference room to join other members of our party and the Russian party.

4:40 [The president] to front porch of the house—facing barrage of cameras and press and large, large crowd with Chairman Kosygin beside him. Remarks—giving report on what the two men had discussed. Chairman Kosygin then replied. The President then escorted him to his car and stood by the front steps of the house at the Chairman's motorcade and the Chairman smiled and waved at the President. An interesting sidelight—as the Chairman's car reached almost the rear of the house, he responded to the screams of the crowd and got out of his car and, almost like the President does, went to the fences touching hands.

4:47 The President back in the house—and to the conference room—with Rusk, McNamara, Bundy, Thompson, Rostow, Christian, Watson.

Sunday

The above account is of the meeting on Friday, June 23. Late that day it was decided to have a second meeting, and two days later, Johnson, Kosygin and the two delegations returned to Glassboro, where they were together for another six hours. For much of that time the two leaders were closeted alone with their interpreters.

The indefatigable M.F. was again on hand but this time she was able to take notes only on the social side of the meeting. It may have been that her note-taking on Friday had been thought too obtrusive and that she had new instructions. Not that the social aspects lacked interest, because on this second occasion Lady Bird and Lynda Bird Johnson were present, as was Lyudmila Gvishiana, thirty-eight-year-old daughter of Kosygin. The ladies detached themselves from the main group at the start, repairing to a nearby lake house owned by Governor and Mrs. Hughes for a separate lunch. (They did not need an interpreter, as Mrs. Gvishiana spoke good English.) The president exercised some executive supervision over these proceedings as well—as the Soviet party was arriving, M.F. overheard him telling Mrs. Johnson "to be sure and offer Mrs. Gvishiana a chance to go to the ladies room and freshen up before leaving [for the Lake House] for she has just had a two-hour drive." Apparently determined to fill her notepad, M.F. also recorded the luncheon menu, as follows:

Crabmeat Salad Ring
Broiled Lamb Chops
(Beaulieu Cabernet Sauvignon)
Parsley Potatoes
Stuffed Eggplant
Fresh Fruit Kirsch
Petits-fours

Adequate to assuage hunger, one might think, but without inducing torpor.

The flight of the president and his party back to Washington was also not without interest.

> During this flight, the President worked on his statement to make to the American people. . . . The flight was to be speeded up as much as possible for the President was in a race with time. . . . [H]e wanted to make his statement on live television at the White House prior to Chairman Kosygin's televised press conference in New York. . . . [When the plane landed, the] President and the occupants of his helicopter quickly lined up at the back door . . . so that they could go directly to the waiting helicopter with a minimum of time. However, as the door opened, it was discovered that the steps had been placed, by mistake, at the front of the plane, so as the President and party raced through the plane, it could be heard over the intercom, "Make way for the President!" As [one member of] the press pool observed, it looked like one of the old silent movies in which a comedy of errors occurred.

Apparent Results

Despite the intensity of the discussions and all the attendant felicity, it appeared to President Johnson that little progress was made at Glassboro. As he wrote in his memoirs: "Kosygin had apparently come to Glassboro with a block against this subject [arms limitation]. . . . As soon as I brought up strategic arms talks, he changed the subject to the Middle East. . . . Each time I mentioned missiles Kosygin talked about Arabs and Israelis."[2] Dean Rusk's view is that Kosygin "obviously had not been fully briefed on the subject [arms limitation]," had no instructions about it from the Politburo, and was therefore unable to react at once to the discussion.[3] Other accounts indicate, however, that while he lacked authority to name a time and place for strategic arms talks Kosygin was indeed impressed with the logic and force of the American presentation. Dean Rusk has suggested, in fact, that Glassboro may have been the start of SALT for the Russians.[4]

Notes

1. Box 15, LBJ Library.
2. Johnson, *The Vantage Point*, p. 483.
3. Private conversation, March 13, 1986.
4. Newhouse, *Cold Dawn*, p. 95.

33
'Twixt Cup and Lip

That year that was lost between when Johnson wanted to start [SALT] negotiations and when they actually started was a terrible year to lose.
—Walt Rostow[1]

The ABM Decision

However impressed Kosygin may have been at Glassboro, the impact was not yet sufficient to move the Soviet leadership to the bargaining table. The prolonged delay weakened McNamara's hand in holding off the pressures for deployment of a U.S. ABM system. Accordingly, on September 18, 1967, at the end of a long speech in which he argued the futility of a "heavy" system to protect against the Russians, McNamara announced a "light" one to defend against the Chinese. He indicated that the system would also be able to deal with an accidental launch by the Soviets and to defend some missile silos. The system was to be called SENTINEL and was to consist of twelve sites and something like a thousand launchers, a far larger system than the one the Soviets seemed to be installing.

Adrian Fisher hastened to reassure the ENDC the day after McNamara's announcement that the American decision did not represent an acceleration of the superpower arms race. The arms race accelerated, nevertheless. On December 13, 1967, John S. Foster, the director of defense research and engineering, stated that the United States was developing missiles that could drop multiple, independently targeted, thermonuclear warheads (MIRVs) as they flew over enemy territory. Foster stated bluntly that this development was intended as a reply to new Soviet offensive and defensive missile deployments.[2] It was repeatedly argued within the government that MIRVs were needed to overwhelm the anticipated deployment by the Soviet Union of a nationwide ABM system. (But when it subsequently became clear that no such nationwide Soviet deployment was in prospect, the development of MIRVs carried on unabated.)

Agreeing to Talk

Meanwhile, President Johnson continued his pursuit of Kosygin. On January 22, 1968, four days after the two powers had submitted their first joint draft of a nonproliferation treaty, the president wrote again to the Soviet leader, expressing satisfaction over progress on the NPT and urging that missile talks begin promptly. In discussing both the NPT and arms limitation in the same letter, the president was again subtly implying linkage between the two. As Walt Rostow writes, "[B]oth Washington and Moscow understood that, over a period of time, the NPT was unlikely to survive if the two nuclear superpowers conducted an uninhibited race."[3]

At length, late in the spring of 1968, positive signals began to come from Moscow. On May 20, First Deputy Foreign Minister Kuznetsov told a UN body that the Soviet Union was "ready to reach an agreement on practical steps" to limit and then reduce the number of strategic delivery vehicles. On June 21, Kosygin wrote to President Johnson saying that he hoped it would soon be possible to have a more concrete exchange of views.[4] Then on July 1, as the NPT was opened for signature in Washington, London, and Moscow, the United States and the Soviet Union announced their intention to enter into near-term talks "on limitation and reduction of offensive strategic nuclear weapons delivery systems as well as systems of defense against ballistic missiles."

Preparing the U.S. Position

Having pressed so long and so hard for these talks, the United States might have been expected to have some proposals ready. But such was not the case. Following the announcements of July 1, therefore, there ensued a frenzied period of staff work. One early step was a meeting of the Committee of Principals on July 8 for what Secretary Rusk, presiding as usual, termed a "preliminary consideration of the U.S. position." A draft position paper prepared by ACDA had been distributed prior to the meeting.

A remarkable feature of this meeting was the militant attitude of Rusk. He seldom expressed strong views in his position as chairman of the committee.* As the Johnson administration drew to a close, however, one could detect in Rusk a mounting impatience with the excessive caution of the military, with their apparent unwillingness to take any risks whatever to stop the arms race. A theme he now began to sound again and again was that the cost of a continued arms race would be "ruinous," both financially and in terms of increasing insecurity, and that some bold steps were needed to bring it to a close. This was, of course, the view that McNamara had consistently voiced while in government. With McNamara's departure on February 28, 1968, to become head of the World Bank,† Rusk seemed to assume more of the burden of espousing what probably had been their common viewpoint.

At the Principals meeting,

Rusk said that President Johnson had worked hard on Kosygin last year at Glassboro to get started on the missile talks. With the Kremlin's apparent assent, it was imperative now to bring the arms race under control. The Soviets had not yet indicated when they would like to start discussions; it wasn't clear what Kosygin meant by "near future" [the term used in the July 1 announcement]. Clifford‡ thought we should not make any concessions at the start of negotiations. He said he would like to hear Soviet views before stating our own. He would like to make them demonstrate that they were sincere, which he said was open to question. While he had been impressed by the

---

*This is not to imply that he did not have strong views. As McGeorge Bundy wrote in 1965, "The point is that he gives his advice to the President and not to the Deputy Assistant Secretary of State. Moreover, when he has a difference with the Defense Department, he prefers to take it direct to Bob McNamara rather than to let his subordinates start wrangling with the lower echelons of the Pentagon. The result is that relations between the two departments have never been more harmonious" (Bundy to President, 7/7/65, National Security File, Memos to President—McGeorge Bundy, Vol. 12, LBJ Library).

†Officially, McNamara's departure was treated as voluntary. It was widely believed, however, that President Johnson, learning of the vacancy in the World Bank, had sought and obtained the job for McNamara. The president was thought to feel that he needed as secretary of defense someone who shared his views on the Vietnam War. McNamara had significantly softened on the war.

‡Clark Clifford, McNamara's successor as secretary of defense. Clifford was a Washington-based corporate lawyer, had been friendly with Lyndon Johnson for twenty-five years, and had been an outspoken "hawk" on Vietnam. Although Johnson denied this, Clifford's change of position on the war after several months in office is thought by many to have been one of the key factors that persuaded Johnson to abandon his quest for victory in Vietnam and to bow out of the 1968 presidential election.

letters Kosygin had written to the president, he wanted to know what the Soviets intended to accomplish in the talks. Turning to specifics, Clifford wondered whether the Russians would have anything new to offer on verification. He did not think we should accept verification limited to our own national technical means (as opposed to onsite inspection). He emphasized that we should not take any risks with our national security. He felt our opening statement at the talks should be confined to administrative and procedural matters.

Rusk disagreed with Clifford about the opening statement. He pointed out that it had been the United States that had pressed for the talks for over a year and that we would be in an untenable position if we didn't have something definite to propose. It went without saying, Rusk added, that we all had the security of the United States uppermost in our minds; to continue the way things were going in the arms race, however, could only lessen our security, and it would be most unfortunate to have to spend all the resources that would be necessary if we continued along the present paths. Rusk acknowledged that he also was uncertain about Soviet motives in the talks. It would be a bad situation if they only wanted to impress the non-nuclear nations and didn't have any serious intention to pursue the talks to a successful conclusion. Possibly even worse would be if they intended to make another of their sweeping, far-fetched disarmament proposals in order to gain a propaganda advantage. Rusk asked Bohlen* what he thought Soviet motives might be. Bohlen said this was very difficult to judge. Either of the alternatives Rusk suggested was a possibility; on the other hand, they might have very honest intentions.

Rusk said that verification would be a very important issue if any treaty were submitted to Congress and he asked [CIA Director Richard] Helms to indicate the capabilities of verification by national means. Helms said a study made a year ago was being updated; it would be ready in ten days.

[Deputy Secretary of Defense Paul] Nitze suggested that a fact sheet should be prepared on each proposal in the position paper so that each could be thoroughly reviewed before being surfaced in discussions with the Soviets. Foster said this implied we were in a new ball game requiring a lot of new study. This was most strange since we had been studying arms limitation pro-

---

*Charles E. Bohlen, deputy under secretary of state for political affairs, former ambassador to the Soviet Union and to France.

posals for years. At this point Rusk interposed that if we could solve the problem of verification perhaps the best solution of all would be to return to the very sweeping Baruch Plan of 1946.

I observed that the position paper seemed to suggest no limitation on advances in technology, and asked confirmation that a treaty based on the paper would permit us to continue developing the warhead for the ABM, on which there was still much work to do. Rusk and Foster agreed that the proposed U.S. position did not preclude warhead development. I agreed with Rusk that we should offer something substantive in our opening statement, and with Clifford that we should start off by asking for some degree of inspection, restricting ourselves to national technical means of verification only as a fall-back position.

Fisher suggested that during upcoming congressional testimony on the Nonproliferation Treaty we should all be very general in what we said about impending missile talks—perhaps just saying that the question was still under study.

Rusk then made a plea that we not let quibbling over details stand in the way of major accomplishments as we had done in so many previous attempts at arms limitation.

This concluding remark by the secretary undoubtedly reflected the wishes of President Johnson. As Rusk said later, the president "wanted to present the Russians with a clear program for the opening of the talks. He knew that SALT would become lengthy and very complicated. But he didn't want it to get bogged down in a lot of detail at the start."[5]

The Pentagon's Proposal

But still there was no opportunity to present the U.S. program. Notwithstanding the dual announcements of July 1, the Soviets would not agree on a date to start talking. On July 30, Rusk tried to put the best face on things, telling a news conference that he expected agreement on a time and place "rather soon." President Johnson, seeing his administration ebbing away, was less able to conceal his impatience. On July 31, also at a news conference, the president said that he was determined to succeed in the missile talks and that the United States was "ready, willing, and waiting."

The question was now arising in many minds whether the Soviets really intended to negotiate with Johnson at all, or whether they preferred to wait for his still unchosen successor. (The president had made his "I will not seek . . . I will not accept" declaration on March 31.) There were advantages to dealing with Johnson; his evident eagerness for an agreement seemed to offer Moscow opportunities for a favorable deal. But perhaps the Soviets foresaw difficulty in starting what was likely to be a long process with someone who would not be able to carry it to its conclusion and who might not be able to commit his successor.

The delay in getting started gave our side a chance to catch up on its staff work. On July 31, a revised position paper was laid before the Principals. It was prepared by an intragovernmental committee with representation from the Office of the Secretary of Defense, the Joint Chiefs of Staff, the CIA, State, and ACDA. John Newhouse states that the document was mainly a product of the Pentagon, most particularly of Morton Halperin, then a thirty-year-old defense intellectual attached to the office of the assistant secretary of defense for international security affairs (Paul C. Warnke), and a staff of middle-level Pentagon employees reporting to Halperin.[6] It was thought necessary to have the U.S. position gestate in the Pentagon because the Joint Chiefs of Staff had developed a mistrust of the ACDA staff, whom they regarded as "ritual disarmers." This feeling had been exacerbated by some personal friction between Foster and General Wheeler that arose out of the Seabed Treaty discussions. A key figure in bringing the Pentagon's paper to fruition was General Royal B. Allison, who worked tirelessly during the summer of 1968 as, in Newhouse's description, "a broker between the interests of the Joint Chiefs of Staff and those of Halperin and his allies."[7] Allison, whom Rostow describes as "one of the most admirable people I dealt with in the bureaucracy,"[8] was later to be a member of the U.S. SALT I delegation.

The position paper took the form of a draft treaty outline about three pages long. The memorandum accompanying it suggested that not all the individual provisions had to be presented to the Soviets at one time. The memorandum also made clear that the proposal did not deal at all with *reductions* in strategic forces, although it recognized that the United States might have to deal with this subject "at some appropriate stage in the talks." (As we now know, reductions did not figure at all in SALT I, and hardly at all in SALT II. The issue was expected to be addressed in a SALT III.)

In accordance with the president's wishes, the treaty outline itself was kept as simple and brief as possible. It contemplated, first, a prohibition on the construction of any additional ICBM launchers and stated that "[u]nder no circumstances would either side be permitted to deploy more than 1,200 ICBM launchers." *There were to be no numerical restrictions on MIRVs;* the Joint Chiefs insisted on this. The number of fixed land-based launchers for intermediate-range ballistic missiles (IRBMs) and medium-range ballistic missiles (MRBMs) were to be frozen. Technological improvements of fixed land-based missiles and launchers was to be permitted. A complete ban was to be imposed on all mobile strategic offensive missile systems. (These would be difficult to verify.) Additional strategic-missile-firing submarines and additional launchers on existing submarines were to be banned, as was fitting out any surface ships to fire ballistic missiles. After five years, missile-firing submarines could be replaced on a one-for-one basis. As to ABMs, the proposal would have banned the deployment of more than a "set and equivalent number" but, at the Joint Chiefs' reported insistence, it did not specify what that number should be.[9] None of the ABM launchers deployed, however, was to be mobile. The treaty was to be reviewed in nine years.

Essentially, then, what was being proposed was a quantitative, but not a qualitative, freeze on strategic missile launchers, and an agreement to limit ABMs on both sides to an equal, but as yet unspecified, number. It was a way to prevent eruption of the arms race into the ruinous escalation that both McNamara and Rusk predicted might follow extensive ABM deployment by either side. As Bertrand Goldschmidt has written of the ultimate SALT I agreements, which followed the general pattern of the Johnson administration's proposals, the restrictions "did not imply a disarmament, but merely set limits to overarmament."[10] An ominous limitation of the proposal, however, was that it did not restrict MIRVs. Thus, while the number of missile launchers might be held steady, the number of warheads could increase significantly.

LBJ's Final Disappointment

Following completion of the U.S. position paper, events began to move forward with relative rapidity. The Committee of Principals approved the proposed treaty outline on August 7, 1968, and sent it to the president, who also approved it "in principle." Then, on Au-

gust 19, the Soviet Union finally agreed to schedule a summit conference that would initiate the talks. The date was to be in the first ten
days of October, the site probably Moscow. A joint announcement
was agreed to; it was to be released on the morning of August 21.
The White House press corps was alerted. On the night of August 20
(Washington time), however, armored units of the Soviet Union and
several other Eastern bloc nations rumbled into Czechoslovakia to
bring to a halt the liberalization initiatives of the Dubček regime.
Ambassador Dobrynin personally delivered information about the invasion to President Johnson at 8 P.M. that evening. His message concluded with the hope that "the current events should not harm Soviet–
American relations, to the development of which the Soviet Government as before attaches great importance."[11] Later that night, following an urgent meeting of his top advisers, the president instructed
Rusk to call Dobrynin and insist that he call Moscow immediately to
tell them not to issue the summit conference announcement the following morning. Johnson realized that, in the general state of outrage
over the invasion, it was impossible to proceed as scheduled.

A few days later Rusk asked Dobrynin what the Soviet Union had
had in mind in timing the invasion to occur a few hours before the
scheduled announcement of a summit conference to initiate strategic
arms talks. (The secretary is reported to have told Dobrynin that the
Soviet action had been "like throwing a dead fish in the face of the
president."[12]) Dobrynin's explanation was that the two subjects had
"doubtless been on different tracks" and had never come together in
the minds of the Kremlin leadership.* Rusk states that he found this
explanation "a little hard to take," adding: "Theoretically, I suppose
it was possible; but that these two things had not come together
somehow within that relatively small Politburo was a little hard for
me to understand."[13]

Walt Rostow also expresses deep skepticism about Dobrynin's
explanation. He believes that the Soviets were much too sophisticated
to behave in such a mindless manner. He recalls that just before the
invasion they were offering us various "sweeteners" on relatively minor matters such as scientific and cultural exchanges. These were
designed, Rostow believes, to soften our reaction to the impending
move on Czechoslovakia.[14] Under such an interpretation, the pro-

---

*Newhouse, *Cold Dawn*, p. 130f. Newhouse reports this query was made by a "senior official."
Rusk acknowledges that he was the official involved (private conversation, March 13, 1986).

spective timing of the announcements on SALT might itself have been considered a device to make President Johnson "swallow" the invasion.

Cruelly disappointed once again, President Johnson persisted in hoping that the arms limitation negotiations could yet be launched before his term expired. Johnson never envisioned that SALT would be completed on his watch. He merely wanted to start it, possibly— though he denied this in his memoirs—so that he could leave office on a positive note having to do with something other than Vietnam. The sequence that Johnson had in mind was as follows:

> First, there would be an exchange of technical papers in which we and the Soviets would set forth our general positions on limiting strategic arms, offensive and defensive.
> Second, the Soviet leaders and I would meet at the summit conference and try to reach agreement on broad principles to guide the negotiators on both sides. We would also discuss other world problems at the meeting, especially the Middle East and Southeast Asia.
> Finally, there would be a continuation of the technical negotiations based on the agreed principles, but under the full control of the new President.[15]

In conformity with this agenda, work continued on putting together various details of the U.S. position while striving to get the derailed summit back on the tracks. On October 16, Undersecretary of State Katzenbach told a conference in Europe that dialogue with the Soviet Union must continue despite Czechoslovakia. The Russians appeared to be ready when we were ready. On November 11, Robert McNamara, visiting Moscow with his wife as a tourist, was invited by Kosygin to the Kremlin and they were reported to have discussed SALT for three hours. The following day Soviet Ambassador Y. A. Malik told the UN General Assembly's Political Committee that the Soviet Union was ready "without delay" for a "serious exchange of views."

In reality, all depended on President-elect Nixon. Neither Johnson nor the Kremlin wished to proceed without his assent since he could later disavow anything that was done and make it pointless. Johnson therefore invited Nixon to accompany him to the summit meeting and, after that invitation was declined, to designate "a trusted advisor" to go. Nixon appears to have toyed with the latter option— tentatively selecting retired diplomat Robert D. Murphy for the assignment[16]—and decided against it. Ambassador Thompson suggested to Gromyko on November 29 that a summit be held just before Christmas but by that time it was clear that the Soviets were no longer interested. Johnson speculates in his memoirs that they were encouraged in that negative attitude by Nixon's representatives.[17] Walt Rostow is more specific. He says: "The Russians were quite willing to go ahead without Nixon but his people told them: 'You do that and you'll damage your relations with us.' "[18] Nixon himself writes that during the transition period Henry Kissinger met with a Soviet diplomat and told him that if a preinauguration summit meeting were held with Johnson, he, Nixon, would have to state publicly that he would not be bound by it.[19]

And so the task of carrying forward the missile talks that Johnson and McNamara had conceived and ardently sought passed to a new administration. Of all the tragedies that befell Lyndon Johnson, this must rank among the most grievous.

Sequels

It lies outside the time frame of this book to attempt a detailed description of SALT I and the resulting agreements. Excellent accounts are available.[20]

SALT did not in fact begin until November 1969. When the United States finally indicated it was ready to proceed—this was in June 1969—the Soviet side waited another five months before assenting. There was early agreement on the desirability of limiting ABMs, but the asymmetry between the offensive forces of the two sides led to difficulties in reaching a more comprehensive agreement. The Soviets then sought to limit negotiations to ABMs, but the United States, fearing an unlimited growth in the Soviet Union's burgeoning ICBM arsenal, insisted that offensive weapons be included as well. After a prolonged deadlock, it was decided to negotiate a permanent treaty limiting ABMs and, as a holding action, to add an interim agreement restricting the growth of offensive arms for five years.

The ABM Treaty and the Interim Agreement on Strategic Offensive Arms were signed by Nixon and Brezhnev on May 26, 1972, in Vienna. The Senate endorsed both accords by overwhelming margins. The ABM Treaty limited each side to two systems of one hundred launchers each, one to protect the national capital, the other to protect a missile complex. By later amendment, each side was limited to only one of these choices. The United States has never deployed its allowed ABMs. The Soviet Union continues to have its Galosh system, defending Moscow.

The Interim Agreement has been admirably summarized in *Nuclear Arms Control, Background and Issues,* a 1985 publication of the National Academy of Sciences, as follows (p. 29):

> The agreement essentially froze at existing levels the number of strategic ballistic missile launchers, operational or under construction, on each side. It did permit construction of additional SLBM launchers up to an agreed level for each party, provided that an equal number of older ICBM or SLBM launchers were destroyed. Within these limitations, modernization and replacement of missiles were permitted. But to prevent further increases in the number of the very large Soviet ICBMs, . . . launchers for light or older ICBMs could not be converted into launchers for modern heavy ICBMs. The Interim Agreement also formalized the principle of verification by National Technical Means. . . . These means included all sources of technical intelligence in space or outside the boundaries of the country being monitored. Limitations were stated in terms of "launchers," . . . rather than in terms of total missiles, which could not be verified by National Technical Means alone. Among the systems and characteristics not limited by the Interim Agreement were strategic bombers, forward based systems, mobile ICBMs, MIRVs, and missile accuracy.

President Nixon, Henry Kissinger, Gerard Smith, and others in the Nixon administration deserve much credit for guiding these first arms limitation negotiations to a moderately successful conclusion. It should not be overlooked, however, that there might have been no negotiations at all but for the earnest and tireless efforts of Lyndon Johnson and Robert McNamara. It was McNamara, more than anyone else, who first saw the need and then sold the idea, both to the U.S. government and to the Soviet government. Walt Rostow has justly written:

> I am inclined to believe that McNamara's role in forcing America, its allies, and the Soviet Union to view the nuclear problem in, roughly, similar terms may well be judged his greatest contribution as a public servant.[21]

After a soul-searching inquiry, President Johnson, to his credit, recognized the validity of McNamara's approach, and committed his personal prestige in a long and ultimately successful effort to bring the Soviet Union to the bargaining table.

While we consider with some satisfaction the results of SALT, and allocate praise for their achievement, it is well that we consider also the cost of the delay in bringing them about. During the period between September 1968, when the talks were first scheduled to start, and November 1969, when they actually did start, the arms race entered a major new phase of danger. In a conversation in March 1986, Dean Rusk put it well:

> If those talks had started in, say, early September 1968, the state of the art in MIRVs was such that we might have been able to get them under control. But that move into Czechoslovakia delayed the talks. And then when the Nixon administration came in they had to spend nearly a year getting their ducks in a row so that by the time serious talks could begin with the Soviet Union the MIRV problem had gotten out of control—the horses had cleared the stable.

Walt Rostow emphasizes the same point. He says that President Johnson was passionately interested in getting an early start on SALT "not because—as Kissinger and Nixon intimated—he wanted a last hurrah before he left office but because he knew that the clock was ticking on this technology [MIRV]. The year that was lost between when Johnson wanted to start negotiations and when they actually started was a terrible year to lose."[22]

The MIRVs transformed what had become an essentially stable "balance of terror" into one where each side could threaten in a first strike to destroy the other's land-based ICBMs. Here we see illustrated the tragic consequences of the unequal struggle so far waged between the arms race and arms control. While arms control negotiations nibble at the edges, trying to make progress in what Dean Rusk called "bits and pieces," major new arms systems follow each other from designers' desks into production into deployment. The result is, as Averell Harriman said, that "each time we negotiate it is at a higher and more dangerous level."

One is reminded of a story Edward R. Murrow told about a particular broadcast he made during the Nazi blitz on London in World War II. As he was reading the night's bulletins in his usual calm voice there came a timid knock on the door, followed by a brief communication. "I hate to disturb you," said the visitor, "but the building is on fire."

Notes

1. Private conversation, May 31, 1985.
2. Larson, *Disarmament and Soviet Policy,* p. 260.
3. Rostow, *The Diffusion of Power,* p. 382.
4. Johnson, *The Vantage Point,* p. 485.
5. Newhouse, *Cold Dawn,* p. 103.
6. Ibid., pp. 111–113.
6. Ibid., p. 110.
7. Newhouse, *Cold Dawn,* p. 114.
8. Private conversation, May 31, 1985.
9. Newhouse, *Cold Dawn,* p. 128.
10. Goldschmidt, *The Atomic Complex,* p. 221.
11. Johnson, *The Vantage Point,* p. 487f.
12. Transcript, John M. Leddy Oral History Interview, 3/12/69, by Paige E. Mulhollan, tape 1, p. 19, LBJ Library.
13. Private conversation, March 13, 1986.
14. Private conversation, May 31, 1985.
15. Johnson, *The Vantage Point,* p. 489.
16. Ibid., p. 490.
17. Ibid., p. 489f.
18. Private conversation, May 31, 1985.
19. Nixon, *RN,* p. 348.
20. See, in particular, Gerard Smith, *Doubletalk,* and John Newhouse, *Cold Dawn.*
21. Rostow, *The Diffusion of Power,* p. 384.
22. Private conversation, May 31, 1985.

Part X
Epilogue

Uneasy is the peace that wears a nuclear crown.

Lyndon B. Johnson
August 26, 1966

34
Reflections

If a man from Mars should suddenly visit among us, he would look at both sides and say: "Are you people crazy? Can't you find some way to stop this?"

—Dean Rusk
July 1968[1]

On the Value of Arms Control

Out of this nettle, danger, we pluck this flower, safety.
—Shakespeare, *Henry IV*, Part I

At a meeting of the Committee of Principals on June 3, 1968 (chapter 30), Joint Chiefs of Staff Chairman General Earle G. Wheeler complained that arms control negotiations were placing the United States in a strategic straitjacket. A quite similar, but more pointed, statement was made in January 1984 by Richard Perle, assistant secretary of defense for international security policy in the Reagan administration. At a meeting of a small group of administration policymakers gathered together to consider the next move in the Strategic Arms Reduction Talks (START), Perle said: "This stuff [arms control] is soporific. It puts our society to sleep. It does violence to our ability to maintain adequate defenses."[2]

Opponents of arms control appear to believe that the United States must rely for its security wholly on its ability to make war, especially nuclear war, whether or not such a policy leads to confrontation with the Soviet Union. There seems to be a belief that by multiplying and perfecting our nuclear weapons we can effect basic changes in the world situation that would be to our benefit. The policy of renouncing arms control for continued competition in nuclear arms also seems to rest on an assumption that the Soviet Union lacks both the technological skills and the economic strength to keep pace with the United States if we push the arms race into new realms. One cannot be certain that this thesis is wrong, although it is belied by the history of the last forty years. One can be quite certain that it is dangerous in the extreme. As has been eloquently stated: "U.S. attempts to accelerate President Reagan's vision of putting the Soviet system on the 'ash heap of history' could all too easily result in two ash heaps and no history."[3]

If the nuclear arms race were to proceed virtually unchecked, such results as the following seem inevitable:

> Less warning time of an attack as the weapons of each side become swifter and in some cases based closer to their targets.*

> Gradual replacement of human control by computer control, increasing the danger of launch by accident, error, or miscalculation.

> Increased nervousness on each side as it considers the other side's growing first-strike capabilities.

> A poisoning of the political atmosphere, strengthening repressive and militaristic tendencies in both societies.

> A greater potential for the destruction of higher forms of life in a nuclear exchange.

> Increasing insecurity for both sides, despite expenditures mounting now into the trillions of dollars.

> This above all: *increased likelihood of nuclear war.*

I consider it far preferable that the United States get back on the track pursued by the five presidents before Reagan, and that is to seek, through negotiation, reasonable arms control accommodations with the Soviet Union.

There are those who say that the arms control process as pursued to date has been a failure in that the nuclear arsenals of the major powers have continued to grow in quantity and quality during all the years when arms control has been in process. Indeed, some of the agreements achieved to date have seemed more to validate than to

---

*Lowell Wood, a leader in Livermore's Star Wars effort, has said: "The situation in which we are now looks to me like it is getting ever less stable because of the supershort time lines, if nothing else. Ignore the hard-target killers. Just consider their submarines off our coasts and our Pershings in Germany. Things can happen very quickly." (Quoted in Broad, *Star Warriors,* p. 198.)

impede such growth. But those who allege that arms control has been a failure have a hard case to prove. They would have to have a pipeline into the unknown and be able to say what would have been the situation of the world had not the Limited Test Ban Treaty done away with atmospheric tests, the ABM Treaty prevented a race in defensive arms, the Interim Agreement and SALT II placed a cap on the multiplication of offensive arms, and the Nonproliferation Treaty discouraged additional entries into the nuclear club. Bad as things are, I believe that without the effects of those agreements they would be far worse.

Moreover, some of the indictments of nuclear arms control have misconstrued its purposes. Arms control is different from disarmament. It does not seek to abolish nuclear arms; realistically, that is hardly possible at present and may never again be possible. Instead, it seeks to defuse the nuclear arms competition in various ways, such as by bringing about more moderate and stable levels of nuclear arms, by eliminating the more provocative and threatening weapons or deployments, and by preventing dangerous, further stages in the arms race. Through such means, arms control aims to change the messages that nations send to each other and to bring about the conditions for political change and ultimately, perhaps, a large degree of nuclear disarmament. Above all, the purpose of arms control is, as Representative Les Aspin has stated it, "to reduce the chance of nuclear war breaking out."[4]

On the Need for Presidential Involvement

The experience of the Johnson years can teach us much about what is and what is not conducive to progress in arms control. It tends to bear out, for one thing, what has been apparent in other presidencies, that significant arms control achievements can be brought about only when the president takes a personal and an affirmative interest. A prime reason for this is that national security policy, including arms control, affects many interests and constituencies with diverging purposes and views. Without a firm presidential hand on the wheel—or at least that of a single strong surrogate—the making and execution of national security policy will be like the progress of a rudderless ship, zigging and zagging and sometimes reversing course and sowing confusion in the country and the world.

Examples of the importance of presidential leadership abound—some quite recent—but let us consider only the record during the Johnson years. It was a period when the rival constituencies were readily apparent. The armed forces, as represented by the Joint Chiefs of Staff, continually sought to minimize potential restrictions on their freedom of action from proposed arms control agreements. There was a strong faction in the State Department especially concerned about the interests and sensitivities of our NATO allies; this group's espousal of the MLF was for a while a prime obstacle to negotiation of the Nonproliferation Treaty. The Arms Control and Disarmament Agency adopted an NPT as its primary objective and, at first, in its zeal to get an agreement, seemed to us in the AEC too ready to sacrifice an essential element of the treaty, namely, adequate safeguards. The AEC must itself have seemed to others to be a somewhat parochial interest group as we pushed our pet projects, safeguards being one and the Plowshare program another. Certain centrally placed individuals—for example, Rusk, McNamara, and McGeorge Bundy—presented independent points of view.

When President Johnson held himself aloof from the controversies generated by the differing points of view in his administration, the decision-making process within the government often seemed disorderly and unproductive. A prime example was the prolonged confusion about the U.S. position on the MLF and alternative proposals, which persisted even after President Johnson appeared to have settled the issue in December 1964. Another example was the on-again, off-again CABRIOLET project (chapter 25) and its unprecedented submission to "binding arbitration." On the other hand, when the president became actively involved, issues tended to be resolved with greater speed and clarity. This was true, for example, when the president let it be known in mid-1966 that he was personally interested in obtaining a nonproliferation agreement on reasonable terms and requested his principal assistants to seek the necessary accommodations with the Soviet Union and with our allies. It was true again when the president became personally convinced of the need for agreements with the Soviets to head off the consequences of an escalating competition in strategic arms and succeeded in persuading the Soviet Union to begin negotiations toward this end.

Although the Johnson administration, overall, achieved these favorable results in arms control, I think the results might have been even better had the president immersed himself more deeply in the substance of the principal proposals. This was particularly the case as regards the development of the initial U.S. position on limiting strategic arms. In the absence of more active participation by the president, the Pentagon was able to exert a predominant influence in formulating a proposal that placed no limits on the development, testing, or deployment of MIRVs. MIRV survived SALT unscathed, and the vision that drove President Johnson to seek the talks—that an escalation in the strategic arms race might thus be avoided—was largely vitiated.

One may argue, of course, that it is not incumbent on a chief executive to become enmeshed in detail—that delegation of responsibility to trusted subordinates is essential to effective administration.* This may be an effective way of presiding over corporate enterprises, and even over many government endeavors, but I submit that the subjects of nuclear arming and arms control cannot safely be handled that way. I agree wholeheartedly with comments that McGeorge Bundy has made based on President Truman's manner of deciding the H-bomb controversy in 1950. Truman, it will be recalled, appointed a group of three advisers (Dean Acheson, David Lilienthal, and Louis Johnson) to recommend what his policy should be, then promptly accepted their recommendation virtually without discussion or debate. Bundy writes:

> [T]he president's duty in nuclear matters is not simply to decide; it is to understand for himself. . . . I conclude, not from this case alone, that analysis of these matters will seldom be more searching than what a president requires, and even undertakes for himself. There are later and happier cases which do tend to show that a president who makes this matter his own business can get near the root of it—most of them are to be found, I currently believe, in the years of Eisenhower and Kennedy. When serious scientists have three views, the president should understand them all; when military men contest priorities, the president should understand their claims too and not simply quell the debate. Finally, when the conflicting claims of common danger and national defense are presented as a crude choice between racing ahead and falling behind, it is the president above all others who should ask for something better.[5]

---

*A classic statement of this management philosophy was made by President Reagan in a recent interview: "Surround yourself with the best people you can find, delegate authority, and don't interfere." (What Managers Can Learn from Manager Reagan," *Fortune*, September 15, 1986.)

On Deference to Military and Other Experts

Experts should be on tap but not on top.
—Lord Cecil

In a recent conversation, Dean Rusk noted that there is a widespread tendency to be "hypnotized by the sight of a man in uniform." Members of Congress are not immune to this spell. Those on the Armed Service Committees, in particular, have frequently insisted that the advice of military leaders must be followed on matters having to do with strategy and levels of arming.

Because of the deference paid to them, the influence of the Joint Chiefs of Staff on Congress has been critical to the fate of several arms control agreements. The presumption has grown that the Joint Chiefs can generally muster the needed votes—one-third of the Senate—to defeat any treaty they oppose. In recognition of this reality, the Chiefs have repeatedly been offered "sweeteners" to gain their support for, or benevolent neutrality toward, pending arms control treaties. Thus, President Kennedy paid a high price to gain JCS support for the Limited Test Ban Treaty, namely, his agreement to the four national security safeguards that so diminished the pacific effect of the treaty (see chapter 17). Similarly, the proposal submitted by the United States for SALT I, at JCS insistence, lost much of its significance by allowing for the testing and deployment of MIRVs. After the SALT I agreements were signed, the Defense Department conditioned its support during the ratification process on congressional approval of new programs for strategic arms.[6] One of these was the B-1 bomber, a much-criticized weapons system whose production and maintenance may cost the taxpayers in excess of $100 billion. A "sweetener" offered to gain the Joint Chiefs' support for SALT II was the MX missile, estimated to cost $50 billion.[7]

The views expressed by weapons laboratory scientists and technicians have also had a pivotal influence on U.S. weapons and arms control policy at various critical junctures. An example occurred when the directors of the Los Alamos and Livermore laboratories met with President Carter during the summer of 1978—at a time when negotiations for a comprehensive test ban treaty seemed likely to succeed—and persuaded him to withdraw U.S. support for the proposed treaty (chapter 20).

The deference paid to military and other experts on questions of nuclear arming seems to be based on the notion that such matters are immensely complicated and beyond the understanding of average citizens and their political representatives. But this is a profound misconception. To design a nuclear weapon is indeed a technical matter requiring expert knowledge. But to decide on whether to build or deploy that weapon or any weapon, and to decide whether to enter into arms control negotiations or specific agreements with the Soviet Union, are not primarily technical issues. The case is well stated by Herbert York:

> Much of the confusion and dispute that have arisen over this matter of the role of the expert derives from a failure to recognize the very fundamental differences between the kind of expertise and knowledge needed to design a weapons system and the entirely different kind of knowledge and wisdom needed to judge one. To take an easier case, consider the lunar landing. If you want to know how to get to the moon, ask a rocket expert; if you want to know who should pilot the spacecraft, ask experts in space medicine and psychology; if you want to know what ought to be done after getting there, ask a geophysicist. But if you want to know whether someone should go there in the first place, ask any sensitive informed person.[8]

The judgments that have to be made in deciding on the overall direction of arms control policy are political, psychological, moral, and philosophical more than they are technical. It was in recognition of this fact that Averell Harriman included no technical expert on the small negotiating team that he took to Moscow for the test ban negotiations, although there was a technical expert with the delegation in case he was needed. Some years later Harriman expressed his views on this matter in Senate testimony, as follows:

> These matters have got to be left to the political leaders of our Nation. The expert is out to point out all the difficulties and dangers . . . but it is for the political leaders to decide whether the political, psychological and other advantages offset such risks as there may be.[9]

A similar view was expressed by President Kennedy. He observed that experts are essential, but one has to be alert to the factors they leave out of account that might be crucial.[10]

The undue weight given to the guidance of professional military men and weapons scientists on both sides tends to exacerbate the arms race. They tend to lack complete confidence in their own arsenals, knowing what can go wrong. At the same time they feel a professional responsibility to take a worst-case view of the other side's capabilities and intentions. As a Soviet SALT delegate observed, each side tends to look at the other's forces through the small end of a telescope and at its own through the large end.[11] Each therefore feels the need to ask for more, newer, and better weapons to prepare for extreme contingencies. This only provokes their counterparts on the other side to do the same. The appearance of an ABM system around Moscow in the 1960s, for example, led to a U.S. decision to develop a whole new generation of offensive weapons, as well as to pressures for extensive missile defenses of our own; this despite the fact that our own work on defensive weapons made it seem very implausible that the Soviet system could effectively defend against such an attack as we were already capable of launching.

The military approach was epitomized in the discussion of a proposed Seabed Treaty in the May 14, 1968, meeting of the Committee of Principals (chapter 30). At that meeting, it will be recalled, Deputy Secretary of Defense Paul Nitze and Joint Chiefs of Staff Chairman Earle Wheeler objected to the proposed agreement on the grounds that, although there were no existing plans to place nuclear weapons on the ocean floor, it might be advantageous to do so at some time in the future. What Wheeler was expressing, in essence, was the military's unwillingness to surrender any option, to take any chances at all in the interest of reducing the risks inherent in an unbridled arms race. The military establishment sees in arms control only a threat to its future freedom of action.

What this approach overlooks is the matter of relative risks. The military man is expert in portraying the risk that may arise from an arms control agreement that might deny him certain weapons. While the civilian policymaker must take these risks into consideration, he also has a duty to consider the risks that can arise in the absence of that arms control agreement—the risks, namely, of further escalation in the numbers and deadliness of nuclear weapons. In the performance of his responsibility the military man is loath to accept risks. The policymaker has no choice—it is one risk or the other.

On the Need for a National Debate

I know of no safe depository of the ultimate powers of the society but for the people themselves; and if we think them not enlightened enough to

exercise their control with a wholesome discretion, the remedy is not to
take it from them but to inform their discretion by education.
—Thomas Jefferson

Although the basic issues involved in determining our national policy
toward arms control are not technical in nature, they can be intel-
lectually demanding, and only a small minority among the general public appears willing to undertake the effort needed to comprehend the
subject matter. Repeated studies have shown that public opinion on
arms control matters is highly unstable and volatile, with a strong
tendency for the average citizen to endorse the views of political leaders with whom they identify on other, more immediate issues. It was
distressing, for example, to observe how large a proportion of the
public registered "approval" of the U.S. performance at Reykjavik
following the simplistic accounts by the president and others of that
fiasco. Other polls have indicated that in recent years the public has
accorded arms control a very low relative importance among the issues confronting the nation.

Here we face a great danger. The theory of our society requires
that decisions on transcendent issues be made ultimately by an informed populace. If the public is uninformed and apathetic, the danger is that major decisions on nuclear arming and arms control will
be dictated by military representatives (in or out of uniform) or others
with special interests in weapons, such as defense contractors, local-
ities that benefit economically from weapons activities, their political
representatives, and weapons laboratories. It would be contrary to
human nature to expect policies so determined to favor any other
course but a continuation of the arms race.

I am convinced that greater public participation in the process by
which our country's nuclear arming and arms control decisions are
made would improve the quality of the decisions. I therefore feel it
essential that there be a greatly increased effort to educate and interest
the public in the content of the arms control debate. There is an
extensive literature on the subject but, by and large, it is not presented
in accessible terms or in media that reach the public. There are prominent individuals who speak out from time to time when particular
issues arise, but too frequently it is to a specialized audience—they end
up preaching to the choir. Not enough of my fellow scientists have
shown themselves willing to leave their ivory towers and mingle in
the argument. It would be of immense benefit if a way could be found

to enlist the popular media in presenting over a period of weeks and months a great national debate in which arms control issues were thoroughly ventilated to a mass audience. Televised congressional hearings might be a suitable device, especially if the commercial networks could be induced to give them some air time.

On Arms Control as Propaganda

Most arms control proposals advanced by both superpowers have been insincere. They have included features known in advance to be unacceptable to the other side, thereby insuring they would be rejected. The calculation has been that since the proposals seemingly involved some self-sacrifice, they would earn credit in world opinion as peaceful initiatives, whereas the rejecting side would be condemned for its intransigence. Arms control has thus frequently been "debased into a species of propaganda"[12] and arms control negotiations into forums for invective.

To cite all the examples of this cynical behavior would require us to recount virtually the entire history of arms control proposals beginning with the Baruch Plan of 1946 and extending to the current day. Suffice it to review some examples mentioned in the present volume.

The Baruch Plan itself was a prime example. For reasons given in chapter 7, it would have placed the Soviet Union in an unacceptably subservient and vulnerable position for an indeterminate period. To mitigate the propaganda defeat resulting from their rejection of the scheme, the Soviets countered with a proposal—to do away with all atomic weapons forthwith—that they knew we could not accept, and thus the propaganda contest over nuclear arms control was launched.

The Soviet Union proposed at one time destroying all bomber aircraft. The Soviets could be sure that the United States would reject the idea because at the time we had many more bombers than they did. The U.S. counterproposal, equally certain to be rejected, was to destroy equal numbers of bombers, leaving us with a proportionally greater numerical advantage.

An American deception repeated several times during the Johnson years was the claim that we advocated a comprehensive test ban, whereas there was strong and controlling opposition to such a measure within the administration. During 1967 and 1968, especially, a CTB would have been inconsistent with a national policy to develop a new generation of offensive and defensive weapons in response to the Soviet ABM deployment. Knowing that overt abandonment of our avowed position on a comprehensive test ban risked a setback on the public opinion front, our negotiators contrived various tactical maneuvers, such as insisting on on-site verification, which the Soviets could be expected to reject (chapter 20).

The Soviets repeatedly included in their arms control proposals requirements that would have struck down arrangements between the United States and its allies, such as doing away with all foreign bases, and forbidding the deployment of nuclear weapons outside the owner's territory. Because acceptance of such ideas would have spelled the end of NATO, the Soviets knew they could count on American rejection and our consequent political embarrassment.

Through the first two years of the Johnson presidency, the United States repeatedly pressed for adoption of its proposal to cut off the production of fissionable materials and transfer proportional quantities to peaceful uses. This was at a time when our stockpile of fissionable materials was vastly greater than that of the Soviet Union. We ceased to push the idea in later years when our intelligence indicated that the size of Soviet stockpiles was rapidly closing the gap. And so it went.

The question arises: since each side is alive to the other's tactics, what real harm is done by these propaganda charades? I think much harm is done by trifling with the hopes of mankind for an end to the threat of nuclear annihilation. In time, the deception becomes apparent to the leading politicians and opinion makers around the world, resulting in an impairment of the moral position of the great powers and of their ability to provide leadership toward a better world. I am convinced that much of the anti-American sentiment one witnesses in other countries, including those allied with us, comes from the perception that the United States is intent on pursuing the arms race behind a facade of pretending to oppose it. The idea has grown, indeed, that the superpowers are actually engaged in a conspiracy to this end. Further, to the extent that the superpowers consume the time and energy of world bodies and leading statesmen in a fruitless debate over sterile propositions, so much less time and energy are left for constructive effort. Also, the empty posturing engenders a cynicism and a sense of despair that taints the atmosphere of negotiation and creates a soil inhospitable to genuine and fruitful endeavors.

The notion that the United States and the Soviet Union are deceptive and untrustworthy also can influence the policies of other governments in a major way. We have witnessed (chapter 27) how the adherence of nonnuclear powers to the Nonproliferation Treaty was won by the superpowers' pledge in Article VI to "pursue negotiations in good faith on effective measures relating to cessation of the nuclear arms race at an early date." General agreement that the superpowers have failed to carry out this pledge, now nearly twenty years old, and an implication that they did not intend to comply with it, is considered to be the greatest overhanging threat to the NPT when a vote on its extension is taken in 1995.

Arms control is a tempting tool for propaganda because it is so vitally important for so many people. It is precisely because arms control is so important that this fraudulent misuse of it must cease.

On Animosity

The nation that indulges toward another an habitual hatred . . . is in some degrees a slave. It is a slave to its animosity . . . which is sufficient to lead it astray from its duty and its interests. . . . Antipathy in one nation against another disposes each more readily to offer insult and injury, to lay hold of slight causes of umbrage, and to be haughty and intractable when accidental or trifling occasions or disputes occur.

—George Washington

It is axiomatic to Americans that our society is superior to Soviet society. There can be no doubt that the greater degree of liberty we enjoy makes this country a better place to live. One can argue further that the expansion of Soviet influence beyond historic Russian borders has impinged on the liberties of other countries and that further expansion of Soviet influence is something we should oppose.

Nevertheless, there are limits beyond which it is not just or of any good purpose to denigrate Soviet society or the motives of the Soviet government. I think those limits have been passed in much that has been said, such as in President Reagan's statement that the Soviet Union is "the focus of evil in the modern world." We should recognize that extreme characterizations of the Russians as ten feet tall and bent exclusively on evil may be motivated by a desire to support military budgets or defeat arms control proposals. It is alarming to observe how similar anti-Soviet portrayals in the popular media have become to what has historically been reserved for nations with whom we were already or soon to be at war—for example, the anti-"Hun" propaganda of World War I and the anti-"Jap" portrayals of World War II.

What most Americans do not recognize is that a similar process goes on in the Soviet Union. Scholars reveal that there has been a continuing conflict of opinion in the Soviet Union about the capabilities and intentions of the United States. One group characterizes us as having imperialist designs, even being bent on world conquest. While we may not recognize any reality in such characterizations, there may be a similar lack of reality in some American characterizations of the Soviet Union.

The end result of such reciprocal distortion can be exceedingly dangerous. It has contributed to a loss of many of the contacts between the two societies that in the past helped each to recognize the other as human. It has added to the belief on each side that the other might indeed attack. It was revealed recently, for example, that in 1981, when President Reagan's anti-Soviet rhetoric was at its most unrestrained, the KGB alerted its stations abroad that an American attack on the Soviet Union was imminent.[13] Thus we stretch more taut the tripwire whose release could lead to holocaust.

We hear much these days about the marked effect that emotions can have on human health. This is true as well of the health of a nation or the family of nations. It should be recognized that deterrence is as much a matter of psychological attitudes as of the number of weapons deployed on each side. If we become persuaded that the Russian is bent on evil and is ten feet tall, then we may not feel safe unless there is an American weapon aimed at every Soviet target and unless every American weapon is protected. A U.S. public conditioned by such attitudes might inevitably conclude that a further huge build-up in strategic arms is our only protection. This is exactly the state of mind that many extreme opponents of arms control wish to foster.

The argument here, then, is not that the Soviet Union is a benign society deserving of emulation or admiration. It is rather that our own national interest requires reduced and more stable levels of nuclear arms and that these are only to be obtained by negotiating agreements with the Soviet Union. The alternative, an unrestrained military competition aimed at humbling the Soviet Union, is unlikely to succeed in its objective and carries with it an unacceptably high risk of bringing on a nuclear war that can be in nobody's interest.

And so I come back to what President Johnson had to say on

relations with the Soviet Union. It was the approach that animated
his efforts and that of his administration to make progress in arms
control. It was the aproach that led to two significant accomplishments—the Nonproliferation Treaty and the beginnings of SALT—
and some lesser ones. That more was not accomplished in the Johnson years can be laid at the door of indifferent execution—some by
the president himself—and inhospitable world conditions. But the
president's address to the problem, as expressed in these words, was
exactly right. They should be adopted as an immutable statement of
national purpose. To repeat, the president said:

> [W]hile differing principles and differing values may always divide
> us, they should not, and must not, deter us from rational acts of
> common endeavor. The world must not now flounder in the back-
> waters of the old and stagnant passions. For our test really is not to
> prove which interpretation of man's past is correct. Our test is to
> secure man's future.[14]

Notes

1. Senate Committee on Foreign Relations, *Nonproliferation Treaty Hearings,* p. 38.
2. Quoted in Talbott, *Deadly Gambits,* p. 348.
3. *The Defense Monitor,* November 3, 1986, p. 11.
4. *Arms Control Today,* January 2, 1986, p. 22.
5. Bundy, "The Lost Chance to Stop the H-Bomb," p. 20.
6. Smith, *Doubletalk,* p. 30.
7. Fallows, *National Defense,* p. 169n.
8. York, *Race to Oblivion,* p. 219.
9. Senate Comm. on Foreign Relations, *Hearings on Promoting a Comprehensive Test Ban Treaty,* p. 106.
10. Rostow, *The Diffusion of Power,* p. 127.
11. Smith, *Doubletalk,* p. 87f.
12. Editorial, *Bulletin of the Atomic Scientists,* January 1984, p. 2.
13. *Washington Post,* August 8, 1986.
14. *Documents on Disarmament 1966,* p. 621.

Appendix: Treaty on the Nonproliferation of Nuclear Weapons, July 1, 1968

The States concluding this Treaty, hereinafter referred to as the "Parties to the Treaty",

Considering the devastation that would be visited upon all mankind by a nuclear war and the consequent need to make every effort to avert the danger of such a war and to take measures to safeguard the security of peoples,

Believing that the proliferation of nuclear weapons would seriously enhance the danger of nuclear war,

In conformity with resolutions of the United Nations General Assembly calling for the conclusion of an agreement on the prevention of wider dissemination of nuclear weapons,

Undertaking to cooperate in facilitating the application of International Atomic Energy Agency safeguards on peaceful nuclear activities,

Expressing their support for research, development and other efforts to further the application, within the framework of the International Atomic Energy Agency safeguards system, of the principle of safeguarding effectively the flow of source and special fissionable materials by use of instruments and other techniques at certain strategic points,

Affirming the principle that the benefits of peaceful applications of nuclear technology, including any technological by-products which may be derived by nuclear-weapon States from the development of nuclear explosive devices, should be available for peaceful purposes to all Parties to the Treaty, whether nuclear-weapon or non-nuclear-weapon States,

Convinced that, in furtherance of this principle, all Parties to the Treaty are entitled to participate in the fullest possible exchange of scientific information for, and to contribute alone or in cooperation with other States to, the further development of the applications of atomic energy for peaceful purposes,

Declaring their intention to achieve at the earliest possible date the cessation of the nuclear arms race and to undertake effective measures in the direction of nuclear disarmament,

Urging the cooperation of all States in the attainment of this objective,

Recalling the determination expressed by the Parties to the 1963 Treaty banning nuclear weapon tests in the atmosphere, in outer space and under water in its Preamble to seek to achieve the discontinuance of all test explosions of nuclear weapons for all time and to continue negotiations to this end,[71]

Desiring to further the easing of international tension and the strengthening of trust between States in order to facilitate the cessation of the manufacture of nuclear weapons, the liquidation of all their existing stockpiles, and the elimination from national arsenals of nuclear weapons and the means of their delivery pursuant to a treaty on general and complete disarmament under strict and effective international control,

Recalling that, in accordance with the Charter of the United Nations, States must refrain in their international relations from the threat or use of force against the territorial integrity or political independence of any State, or in any other manner inconsistent with the Purposes of the United Nations, and that the establishment and maintenance of international peace and security are to be promoted with the least diversion for armaments of the world's human and economic resources,

Have agreed as follows:

Article I

Each nuclear-weapon State Party to the Treaty undertakes not to transfer to any recipient whatsoever nuclear weapons or other nuclear explosive devices or control over such weapons or explosive devices directly, or indirectly; and not in any way to assist, encourage, or induce any non-nuclear-weapon State to manufacture or otherwise acquire nuclear weapons or other nuclear explosive devices, or control over such weapons or explosive devices.

Article II

Each non-nuclear-weapon State Party to the Treaty undertakes not to receive the transfer from any transferor whatsoever of nuclear weapons or other nuclear explosive devices or of control over such weapons or explosive devices directly, or indirectly; not to manufacture or otherwise acquire nuclear weapons or other nuclear explosive devices; and not to seek or receive any assistance in the manufacture of nuclear weapons or other nuclear explosive devices.

Article III

1. Each non-nuclear-weapon State Party to the Treaty undertakes to accept safeguards, as set forth in an agreement to be negotiated and concluded with the International Atomic Energy Agency in accordance with the Statute of the International Atomic Energy Agency[72] and the Agency's safeguards system, for the exclusive purpose of verification of the fulfillment of its obligations assumed under this Treaty with a view to preventing diversion of nuclear energy from peaceful uses to nuclear weapons or other nuclear explosive devices. Procedures for the safeguards required by this article shall be followed with respect to source or special fissionable material whether it is being produced, processed or used in any principal nuclear facility or is outside any such facility. The safeguards required by this article shall be applied on all source or special fissionable material in all peaceful nuclear activities within the territory of such State, under its jurisdiction, or carried out under its control anywhere.

2. Each State Party to the Treaty undertakes not to provide: (a) source or special fissionable material, or (b) equipment or material especially designed or prepared for the processing, use or production of special fissionable material, to any non-nuclear-weapon State for peaceful purposes, unless the source or special fissionable material shall be subject to the safeguards required by this article.

3. The safeguards required by this article shall be implemented in a manner designed to comply with article IV of this Treaty, and to avoid hampering the economic or technological development of the

Parties or international cooperation in the field of peaceful nuclear activities, including the international exchange of nuclear material and equipment for the processing, use or production of nuclear material for peaceful purposes in accordance with the provisions of this article and the principle of safeguarding set forth in the Preamble of the Treaty.

4. Non-nuclear-weapon States Party to the Treaty shall conclude agreements with the International Atomic Energy Agency to meet the requirements of this article either individually or together with other States in accordance with the Statute of the International Atomic Energy Agency. Negotiation of such agreements shall commence within 180 days from the original entry into force of this Treaty. For States depositing their instruments of ratification or accession after the 180-day period, negotiation of such agreements shall commence not later than the date of such deposit. Such agreements shall enter into force not later than eighteen months after the date of initiation of negotiations.

Article IV

1. Nothing in this Treaty shall be interpreted as affecting the inalienable right of all the Parties to the Treaty to develop research, production and use of nuclear energy for peaceful purposes without discrimination and in conformity with articles I and II of this Treaty.

2. All the Parties to the Treaty undertake to facilitate, and have the right to participate in, the fullest possible exchange of equipment, materials and scientific and technological information for the peaceful uses of nuclear energy. Parties to the Treaty in a position to do so shall also cooperate in contributing alone or together with other States or international organizations to the further development of the applications of nuclear energy for peaceful purposes, especially in the territories of non-nuclear-weapon States Party to the Treaty, with due consideration for the needs of the developing areas of the world.

Article V

Each Party to the Treaty undertakes to take appropriate measures to ensure that, in accordance with this Treaty, under appropriate international observation and through appropriate international procedures, potential benefits from any peaceful applications of nuclear explosions will be made available to non-nuclear-weapon States Party to the Treaty on a nondiscriminatory basis and that the charge to such Parties for the explosive devices used will be as low as possible and exclude any charge for research and development. Non-nuclear-weapon States Party to the Treaty shall be able to obtain such benefits, pursuant to a special international agreement or agreements, through an appropriate international body with adequate representation of non-nuclear-weapon States. Negotiations on this subject shall commence as soon as possible after the Treaty enters into force. Non-nuclear-weapon States Party to the Treaty so desiring may also obtain such benefits pursuant to bilateral agreements.

Article VI

Each of the Parties to the Treaty undertakes to pursue negotiations in good faith on effective measures relating to cessation of the nuclear arms race at an early date and to nuclear disarmament, and on a treaty on general and complete disarmament under strict and effective international control.

Article VII

Nothing in this Treaty affects the right of any group of States to conclude regional treaties in order to assure the total absence of nuclear weapons in their respective territories.

Article VIII

1. Any Party to the Treaty may propose amendments to this Treaty. The text of any proposed amendment shall be submitted to the Depositary Governments which shall circulate it to all Parties to the Treaty. Thereupon, if requested to do so by one-third or more of the Parties to the Treaty, the Depositary Governments shall convene a conference, to which they shall invite all the Parties to the Treaty, to consider such an amendment.

2. Any amendment to this Treaty must be approved by a majority of the votes of all the Parties to the Treaty, including the votes of all nuclear-weapon States Party to the Treaty and all other Parties which, on the date the amendment is circulated, are members of the Board of Governors of the International Atomic Energy Agency. The amend-

ment shall enter into force for each Party that deposits its instrument of ratification of the amendment upon the deposit of such instruments of ratification by a majority of all the Parties, including the instruments of ratification of all nuclear-weapon States Party to the Treaty and all other Parties which, on the date the amendment is circulated, are members of the Board of Governors of the International Atomic Energy Agency. Thereafter, it shall enter into force for any other Party upon the deposit of its instrument of ratification of the amendment.

3. Five years after the entry into force of this Treaty, a conference of Parties to the Treaty shall be held in Geneva, Switzerland, in order to review the operation of this Treaty with a view to assuring that the purposes of the Preamble and the provisions of the Treaty are being realized. At intervals of five years thereafter, a majority of the Parties to the Treaty may obtain, by submitting a proposal to this effect to the Depositary Governments, the convening of further conferences with the same objective of reviewing the operation of the Treaty.

Article IX

1. This Treaty shall be open to all States for signature. Any State which does not sign the Treaty before its entry into force in accordance with paragraph 3 of this article may accede to it at any time.

2. This Treaty shall be subject to ratification by signatory States. Instruments of ratification and instruments of accession shall be deposited with the Governments of the United States of America, the United Kingdom of Great Britain and Northern Ireland and the Union of Soviet Socialist Republics, which are hereby designated the Depositary Governments.

3. This Treaty shall enter into force after its ratification by the States, the Governments of which are designated Depositaries of the Treaty, and forty other States signatory to this Treaty and the deposit of their instruments of ratification. For the purposes of this Treaty, a nuclear-weapon State is one which has manufactured and exploded a nuclear weapon or other nuclear explosive device prior to January 1, 1967.

4. For States whose instruments of ratification or accession are deposited subsequent to the entry into force of this Treaty, it shall enter into force on the date of the deposit of their instruments of ratification or accession.

5. The Depositary Governments shall promptly inform all signatory and acceding States of the date of each signature, the date of deposit of each instrument of ratification or of accession, the date of the entry into force of this Treaty, and the date of receipt of any requests for convening a conference or other notices.

6. This Treaty shall be registered by the Depositary Governments pursuant to article 102 of the Charter of the United Nations.

Article X

1. Each Party shall in exercising its national sovereignty have the right to withdraw from the Treaty if it decides that extraordinary events, related to the subject matter of this Treaty, have jeopardized the supreme interests of its country. It shall give notice of such withdrawal to all other Parties to the Treaty and to the United Nations Security Council three months in advance. Such notice shall include a statement of the extraordinary events it regards as having jeopardized its supreme interests.

2. Twenty-five years after the entry into force of the Treaty, a conference shall be convened to decide whether the Treaty shall continue in force indefinitely, or shall be extended for an additional fixed period or periods. This decision shall be taken by a majority of the Parties to the Treaty.

Article XI

This Treaty, the English, Russian, French, Spanish and Chinese texts of which are equally authentic, shall be deposited in the archives of the Depositary Governments. Duly certified copies of this Treaty shall be transmitted by the Depositary Governments to the Governments of the signatory and acceding States.

In witness whereof the undersigned, duly authorized, have signed this Treaty.

Done in triplicate, at the cities of Washington, London and Moscow, this first day of July one thousand nine hundred sixty-eight.

Signatories and Parties as of December 1986

Country	Date of Signature	Date of Deposit of Ratification	Date of Deposit of Accession (A) or Succession (S)
Afghanistan	7/1/68	2/4/70[1]	
Antigua and Barbuda			6/17/85 (S)
Australia	2/27/70	1/23/73	
Austria	7/1/68	6/27/69	
Bahamas, The			8/11/76 (S)
Bangladesh			8/31/79 (A)
Barbados	7/1/68	2/21/80	
Belgium	8/20/68	5/2/75	
Belize			8/9/85 (S)
Benin	7/1/68	10/31/72	
Bhutan			5/23/85 (A)
Bolivia	7/1/68	5/26/70	
Botswana	7/1/68	4/28/69	
Brunei			3/26/85 (A)
Bulgaria	7/1/68	9/5/69	
Burkina Faso	11/25/68	3/3/70	
Burundi			3/19/71 (A)
Cameroon	7/17/68	1/8/69	
Canada	7/23/68	1/8/69	
Cape Verde			10/24/79 (A)
Central African Republic			10/25/70 (A)
Chad	7/1/68	3/10/71	
Colombia	7/1/68	4/8/86	
Congo			10/23/78 (A)
Costa Rica	7/1/68	3/3/70	
Cyprus	7/1/68	2/10/70	
Czechoslovakia	7/1/68	7/22/69	
Denmark	7/1/68	1/3/69	
Dominica			8/10/84 (S)
Dominican Republic	7/1/68	7/24/71	
Ecuador	7/9/68	3/7/69	
Egypt	7/1/68	2/26/81[1]	
El Salvador	7/1/68	7/11/72	
Equatorial Guinea			11/1/84 (A)
Ethiopia	9/5/68	2/5/70	
Fiji			7/14/72 (S)
Finland	7/1/68	2/5/69	
Gabon			2/19/74 (A)

Country	Date of Signature	Date of Deposit of Ratification	Date of Deposit of Accession (A) or Succession (S)
Gambia, The	9/4/68	5/12/75	
German Democratic Republic	7/1/68	10/31/69	
Germany, Federal Republic of	11/28/69	5/2/75[1,2]	
Ghana	7/1/68	5/4/70	
Greece	7/1/68	3/11/70	
Grenada			9/2/75 (S)
Guatemala	7/26/68	9/22/70	
Guinea			4/29/85 (A)
Guinea-Bissau			8/20/76 (A)
Haiti	7/1/68	6/2/70	
Holy See			2/25/71 (A)[1]
Honduras	7/1/68	5/16/73	
Hungary	7/1/68	5/27/69	
Iceland	7/1/68	7/18/69	
Indonesia	3/2/70	7/12/79[1]	
Iran	7/1/68	2/2/70	
Iraq	7/1/68	10/29/69	
Ireland	7/1/68	7/1/68	
Italy	1/28/69	5/2/75[1]	
Ivory Coast	7/1/68	3/6/73	
Jamaica	4/14/69	3/5/70	
Japan	2/3/70	6/8/76[1]	
Jordan	7/10/68	2/11/70	
Kampuchea			6/2/72 (A)
Kenya	7/1/68	6/11/70	
Kiribati			4/18/85 (S)
Korea, Democratic People's Republic of			12/12/85 (A)
Korea, Republic of	7/1/68	4/23/75	
Kuwait	8/15/68		
Laos	7/1/68	2/20/70	
Lebanon	7/1/68	7/15/70	
Lesotho	7/9/68	5/20/70	
Liberia	7/1/68	3/5/70	
Libya	7/18/68	5/26/75	
Liechtenstein			4/20/78 (A)[1]
Luxembourg	8/14/68	5/2/75	
Madagascar	8/22/68	10/8/70	
Malawi			2/19/86 (A)
Malaysia	7/1/68	3/5/70	

Country	Date of Signature	Date of Deposit of Ratification	Date of Deposit of Accession (A) or Succession (S)
Maldives	9/11/68	4/7/70	
Mali	7/14/69	2/10/70	
Malta	4/17/69	2/6/70	
Mauritius	7/1/68	4/8/69	
Mexico	7/26/68	1/21/69[1]	
Mongolia	7/1/68	5/14/69	
Morocco	7/1/68	11/27/70	
Nauru			6/7/82 (A)
Nepal	7/1/68	1/5/70	
Netherlands	8/20/68	5/2/75[3]	
New Zealand	7/1/68	9/10/69	
Nicaragua	7/1/68	3/6/73	
Nigeria	7/1/68	9/27/68	
Norway	7/1/68	2/5/69	
Panama	7/1/68	1/13/77	
Papua New Guinea			1/13/82 (A)
Paraguay	7/1/68	2/4/70	
Peru	7/1/68	3/3/70	
Philippines	7/1/68	10/5/72	
Poland	7/1/68	6/12/69	
Portugal			12/15/77 (A)
Romania	7/1/68	2/4/70	
Rwanda			5/20/75 (A)
San Marino	7/1/68	08/10/70	
Sao Tome and Principe			7/20/83 (A)
St. Lucia			12/28/79 (S)
St. Christopher and Nevis			11/2/83[4]
St. Vincent and the Grenedines			11/6/84 (S)
Senegal	7/1/68	12/17/70	
Seychelles			4/8/85 (A)
Sierra Leone			2/26/75 (A)
Singapore	2/5/70	3/10/76	
Solomon Islands			6/17/81 (S)
Somalia	7/1/68	3/5/70	
Sri Lanka	7/1/68	3/5/79	
Sudan	12/24/68	10/31/73	
Suriname			6/30/76 (S)
Swaziland	6/24/69	12/11/69	
Sweden	8/19/68	1/9/70	

Country	Date of Signature	Date of Deposit of Ratification	Date of Deposit of Accession (A) or Succession (S)
Switzerland	11/27/69	3/9/77[1]	
Syrian Arab Republic	7/1/68	9/24/69[1]	
Thailand			12/2/72 (A)
Togo	7/1/68	2/26/70	
Tonga			7/7/71 (S)
Trinidad and Tobago	8/20/68		
Tunisia	7/1/68	2/26/70	
Turkey	1/28/69	4/17/80[1]	
Tuvalu			1/19/79 (S)
Uganda			10/20/82 (A)
Union of Soviet Socialist Republics	7/1/68	3/5/70	
United Kingdom	7/1/68	11/27/68[5]	
United States	7/1/68	3/5/70	
Uruguay	7/1/68	8/31/70	
Venezuela	7/1/68	9/25/75	
Vietnam, Socialist Republic of			6/14/82 (A)
Western Samoa			3/17/75 (A)
Yemen Arab Republic (Sana)	9/23/68	5/14/86	
Yemen, People's Democratic Republic of (Aden)	11/14/68	6/1/79	
Yugoslavia	7/10/68	3/4/70[1]	
Zaire	7/22/68	8/4/70	
Taiwan[6]	7/1/68	1/27/70[6]	

Dates given are the earliest dates on which a country signed the Treaty or deposited its instrument of ratification or accession—whether in Washington, London, or Moscow. In the case of a country that was a dependent territory which became a party through succession, the date given is the date on which the country gave notice that it would continue to be bound by the terms of the Treaty. Data from the Office of the Legal Adviser, Department of State.

1. With Statement.
2. Applicable to Berlin (West).
3. Extended to Netherlands Antilles.
4. Date of general declaration to the Secretary General of the UN concerning continuing treaty obligations applicable prior to independence. The United States considers each of these countries bound by the obligations in the treaty in accordance with its general declaration, but not a party pending deposit of an instrument of succession or accession.
5. Extended to Anguilla and territories under the territorial sovereignty of the United Kingdom.
6. On January 27, 1970, an instrument of ratification was deposited in the name of the Republic of China. Effective January 1, 1979, the United States recognized the People's Republic of China as the sole legal government of China. The authorities on Taiwan state that they will continue to abide by the provisions of the Treaty and the United States regards them as bound by its obligations.

List of Works Cited

Books

Anders, Roger M., ed., *Forging the Atomic Shield: Excerpts from the Office Diary of Gordon E. Dean* (Chapel Hill: University of North Carolina Press, 1987).

Anderson, Patrick, *The President's Men* (Garden City, N.Y.: Doubleday & Co., 1968).

Bader, William B., *The United States and the Spread of Nuclear Weapons* (New York: Pegasus, 1968).

Bechhoefer, Bernhard G., "The Historical Evolution of International Safeguards," in Willrich, ed., *International Safeguards.*

Bloomfield, Lincoln Palmer, *Disarmament and Arms Control* (New York: Foreign Policy Association, 1968).

Broad, William J., *Star Warriors* (New York: Simon and Schuster, 1985).

Buchan, Alastair, "The Multilateral Force, An Historical Perspective," Adelphi Papers No. 13 (London: The Institute for Strategic Studies, 1964).

Cleveland, Harlan, *NATO: The Transatlantic Bargain* (New York: Harper & Row, 1970).

Coffey J. I., "The Confrontation," in Rabinowitch and Adams, eds., *Debate the Antiballistic Missile.*

Craig, Paul P., and John A. Jungerman, *Nuclear Arms Race: Technology and Society* (New York: McGraw-Hill Book Company, 1986).

Dean, Arthur H., *Test Ban and Disarmament: The Path of Negotiation* (New York: Harper & Row for Council on Foreign Relations, 1966).

Dougherty, James E., *Arms Control and Disarmament, The Critical Issues* (Washington: The Center for Strategic Studies, 1966).

Drosnin, Michael, *Citizen Hughes* (New York: Holt, Rinehart, and Winston, 1985).

Dunn, Lewis A., *Controlling the Bomb: Nuclear Proliferation in the 1980s*. A Twentieth Century Fund report (New Haven: Yale University Press, 1982).

Dyson, Freeman, *Weapons and Hope* (New York, Harper & Row, 1984).

Enthoven, Alain C., and K. Wayne Smith, *How Much Is Enough? Shaping the Defense Program, 1961–1969* (New York: Harper & Row, 1971).

Epstein, William, "Retrospective of the NPT Review Conference" (Muscatine, Iowa: The Stanley Foundation, 1975).

Fallows, James M., *National Defense* (New York: Random House, 1981).

Geyelin, Philip, *Lyndon B. Johnson and the World* (New York: Frederick A. Praeger, 1966).

Goldschmidt, Bertrand, *The Atomic Adventure: Its Political and Technical Aspects* (1962), translated from the French by Peter Beer (Oxford: Pergamon Press, 1964).

Goldschmidt, Bertrand, *The Atomic Complex* (Paris: Librarie Artheme Fayard, 1980), translated from the French by Bruce M. Adkins (La Grange Park, Ill.: American Nuclear Society, 1982).

Halberstam, David, *The Best and the Brightest* (New York: Random House, 1969).

Halsted, Thomas A., "The Spread of Nuclear Weapons—Is the Dam About to Burst?" in Kincade and Porro, eds., *Negotiating Security*.

Hanrieder, Wolfram F., ed. *Technology, Strategy, and Arms Control* (Boulder, Colo.: Westview Press, 1986).

Herken, Gregg, *The Winning Weapon: The Atomic Bomb in the Cold War, 1945–1950* (New York: Alfred A. Knopf, 1980).

Hewlett, Richard G., and Oscar E. Anderson, Jr., *The New World: A History of the United States Atomic Energy Commission, Volume I, 1939/1946* (University Park, Pa.: Pennsylvania State University Press, 1962).

Hewlett, Richard G., and Francis Duncan, *Atomic Shield: A History of the United States Atomic Energy Commission, Volume II, 1947/1952* (University Park, Pa.: Pennsylvania State University Press, 1969).

Hoover, Robert A., "Strategic Arms Limitation, Negotiations and U.S. Decision Making," in Hanrieder, ed., *Technology, Strategy, and Arms Control.*

Jacobson, Harold Karan, and Eric Stein, *Diplomats, Scientists, and Politicians: The United States and the Nuclear Test Ban Negotiations* (Ann Arbor: University of Michigan Press, 1966).

Johnson, Lyndon B., *The Vantage Point: Perspectives of the Presidency, 1963–1969* (New York: Holt, Rinehart and Winston, 1971).

Kearns, Doris, *Lyndon Johnson and the American Dream* (New York: Harper & Row, 1976).

Kelleher, Catherine McArdle, *Germany and the Politics of Nuclear Weapons* (New York: Columbia University Press, 1975).

Kertesz, Stephen D., ed., *Nuclear Non-Proliferation in a World of Nuclear Powers* (Notre Dame, Ind.: University of Notre Dame Press, 1967).

Kincade, William H., and Jeffrey D. Porro, eds., *Negotiating Security: An Arms Control Reader* (Washington: The Carnegie Endowment for International Peace, 1979).

Kissinger, Henry A., *The Troubled Partnership: A Re-appraisal of the Atlantic Alliance* (New York: McGraw-Hill, 1965).

Kissinger, Henry A., *White House Years* (Boston: Little Brown & Co., 1979).

Kistiakowsky, George B., *A Scientist at the White House* (Cambridge, Mass.: Harvard University Press, 1976).

Kolkowicz, Roman, et al., *The Soviet Union and Arms Control, A Superpower Dilemma* (Baltimore: The Johns Hopkins University Press, 1970).

Kurzman, Dan, *Day of the Bomb: Countdown to Hiroshima* (New York: McGraw-Hill Book Company, 1986).

Larson, Thomas B., *Disarmament and Soviet Policy: 1964–1968* (Englewood Cliffs, N.J.: Prentice-Hall, 1969).

Mastny, Vojtech, *Disarmament and Nuclear Tests: 1964–1969* (New York: Facts on File, Inc., 1970).

Myrdal, Alva, *The Game of Disarmament: How the United States and Russia Run the Arms Race* (New York: Pantheon Books, 1976).

National Academy of Sciences, *Nuclear Arms Control: Background and Issues* (Washington: National Academy Press, 1985).

Newhouse, John, *Cold Dawn: The Story of SALT* (New York: Holt, Rinehart and Winston, 1973).

Nixon, Richard, *RN: The Memoirs of Richard Nixon* (New York: Grosset & Dunlap, 1978).

Polach, Jaroslav G., *Euratom* (Dobbs Ferry, N.Y.: Oceana Publications, 1964).

Pringle, Peter, and James Spigelman, *The Nuclear Barons* (New York: Holt, Rinehart and Winston, 1981).

Rabinowitch, Eugene, and Ruth Adams, eds., *Debate the Antiballistic Missile* (Chicago: Bulletin of the Atomic Scientists, 1967).

Richardson, J. L., *Australia and the Non-Proliferation Treaty* (Canberra: Australian National University Press, 1968).

Roberts, Chalmers M., *The Nuclear Years: The Arms Race and Arms Control, 1945–70* (New York: Praeger Publishers, 1970).

Rostow, Walt W., *The Diffusion of Power* (New York: The Macmillan Co., 1972).

————., *Open Skies: Eisenhower's Proposal of July 21, 1955* (Austin: University of Texas Press, 1982).

Schlesinger, Arthur M., Jr., *A Thousand Days: John F. Kennedy in the White House* (Boston: Houghton Mifflin Company, 1965).

Schlesinger, James, "Nuclear Spread: The Setting of the Problem," in Kertesz, ed., *Nuclear Non-Proliferation in a World of Nuclear Powers.*

Seaborg, Glenn T., *Kennedy, Khrushchev, and the Test Ban* (Berkeley: University of California Press, 1981).

Seaborg, Glenn T., and William R. Corliss, *Man and Atom* (New York: E. P. Dutton & Co., 1971).

Shaker, Mohamed I., *The Nuclear Non-Proliferation Treaty, Origin and Implementation, 1959–1979* (London: Oceana Publications, Inc., 1980).

Smith, Gerard, *Doubletalk: The Story of the First Strategic Arms Limitation Talks* (New York: Doubleday & Co., Inc., 1980).

Sorensen, Theodore C., *Kennedy* (New York: Harper & Row, 1965).

Szasz, Paul C., "International Atomic Energy Safeguards," in Willrich, ed. *International Safeguards.*

Willrich, Mason, ed., *International Safeguards and Nuclear Industry* (Baltimore: The Johns Hopkins University Press, 1973).

Willrich, Mason, *Non-Proliferation Treaty: Framework for Nuclear Arms Control* (Charlottesville, Va.: The Michie Co., 1969).

Wilson, Harold, *A Personal Record: The Labour Government 1964–1970* (London: Weidenfeld and Nicholson, and Michael Joseph, 1971).

York, Herbert, *Race to Oblivion: A Participant's View of the Arms Race* (New York: Simon and Schuster, 1970).

Young, Elizabeth, *A Farewell to Arms Control?* (Harmondsworth, England: Penguin Books, 1972).

Young, Elizabeth, "The Control of Proliferation: The 1968 Treaty in Hindsight and Forecast," Adelphi Paper No. 56 (London: The International Institute for Strategic Studies, 1969).

Articles

Albright, David, and Andre Carothers, "Fragile Consensus on Non-Proliferation Treaty," *Bulletin of the Atomic Scientists,* December 1985.

Arkin, William M., Thomas B. Cochran, and Milton M. Hoenig, "Fueling the Arms Race," *Arms Control Today,* April 1982.

Bader, W. B., "Nuclear Weapons Sharing and 'The German Problem,'" *Foreign Affairs,* July 1966.

Boyer, Paul, "From Activism to Apathy: America and the Nuclear Issue, 1963–1980," *Bulletin of the Atomic Scientists,* August/September 1984.

Bundy, McGeorge, "The Last Chance to Stop the H-Bomb," *The New York Review,* May 13, 1982.

DeWitt, Hugh E., and Gerald E. Marsh, "Weapons Design Policy Impedes Test Ban," *Bulletin of the Atomic Scientists,* November 1985.

Foster, William, "New Directions in Arms Control," *Foreign Affairs,* July 1965.

Ganguly, Sumit, "Why India Joined the Nuclear Club," *Bulletin of the Atomic Scientists,* April 1983.

Goldblatt, Jozef, "Will the NPT Survive?", *Bulletin of the Atomic Scientists,* January 1986.

Greb, G. Allen, and Warren Heckrotte, "The Long History: The Test Ban Debate," *Bulletin of the Atomic Scientists,* August 1983.

Halperin, Morton H., "Arms Control: A Twenty-Five-Year Perspective," *Journal of the Federation of American Scientists,* June 1983.

Humphrey, David C., "Tuesday Lunch at the Johnson White House: A Preliminary Assessment," *Diplomatic History,* Winter 1984.

Inglis, David R., and Carl L. Sandler, "Prospects and Problems: The Non-Military Uses of Nuclear Explosives," *Bulletin of the Atomic Scientists,* December 1967.

Larsson, Christer, "Build a Bomb!" Published in Swedish in *Ny Teknik* (Stockholm), April 25, 1985.

Newhouse, John, "The Multilateral Force: An Appraisal," *Bulletin of the Atomic Scientists,* September 1964.

Norris, Robert S., Thomas B. Cochran, and William M. Arkin, "History of the Nuclear Stockpile," *Bulletin of the Atomic Scientists,* August 1985.

Seaborg, Glenn T., "Seaborg proposal: Support a comprehensive test ban," *Chemical and Engineering News* (letter to editor), June 13, 1983.

Silard, John, "The Multilateral Force: The Case Against," *Bulletin of the Atomic Scientists,* September 1964.

Smith, R. Jeffrey, "The Allure of Nuclear Testing," *Science,* May 18, 1984.

Sommer, Theo, "Bonn Changes Course," *Foreign Affairs,* April 1967.

Stratton, James H., "Sea-Level Canal: How and Where?", *Foreign Affairs,* April 1965.

York, Herbert, and G. Allen Greb, "The Comprehensive Test Ban," discussion paper
No. 84, Santa Monica (California) Seminar on Arms Control and Foreign Policy,
1979.

Unpublished Material

AEC 1140, "History of Expansion of AEC Production Facilities," unpublished report
prepared in the Atomic Energy Commission Historian's Office under the direc-
tion of Richard E. Hewlett, 1963, Department of Energy Archives.
Barnes, Harley Hassinger, Jr., "The Nuclear Non-Proliferation Treaty: Participants,
Interests and Processes in American Foreign Policy," Ph.D. dissertation, Rutgers
University, 1976.
Lambert, Robert W., "Background Information on the Strategic Nuclear Delivery
Vehicles Freeze, 1964–1967," an unpublished ACDA research paper, 1968.
The Ploughshares Fund (San Francisco), "Press Kit on Comprehensive Test Ban
Treaty," 1986.
U.S. Arms Control and Disarmament Agency, "Negotiations on a Comprehensive
Test Ban, 1965–1967," unpublished research paper, 1968.
Williamson, Richard L., "Peaceful Nuclear Explosions: Implications for Arms Con-
trol," Ph.D. dissertation, American University, 1976.

Government Documents

Report of the Atlantic–Pacific Interoceanic Canal Study Commission (Washington:
Government Printing Office, 1970, No. 1971 0-410-974).
U.S. Arms Control and Disarmament Agency, *Arms Control and Disarmament
Agreements: Texts and Negotiations,* 1982 edition.
———, *Documents on Disarmament,* published annually.
———, *International Negotiations on the Treaty on the Nonproliferation of Nuclear
Weapons,* 1969.
U.S. Congress, House, Committee on Foreign Affairs, *Hearings on Arms Control and
Disarmament Act Amendments, 1968,* February 1968.
U.S. Congress, Senate, Committee on Foreign Relations, *Hearings on Nonprolifera-
tion Treaty,* 90th Cong., 2d sess., July 1968.
U.S. Congress, Senate, Committee on Foreign Relations, *Hearings on Promoting a
Comprehensive Test Ban Treaty,* 93rd Cong., 1st sess., May 1, 1973.
U.S. Congress, Senate and House, Joint Committee on Atomic Energy, *International
Agreements for Cooperation, Hearings,* 88th Cong., 1st and 2d sess., September
1963–June 1964.
U.S. Congress, Senate and House, Joint Committee on Atomic Energy, *Nonprolifer-
ation of Nuclear Weapons, Hearings,* 89th Cong., 2d sess., February–March
1966.
U.S. Congress, Senate and House, Joint Committee on Atomic Energy, *Peaceful Ap-
plications of Nuclear Explosives—Plowshare, Hearings,* 89th Cong., 1st sess.,
January 5, 1965.

U.S. Department of Energy, "Announced United States Nuclear Tests," NVO-209 (Rev. 5) January 1985.

U.S. Library of Congress, Congressional Research Service, "Soviet Compliance with Arms Control Agreements (excluding SALT I)," October 16, 1978.

Index

About the Authors

G LENN T. SEABORG shared the 1951 Nobel Prize in Chemistry with E. M. McMillan for their work in the chemistry of transuranium elements. From 1961 to 1971 he was chairman of the Atomic Energy Commission, which had national responsibility for programs relating to both the military and civilian uses of nuclear energy. As a member of the intragovernmental Committee of Principals during these years he participated actively in the formulation of U.S. arms control policy. While AEC chairman he headed the U.S. delegation to the annual General Conference of the International Atomic Energy Agency. He also served on the National Aeronautics and Space Council and the Federal Council on Science and Technology.

Dr. Seaborg has been a member of the chemistry faculty of the University of California (Berkeley) since 1939, serving currently as University Professor of Chemistry, the highest rank awarded by the university, as chairman of the Lawrence Hall of Science, and as an associate director of the Lawrence Berkeley Laboratory. From 1958 to 1961 he was chancellor of the Berkeley campus. In his academic work, Seaborg is one of the discoverers of ten transuranium elements. With his colleagues, he is responsible for identifying more than one hundred isotopes throughout the periodic table of elements, many with practical applications in medicine and industry. He served on the National Commission on Excellence in Education, which published *A Nation at Risk* in April 1983, and is recognized as a national spokesman on the crisis in mathematics and science education. He has received fifty honorary degrees.

Dr. Seaborg has written numerous books and articles. His most recent book, *Kennedy, Khrushchev and the Test Ban,* describes the events and negotiations leading to the Limited Test Ban Treaty of 1963.

BENJAMIN S. LOEB received the Ph.D. degree from Columbia University. He is now retired from a career as an economist and writer in federal agencies, including the Atomic Energy Commission and the Nuclear Regulatory Commission. He also served for two years with the International Atomic Energy Agency. While with the AEC he edited a number of the agency's "Understanding the Atom" booklets and coauthored *Radioisotopes and Radiation* (McGraw Hill, 1964). He collaborated with Glenn T. Seaborg in the writing of *Kennedy, Khrushchev and the Test Ban* (University of California Press, 1981).